Convivencia

Jews, Muslims, and Christians in Medieval Spain

por la dell otro pierde. En estos .xij.
iuegos delos dados que aqui auemos
puestos. se pueden entender todos los otros
q iuegan en las otras tras q son fec
hos o se pueden fazer daqui adelant de
que nos non sabemos.

Convivencia

Jews, Muslims, and Christians in Medieval Spain

EDITED BY

Vivian B. Mann
Thomas F. Glick
Jerrilynn D. Dodds

George Brazziller

IN ASSOCIATION WITH

The Jewish Museum

NEW YORK

THE JEWISH MUSEUM IS UNDER THE AUSPICES OF
THE JEWISH THEOLOGICAL SEMINARY OF AMERICA

Published in 1992 by George Braziller, Inc.

For information, address the publisher:
George Braziller, Inc.
171 Madison Avenue
New York, N.Y. 10016

Library of Congress Cataloging-in Publication Data:
Convivencia: Jews, Muslims, and Christians in Medieval Spain
edited by Vivian B. Mann, Jerrilynn D. Dodds, and Thomas F. Glick.
p. cm.
Published in conjunction with an exhibition of the same name held at The Jewish Museum, New York.
Includes bibliographical references (p.)
ISBN 0-8076-1283-9 (cloth).—ISBN 0-8076-1286-3 (pbk.)
1. Jews—Spain—Civilization. 2. Spain—Civilization—711-1516.
3. Spain—Civilization—Jewish influences. 4. Spain—Ethnic relations:
I. Mann, Vivian B. II. Dodds, Jerrilynn Denise.
III. Glick, Thomas F. IV. Jewish Museum (New York, N.Y.)
DS135.S7C585 1992
946'.004924—dc20 92-10069
CIP

Title page illustration: Alfonso X El Sabio, *Libro de ajedrez, dados, y tablas* (Book of Chess, Backgammon, and Dice), finished in 1283 in Seville, Biblioteca de El Escorial, Madrid, T.I.6, fol. 71v. Jews and Muslims are shown playing together in a garden setting.

This volume was designed by H Plus Incorporated.
The text and display are typset in Adobe Caslon.
Printed and bound in China

Table of Contents

vii	Foreword	*Joan Rosenbaum*
xi	Preface	*Vivian B. Mann*
1	*Convivencia:* An Introductory Note	*Thomas F. Glick*
11	Jews, Christians, and Muslims in Medieval Iberia: *Convivencia* through the Eyes of Sephardic Jews	*Benjamin R. Gampel*
39	Hebrew Poetry in Medieval Iberia	*Raymond P. Scheindlin*
61	Social Perception and Literary Portrayal: Jews and Muslims in Medieval Spanish Literature	*Dwayne E. Carpenter*
83	Science in Medieval Spain: The Jewish Contribution in the Context of *Convivencia*	*Thomas F. Glick*
113	Mudejar Tradition and the Synagogues of Medieval Spain: Cultural Identity and Cultural Hegemony	*Jerrilynn D. Dodds*
133	Hebrew Illuminated Manuscripts from the Iberian Peninsula	*Gabrielle Sed-Rajna*
157	Material Culture in Medieval Spain	*Juan Zozaya*
177	Catalogue	
251	Bibliography	
261	Contributors	
263	Lenders to the Exhibition	

DONORS TO THE EXHIBITION

"*Convivencia:* Jews, Muslims, and Christians in Medieval Spain" was made possible, in part, by generous grants from the National Endowment for the Humanities, a federal agency.

Major funding for the exhibition has been provided by Sara and Axel Schupf.

Other significant funds have been received from the Louis and Anne Abrons Foundation, Maurice Amado Foundation, Virginia and Alan B. Slifka, and the National Endowment for the Arts.

Additional support has been provided by the New York State Council on the Arts, the City of New York Department of Cultural Affairs, Leonard B. Stern, and other generous donors.

The catalogue is published with the generous assistance of the Lucius N. Littauer Foundation and The Reed Foundation. Poster design has been contributed by Joan Vass.

Special considerations have been provided by Iberia Airlines.

The exhibition has been formally designated as an official project of the Spain '92 Foundation.

Spain '92 Foundation

Foreword

Remaining a Jew while participating fully as a citizen in the life of a particular country has been a continuing challenge in Jewish life for centuries. The experience of Jews living in medieval Iberia, particularly in the period of Muslim rule, provides a model of achievement for simultaneously flourishing Jewish religious and secular life. Our exhibition, *Convivencia*, explores the interaction of three religious groups and looks at the resulting material culture in the period that begins in 711 with the Muslim Conquest and ends in 1492 with the expulsion of the Jews and the defeat of the last Muslim ruler.

A new consciousness of the cultural interactions influencing American history and daily life has marked this Quincentennial year. *Convivencia* has provided a welcome opportunity to highlight a multicultural society that reflects the achievement of three groups as revealed in literature, scientific endeavors, architecture, and decorative arts.

The exhibition was created and developed in the Judaica department of The Jewish Museum, with invaluable assistance from scholars of The Jewish Theological Seminary of America and other academic institutions. Vivian Mann, Morris and Eva Feld Chair of Judaica at the Museum, served as project director, skillfully charting the project through the three-year course of planning, development, and execution. Co-Curator Jerrilynn Dodds, Associate Professor of Architectural History at the City University of New York, brought important expertise in medieval Spanish art. Raymond Scheindlin, Professor of Hebrew Literature, and Benjamin Gampel, Associate Professor of Jewish History, both at The Jewish Theological Seminary of America, not only contributed essays to this publication, but were important consultants throughout the development of the exhibition. Professor Thomas Glick of Boston College joined in editing this volume and in shaping the sections on science. Lynne Breslin, Adjunct Assistant Professor of Architecture at Columbia University, also shared many hours of consultation in addition to creating a beautiful exhibition design.

Within the Museum's Judaica Department, Curatorial Assistant Claudia Nahson's linguistic abilities and administrative and scholarly talents greatly benefitted the project. Editorial and administrative details of both the exhibition and this volume were ably handled by Administrative Assistant, Sharon Wolfe. Assistant Director for Programs, Ward Mintz, was an enthusiastic supporter of the concept of *Convivencia*, providing guidance throughout. Former Exhibition Administrator Diane Farynyk and Registrar Susan Palamara and her staff deftly handled the complex assignment of bringing together a variety of loans from many collections around the world. The Development Department, particularly Philip Meranus and Lori Gordon, and former Assistant Director Barbara Perlov, worked to ensure the viability of the project. Also engaged in bringing *Convivencia* to the public eye were our Public Relations Department headed by Anne Scher, and the Education Department headed by Judith Siegel. All aspects of the budget were given patience and care by Assistant Director of Administration, Claudette Donlon, and Comptroller Donna Jeffrey.

As of this publication date, the list of funders is incomplete. However, we are able to acknowledge, with tremendous gratitude, the generous support of the National Endowment for the Humanities, and the additional support of Axel and Sara Schupf, the Louis and Anne Abrons Foundation, Maurice Amado Foundation, Virginia and Alan B. Slifka, the National Endowment for the Arts, the New York State Council on the Arts, the City of New York Department of Cultural Affairs, the Lucius N. Littauer Foundation and the Reed Foundation, and Leonard B. Stern. The lenders, noted on page 263 of this volume, provided a generosity that enabled the museum to bring together the objects that tell the story of *Convivencia*. Sharing this material from private and public collections has helped accomplish an important historical and art historical investigation.

Just as the subject of this exhibition reflects a collaboration in medieval Spanish society among cultural groups, so does this exhibition reflect a collaboration among people with a variety of interests and expertise. The more one understands the concept of *convivencia,* the more one appreciates the necessity of maintaining it, even with its intrinsic tension, as a model for many endeavors both within the museum and without.

We are especially grateful to the following people in other institutions who were helpful and lent their expertise: Dr. Liba Taub, Associate Curator, and Kate Desulis, Curatorial Assistant, Adler Planetarium, Chicago; Father Leonard Boyle, Biblioteca Apostolica Vaticana; Dwayne Carpenter, Associate Professor of Spanish, Boston College; Dr. Stefan Reif, Director and Senior Under-Librarian, Taylor-Schechter Genizah Research Institute, Cambridge University Library; Dorothy Shepherd Payer, retired Curator, Cleveland Museum of Art; Olivia Ramie Constable, Assistant Professor of History, and George Saliba, Chairman, Department of Middle Eastern Languages and Culture, Columbia University, New York; Milton Sonday, Curator of Textiles, The Cooper-Hewitt Museum, Smithsonian Institution, New York; Dr. Thomas Kren, Curator of Manuscripts and Adjunct Curator of

Paintings, and William Noel, Assistant Curator of Manuscripts, J. Paul Getty Museum, Malibu; Dr. Mayer Rabinowitz, Librarian, Rabbi Jeremy Schwarzbard, and Sharon Lieberman-Mintz, The Library of The Jewish Theological Seminary of America, New York; Dr. Menahem Schmelzer, Professor of Medieval Hebrew Literature and Jewish Bibliography, The Jewish Theological Seminary; Dr. Marilyn Jenkins, Curator, and Daniel Walker, Curator in Charge, Department of Islamic Art, and William Wixon, Chairman, Medieval Art and The Cloisters, Charles Little, Curator Medieval Art, and Timothy Husband, Curator in Charge, and Daniel Kletke, The Cloisters, The Metropolitan Museum of Art, New York; Dr. Francisco Godoy Delgado, Director, Museo Arqueológico Provincial, Córdoba; Dr. Juan Zozaya, Deputy Director, Museo Arqueológico Nacional, Madrid; Dr. Purificación Marinetto Sánchez, Assistant Director and Curator, Museo Nacional de Arte Hispano-Musulmán, Granada; Ana María López Alvarez, Director, and Santiago Palomero Plaza, Assistant Director and Curator, The Museo Sefardí, Toledo; Jaime D. Vicente Redón, Director of the Museo de Teruel; Dr. Robert Rainwater, Curator of the Spencer Collection, and Margaret Glover, Librarian II, The New York Public Library; Mary Wyly, Associate Librarian, The Newberry Library, Chicago; Julio de La Guardia García, Consejero Gerente, Patrimonio Nacional, Madrid; Renata Holod, Associate Professor and Chairman of the History of Art, University of Pennsylvania, Philadelphia; William Voelkle, Curator of Medieval and Renaissance Manuscripts, The Pierpont Morgan Library, New York; Bernard Goldstein, Professor of Religious Studies, University of Pittsburgh; Dr. Ulf Haxen, Librarian, The Royal Library, Copenhagen; Dr. Volkmar Enderlein, Director, Islamisches Museum of the Staatliche Museen zu Berlin; Evelyn Cohen, Assistant Professor of Art History, Stern College; Dr. Carol Bier, Curator of Eastern Hemisphere Collections, The Textile Museum, Washington DC; and Norman Roth, Professor of Hebrew and Semitic Studies, University of Wisconsin, Madison.

Special thanks to Paloma Acuña, Director, Fundación Toledo; Dr. Elena Romero, Instituto Arias Montanas; Gerardo Bugallo, Consul for Cultural Affairs, and Elisabeth Cuspinera, Cultural Affairs Officer, Spanish Consulate, who answered numerous queries and gracefully forged links between The Jewish Museum and Spanish institutions. Many thanks also to Adrienne Baxter, Art Editor, and Gavin Lewis, copy editor, of George Braziller Publishers, who saw this volume through the complicated process of publication.

Final thanks to the Board of Trustees of The Jewish Museum and in particular Axel Schupf, Chairman, whose encouragement helped to make the exhibition possible.

Joan Rosenbaum
Director
The Jewish Museum

Preface

For many, and particularly for those who received a Jewish education, Spain is synonymous with the "Golden Age." The phrase connoted scholarly achievements in rabbinics like the great law codes of Rabbi Jacob ben Asher and Maimonides; the creation of innovative Hebrew poetry by Solomon ibn Gabirol, Samuel ibn Nagrela, Judah Halevi, and others; and, notable Jewish contributions to science and to the translation of ancient texts into the spoken languages of medieval Europe. Above all, the words "Golden Age" connoted a Jewish community living in harmony with its neighbors and, therefore, free to explore its creative potential in a wide variety of fields.

The Golden Age of Spanish Jewry always seemed tangible. It was personified above all by Maimonides, (even though he had left the peninsula as a young man). Maimonides: his name brings to mind the towering genius who wrote a commentary on the Mishna at the age of twenty-three, who codified all Jewish law known in his time, who was a physician and wrote on science, and still managed to lead the Jewish community of old Cairo. His posthumous turbaned portrait and his signature adorned our Hebrew notebooks and gave a face to all we learned about the Golden Age.

In addition to these general Jewish associations, familie who traced their ancestry to Spain or Portugal, the Sephardim, had direct links to the heritage of the Golden Age. Their family names often derived from Spanish cities (Soria or Toledano) or from families famous for their roles in Iberian Jewish life (Abravanel). These families preserved the lingua franca of Sephardi Jewry, Ladino, that mixture of Castilian and Hebrew, and the literature and folklore of the Sephardi past. For them, as they sang the songs of Gabirol and Halevi around the dinner table on Friday nights, the Golden Age seemed very real.

But was it? This year, 1992, does not celebrate a positive event. It commemorates the nadir of Jewish life on the Iberian peninsula, the expulsion of all Jews from Castile and Aragon, and the defeat of the last Muslim ruler of Granada. The negative force of this anniversary demands that we review the myths and reassess the Golden Age. Historians prefer the word *convivencia,* best translated as "coexistence," to describe the living together of Jews, Muslims, and Christians from 711 until 1492.

As an institution devoted to the arts and culture of the Jewish people, The Jewish Museum has chosen to examine the ways in which Jews, Muslims, and Christians interacted in the spheres of art and learning. Thomas Glick first explores the cultural and social dynamics underlying *convivencia.* Benjamin Gampel discusses the limits and possibilities of *convivencia* as it affected the Jewish minority over the entire period when Jews, Muslims, and Christians lived together on the peninsula, and he shows how cultural achievements often occurred in difficult political environments. Raymond Scheindlin examines the extraordinary impact of Arabic poetry on Hebrew writers, which stimulated them to create, among other things, the first Hebrew secular poetry, as well as new verse forms and new imagery. One is startled to learn that this whole outpouring of Jewish literary creativity went unnoticed by Muslim intellectuals.

This creative impulse continued into the age of Christian rule. Dwayne Carpenter studies medieval Spanish literature from the opposite perspective. He reviews the portrayal of Muslims and Jews in the Christian literature of Spain. Although some positive traits are ascribed to Muslims and Jews, most often they are seen through negative stereotypes.

Thomas Glick's essay on science considers the diffusion of scientific ideas and technology from East to West and their reinterpretation in Iberia in the context of cultural interchange among Muslims, Jews, and Christians. If this chapter examines the one enterprise truly shared by the three groups, then the chapter on architecture discusses a shared language of forms. Jerrilynn Dodds considers how Jews and, to a lesser extent, Christians, employed a Mudejar language of forms grafted onto traditional plans for their houses of worship.

The final two chapters examine shifts in areas of cultural creativity that reflect changes in political rule on the peninsula. As Gabrielle Sed-Rajna writes, the earliest illuminated Hebrew manuscripts from Spain follow oriental models in terms of iconography and style. By the fourteenth century, there is a progressive adaptation to Gothic style and the introduction of narrative illustrations. A similar process can be seen in the sphere of material culture. Juan Zozaya surveys the continuity of Muslim forms and the imitation of Mudejar life style long after the establishment of Christian rule in the south. Only after the Reconquest was orientalizing taste slowly superseded by European fashions and habits.

The picture that emerges is nuanced, shaded. There is no longer a pure Golden Age, but a *convivencia* that is not total harmony. Medieval Spain was a pluralistic society in which the separate communities engaged in business with each other and influenced each other with their ideas and their cultural forms. At the same time, these groups mistrusted each other and were often at war with one another. Culture flourished despite politics, but flourished it did and left such a rich legacy that for centuries after men and women thought it had been created in an age that was "Golden" in every sense of the term.

Vivian B. Mann
Morris and Eva Feld Chair of Judaica
The Jewish Museum

Convivencia: An Introductory Note

Thomas F. Glick

This volume, and the exhibition that it accompanies, explore the history of cultural interaction among Christians, Muslims, and Jews in the Iberian peninsula. The exhibition presents the products of this interaction, from works of art and literature through scientific instruments to legal documents and articles of daily use; the essays in this volume consider both these objects and the social relations that configured them. In this way, it is hoped to convey something of the richness and complexity, and at the same the vital significance in the intellectual, cultural, and social life of Europe as a whole, of what a distinguished school of Spanish historians has called *convivencia.* The word, as we use it here, is loosely defined as "coexistence," but carries connotations of mutual interpenetration and creative influence, even as it also embraces the phenomena of mutual friction, rivalry, and suspicion. Accordingly, it is the aim of this opening essay to explore these connotations and the way in which they were acquired.

The word *convivencia* as we use it can be traced back as far as Ramón Menéndez Pidal, the great philologist and historian, who in his history of the Spanish language (*Orígenes del español*) used the term "coexistence of norms" (*convivencia de normas*) to characterize the contemporaneous existence of variant forms in the early Romance languages of the peninsula, for example the diphthongs of the open *o,* as in Castilian *puerto, puorto, puarto.* These norms he saw, in conformity with prevailing notions of cultural evolutionism, as competing with one another until all the variants but one were selected out.[1]

It was, however, Menéndez Pidal's disciple, Américo Castro, who first used *convivencia* in the sense in which we will use it in this book.[2] Castro retains something of Menéndez Pidal's usage, presenting medieval Iberian culture as a kind of a field of interaction among all kinds of cultural elements originating in the different confessional groups that, in his characterization, functioned like castes [fig. 1]. But Castro's concept is more idealistic, for he sees the interaction of cultural elements, which for Menéndez Pidal was competitive and mechanistic, as intelligible only if filtered through the collective consciousness of the three castes. The filters were in large part ethnic: the castes possessed cultural elements and values that were idiosyncratic to them and that were selectively available for appropriation by members of the other, competing castes. The sense of self possessed by members of each caste was generated through the experience (*vividura*) of opposing the other two.[3] Thus far, *convivencia* still retains the competitive sense intended by Menéndez Pidal. But Castro imposes the further condition that the interactions be "historifiable" (*historiable*). For Castro, peoples only become ethnic actors when collectively possessed of self-awareness. Upon self-awareness Castro superimposes a teleological notion of destiny, of a people's "becoming something": the culture that the group projects is something that it itself recognizes as worthy. Finally, the cultural group must attain the ability to express this self-awareness in some form of high culture that becomes, thereby, the moving force of the society. Within this idealist construct it therefore follows that the Christians' struggle with Jews and Muslims takes place within the consciousness of Christians; and the same is true, *mutatis mutandis,* for the other two castes. It is here that *convivencia* attains its special meaning: it is the coexistence of the three groups, but only as registered collectively and consciously in the culture of any one of them.[4]

Not surprisingly, historians have had a great deal of difficulty dealing with Castro's labored idealist notions. He conveys no sense of the social dynamics of contact and conflict among the three groups. Mental processes are all that matter, and he fails to understand that those processes are shaped and to a certain extent determined by a social dynamic. For this reason, recent historians of ethnic relations in medieval Spain have preferred the term "coexistence," rather than *convivencia.* They have rejected Castro's view of intergroup relations as idealized, romanticized, and idyllic, presenting only the positive aspects of cultural contact and underrating the negative ones.

Here I would like to state how that social dynamic is presently perceived in post-Castro historiography, and then attempt to retrieve Castro's social psychological component and restate it in sociological terms.

II

To reformulate the question, we must inquire to what extent, and how, social distance configures the nature of cultural interchange. Any answer to this question must take full account of the complexities of the social dynamics of cultural interaction, and of the fact that the

Figure 1

Feudal Customs of Aragon called "Vidal Mayor," Aragon, second half of the 13th century, Collection of the J. Paul Getty Museum, Malibu, 83.MQ.165 (Ms. Ludwig XIV 6), fol. 175 v (cat. no. 24)
This miniature depicts a Jew and a Christian engaged in economic activity (at right) and then appealing to the king to resolve their dispute (at left). *Convivencia* as cultural interaction was partly based on each group's perception of the others formed during activities such as those shown here.

relationship between cultural and social processes changes over time and according to specific contexts. It is also well to bear in mind Mark Meyerson's distinction between assimilation and integration.[5] To the extent that both Jews and Muslims were expelled, they were never assimilated by Christian society, and hence it is easy to argue that they were never acculturated either. But if they were not assimilated, they were indeed integrated; and integration, a process of normalization of day-to-day interactions, provides the immediate social context for cultural exchange.

Convivencia, under any kind of operational definition, must encompass the ability of persons of different ethnic groups to step out of their ethnically bound roles in order to interact on a par with members of competing groups. We admit, however, that many kinds of interactions are conditioned by ethnic role playing. Are there roles not ethnically bound? The ability of medieval peoples to assume them was limited, or rather interactions were sharply structured both by ethnic/religious ascription as well as by social class. Nevertheless one person can play multiple roles, some of which are more ethnically bound than others.

Elena Lourie, in her exploration of the differing roles that Jews and Mudejars (Muslims living under Christian rule) could successfully play in the medieval kingdom of Aragon, states that those Mudejars who had military skills were successful in playing the role of soldier in Christian units, regardless of ethnicity.[6] But Jews she views as unable to play multiple roles except in very limited, mainly socially marginal, contexts, as when Jewish and Christian criminals conspired without respect to ethnic identity, or in the specific case she describes, built on the ethnic connotations of moneylending in order to set up a clever confidence game.[7]

But what of less exceptional interactions? Lourie may be right in referring to St. Thomas's admiring citation of Maimonides as merely an instance of academic courtesy,[8] but the same cannot be said of Jews and Christians who formed translation teams. As we shall see,[9] in twelfth- and thirteenth-century Christian Spain, Christian translators were frequently subordinate to Jewish scholars whom they addressed as their "masters."

One of Lourie's goals is to test the "relative vulnerability" of Jews and Muslims to persecution in Christian Spain. One of her conclusions is that Mudejars ran less risk of mass assault (that is, pogroms) than Jews did, but greater risk of individual kidnapping and enslavement.[10] What were the cultural concomitants of vulnerability? On the face of it, there was an inverse relationship between vulnerability and cultural openness. As a group, Muslims were less vulnerable to persecution than Jews; yet their culture was more highly bounded and impervious to Christian pressures. Such a conclusion, while standing on its head the commonsense expectation that tolerance would encourage acculturation, has a certain kind of psychological logic arising from the dependence of the persecuted on the persecutor. I raise the issue only to state, in another form, that the relationship between cultural dynamics and social dynamics is a complicated one and cannot be left to insight or ideology.

As Lourie also makes clear, the different social structures of Muslim and Jewish minority communities in Christian Spain affected differentially the reactions of each to pressures from the dominant caste. The Jewish community was internally stratified to a much greater degree than were the Mudejars.[11] It is precisely in the pattern of class stratification that we can locate the ability of Jewish *maiores* to interact with Christians, notably in the marketplace and in the financial departments of royal administration, by stepping out of their ethnic roles. This in turn makes intelligible the conversion of Jewish magnates and intellectuals in the fifteenth century, for substantial acculturation must be assumed to have been characteristic of members of this group prior to their conversion. Indeed, the working out of the cultural concomitants of class stratification among late medieval Jews will provide the necessary social grounding to strengthen and make more intelligible Castro's pioneering study of the Jewish presence in Spanish literature.[12] Castro, incidentally, wisely observed that class stratification among Christians strongly affected the different relationships of members of that caste to the Jews.[13]

In assessing the variety and range of cultural elements exchanged, we must recognize that these did not merely include vocabulary, techniques, or manners of speech, dress, or diet, and that acculturation involved conscious shifts of the most subtle and intimate nature. For example, in northern Europe, Jews living among Christians acquired from them a distinctive consciousness of self that distinguished both groups from their coreligionists in the Mediterranean world. Any notion that borrowing across cultural boundaries is merely superficial is wishful thinking.[14] The image of a sealed, pristine, pure, and uncontaminated culture that ethnic groups typically ascribe to themselves (even if only to lament its loss) is contrary not only to all the evidence but to everyday experience. There are no cultural isolates, not in remote jungles, and much less in the cosmopolitan towns of medieval Spain.

In both al-Andalus and Christian Spain the dominant caste wanted to isolate minorities religiously but not economically, creating an inevitable tension in intergroup relations.[15] This tension, however, opened up avenues for cultural interchange by making the market a place where ethnic distinctions mattered less than in other walks of life. A similar tension is revealed in the ethnic exclusivity of guilds. Meyerson notes that Christian guilds in late medieval Valencia feared revealing their technological secrets to Muslim rivals, at least in periods when the rattle of war could be heard from the frontier.[16] Muslims conveyed similar fears: thus ibn ʿAbdūn, in his treatise on regulation of the market, warns Muslims against selling books of science to Jews or Christians.[17] Such strictures, however, more than likely reflect the intensity of technical and scientific interchange that attracted the attention of religious zealots but was impossible to stop.

III

The social dynamic among the three castes can be described comparatively in a series of triangles or triads for each particular trait or context. For example, Jewish scholars acknowledged Muslims as their masters in al-Andalus, as Christian did Jews in Castile and Catalonia. Did Muslims so acknowledge Jews or Christians? Ibn Juljul, a Muslim physician, recounts the visit of the physician Yaḥyā ibn Isḥāq to a monastery to consult a monk about an ear ailment of the Caliph ʿAbd al-Raḥmān III and, later in the tenth century, ibn al-Kattānī (ca. 949–1029) studied with the Mozarab bishop Abūʾl-Ḥārith, along with Muslim masters.[18] In al-Andalus it might have been rare for a Muslim to study medicine with a Christian or a Jew; but Mudejars of the fourteenth and fifteenth centuries living under Christian rule were totally integrated into the Christian medical system, trained by Christians, and examined by Christian medical tribunals on scholastic texts.[19] Patterns of medical examination of minority candidates differed from place to place: in fourteenth-century Catalonia, Jews were generally examined by Jewish doctors, but in Valencia and Castile both Jewish and Muslim candidates were examined by Christians.[20] Such divergences from the general medieval model whereby minority candidates were to be examined by members of their own ethnic group reflect the pace of acculturation of minority groups to the dominant culture, the steady extension of control by Christians over the two minorities, and permutations in the dynamics of social interaction in those places that diverged from the model. The pace of acculturation naturally increased over time. In the fourteenth century, Spanish Jews, who had typically been teachers of medicine, now learned Latin scholastic medicine and philosophy from Christians.[21] By the late sixteenth century, so many Moriscos (Muslims resident in Iberia after 1492) were studying medicine in Spanish universities that one commentator complained that soon all physicians would be Moriscos.[22] A negative reading of these changes would conclude that despite the lessening of cultural distance among the three castes, social distance remained unchanged. A more positive view would be that movement in social distance lagged behind that of cultural distance because of the drag of blood-purity statutes and other instances of racialist prejudice.

The *dhimma* contract in al-Andalus that regulated the social interaction between Muslims and the minority communities also ensured that in the normal course of events such relations would be less supercharged emotionally.[23] Lourie's assertion that the caste hierarchy in Christian Spain was the "mirror image" of Islamic law[24] is not true as stated. The fact that the *dhimma* contract was a religious obligation upon Muslims provided those relationships with a solidity that the shifting sands of Christian administration and politics could in no way provide, although the *dhimma* model is clear. The Christians borrowed the model but implemented it as civil, not religious, law; therefore the borrowed version lacked the universal sanction of the original concept.[25]

Jewish religious doctrine was more threatening to Christians than to Muslims.[26] What statements could be made about the threat that Islam or Christianity held for the other groups? The employment of craftsmen of one caste by members of the others was, of course, commonplace and here the lines conjoining the triad would be of more equal value. By filling in many such triads the complex weave of the dynamic of social interaction could be reconstructed.

Historians' views of cultural contact frequently conceal two ideological modes or sets of preconceptions: one that emphasizes conflict and one that, while recognizing the reality of conflict, stresses cultural congruence and creative interaction. In Jewish history, for example, the first view—the "neo-lachrymose" view, as it has been called,[27] is promoted as a corrective to an older school that is considered to have portrayed various "golden ages" of the Jewish past in too idyllic and optimistic terms. In Spanish history a similar polarity characterized the polemic between Américo Castro and his detractors such as Claudio Sánchez Albornoz, who remarked that the symbiosis of the three castes as Castro depicted it was more nearly an "antibiosis."[28] Such polemics are the result of inadequate theoretical grasp of the relationship between social relations and cultural interchange, between social distance and cultural distance.

Castro's *convivencia* survives. What we add to it is the admission that cultural interaction inevitably reflects a concrete and very complex social dynamic. What we retain of it is the understanding that acculturation implies a process of internalization of the "other" that is the mechanism by which we make foreign cultural traits our own.

NOTES

1. See my article "Darwinismo y filología española," *Boletín de la Institución Libre de Enseñanza,* n.s., no. 12 (October 1991): 35–41.

2. Castro's cultural terminology, which was not clearly defined in Spanish, became distorted in English. Thus in *The Spaniards,* trans. by Williard F. King and Selma Margaretten (Berkeley, Calif., 1971), *convivencia* is rendered as "living-togetherness" (584). See my comment on Castro's terminology in *Islamic and Christian Spain in the Early Middle Ages* (Princeton, N.J., 1979), 292–93.

3. Castro, *The Spaniards,* 86.

4. The fact that the unconscious nature of most cultural processes eluded Castro need not detract from his understanding of experience registered consciously.

5. Mark D. Meyerson, *The Muslims of Valencia in the Age of Fernando and Isabel: between Coexistence and Crusade* (Berkeley, Calif., 1991), 216.

6. Elena Lourie, "Anatomy of Ambivalence: Muslims under the Crown of Aragon in the Late Thirteenth Century," in *Crusade and Colonisation: Muslims, Christians and Jews in Medieval Aragon* (Hampshire, 1990), 73. The case of Abraham el Genet, a Jewish member of a Muslim mercenary band in the service of the King of Aragon, may be the exception that proves the rule; Lourie, "A Jewish Mercenary in the Service of the King of Aragon," *Revue des Etudes Juives* 137 (1978): 367–73.

7. Elena Lourie, "Complicidad criminal: un aspecto insólito de convivencia judeo-cristiana," *Actas del III Congreso Internacional 'Encuentro de las Tres Culturas'* (Toledo, 1988), 93–108.

8. Lourie, "Anatomy of Ambivalence," 72.

9. See below, "Science in Medieval Spain: The Jewish Contribution in the Context of *Convivencia.*"

10. Lourie, "Anatomy of Ambivalence," 2, 61.

11. Ibid., 2, 35, 41.

12. Américo Castro, *The Structure of Spanish History,* trans. by Edmund L. King, (Princeton, N.J., 1954) chapter 14. This chapter and the previous one ("The Spanish Jews") were omitted from the later recension of Castro's *magnum opus* (*The Spaniards,* n. 2 above).

13. Ibid., 489. For Castro, anti-Semitism was the mark of the lower classes, cultural exchange that of the upper.

14. On consciousness of self, see John E. Benton, "Consciousness of Self and Perceptions of Individuality," in *Renaissance and Renewal in the Twelfth Century,* ed. Robert L. Benson and Giles Constable (Cambridge, Mass., 1982), 291, n. 89. On cultural borrowing, see, for example, my comment on Sánchez Albornoz's views in my *Islamic and Christian Spain,* 279–80.

15. Meyerson, *Muslims of Valencia,* 46.

16. Ibid., 128.

17. Noted by Marie-Thérèse d'Alverny, "Translations and Translators," in *Renaissance and Renewal in the Twelfth Century,* 440, where she presumes that such prohibitions may account for a hiatus in scientific activity in Christian Spain in the eleventh century.

18. On Yaḥyā ibn Isḥāq: Juan Vernet, "Los médicos andaluces en el 'Libro de las Generaciones de Médicos,' de ibn Yulyul," *Anuario de Estudios Medievales* (Barcelona) 5 (1968): 457; on Ibn al-Kattānī: D. M. Dunlop, "Philosophical Predecessors and Contemporaries of ibn Bajjah," *Islamic Quarterly* 2 (1955): 107.

19. Luis García Ballester, *Historia social de la medicina en España de los siglos XIII al XVI, I: La minoria musulmana y morisca* (Madrid, 1976), p. 43. García Ballester goes on to say that these Mudejar physicians were thereby cut off from "their own" scientific tradition, but that of course entails the unnecessary assumption that the culture of specified social groups is normally expected to remain intact.

20. Ibid., 47–48.

21. Ibid., 10.

22. Ibid., 111.

23. As Meyerson, *Muslims of Valencia,* 3–4, observes, one function of the autonomy of religious minorities was to isolate them from the majority. But another function was to provide rules for social and cultural interaction that, if followed, were designed to prevent or minimize conflict.

24. Lourie, "Anatomy of Ambivalence," 70.

25. See my discussion in *Islamic and Christian Spain,* 168–69.

26. A point made by many authors, such as Lourie, "Anatomy of Ambivalence," 56; Mark M. Cohen, "The Neo-Lachrymose Conception of Jewish Arab History," *Tikkun* 6, no. 3 (May–June 1991): 58.

27. Ibid., and Norman A. Stillman, "Myth, Countermyth, and Distortion," 60–64.

28. Claudio Sánchez Albornoz, *España: Un enigma histórico,* 2 vols. (Buenos Aires, 1956), 1:249: the decline in intellectual curiosity of the Christians was in part owing to their directing most of their energy to fighting the Muslims, "an effect provoked by Christian-Islamic antibiosis in the temperamental inheritance of the northern Spaniards."

Jews, Christians, and Muslims in Medieval Iberia: *Convivencia* through the Eyes of Sephardic Jews

Benjamin R. Gampel

The Muslim conquest of the Iberian peninsula in 711 inaugurated the relationship among the three faith-communities of the peninsula, and the expulsion of the Jews in 1492 brought these interactions, at least officially, to an end. The contours of this *convivencia,* its limits in times of cultural openness, and its possibilities even in time of great decline, are our guiding theme.

When we employ the term *convivencia* in this essay, we are not attempting to conjure up an image of total harmony, of a cosmopolitan setting wherein all faith-communities joyfully infused each other with their particular strengths. Rather we are evoking images of a pluralistic society where communities often lived in the same neighborhoods, engaged in business with each other, and affected and infected each other with their ideas. At the same time, these groups mistrusted each other and were often jealous of each other's successes, and the ever-present competition among them occasionally turned to hatred.

Figure 5 *(opposite)*
Textile with Drinking Ladies, Spain, 13th century, The Cooper-Hewitt Museum, National Museum of Design, Smithsonian Institution, New York, Gift of J. P. Morgan from the Miguel y Badia Collection, 1902-1-82 (cat. no. 106)
Under the caliphate, the norms of Islamic life were often observed in a lenient manner. Sensual pleasures such as the drinking of wine were routinely pursued.

The relationship of the Jewish minority to other groups within Iberian society dates well before the arrival of the Muslims. Indeed, the first bit of data that points to the existence of Jews in Iberia is also testimony to their integration into Hispano-Roman society. This evidence is a third-century tombstone, now lost, that commemorated the death of a girl, Annia Salomonula, at the age of one year, four months, and one day. In many ways this tombstone is an appropriate starting point for our story. The tombstone, on which the Latin word "IVDAEA" (Jewess) is inscribed, indicates Jewish acculturation to the norms of the ruling classes of Roman society even as it calls attention to the Jewish wish to be buried among one's own and for their religion to be identified.[1]

The Jews had probably arrived in the peninsula alongside the Roman colonizers. In the early years of their community it appears that, aside from matters of faith, Jews could not be distinguished from the Romans. This situation caused much consternation to the leaders of the nascent Christian Church, which was much concerned with keeping the Christian community separate from other peninsular inhabitants and insisted that its members be possessed of a clearly defined religious identity. At a council that met around 313 in the town of Iliberis (Elvira), local churchmen attempted to regulate the practice of Christianity in Hispania or at least in the immediately surrounding area. The references to Jews in the canons of this council reflect the nature of Jewish interaction with the Christians; the local ecclesiastical authorities found these relations troubling.

The sixteenth canon of the council, which prohibited daughters of Christians from marrying sons either of heretics or of Jews, underscored the defensive nature of early Christianity. The main concern of these clerics was the preservation of their religion: had the daughters of Christians married men other than those of their own faith, the young women, the churchmen feared, would be forever lost either to Judaism or to unsanctioned forms of Christianity. The punishment for this offense—excommunication for five years—was inflicted on the parents of the girls. Evidently, not only were such marriages being celebrated, but, strikingly, it was the parents of these youngsters who arranged these matches.

Other canons of the council further served to restrict the interaction of Jews and Christians. One forbade clerics or lay Christians to eat with Jews, a rule that was probably intended to prevent Christians from participating in rituals that accompanied Jewish meals, especially those taken on the Sabbath and holidays. Canon 49 reflects the remarkable relationship that existed between Jews and Christians and indeed between Judaism and Christianity, and speaks volumes about Jewish symbiosis with the Christian inhabitants of the peninsula. It decreed that Christian farmers who had their crops blessed by the Church were not allowed to have their fields blessed as well by Jews. Evidently, not only were Christian farmers, after they had already besought the help of their priests, also requesting Jewish holy men to pray for the success of their harvest, but the Jews who were asked to perform the ritual may have been complying. Otherwise, there would have been no need to ban such activity. Christians and Jews may not have seen themselves as distinct peoples, despite the efforts of these religious leaders to create boundaries among people whose relationships may have been marked by great fluidity.[2]

When charting the elusive path of *convivencia,* it is important to realize the limits of cooperation between Jews and the dominant monotheistic cultures of the Middle Ages. Christian theological attitudes to, and estimation of, Judaism provided the ground rules by which

Figure 2
Basin with Trilingual Inscription, Tarragona, 5th century, marble, Museo Sefardí, Toledo
This is one of the few Jewish works extant from Visigothic Spain. Although its symbols (a menorah and tree of life) as well as its Hebrew inscription make Jewish usage indubitable, its exact function is uncertain.

these two faith-communities could interact in Christian lands. According to Christian theology, Jews were to be kept in a debased status because of their refusal to recognize Jesus as the Son of God, and God's rejection of them as his chosen people. In addition, they were to be kept separate from Christians so that the "True Israel" would not be influenced by the Jews' religious activities. Christians held out the hope that Jews who had rejected Jesus would in the "fullness of time" return to him in grace. While within these limits we can still observe evidence of interaction in late antiquity, we also note a gradual movement toward the debasement of Jews and even their exclusion from Christian society.[3]

In the fourth century Christianity became the official religion of the Roman Empire and there are indications that Jewish status within Iberian society was threatened. In a letter attributed to Severus, bishop of Minorca, street fighting was reported between Jews and Christians in the island town of Mahón around the year 418; the synagogue was destroyed and Jewish books were burned. According to the account, many Jewish women and children martyred themselves while the most distinguished of the Jewish men converted after a debate with Christian clergy. While some of the details of this account are open to question, the existence on the island of both a Jewish community and a synagogue in the fifth century and its destruction by Christian mobs seem to be without doubt.[4]

By the end of the fifth century, new rulers were in place in most of the peninsula. Rome and the western half of the empire had fallen and most of Iberia had been overrun by Visigothic tribes. At the outset, the Arian Visigoths must have viewed the Jews as yet another indigenous element within their new kingdom. Their first law code, a summary of the Theodosian Code compiled under the aegis of Alaric II in 506, retained only ten of the fifty-three provisions of the code relating to the Jews. Acknowledging the Jews' existing status and keeping only those Jewish-related laws that were relevant to the governance of the peninsula, the Visigoths were not preoccupied with the Jewish question [fig. 2].[5]

The Visigoths' attitude toward the Jews appears to have remained static until the accession of Reccared to the throne in 586. Reccared converted to the Catholic faith in the following year and seemingly in the wake of that decision issued a number of anti-Jewish laws. Almost thirty years later, in 613, Sisebut brought about an abrupt change in the status of the peninsular Jews when he ordered the forced conversion of all Jews within his dominions. Theories abound as to why Sisebut chose this course of action, the speculation ranging from religious to economic motivations, but his reasons remain a mystery. Forced conversion was contrary to the Christian teachings of his day and the publication of this edict does not appear to have been preceded by any policies pointing in its direction.

The policy of forced conversion was not particularly effective, but a number of Jews who wished to return to their former religion were not permitted to do so. By midcentury, whatever the reasons had been for the forced conversion and whatever the Jews' reactions might have been, the "baptized and unbaptized" Jews had not been successfully integrated into Christian society. The rulers became increasingly frustrated at their apparent lack of success and flailed about attempting to resolve this problem through laws, admonitions, and exhortations.

Suspicion of the loyalty and true affiliation of these converts plagued the ruling Visigoths. In 694, the Visigoths claimed, based on evidence obtained from "confessions," that Jews were conspiring with newly organized and triumphant Islam to overthrow them. In the absence of corroborating data, the most historians can assert is that Jews, converted or otherwise, may well have wished to rid themselves of their oppressive overlords.[6]

In 711 the Muslims conquered the peninsula. Paradoxically, the rare interplay among the three civilizations of Islam, Judaism, and Christianity—what is being labeled *convivencia*—emerged as a result of military adventure. According to the theological constructs of the victorious religion, soon to find expression in its classical form in the Covenant of ᶜUmar, Jews and Christians, although to be debased and treated as second-class citizens, were to be tolerated. As "people of the book," they were *dhimmis*, protected minorities, who while not enjoying the societal benefits that were solely the prerogative of Muslims, were not classified as pagans who could theoretically be put to the sword [fig. 3].

Ideally, the *dhimmis* were protected from injury to their persons and property; were granted freedom to pursue any occupation as long as it did not involve hegemony over Muslims; were allowed freedom of settlement and movement; and significantly were permitted freedom of religion that included the license to manage the affairs of their own faith-community. While the stipulations later developed in the Covenant of ᶜUmar were not the rule of the day in the immediate aftermath of the conquest, the Muslims did tolerate Jewish faith and

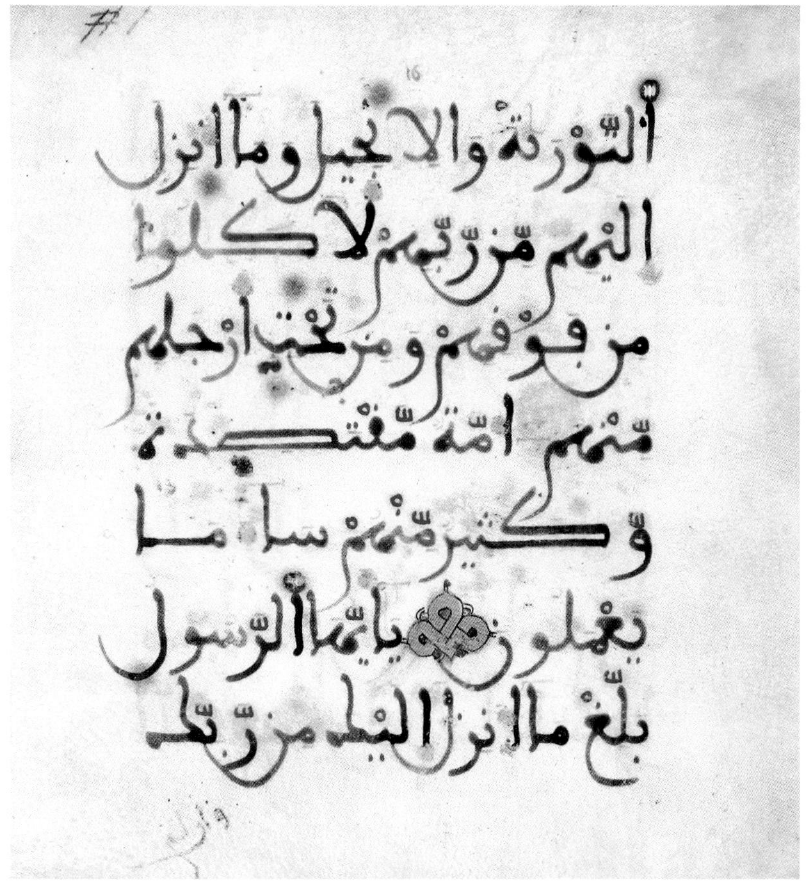
التوراة والانجيل وما انزل
اليهم من ربهم لاكلوا
من فوقهم ومن تحت ارجلهم
منهم امة مقتصدة
وكثير منهم ساء ما
يعملون يايها الرسول
بلغ ما انزل اليك من ربك

Figure 3
Leaf from Qurʾān, North Africa, ca. 1300, The Metropolitan Museum of Art, New York, Rogers Fund, 1921 (21.28) (cat. no. 4)
Muslims share with Jews a strict iconoclasm regarding the decoration of biblical texts read for ritual purposes. Muslim calligraphers consequently emphasized decorative scripts and beautiful inks and materials.

practice: a policy that surely was enthusiastically welcomed after the horrors of the Visigothic period. Although this toleration was celebrated and may have been perceived by some as a manifestation of divine deliverance, the relationship between the Jews and the conquering Muslims was not yet what later historians would call *convivencia*.[7]

The first glimmers of such symbiosis can be observed in the tenth century when the Umayyad emir ʿAbd al-Raḥmān III, who ruled the peninsula, from Córdoba declared his independence from the nominal authority of the Abbasid caliph in Baghdad. ʿAbd al-Raḥmān, like his father before him, pursued an ethnically and religiously inclusive policy dedicated to the pacification and unification of the Islamic Iberian state of al-Andalus. From his capital at Córdoba, ʿAbd al-Raḥmān greatly supported the arts and sciences, sparking a general cultural efflorescence. He stimulated the protected minorities to further their own intellectual interests by furnishing them with a model of how to proceed.

The Christians, having enjoyed political power in the peninsula under the previous rulers, accepted their second-class status with much reluctance, and consequently their community was often plagued by social and religious turmoil. The Jews, relishing their newly granted autonomy after their sufferings under the Visigoths, more easily adapted to these beneficent overlords. At any rate, as ʿAbd al-Raḥmān III brought scientists, poets, musicians, and religious scholars to his glittering capital at Córdoba and supported their endeavors, his *dhimmi* subjects followed suit [fig. 4].[8]

It was precisely this complex interaction among the three civilizations that made possible this brief moment of cultural sharing. But the source of Jewish religious vitality came not from the peninsula itself but from the east, from the center of the Abbasid caliphate in Baghdad. From that nerve center of political power and intellectual achievement flowed biblical and Talmudic learning, knowledge of philosophy and the sciences, mastery of Hebrew and the art of the poet. Over the course of the two centuries since the Muslim conquest of Iberia, people and their learning—both Muslim and Jewish—had streamed from east to west, and Iberian Jewry slowly began to participate in the efflorescence of rabbinic and Muslim culture that emanated from Baghdad.

But from these sources alone a Golden Age did not emerge. The simple accumulation of eastern learning was not sufficient. The additional catalyst was provided by Muslim society in al-Andalus. As part of his policy of having all the local ethnic and religious groups participate in his rule, ʿAbd al-Raḥmān looked to the highest-ranking government officials belonging to each minority and viewed them as the effective heads of their communities. These individuals were chosen—for example in the Jewish case—because of their value as members of the royal court and not as a result of their distinguished place within Jewish society or their mastery of Jewish lore. Such a courtier more often than not was a wealthy man, an aristocrat, often a physician, well versed in many languages: a person who mixed well with the royal entourage.

Figure 4
Córdoba Synagogue, south wall, Córdoba, 1314–15 (see also cat. no. 56 a, b). The seat of the caliphate was in Córdoba.

The man chosen by ʿAbd al-Raḥmān III as the nominal head of the Jews, however, was also viewed by the Jewish community as a fine representative of its interests. Ḥasdai ibn Shaprūṭ was born in Jaén in 910 to an aristocratic family, knew Arabic and Latin, was a physician by profession, and first came to the attention of the caliph through his medical expertise. He was later appointed tax collector at the Andalusian ports. Since ʿAbd al-Raḥmān viewed Ḥasdai as the leader of the Jewish community, the Jews in turn saw him as their *nasi*—their prince.[9]

Ḥasdai's career was prototypical of the Jewish courtiers whose activities as representatives of Andalusi Jewry at the royal court can be traced from the tenth up through the end of the fifteenth century and the expulsion of the Jews from the Iberian Christian kingdoms. The foremost obligation and responsibility of Ḥasdai, as of all courtiers, was to be a faithful servant to the caliph, or whoever occupied the seat of central power, since he served at the ruler's discretion. There were structural tensions inherent in this reality, especially those that continually erupted between the courtier and the organized Jewish community. Clearly, their goals were not always the same. Ḥasdai fulfilled his commission in an exemplary fashion, serving both the Jewish community and ʿAbd al-Raḥmān, and additionally, often without apparent mandate, acting as a representative of Andalusi Jewry to other Jewish communities.

At home in al-Andalus, Ḥasdai patterned himself after the Muslim example, specifically the cultural stewardship of the caliph, by inviting and attracting scholars to the peninsula: individuals trained in the traditional fields of Bible and Talmud scholarship, as well as philosophers, scientists, students of the Hebrew language, and professional poets. It was not simply the store of learning that had accumulated since the downfall of the Visigoths and the immigration of knowledgeable Jews to these western Mediterranean shores that provided the impetus for this golden age. Rather the ideal that Islamic society presented to Andalusi Jews embodied in its glorious architecture, Qurʾānic and Arabic scholarship, and glittering intellectual contributions in the poetical arts and in the sciences, challenged the Jews' self-definition and self-perception. The Jews strove mightily to display within this society of many cultures that they too possessed a rich and multifaceted civilization.

Jewish scholars were spurred on by Muslim achievements. If the Muslims studied the Qurʾān and the *hadith* (an appendix to the Qurʾān containing traditions related to Mohammed) and were doctors of the *sharīʾa* (Muslim law), then Jews perforce would investigate the Bible, Talmud, and *halakhah* (Jewish law). If the Muslims were advanced in their study of Arabic and believed that Arabic was suited more than any other tongue to the creation of verse, then the Jews for the first time would subject the Hebrew language and its structures to close scrutiny and expend much effort to create spiritual and sensual verse in Hebrew, as well as in Arabic. The ideal of *ʿarabiyya,* "the utter perfection of classical Arabic and its poetry...and the religious doctrine of the inimitable perfection of the Qurʾān,"[10] furnished the reference point for the Jewish intellectual and courtier. Ḥasdai, like the Muslims and the

Jewish aristocrats who followed his lead, employed family poets whose responsibilities included composing verses in praise of their patron, his family, and his entourage, and presenting them in the most favorable light to both Muslim and Jewish society. Blessed with the financial support of these benefactors, these poets were also able to produce religious and secular poetry of great beauty and significance.

Such conditions made Andalusi Jewry ripe for a religious renaissance. The existence of a wealthy commercial class living in the midst of a politically, economically, and religiously confident Islamic society enabled a new and highly motivated Jewish intellectual class to be born. Menaḥem ben Saruq, Ḥasdai's personal secretary and family poet, while attending to his primary duties, was a masterful writer of Hebrew poetry, which he composed according to biblical meter, and blazed new paths as a pioneer in the scientific study of the Hebrew language. He fell out of favor with Ḥasdai for reasons that remain obscure, and was replaced by Dunash ibn Labrat. Born in Fez and trained in Baghdad, Dunash brought with him such radical notions as studying Hebrew, the holy tongue, by paying attention to its cognate languages such as Arabic, and creating Hebrew verse that did not hew to traditional Hebrew meter but followed the metrical system that Muslims employed in their Arabic compositions.[11]

Drawing upon Jewish traditions of communal responsibility and viewing himself as part of a larger cosmopolitan Mediterranean society, Ḥasdai saw in his position as *nasi* of Andalusi Jewry a mandate to be a spokesman for Jewry in general. Ḥasdai sent a personal emissary to southern France in an attempt to put an end to a Christian custom of having Jews render thirty pounds of wax to churches on Palm Sunday, on which occasion the Jews received a ceremonial slap. He wrote a threatening letter to the former queen mother of Byzantium warning that if the Jews continued to be mistreated in that empire, the Christian population in al-Andalus would find itself in a difficult position. Ḥasdai also sent a letter, written by his secretary Menaḥem, to the khan of the Khazars, who with his people had converted to Judaism, inquiring about his fabled kingdom. He asked the monarch if he had any knowledge of the whereabouts of the ten lost tribes, or if he possessed any information about whether the messiah was bestirring himself in the king's corner of the globe.[12]

Even with the downfall of ʿAbd al-Raḥmān's caliphate in the next century and the splitting of al-Andalus into over twenty small *taifa* (party) kingdoms, the three cultures continued to thrive. Each of the rulers of these tiny polities wished to support as sparkling a culture as that which had been fashionable in Córdoba. And it is in one of these kingdoms, the Berber state of Granada, that we encounter another glittering star of the Jewish courtier class, whose career, and that of his son, sketches for us the extraordinary possibilities yet, simultaneously, the harsh limits of *convivencia*.[13]

Samuel ibn Nagrela was born in 993 in Córdoba to an aristocratic family that had originated in Mérida. He had the best Hebrew and Arabic education, was accomplished in Latin, Romance, and Berber, and studied with the leading Hebrew grammarians and halakhists of his day. With the downfall of the caliphate, his family fled to Málaga, which was subject to the small kingdom of Granada. He entered government service and was extremely successful. But that was not the only arena in which Samuel shone. He produced over two thousand poems in Hebrew and Arabic, was a significant Hebrew grammarian, wrote a polemic against Islam—an activity that took much courage—displayed himself as a superb Arabic scholar, and exhibited a remarkable knowledge of the Talmud and rabbinic literature. While his rise into the upper echelons of governmental service was not without a hitch, by 1027 we see him referred to as the *nagid* (ruler), and by the 1030s he was no less than the vizier to Ḥabbūs, the Berber king of Granada.

In his role as leader of the Jewish community of Granada, Samuel, like Ḥasdai, was a great patron of Jewish learning, supporting scholars both at home and abroad and corresponding with Jewish scholars all over the world. In his activities on behalf of the king, Samuel proved himself a master diplomat and military strategist. In an intriguing combination of his rare talents, he apparently wrote poems on the battlefield. His poetry testifies to the external enemies of Granada who taunted Samuel because of his faith and criticized the Granadan king for employing a Jew in such an influential position. He also wrote of his internal enemies within the kingdom who wished to replace him in his role as vizier. These Muslim foes of Samuel were as motivated by their jealousy of his position as they were by their antagonism to the faith that he professed.

Surrounded as he was by enemies, Samuel's greatest accomplishment was to die of natural causes in 1056 at the age of sixty-three. He was succeeded in the post of vizier by his son Yehosef who was learned in Jewish subjects and an accomplished poet. We cannot determine whether or not Yehosef was as diplomatically gifted as was his father, but we do know that beset by all the palace intrigue in which he, like his father, was necessarily involved, he probably made a tactical mistake and was killed. Upon Yehosef's death a pogrom broke out in the streets of Granada, and the Jewish community was destroyed. Three hundred Jews were murdered.[14]

The Granada pogrom shows that Jews were able to attain lofty positions in the courts of the Andalusi monarchs despite the undercurrent of anti-Judaism in eleventh-century Islamic Iberia. The Jewish courtier was trusted precisely because both he and the royal authorities were aware that if he fell out of favor, the entire Jewish community could be made to suffer. The latent anti-Judaism that the royal authorities held in check was always in danger of being released.

The eleventh century was truly an insecure time for the Jews. The small kingdoms that emerged with the downfall of the caliphate were continually at war with each other. Most of the inhabitants of the peninsula suffered constantly, either as a result of the wars or because of continual famine. Whatever the nature of the *convivencia* during the period of the *taifa* kingdoms, it was always tenuous and at best enjoyed only by a tiny elite.

These glories, such as they were, were not to last. The small Christian kingdoms, which had survived in the far north of the peninsula during the years of Muslim hegemony, increased their political and military strength and soon posed a clear danger to the survival of Islam's dominion in Iberia. With the constant warring among the *taifa* kingdoms and the resurgence of the small Christian states, the situation of the Jews deteriorated. At first the *taifa* kings turned to the Almoravids, an ascetic Muslim sect that had recently gained control over North Africa and disdained the material and intellectual culture created by their coreligionists in al-Andalus. During the first Almoravid campaign in Iberia, the newcomers became quite upset over the loose way that they perceived that the Andalusians were interpreting the Qurʾān and the Islamic tradition. Sensual pleasure was celebrated [fig. 5, p. 10]; *dhimmis*—both Jews and Christians—occupied positions that granted them power over Muslims; taxes were collected that were not approved in Islamic law; and activities that were simply not in consonance with the pattern of life that a devout Muslim was to follow, such as the drinking of wine, were countenanced.[15]

After defeating the Christians, the Almoravids returned to North Africa, but as the military equilibrium in the peninsula shifted again in favor of the Christians, the Almoravids were invited back. This time they stayed and put their own Islamic ideas into practice in al-Andalus. Some highly placed Jews in government service lost their positions and the glittering society that was al-Andalus began to lose its luster. Over time, though, as the Almoravids extended their sojourn in the peninsula, they were swept away by the mood of Andalusi Islam. Creative juices still flowed through and amongst the Jewish intelligentsia, and the poetry of Moses ibn Ezra was a prime example of the symbiosis that continued to exist with the surrounding Muslim culture.[16]

When the Almoravids' base of operations in North Africa came under attack from other Muslim tribes, the Almoravids retreated from the peninsula. When Andalusi Muslims needed further military help against the Christians, they again turned southward to the tribes that had replaced Almoravid power in the Maghreb. The Almohads were even fiercer guardians of the strict interpretation of Islamic tradition than were the Almoravids. They saw little place for the protected *dhimmis* within Islamic society and initiated a policy of forced conversion, the second time in peninsular history that the Jews were forced under penalty of death to abandon their religion. Some Jews fled the peninsula to other Islamic lands, the young Maimonides and his family being the most famous among them. Yet many traveled northward within Iberia. The memory of their treatment at the hands of the Visigoths did not have any discernible effect on the Jews' choice to put down roots in the growing Christian kingdoms.[17]

As the Christians emerged victorious and as the Muslim tribes pursued a course of intolerance, the center of gravity of Jewish and of course Christian culture shifted to the north. In the newly dominant Christian states of Portugal, Castile, Navarre, and Aragon, Jews were granted high diplomatic and cultural positions by the local rulers since their financial, administrative, and diplomatic expertise was sorely needed. These same rulers treated their Muslim population warily because of their potential as political adversaries.

The Jews, skilled in crafts and commerce, were crucial to the continuity of urban life in the areas conquered from the Muslims. The Christians, who were mainly devoted to agriculture and herding, were not yet capable of performing these tasks. Jews were also helpful to their new overlords in the distribution of conquered land and in acting as diplomats and middlemen between the conquered Muslims and the newly victorious Christians. While the Jews' social and economic status markedly improved under the Christians, it took much longer for Jewish culture to flourish.[18]

Eventually, however, halakhists, poets, and Talmudic and biblical commentators all began to develop their traditions in Christian countries. But some aspects of the Jews' creativity only found full expression in settings in which Jews worked alongside Christians and Muslims. Members of all three faith-communities were to be found in thirteenth-century Toledo, serving the Castilian court. Jews and Muslims were utilizing their intimacy with Muslim language and culture to translate and thus help transmit the cultural glories of Islam to Christian society [fig. 6]. Under the rule of Alfonso X, the Wise, a Castilian cultural efflorescence was nurtured and carefully cultivated, as the monarch attempted to create an indigenous Christian Iberian culture in the Romance vernacular. The Muslims and Jews had their own areas of expertise: the Mudejars (Muslims living under Christian rule) were distinguished, for example, by their knowledge of art and architecture, the Jews by their astronomical expertise.[19]

While the thirteenth century was enlivened by unusually positive interplay among the three faith-communities, we cannot help but notice that with Iberia now the southwesternmost appendage of European civilization, the prejudices of that culture toward other monotheisms began to infiltrate the Christian kingdoms of the peninsula. So while James I the

Conqueror of Aragon employed Jews in the highest administrative posts within his realm, he also presided over the first great public disputation between Jews and Christians, designed by the newly fashioned Christian Mendicant orders among whose goals was the conversion of Jews to the Christian faith.

Figure 6

Avicenna, *The Canon,* Spain, 14th century and 1468, Courtesy of The Library of The Jewish Theological Seminary of America, New York, Mic. 8184, fol. 58r (cat. no. 28)

Avicenna, or Abu Ali al-Hussein ibn ʿAbdallah ibn Sina (980-1037), was a physician, scientist, and outstanding Muslim philosopher. His *Canon of Medicine* was very popular during the Middle Ages among scholars of all religions, as is attested to by the many Arabic, Hebrew, and Latin manuscripts still in existence.

In 1263 in Barcelona, Rabbi Moses ben Naḥman (Nahmanides), was summoned by James I, and ordered to appear in a religious disputation with Paulus Christiani, a Jew who had converted to Christianity. The organizers of the disputation were eager for the public opportunity to test a method that they hoped would be effective in helping Jews recognize the true faith. Recently developed in southern France, this innovative approach, pioneered by the Mendicants, involved the use of the Talmud and rabbinic literature, the Jews' own teachings, to prove that Jesus was the messiah whom the Old Testament had prophesied. It was Jewish sources, they hoped, that would underscore that Christianity indeed was the true religion. While Nahmanides put up a valiant fight against his Christian interlocutors, often taking control of the "debate," he had no opportunity to prevail since the goal of the disputation was simply the testing of the new method. Immediately following the conclusion of the disputation, Aragonese Jews were compelled to attend Christian sermons in their synagogues, where local preachers put these new ideas to use.[20]

Such was the nature of coexistence in the thirteenth century. On the one hand, at Alfonso's court, Jews, Christians, and Muslims could mix freely while contributing to a royally mandated intellectual agenda. On the other, the same Alfonso could also give voice to the Christian blood libel (though the king clearly stated that such charges against Jews would have to be proven) and the dissemination of anti-Jewish imagery through the publication of the *Cantigas de Santa María,* a collection of poems compiled in honor of the Virgin Mary. And if James I could appreciate more than any other Iberian Christian monarch the value of his Jewish communities, this did not prevent him, as we have just seen, from seeking to fulfill a millennial Christian fantasy that had been given fresh impetus in the thirteenth century: the conversion of the Jewish people.[21]

While political and economic relationships involved the Jews daily with Christians and at times with Muslims as well, the Jews also had an internal life that, while influenced by trends within contemporary Iberian society, owed the forms of its existence to the rhythms and dynamics of the Jewish religion. Organized Jewish communities (*aljamas*) were an ever-present feature of Jewish life in the diaspora and the communal structure that obtained in Sepharad was sophisticated and highly developed. Local governments supported the Jewish *aljama* for their own reasons; they did not wish to police the community alone. And since the main concern of all levels of government was the collection of revenues, it was far more cost-effective, not to say politically expedient, for Jews to assess, collect, and render their own taxes.

Members of the upper social and economic strata of the Jewish population formed the governing body of each *aljama.* Not surprisingly, this arrangement caused much strife between the richer and poorer classes, especially since the council was responsible for the *aljama*'s social and religious needs and for tax collection as well. The central institution of the community was the *bēt dīn* or court of Jewish law. It operated, as was its mandate, according to the *halakhah*, although its members were not necessarily great legal scholars. Additionally, the council empowered various committees to administer educational and charitable institutions, synagogues and prayer halls, ritual baths and slaughterhouses. Groups were also formally constituted to prevent religious and moral laxity and to oversee business practices, especially to supervise weights and measures. Of course a variety of religious functionaries were inscribed on the payroll of the community, from rabbis to schoolmasters, from ritual circumcisers to ritual slaughterers.[22]

It was precisely the *aljamas'* contacts and conflicts with the governments of the cities and towns in which the Jews lived that shaped the mandate of these communities and delimited the extent of their power. Generally, the Jewish community in the Middle Ages, and before and after as well, was very anxious about its authority over its members. The *kahal* (community) was anxious lest its jurisdiction be undermined and was therefore much troubled when Jews sought redress of grievances or adjudication of conflicts at the "courts of the Gentiles." Moral suasion and social pressure aside, the Jewish community had no truly effective means to prevent their coreligionists from attending these courts. Contemporary rabbis inveighed against Jews who resorted to these non-Jewish institutions; reading their remarks brings home so clearly the limits of Jewish power even in, for medieval times, a tolerant society.[23]

And yet, surprisingly, the Jewish courts in Sepharad arrogated powers to themselves that quite outstripped their authority as delineated by Jewish law. We find these communal bodies issuing sentences of corporal punishment such as maiming and cutting off body parts and even ordering particular offenders to be put to death: actions that clearly violated the *halakhah*. The *bēt dīn* would not execute the sentence itself but rather would remand the guilty party to the local government that, for a fee, would carry out the wishes of the Jewish court. These harsh and extralegal punishments were usually meted out to those accused of slandering the Jewish community. This individual labeled a *malshin*—the word covered a variety of sins against one's fellow Jews and even entered the Castilian language as *malsín*—was the most feared and hated person in the organized Jewish community. The treatment of the *malshin* pointed up as clearly as could anything else that despite or rather as a result of the great power that the *aljama* possessed, it was terribly fearful lest anyone erode the integrity of the community.[24]

A curious side-effect of the tolerance, then, that allowed the Jews much autonomy over their communal affairs was their intense anxiety over the loss of their treasured status. It is significant that one of the rationalizations offered for these harsh penalties meted out to social offenders was that Gentiles ordered similar punishments for such crimes. To look at this in another way, it was the mores of the external society that were employed to preserve the inviolability of the internal community. It may have been that the extraordinarily grand self-perception of Sephardim allowed them to acquire rights, such as that of inflicting the death penalty, not permitted to Jewish courts of law since the days of the famed Sanhedrin of Greco-Roman times. Yet what lurked beneath this lofty self-esteem was a crushing insecurity about the enduring strength of the institutions themselves. While the king would encourage slanderers to spy out the closed-door decisions of the Jewish communal governing bodies, he would also allow the Jewish community to catch the slanderer and sentence him to death. Since the former spy became totally useless to the king, it was expedient for the monarch even to carry out the sentence for the Jews because at that juncture it would be in his best interests to strengthen the foundations of the community.

The relationships between Jews and others in Iberian Christian society, while not a major factor in shaping the structure and activities of the Jewish communities, did mold aspects of the social and religious agenda of individual *aljamas*. The influence of Christian Europe and of Christian Iberia upon Jewish culture is also evident. In al-Andalus, the study of philosophy had been considered the capstone of the education of a well-educated man, whether Jew or Muslim. However, as the Christian reconquest achieved its greatest successes in the peninsula, this exalted appreciation of philosophy slowly came under attack. Philosophy was not an unalloyed blessing in the eyes of Christian society nor was it to Jews who lived in Christian realms. This changing attitude toward the study of philosophy was openly manifested in Provence during the fourth decade of the thirteenth century amidst the controversy over the writings of Maimonides. Not coincidentally, the Church was investigating heretical ideas within the Christian community in an attempt to stem the activities of the Cathars and Albigensians in the same region of southern France.[25]

Just as uncertainty about the appropriate role of philosophy within the religious curriculum spread to the Iberian peninsula, theosophical mysticism emanated into Sepharad from sources that also originated in southern France. These mystical reflections found earnest expression in the search for the true meaning of Scripture and of the appropriate prism through which to view rabbinic traditions. Such ideas were given important encouragement by Moses de León and his circle of mystical adepts with the authorship of what would emerge as the classic work of Jewish mysticism written in the Middle Ages: the pseudepigraphic *Sefer ha-Zohar* or *Book of Splendor*. And using the more conventional form of biblical commentary but infusing it with novel mystical ideas, the distinguished Rabbi Moses ben Naḥman, communal leader, profound Talmudist, and representative of Judaism at the Barcelona disputation, was able to introduce many of these concepts to a learned public audience.[26]

The more traditional vehicles of intellectual expression within the Jewish community, biblical and Talmudic commentary, continued to thrive. Talmudic exegesis especially was enriched by the introduction of northern European methods of Talmudic analysis that were publicized in the peninsula by that literary virtuoso, Nahmanides himself. The poets of the period such as Todros ben Judah Abulafia also scaled new heights in the era of the *reconquista* and their poetry assumed new forms, thanks to the influence of Christian society.[27]

It remains difficult to characterize Jewish society in the years that followed the Christian conquests of the thirteenth century and preceded the eruption of the anti-Jewish outbreaks at the close of the fourteenth century. One is tempted either to trace the lingering effects of the new Christian hegemony and concomitantly the important role that Jews played in the society, or to stress aspects of the decline of Jewish power as an adumbration of the erosion of Jewish society that is evident at the end of the fourteenth century. Either way, by the 1300s, after the Christians had completed their most significant conquests within the peninsula, the Christian population gradually began to develop the urban talents in which they had been sorely deficient a century earlier. Their acquisition of commercial skills was especially rapid in the Crown of Aragon and was reflected in the growth of its Mediterranean empire. As a result, Jewish status in that eastern kingdom declined, unlike that of Castilian Jewry, which remained relatively stable.[28]

The Black Death, which devastated Europe's population in the fourteenth century, had a profound impact upon the peninsula including its Jewish communities. Indeed, Jews may have endured greater trauma than others since they were often accused of having instigated the outbreak of this dreaded disease, and in some instances were attacked and even killed. Jewish suffering was especially acute in the Crown of Aragon where the Jewish communities met in 1354 and presented a rare united front to confront the aftermath of the devastation.

In the neighboring kingdom of Castile in midcentury, Jews still held important posts within the royal government, as evidenced by the career of Samuel Halevi, who served as treasurer to King Peter I. When Samuel had a private synagogue (later called El Tránsito) built in the capital city of Toledo [fig. 7], he dedicated the chapel to Peter. Muslim artisans employed in its construction fashioned the building according to the prevailing Mudejar style. In Navarre, the Jews were recuperating from the pernicious effects of the Shepherds' Crusade of the 1320s and the outbreaks of violence that accompanied the end of the Capetian dynasty in 1328. Still the existence of highly placed Jews such as Ezmel de Ablitas and a prevailing atmosphere conducive to the general social and economic integration of the Jews were features of Navarrese society. Portugal, blessed with royal stability, also seemed to provide the necessary conditions for a flourishing Jewish community.[29]

After midcentury, however, Castile was wracked by a long civil war as Henry of Trastámara, half-brother of Peter, challenged Peter's right to occupy the throne. One of Henry's devices in gaining the support of the nobility and others within the kingdom was his promulgation of fierce anti-Jewish sentiments. Such tactics reveal the attractiveness of such arguments to many within Castile. With the progress of the civil war, many Jewish communities, especially the *aljama* in Burgos, were threatened, attacked, and ultimately impoverished. Surprisingly, after the murder of Peter by Henry at Montiel and the accession of Henry to the throne, Jews resumed their elevated positions at the royal court.[30]

Prior to the civil war, there had been plans afoot to harm the Jews physically and financially such as that devised by Gonzalo Martínez de Oviedo, the majordomo of Alfonso XI, but it is impossible to gauge their importance or assess their influence. What we can observe during the 1300s is the persistence of the Christian-Jewish polemic that we first saw emerge publicly in 1263 and that continued dramatically to affect Jewish-Christian relationships in

Figure 7 *(opposite)*
Interior of El Tránsito Synagogue, Toledo, 1357 (see also cat. no. 58 a, b, c)

the peninsula. A significant figure in the religious debates of the time was Alfonso of Valladolid who was born Abner of Burgos and was a practicing physician and prolific Jewish intellectual prior to his conversion to Christianity. As a Christian he continued his profound literary efforts, now directed toward the conversion of his former coreligionists.[31]

While the fourteenth century did witness a decline in Jewish status, an increase in physical attacks against Jews, and an escalating tempo in attempts to convert Jews to Christianity, the pogroms that broke out in June 1391 against the Jews of Seville shocked Jews and Christians alike. The riots rapidly spread to Córdoba, Jaén, Ubeda, Baeza, Carmona, and many other communities throughout Andalusia. Contemporary Hebrew poetry reveals that many of these attacks occurred simultaneously. They were not, however, coordinated; evidently, anti-Jewish sentiment was simmering right beneath the surface. By the onset of summer, Jewish communities in the Crown of Aragon were assaulted. Rioters traveled up the Mediterranean coast wreaking havoc upon Jewish communities in their path. Large and distinguished Jewish communities like that of Barcelona suffered such devastation that they never recovered.[32]

What had happened to the famed *convivencia* of Iberian society? In Seville, Archdeacon Ferrante Martínez of Ecija had been preaching hatred against Jews for more than ten years and encouraging anti-Jewish violence. In 1390, the death of the archbishop of Seville had provided the opportunity to Martínez to act as he wished. Moreover, King John I of Castile had died in the same year, leaving an underage son, and since the royal government frequently acted as the traditional protector of Jewish rights, the Jews were left defenseless. It was the weakness of royal government that had been the crucial factor in the devastation of Navarrese Jewry in 1328, as well as other outbreaks of violence against the Jews in the Middle Ages. In 1391, on the other hand, the throne of Navarre as well as that of Portugal were occupied by strong and capable rulers, so that the Jewish communities in these kingdoms appear to have escaped unharmed.

While the killings of Jews were unexpected, so were other results of the devastation. Jews are recorded as having taken their own lives in response to the choice of baptism or death, but others preferred to convert when faced with the same alternative. It is striking, however, that of the many Jews who converted to Christianity, a number did so willingly. Although volition is hard to establish given the pervasive atmosphere of intimidation and fear, Jews did flock to baptismal fonts across Castile and Aragon. While this wholesale acceptance of the majority religion could be considered a natural extension of *convivencia,* it more accurately reflects a loss of faith on the part of large segments of the Jewish community. This decline of morale was the end result not just of successful integration but of unceasing anti-

Jewish polemic and of relentless Christian preaching to which the "successful" Jewish community had been subjected ever since the heyday of the Reconquest and of the disputation at Barcelona. As the number of those baptized increased over time, the morale of those who remained Jews sank even lower and the tide of conversions surged. The Jews were extremely vulnerable. Attempts at punishment of the rioters and of reconstruction of the communities met with mixed success. Things would never be the same.[33]

Many leaders of the Christian community were energized by the messianic possibilities inherent in the widespread Jewish conversions, and attempted to gather all of the former chosen people—"Israel in the flesh"—into the bosom of Christianity. Vicente Ferrer, the charismatic preacher of the Antichrist and the Second Coming, sparked the desire of the Avignonese Pope Benedict XIII to stage a great public disputation between Judaism and Christianity, and thus to bring about the Messianic Age. From a more earthly perspective, Benedict seized this opportunity to impress those who were wavering in their support of his claim to the papacy. Ferdinand I, the king of Aragon, who as regent of Castile was much influenced by Ferrer, provided the additional impetus for the public debate. Accordingly, a disputation was held in 1413 in Tortosa, at the mouth of the Ebro in Aragon.[34]

The goal of the disputation was to effect the theological grand coup and stampede the remaining Jews to the baptismal font. And try the Christians did. The Jewish representatives were implored to convert and their families were harassed as the "debate" dragged on for over a year and a half, for sixty-nine sessions. During the disputation, converts were often paraded before those assembled to make clear, if it had not already become transparent to all, what the purpose of the debate was. Some Jews did "embrace" Christianity in the wake of the events at Tortosa but in a short time, the three men who were responsible for the planning and production of the debate departed the Iberian stage. Ferdinand I died in 1416, but not before renouncing Benedict XIII, and Vicente Ferrer wandered off to southern France where he died in 1419.

The result of this tumultuous period from 1391 to 1415 was that at least one-third to one-half of Iberian Jewry converted to Christianity. The Jewish communities of the large Castilian cities were decimated. As part of a larger demographic trend involving all Castilians, Jews moved to smaller villages and towns and to areas outside the control of the royal authorities. In Aragon, many Jewries did not recover; only eight were left in Catalonia, five in Valencia, and twenty-two in Aragon. Portuguese Jewry, although escaping the ravages of the pogroms, suffered from anti-Jewish legislation in the early years of the fifteenth century. The Majorcan Jewish community, which suffered greatly in 1391, found its numbers even more depleted by the emigration of many of its members. A ritual murder accusation was leveled against the remaining Jews in 1432 and the case was brought to trial. In 1435 after the Jewish population was physically threatened, many fled, and seemingly all those who remained were converted.[35]

Remarkably, Jews began to recover. Perhaps they did not scale the social and economic heights to which they had ascended before, but they continued to function as artisans, small-scale merchants, and moneylenders. We do not know if these relationships assumed a different texture after the events of 1391, but instances of the greater tolerance—*convivencia,* if you will—that had existed prior to 1391, can still be found in the fifteenth century. In 1433, the Jew Moses Arragel—with the help of two Christian friars—completed a translation of and commentary on the Hebrew Bible for a Christian patron, a Master of the Military Order of Calatrava, Don Luis González de Guzmán. And in these years when most Christians were not interested even in feigning religious dialogue, but rather were openly antagonistic to the culturally weakened Muslim communities, Juan of Segovia produced a trilingual translation of the Qurʾān.[36]

But the fate of the Jews and the destiny of the fragile coexistence that Iberian society had managed to construct was not bound up either with the Jews themselves or with the relationships they maintained with Christians and Muslims. Rather, the large numbers of Jews who had converted to Christianity proved crucial to both the survival of the Jewish community and its relationships with other faith-communities in the peninsula. The New Christians, or *conversos,* as the converts were called, remained at first in the same quarters they had lived in as Jews and continued to work at the same professions. But as the years passed some moved out of their former dwellings and attained positions from which they had been excluded as Jews, such as those of public notary, city magistrate, and other municipal posts.

The converts began to incur the wrath of the Old Christians as they competed for the social and economic benefits Iberian society had to offer. Not only were the erstwhile Jews enjoying the professional opportunities available to Christians, wealthier New Christians were often marrying into the nobility, especially those noble families that had fallen on hard times. Through these unions the *converso* family was able to achieve the social respectability and the noble family the wealth that seemed otherwise to elude the grasp of each. The suspicion emerged among Old Christians that the conversion of so many of these Jews was simply opportunistic and did not reflect a sincere attachment to their newly embraced religion. As these sentiments festered, antipathy toward the neophytes rose and the wrath of the people was now directed against the New Christians. While these events took place in Toledo in 1449, across the peninsula during this same year but apparently unconnected to the events in Castile, riots broke out in Lisbon, but here the target of the attacks was the traditional enemy of the Christians: the Jews.[37]

Thus while the Jews recuperated to some extent following the devastations of the late fourteenth and early fifteenth centuries and in some measure may have recaptured those feelings of *convivencia* that had been understandably destroyed during those years, it was the New Christians who were generally the objects of violence, hatred, and suspicion during the second half of the fifteenth century. Debate erupted at all levels of Castilian society over the question of how to handle the *converso* problem. Whatever the original motivations were that prompted the large-scale conversions at the turn of the century, New Christians, as a group, were perceived as presenting a major problem for Iberian society. Among the many solutions that were suggested, one was chosen as the best means of ascertaining the truth of the *conversos'* actual religious allegiance: to investigate the religious beliefs and practices of the New Christians. Armed with this information, the rulers hoped they would be able to make the appropriate decisions about the treatment of *conversos.*[38]

Ferdinand and Isabella, upon their accession to the thrones of Castile and Aragon (and indeed even earlier), requested Pope Sixtus IV to grant them permission to found an ecclesiastical inquisition that would function in their own kingdoms under crown control. In a politically weak moment for the papacy, Sixtus IV agreed, and the "Spanish Inquisition" was born. Four tribunals were created in Castile in the early 1480s, and in 1485, despite much local opposition, the Aragonese Inquisition was also established. After the earliest inquiries, the officials of the Inquisition decided in 1483—and then effectively persuaded the monarchs—that in order to repress the judaizing practices that they believed were rife among the *conversos* of southern Castile, all Jews needed to be expelled from Andalusia. It was not the New Christians who were the subject of this order. Rather the inquisitors believed that if the Jews were eliminated from Andalusia they would not influence the *conversos* to continue their secret practice of Judaism.

But the rulers did not intend to eliminate Jews from their dominions. There were many within the kingdoms who were in favor of a continued Jewish presence, a policy that appealed to traditional elements within the government. This conservative position was expressed in actions of Ferdinand and Isabella that indicated that the Jewish connection to Iberian society was not being severed but rather was continuing. Jewish communities were protected during the reign of the Catholic Monarchs and through the 1480s and early 1490s Jews still attended the Castilian court as high-ranking officials, among them the great Jewish scholar and financier, Don Isaac Abravanel and the official head of Castilian Jewry, the *rab de la corte,* Abraham Seneor.[39]

During the 1480s and after many more investigations, the Holy Office firmly concluded that the New Christians were generally involved in Jewish rituals and obeyed precepts of the

Jewish religion, and that their heretical behavior should not be tolerated. Ominously, there were also conflicting signals from other groups during the reign of Ferdinand and Isabella about the future treatment and ultimately the protection of the Jews. Jews were still participating in the social and economic life of the kingdoms but there were movements afoot within the Church, the cities, and the Castilian Cortes or parliament to separate Jews from Christians, initiatives that were probably influenced by the Inquisitorial argument that Jews should be prevented from exercising a baneful influence upon the New Christians.[40]

If we read the words that Isaac Abravanel wrote many years later, when he was reflecting on the years before the expulsion, we would imagine that the Jews lived very comfortably in Sepharad, that they were at peace with their neighbors. It would appear that elements of the *convivencia* that the Jews had enjoyed were still more or less intact. But this was to change. In 1490 and 1491, the officials of the Inquisition accused a Jew, Yuce Franco, of the ritual murder of a Christian child—named the Holy Child of Laguardia—and they mounted a show trial. This spectacle also served as a vehicle for the Inquisition to publicize its views about what it believed should be the fate of all the Jewish communities of Castile and Aragon.[41]

Very soon, these views became the policy of the rulers. In January 1492, after a protracted ten-year war, the Muslim emirate of Granada was conquered. The Reconquest was officially over, and so was *convivencia*. On the last day of March of that same year, Ferdinand and Isabella signed the edict banishing the Jews from Castile and Aragon [fig. 8]. The reasons given in the edict were strikingly similar to the arguments that the Inquisition had been articulating in the last few years. The Jews were setting a bad example for the New Christians by their mere presence and, through the performance of their rituals, were proving to be a negative influence on the newcomers to the Christian faith. To safeguard the *conversos*, the Jews needed to be eliminated from Castilian and Aragonese society.[42]

Given the choice of conversion or exile, half of the Jewish population converted. Was conversion a foolhardy decision considering what had happened to the New Christians over the course of the fifteenth century? Did these Jews possess such strongly held beliefs in the possibilities inherent in *convivencia* that they elected to remain in Castile and Aragon? Or was it simply too difficult to give up all their economic, social, and family ties and to depart into the unknown? Those who opted for exile traveled mainly to the remaining Iberian kingdoms that still permitted Jewish residence, Portugal and Navarre. They were accepted in both of these kingdoms but not without much bitter debate among their Portuguese and Navarrese hosts.

Figure 8 *(opposite)*
Edict of Expulsion of the Jews from Spain, Granada, March 31, 1492, Exmo. Ayuntamiento de Avila, Archivo Histórico Provincial de Avila, 1/77 (cat. no. 47)

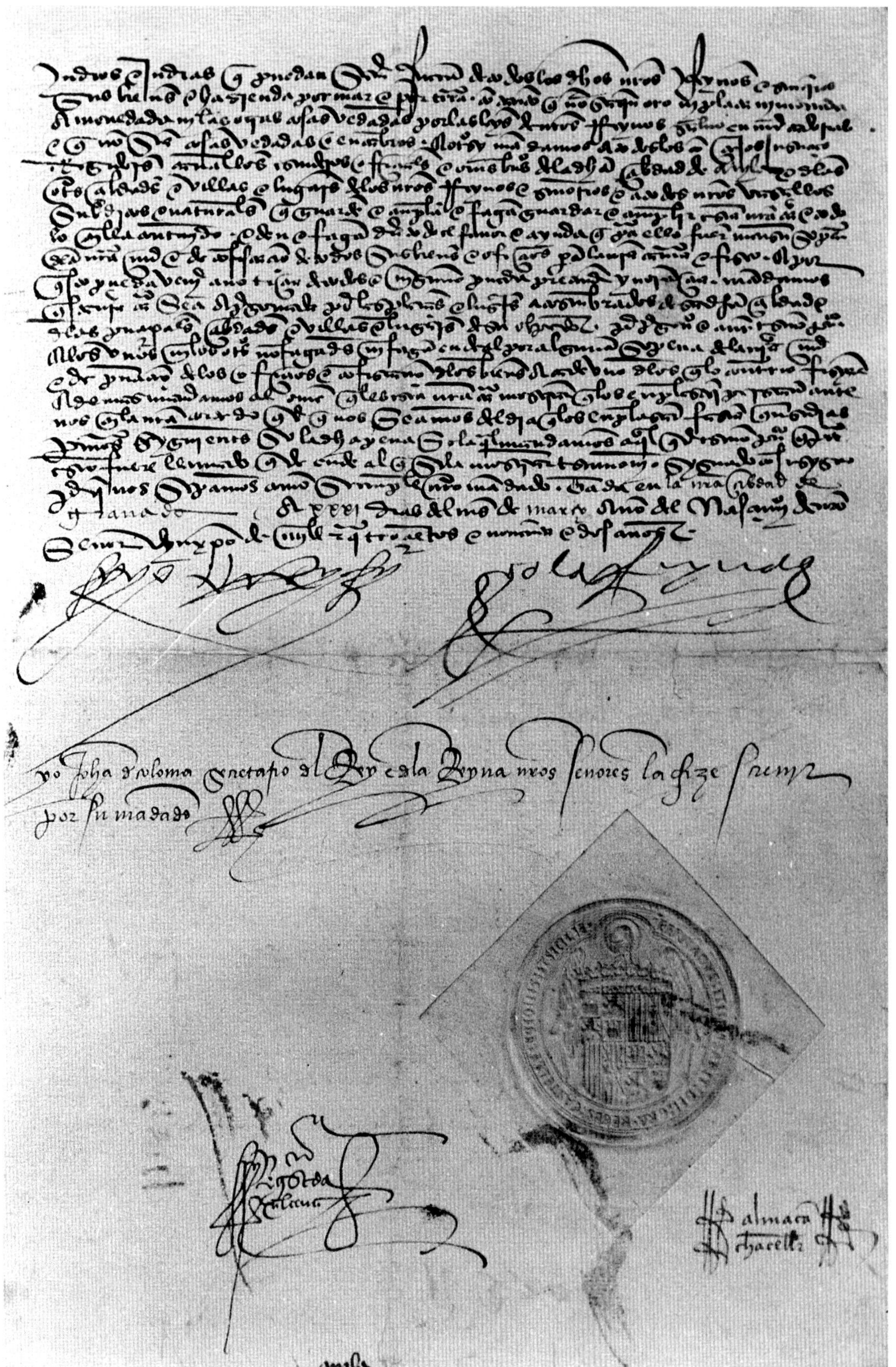

In Navarre, some of the exiles prepared to settle permanently. But Portugal was to prove inhospitable to the immigrants and the situation of the native Jews began to deteriorate as well. Accusations abounded that the immigrant Jews had brought the plague with them. In 1493, when most of the Jews were supposed to leave, their departure was restricted and they were accused of violating the terms of their entry. Many were enslaved and Jewish children were sent to the newly discovered island of São Tomé to test the possibilities of settlement there. When Manuel succeeded John II on the Portuguese throne, he freed the enslaved Jews and seemed to be turning from the anti-Jewish policies of his predecessor. But the rising tide of anti-Judaism in Portugal and the increasing pressure of the Spanish rulers, who insisted on expulsion of the Jews as a condition for Manuel's marriage to their daughter Isabella, led the Portuguese king and his royal council to order the banishment of the Jews in December 1496. But then, probably because there were not enough New Christians in Portugal who could pick up the economic slack for the departing Jews, the king blockaded the harbors in 1497 to prevent their leaving. Instead, almost the entire Portuguese Jewish community was forcibly converted to Christianity. Similarly under pressure from Ferdinand and Isabella, the Navarrese monarchs expelled the Jews in 1498, and having no place to go and no safe passage through which to leave the peninsula, they, too, were obliged to convert.[43]

Although Iberian society had decided that it no longer had any room for Jews or for Judaism, and despite the fact that the expulsion was a time of great hardship and trauma for the exiles, Sephardic Jews preserved aspects of the *convivencia* that was part of their daily lives. Those who left the peninsula took with them their well-defined Sephardic traditions. Included in this baggage was pride in their attachment to the peninsula—after Palestine, their "second homeland"—and the love of Iberian languages, which they continued to express through speaking, writing, and singing in Ladino.[44]

Among those who stayed and converted, there were many who were successful at assimilating into Christian society. Some continued to practice Judaism in secret while publicly continuing their daily involvement in Iberian Christian life. But even for those who attempted to acculturate, their Jewish heritage often fueled their creativity. Some of these *conversos*—such as Fernando de Rojas, the author of *La Celestina*—creatively infused Iberian Christian culture with their own ideas, which they dressed in new religious garb. Other *conversos,* from writers to mystics, attempted to fuse the two cultures together in ways that made sense to them in their lives.[45]

While the *conversos* were harassed by the Inquisition in newly united Spain and in Portugal, the *moriscos*—those Muslims who were forcibly converted over the course of the early sixteenth century, Muslims whose allegiance to the Christian state was doubted and so were considered politically dangerous—were expelled a century later. Moreover, although many descendants of the formerly Jewish *conversos* did lose the memory of their ancestry, a few did not. Many of these individuals left the peninsula as late as the seventeenth century and continued their lives as Jews in countries where Judaism was allowed to flourish. They carried with them what they perceived to be authentic Jewish culture and an awareness of contemporary Iberian intellectual trends. These refugees infused the Jewish communities and the countries where they established their homes with novel syntheses of these disparate ideologies, born of a latter-day though painfully strained *convivencia.*

NOTES

Notes for this essay have been kept brief and to a minimum. I have chosen to emphasize recent works that are readily available and studies that contain detailed bibliographies. Where possible I have cited titles available in English. Robert Singerman, *The Jews in Spain and Portugal: A Bibliography* (New York and London, 1975), is a helpful compilation.

1. L. García Iglesias, *Los judíos en la España antigua* (Madrid, 1978), 53.

2. Ibid., 69–81.

3. See generally Rosemary Ruether, *Faith and Fratricide: The Theological Roots of Anti-Semitism* (New York, 1974).

4. García Iglesias, *Los judíos en la España antigua,* 87–92.

5. Ibid., 93–99 and Alfredo Mordechai Rabello, *The Jews in Visigothic Spain in the Light of the Legislation* [Hebrew] (Jerusalem, 1983), 32–37.

6. Much has been written on Visigothic Jewry in the last few years: for synthetic treatments, see García Iglesias, *Los judios en la España Antigua,* 103–202, Rabello, *The Jews in Visigothic Spain,* 43–85, and also Roger Collins, *Early Medieval Spain: Unity in Diversity, 400–1000* (London, 1983), 129–42.

7. Norman Stillman, *The Jews of Arab Lands* (Philadelphia, 1979), 25–28. On the shift from Christian to Islamic domination and its effects on the inhabitants of the peninsula, see the provocative work by Thomas F. Glick, *Islamic ad Christian Spain in the Early Middle Ages* (Princeton, N.J., 1979), especially, 19-42.

8. W. Montgomery Watt, *A History of Islamic Spain* (Edinburgh, 1965), 39–80, and Eliyahu Ashtor, *The Jews of Moslem Spain* (Philadelphia, 1973) 1: 155–59.

9. Ashtor, *The Jews of Moslem Spain,* 1: 159–63.

10. The quotation is from Raymond P. Scheindlin, "Rabbi Moshe Ibn Ezra on the Legitimacy of Poetry," *Medievalia et Humanistica,* n.s. 7 (Medieval Poetics): 113.

11. Jefim Schirmann, "The Function of the Hebrew Poet in Medieval Spain," *Jewish Social Studies* 16 (1954) 235–52, and Ashtor, *The Jews of Moslem Spain,* 1:228–63.

12. Ibid., *The Jews of Moslem Spain,* 1:163–217.

13. Ashtor, *The Jews of Moslem Spain,* 11:3–40. Also see David Wasserstein, *The Rise and Fall of the Party Kings: Politics and Society in Islamic Spain 1002–1086* (Princeton, N.J., 1985), 190–223.

14. Jefim Schirmann, "Samuel Hannagid: The Man, the Soldier, the Politician," *Jewish Social Studies* 13 (1951): 99–126, and Ashtor, *The Jews of Moslem Spain,* 2: 41–189.

15. Watt, *A History of Islamic Spain,* 95–102.

16. Ashtor, *The Jews of Moslem Spain,* 3: 3–58.

17. On the Almohads, see Watt, *A History of Islamic Spain,* 103–11. Gerson Cohen's edition of Abraham Ibn Daud's *Sefer Ha-Qabbalah* (Philadelphia, 1967) is valuable; see on the period, pp. xvi–xxviii. On the Jews in these Christian kingdoms prior to the major Christian conquests of the thirteenth century, see Francisco Cantera Burgos, "Christian Spain," in *The World History of the Jewish People: The Dark Ages,* ed. Cecil Roth, 357–81. For the early years of the Christian kingdoms, see Collins, *Early Medieval Spain,* 225–68, and Glick, *Islamic and Christian Spain,* 42–50.

18. Yitzhak Baer, *A History of the Jews in Christian Spain* (Philadelphia, 1961) 1: 39–185.

19. On the transfer of Jewish culture, see Bernard Septimus, *Hispano-Jewish Culture in Transition* (Cambridge, Mass., 1982). On the court of Alfonso "el Sabio," see Evelyn S. Procter, *Alfonso X of Castile: Patron of Literature and Learning* (Oxford, 1951) and Robert I. Burns, ed., *Emperor of Culture: Alfonso X The Learned of Castile and His Thirteenth-Century Renaissance* (Philadelphia, 1990).

20. Nahmanides's report on the disputation is in Chaim Chavel, ed. and trans., *Ramban: Writings and Discourses,* (New York, 1978) 2: 657–96. Robert Chazan, "The Barcelona 'Disputation' of 1263: Christian Missionizing and Jewish Response," *Speculum* 52 (1977): 824–42 is an analysis of the debate and its implications.

21. See Dwayne E. Carpenter, *Alfonso X and the Jews: An Edition of and Commentary on* "Siete Partidas" *7.24 "De los judíos"* (Berkeley, Calif., 1986).

22. Baer, *A History of the Jews,* 1: 212–36, and Abraham A. Neuman, *The Jews in Spain,* 2 vols., (Philadelphia, 1942).

23. Yom Tov Assis, "The Jews of Spain in Gentile Courts (13th and 14th centuries)" [Hebrew] in *Culture and Society in Medieval Jewry,* Menahem Ben-Sasson et al., eds. (Jerusalem, 1989), 399–430.

24. Baer, *A History of the Jews,* 1: 322–25, Neuman, *The Jews in Spain,* 1: 134–45, and Eliyahu Ben-Zimrah, "Ha-Malshinut ve-ha-Mesirah be-Mishnatam shel Hakhmei Sefarad" [Slander and informing in the writings of Sephardic sages] in *Studies in Memory of the Rishon le-Zion R. Yitzhak Nissim,* ed. Meir Benayahu (Jerusalem, 1985) 1: 297–321.

25. Baer, *A History of the Jews,* 1:96–110, and Bernard Septimus, "Piety and Power in Thirteenth-Century Catalonia," in *Studies in Medieval Jewish History and Literature,* ed. Isadore Twersky (Cambridge, Mass., 1976), 197–230.

26. See the compilation of Isaiah Tishby, ed., *The Wisdom of the Zohar,* 3 vols., (Oxford and New York, 1989) and Moshe Idel, "We Have No Kabbalistic Tradition on This," in *Rabbi Moses Nahmanides (Ramban): Explorations in His Religious and Literary Virtuosity,* ed. Isadore Twersky (Cambridge, Mass., 1983), 51–73.

27. On Todros, see Hayyim Schirmann, *Hebrew Poetry in Sepharad and Provence* [Hebrew] (Jerusalem and Tel Aviv, 1954–56) 2: 413–48 and T. Carmi, ed., *The Penguin Book of Hebrew Verse* (New York, 1981), 410–16. The essays in Twersky, *Nahmanides,* are illuminating.

28. Baer, *A History of the Jews,* 1:306–78 and 2:1–94 treat Castile and Aragon respectively up to the end of the fourteenth century. For a characterization of the period from the late thirteenth to the mid-fourteenth century, see Julio Valdeon Baruque, *Los judíos de Castilla y la revolución Trastamara* (Valladolid, 1968), 15–25.

29. On synagogues generally, see Don A. Halperin, *The Ancient Synagogues of the Iberian Peninsula* (Gainesville, Fla., 1969). On the Toledan synagogue called today *El Tránsito,* see 49–55. Fourteenth-century Navarrese Jewry is described in Beatrice Leroy, *The Jews of Navarre* (Jerusalem, 1985) and in Yom Tov Assis and Ramón Magdalena, *The Jews of Navarre in the Late Middle Ages* [Hebrew] (Jerusalem, 1990). On Portugal, see J. Mendes Dos Remedios, *Os judeus em Portugal* (Coimbra, 1895), vol. 1, and Maria José Pimenta Ferro, *Os judeus em Portugal no século XIV* (Lisbon, 1979).

30. See generally Valdeon Baruque, *Los judíos de Castilla.*

31. On Abner, see Baer, *A History of the Jews,* 1: 327–54.

32. Ibid., 2: 95–110. Philippe Wolff, "The 1391 Pogrom in Spain: Social Crisis or Not?" *Past and Present* 50 (1971): 4–18 and Don Pagis, "Dirges on the Persecutions of 1391 in Spain," [Hebrew] *Tarbiz* 37 (1968): 355–73.

33. Baer, *A History of the Jews,* 2: 110–66.

34. Ibid., 166–232.

35. A. Lionel Isaacs, *The Jews of Majorca* (London, 1936), 103–17.

36. Baer, *A History of the Jews,* 2: 244–70 and J. N. Hillgarth. *The Spanish Kingdoms 1250–1516* (Oxford, 1978), 2: 156–63, and ff.

37. Baer, *A History of the Jews,* 2: 270–83; Angus MacKay, "Popular Movements and Pogroms in Fifteenth-Century Castile," *Past and Present* 55 (1972): 33–67; Humberto Baquero Moreno, "Movimentos sociais anti-judaicos em Portugal no século XV," in *Jews and Conversos,* ed. Yosef Kaplan (Jerusalem, 1985), 62–73; and Maria José Pimenta Ferro Tavares, *Os judeus em Portugal no século XV* (Lisbon, 1982), 1: 421–23.

38. Haim Beinart, *Conversos on Trial* (Jerusalem, 1981), 1–47.

39. On the policy of Ferdinand and Isabella toward the Jews, see the fine article by Maurice Kreigel, "La prise d'une décision: l'expulsion des juifs d'Espagne en 1492," *Revue Historique* 260 (1978): 49–90.

40. Hillgarth, *The Spanish Kingdoms,* 2: 438–47.

41. See the biography by B. Netanyahu, *Don Isaac Abravanel: Statesman and Philosopher* (Philadelphia, 1968), specifically, 53. On the "Holy Child of La Guardia" trial, see Baer, *A History of the Jews,* 2: 398–423.

42. Baer, *A History of the Jews,* 2: 424–39 and Hillgarth, *The Spanish Kingdoms,* 2: 447–52.

43. On Navarre, see Benjamin R. Gampel, *The Last Jews on Iberian Soil* (Berkeley, Calif, 1989), 71–134. On Portugal, a convenient summary of these years is Yosef H. Yerushalmi, *A Jewish Classic in the Portuguese Language* (Lisbon, 1989), pp. 9–22. This volume, published separately, also serves as an introduction to Samuel Usque, *Consolação as tribulações de Israel,* 2 vols. (Lisbon, 1989). The relevant pages in this format are 19–32. See also Isaiah Tishby, *Messianism in the Time of the Expulsion From Spain and Portugal* [Hebrew] (Jerusalem, 1985).

44. See Haim Hillel Ben-Sasson, "The Generation of Spanish Exiles on Its Fate," [Hebrew] *Zion* 26 (1961): 23–42.

45. Yirmiahu Yovel, *Spinoza and other Heretics,* 2 vols. (Princeton, N.J., 1989). In the first volume, he relies on other scholars; on Fernando de Rojas, see 1: 85–127.

وصنع الفقيه أبو الحسن بن [illegible] قصيدة طائية يصف فيها نواوير الربيع بوصف حسن [illegible] ويمدح بها ابنه الوزير ابن القاضي أدام الله عزه ووطد [illegible] وأنا أذكر منها قطعة تشاكل هذا الباب وهي بعرض [illegible]

كأنما الروض لما وشّت بزا المزن أرضه
بكل حمراء صرف وكل بيضاء بضه
كواكب في سماء من الزبرجد غضه
كأن كل الأقاحي مدامع مرفضّه
أو لؤلؤ فوق أرض من المهى منبضه
كأنما الورد طرا أبقى به اللثم عضه
أو خد غمر فرا أخجلته حال ممضّه
كأنما النهر نظ جلا الصبا فل عرضه
كأنما غدر الماء في المروج الغضه
إذا النسيم مراء أو أترس من فضه
كأنما الشمس في الجو حين تقطع عرضه

المراد جمع مرآة مثل مقواة ومقاوي وهو تشبيه قوي بسوى جراد . قال أبو الوليد فلما بلغني ذلك صنعت قصيدا على ذلك النحو وأنا ذاكر بعضه منه

Hebrew Poetry in Medieval Iberia

Raymond P. Scheindlin

The Jewish community of medieval Iberia was an extraordinarily innovative one that made both distinctive and lasting contributions to the history of Hebrew literature. The catalyst for these innovations was Arabic culture, especially Arabic poetry, which inspired the Jews of al-Andalus to produce the first secular Hebrew poetry since biblical times. In Iberia the Jews also developed completely new types of synagogue poetry, both through the influence of secular poetry and through that of the philosophical and religious ideas that reached them by way of Arabic humanism.

It is customary to divide the literary history of the Iberian Jews chronologically into two parts: first a creative period, often referred to as the "Golden Age," when the majority of Jews lived under Muslim domination (mid-tenth to mid-twelfth century); and second, an epigonic "Silver Age," when the Jews were mostly under Christian control (mid-twelfth century until the expulsion in 1492). This essentially political scheme does not accurately reflect the richness of Iberian Hebrew literary history. While it is true that most of the distinctive forms of secular Hebrew poetry were devised during the earlier period, it is not true that literary creativity came to an end with the *reconquista* or that Christian rule stifled the Jewish literary imagination. This essay will give due attention to the exciting developments of the Hebrew Golden Age, but will call attention to the important achievements of the Christian period as well.

Figure 9 *(opposite)*
Abu'l Walid al-Himyarī (1026-48), *Poems on Spring*, Spain, 14th century, Madrid, Biblioteca de El Escorial, no. 353

For literary purposes it is appropriate to divide the history of Hebrew letters in Spain into three overlapping periods: the period when most Jewish literary figures inhabited an Arabic ambience (ca. 900–ca. 1150); a transitional period (ca. 1100–ca. 1300); and a period when most Jewish literary figures inhabited a Christian ambience (ca. 1250-1492). This formulation stresses not the political status of the Jews as inhabitants of Islamic or Christian states, but rather the cultural environment in which they found themselves.

THE ARABIC PERIOD (CA. 900–CA. 1150)

The Jews of Muslim Spain from the time of the Andalusi Caliph ʿAbd al-Raḥmān III (reigned 912–61) until the invasion of the Almohads in the 1140s had a distinctive character among medieval Jewish communities. No other Jewish community produced as many Jews who achieved positions of status and power in the non-Jewish world; and no other Jewish community produced such an extensive literary culture reflecting the deep impact of an intellectual life shared with non-Jews. These two characteristics were interrelated.

Some of the factors in the uniqueness of al-Andalus were present in other Jewish communities in the Islamic world, but nowhere were they present in such concentrated form. Individual Jews in Iraq, Egypt, and elsewhere had risen to power and wealth before the tenth century, and would continue to do so long after the eclipse of al-Andalus. Jewish literature in the Islamic East had begun to reflect the influence of larger intellectual trends before the tenth century and would be permanently affected by what Jews learned from Muslims in the course of their long subjugation to Islam. But both conditions flowered most brilliantly in Islamic Spain from the mid-tenth until the mid-twelfth centuries. Certainly nowhere in Christendom did the conditions for the creation of such a community and such a literature exist until the Renaissance.

The Andalusi Jewish culture that bursts into view during the reign of ʿAbd al-Raḥmān III is an elite culture. We know virtually nothing about the ordinary Jews of the period, for the Hebrew poetry that is our main historical source emanates from a class of highly educated Jews writing mostly for and about themselves. Even the poetry must be used with caution as a historical source, as it is a stylized literature written in accordance with conventions inherited from Arabic and carefully transplanted into Hebrew.

The first of the individual Andalusi Jews who come into view in the age of ʿAbd al-Raḥmān III already embodies many of the distinctive qualities of this culture. Ḥasdai ibn Shaprūṭ was a Jewish physician in the caliph's court who at various times held important diplomatic and financial positions, as recorded in both Islamic and Jewish sources. He was also a central figure in the Jewish community who made use of his public position to look after the interests of that community and those of communities abroad. Perhaps the most remarkable example is his letter, written in Hebrew, to Helena, the wife of the Byzantine emperor Constantine VII Porphyrogenitus, asking her to protect the Jews of Byzantium from persecution. Within the community his patronage of Hebrew letters and Jewish cultural institutions was a decisive influence on later generations, as we shall see below. In the totality of Ḥasdai's activities he represents the type of the Andalusi Jewish courtier-rabbi, a type that would become more prominent in the *taifa* period, and that, with varying nuances, would remain characteristic of Spanish Jewry until the expulsion.

Ḥasdai was only the first in what was to be a long series of courtier-rabbis. In the early eleventh century Jewish Iberia was dominated by Samuel the Nagid, known in Arabic as Ismāʿīl ibn Naghrāla, who for a time was de facto ruler of Granada. We know of a certain Abraham, also in the Zirid court of Granada; of an anonymous Jewish courtier in Almería; of Abū Faḍl Ibn Ḥasdai in the Hūdid court of Saragossa; of Abraham Ibn Muhājir and Isaac Ibn al-Balia who served the ʿAbbadids of Seville. Many of these dignitaries bore the title of vizier, which, to be sure, had lost its exclusivity in the *taifa* period. Other Jewish grandees like the poet Moses Ibn Ezra and Abraham bar Ḥiyya bore the title *sāḥib al-shurṭa* (literally, "chief of police"; but perhaps simply an honorific). Some of these, particularly Abū Faḍl Ibn Ḥasdai, may have converted to Islam; but the apostates are less surprising than the ones who remained Jewish and active in Jewish communal affairs.

Poetry played a role in the lives of these public Jews unimaginable in our world. The courtier-rabbis adopted their language and all their social institutions from the fashions of the Arab Andalusi courts; one of these institutions was the craft of poetry as it had become crystallized throughout the Arab world.

Arabic poetry served mostly public functions. Especially important was courtly panegyric, used for eulogizing friends, patrons, or allies, and intended partly to flatter the recipient, partly to shape public opinion in a world in which poetry was the chief form of publicity. Related to panegyric in function were both satirical poems, in which the poet's or his patron's enemies were lampooned, and funeral laments, really a species of panegyric. These three genres are united by their predominantly political function as instruments for the regulation of relations within the ruling class. They are serious works of substantial length, thematic complexity, and a studied, formal character.

But poetry was also composed for simple amusement. Members of the courtier class entertained each other by listening to poetry, reciting their own verses, discussing those of others, and setting themes for improvisation for one another. Such literary conversation often took place at wine parties held in gardens and lasting all night [fig. 10]. The poems recited on such occasions often describe the occasion itself. They are short, stylized treatments of certain conventional themes like love, flowers, spring, and the tranquil pleasure of conversation

with sophisticated friends. They deal, in short, with the pleasures of life enjoyed by the Andalusi courtiers, and the regret that life is so short and its pleasures so transient.

The Jews had a native tradition of synagogue poetry going back four or five hundred years before the Hebrew Golden Age. Now, with the adoption of the new, nonliturgical functions of poetry, the Jews also adopted new forms for liturgical poetry deriving from Arabic.

The main body of Arabic poetry written in al-Andalus follows the classical patterns of Arabic verse devised in pre-Islamic Arabia and polished in the Abassid court of Baghdad, the cultural center of the Islamic world in the ninth to eleventh centuries. These poems are written in classical Arabic, never in the vernacular dialects, and are shaped according to rigid

Figure 10 *(opposite)*
Ivory Casket with Musicians and Drinkers, Probably Córdoba, early 11th century, Courtesy of the Board of Trustees of the Victoria and Albert Museum, London, 10-1866 (cat. no. 88)
The scenes portrayed on this work, pairs of figures drinking in gardens, are visual embodiments of one of the themes of Hebrew and Arabic poetry created on the Iberian peninsula.

rules of meter and rhyme. Whether the poem is a formal Arabic ode of a hundred lines or a casual epigram of two, it will consist of a series of very long lines of identical meter and end-rhyme. This was the pattern of all serious poetry in the Arabic-speaking world until modern times.

Hispano-Arabic poets contributed a new verse form to the literary repertoire, the *muwashshaḥ*. Unlike the poems of the classical type described above, these poems are strophic. Each strophe consists of a group of lines with a rhyme that changes from strophe to strophe, followed by another group of lines with a rhyme that remains unchanged throughout the poem, linking all the strophes. The last such group has the peculiarity that unlike the body of the poem, it is often written in the Andalusi dialect of spoken Arabic, in Romance, or in a mixture of both, rather than in classical Arabic. Such an intrusion of the language of everyday speech into Arabic poetry was unprecedented in the Arabic world. The origin and cultural significance of these unusual lines, known as *kharja,* as well as the character of the *muwashshaḥ* as a genre, are topics hotly debated by scholars of Iberian literature. Clearly they attest to the interaction of Arabic and native Hispanic cultural elements in a single literary genre, and thus may be seen as embodying a kind of literary *convivencia.*

Courtier-rabbis like Ḥasdai ibn Shaprūṭ adopted the conventions of upper-class Arabic life, including the various uses and genres of poetry, and thereby created a whole new type of Jewish literature. Instead of writing Jewish poetry in Arabic, however, they did so in Hebrew [fig. 11]. The choice of language was probably dictated by communal pride, linked with the idea, also learned from the Arabs, that a great literature in a classical language is the mark of a great culture. For the Arabs, this great literature consisted of the *Qurʾān* and the body of poetry in classical Arabic. The Jews Hebraized this conception, taking biblical Hebrew as their classical language and the Bible as their classical literature, and created a new body of

Figure 11 *(right)*
Capital, Toledo, 12th or 13th century, Museo Sefardí, Toledo, no. 25 (cat. no. 55)
This capital stems from a now-destroyed Toledan synagogue. Its bilingual inscription in Hebrew and Arabic underscores the linguistic facility of Iberian Jewry.

Hebrew poetry, using biblical diction. They seemed to be telling themselves not to feel ashamed or outclassed in the presence of the great treasures of Arabic literature, and that they could do every bit as well with their own language and their own tradition.

One of the most remarkable developments within Andalusi Jewry was this syncretic literary culture that brought together Arabic and Hebrew ideas and literary forms. The Jewish courtier-rabbis, men like Ibn Shaprūṭ and Ibn Naghrāla, played a major role in fostering this literature.

The Jewish courtiers would have been unable to attain their public positions had they not been prepared for them by an Arabic education similar to that enjoyed by their Muslim peers. It was impossible for a non-Muslim to receive extensive formal training in Islamic religious studies as well as undesirable from a Jewish point of view. But the Arabic humanities—linguistic studies, literature, and the sciences—were available to anyone who knew Arabic and could afford to study. Language was no problem, for the Jews spoke the same vernacular Arabic and Romance as did the majority of Christians and Muslims, and members of the elite could afford to provide their sons with teachers. The same intellectual openness to such studies had to come from both sides, for orthodox Judaism and orthodox Islam shared a strong religious prejudice against the study of "Greek wisdom." But the tolerant atmosphere within the Muslim intellectual class had a broadening effect on the Jewish elite as well, making its members accepting of and eager for such studies; in this period we occasionally even hear of Jews and Muslims studying together under the same teacher. Thus, beginning in the tenth century, Jews like Ḥasdai could have a traditional Jewish education in the Bible and Talmud as well as the Arabic education of an *adīb* ("literary person," "man of culture") or a *failasūf* (loosely, "philosopher," "scientist"). The polymath soon became an honored figure in Andalusi Jewry.

Members of Ḥasdai's Jewish circle joined the larger society by living Arabized lives to the extent possible, within the limits imposed on the one hand by Islamic exclusiveness and on the other by Jewish loyalty. At the same time they imported the style of the larger society into the Jewish community and created new Jewish institutions modeled on Arabic ones. The latter tendency resulted in the creation of a kind of Jewish *adab* (literary culture), with Hebrew as its language.

The Jews of al-Andalus adopted the classicizing concept of *ʿarabiyya*—the Arabic view of the preeminence of classical Arabic—but gave it a Jewish twist: they made biblical Hebrew the Jewish equivalent of classical Arabic and accorded their language a new status as a cultural monument above and beyond its traditional status as "the holy tongue" (*lᵉshon haqodesh*).

In the process they rejected the language of both rabbinic literature and synagogue poetry, products of a millennium of the language's development, and revived the language of the Hebrew Bible. Grammarians laboriously analyzed biblical Hebrew in the light of techniques and concepts learned from Arabic grammarians and lexicographers. Secretaries adopted Arabic epistolary style for formal correspondence in Hebrew. And secular poetry in Hebrew made its first appearance since biblical times.[1]

A breakthrough in the writing of Hebrew secular poetry was achieved by Dunash ben Labrat, who entered the service of Ḥasdai after having been a disciple of the famous rabbi Saadia ben Joseph in Baghdad. Already in Iraq Dunash had devised a way to imitate the prosody of classical Arabic poetry (*ʿarūḍ*) in Hebrew. After he arrived in al-Andalus his innovation displaced such forms as had already been devised for secular Hebrew poetry by his contemporaries such as Menaḥem ben Saruq, another protégé of Ḥasdai. Dunash's techniques enabled Hebrew poets to add to the Arabic contents and functions of their poetry the sounds and rhythms of Arabic.

But Dunash's rival, Menaḥem, describes the work of a Hebrew poet in the service of a courtier-rabbi in terms that show that even before Dunash's arrival the functions of the poet were well established. In a formal rhymed epistle addressed to Ḥasdai he says:[2]

> ...I stood before your father...
> And to the extent of my intellect
> I spoke his praises;
> They are inscribed on the Ark of Testimony
> In the synagogue that he built to his God....
> Then remember the bitter night
> When your noble mother died....
> By God, you came to me on foot at midnight
> To bid me compose a eulogy and rhyme a dirge.
> You found me already writing,
> Obeying before I was commanded....
> When your father died
> I wrote a great eulogy and composed lamentations,
> Which all Israel recited, one each day,
> All the days of mourning....
> I made the pages of your panegyrics swift riders;
> I made the tale of your glory chariot wheels in every city...
> I silenced every rhetorician, I muzzled every rhymster...
> And I am still singing your praises
> And scattering your encomiums
> Like dew on the ground.

As these lines attest, the creation of secular poetry in Hebrew was a social as well as a literary development, part of the tendency of the Andalusi Jewish aristocracy to adopt Arabic social institutions. But by using Hebrew rather than Arabic, the group turned this Arabic institution into an expression of its own communal cohesiveness and ethnic pride. This pride in the Iberian Jewish community's literary achievement is strongly echoed in Moses Ibn Ezra's Arabic book about Hebrew poetry *Kitāb al-muḥāḍara wa 'l-mudhākara* (*The Book of Discussion and Conversation*), and in Judah al-Ḥarizi's Hebrew collection of *maqamāt*—a narrative in rhymed prose—the *Taḥkemoni* (on which, see below).

Poetry came to be as important to the social life of the Jewish aristocracy in al-Andalus as it was to the Muslims. The leading Jewish figures composed formal odes in Hebrew, improvised occasional verses, took pleasure in poetic competition, and employed poets to compose panegyrics, laments for the dead, and lampoon odes, as well as official correspondence in rhymed prose. A tiny class of professional secretaries and poets arose to provide for their needs, but many of the leaders of the community themselves proved to be gifted poets, and nearly anyone with any pretensions to an education tried his hand at it. Four large Hebrew *dīwāns* (collections of poems by a single poet) and thousands of other poems have come down to us from the period before the Almohads, attesting to the tremendous prestige of Hebrew poetry within this social class. Moses Ibn Ezra, the author of one of the great *dīwāns*, also wrote two books in Arabic on the theory of Hebrew poetry, only one of which has been published.[3]

Samuel the Nagid (993-1055 or 1056) is the most spectacular of the courtier-rabbis and one of the greatest of the Hebrew poets. As a courtier of Ḥabbūs, the Zirid ruler of Granada, Ibn Naghrāla helped to secure the succession of Prince Bādīs, and thereafter played a central role in the Zirid state. He even accompanied the Granadan troops on their annual military campaigns, which he described in verse:

> The day was a day of dust cloud and darkness;
> The sun was as black as my heart;
> The clamor of the troops was like thunder, like the sea
> And its waves when it rages in a storm....
> The horses were running back and forth
> Like serpents darting from their den.
> The lances as they were cast
> Were lightning that filled the air with a gleam.
> The arrows were like drops of rain,
> And the backs of men were sieves,
> And the bows in their hands were like snakes,
> And each snake was spitting out a bee.
> The swords over their heads were like torches,
> But falling they put out the light.

His Hebrew poems and their Arabic superscriptions describe the battles, providing details of political events not known from other sources. Like Ḥasdai, Ibn Naghrāla was also a central figure in the Jewish community. He bore the Hebrew title *nagid* (prince), though again we do not know the title's exact communal significance. He not only supported Hebrew poetry and Talmudic scholarship, but was himself one of the most accomplished of his contemporaries in both fields. His brilliant career became a model for ambitious Jewish fathers to hold up to their sons long after the end of the *taifa* period.

Samuel the Nagid recorded the main political and military events of his career, as well as his reflections on those events and on life in general, in three large volumes of poetry. These collections were assembled by his own young sons at his orders; he saw this assignment as part of their education and initiation into the manners of a Jewish grandee. The inclusion of secular poetry in the conception of Jewish education was itself a notable innovation within Judaism, having arisen in direct imitation of the Arabic cultural model.

Not everyone in the Jewish community was pleased with these Arabizing developments. The Nagid was criticized by pietists for writing secular love poetry, and even some of the main exponents of the culture evinced some ambivalence toward poetry. Moses Ibn Ezra's book on poetry reflects second thoughts on the propriety of secular Hebrew poetry, and may have been intended partly as a defense of the whole enterprise. Judah Halevi, the last of the poets who left large *dīwāns,* purportedly vowed to stop writing poetry altogether. In old age he left al-Andalus to make the pilgrimage to Palestine, denouncing the courtly culture in which he himself had been a brilliant participant.[4]

Though not a courtier in the service of a Muslim prince, Solomon Ibn Gabirol (ca. 1020–ca. 1057) enjoyed the patronage of such a courtier (until his patron was assassinated). Thus among the Hebrew poets his career is the one that most closely resembles that of the professional poet in the Arabic world. But he was also a philosopher, much of whose personal poetry reflects the loneliness of his quest for intellectual fulfillment. Fully as ambitious in his inner life as Samuel the Nagid was in his external life, he captured in his poetry the frustration of his quest together with irritability about his lack of recognition. Ibn Gabirol was also one of the first and most influential of the poets to apply the techniques of Arabic poetry to synagogue poetry, laying the foundation for another unique contribution of Spanish Jewry to Hebrew literature, the Spanish *piyyut.*[5]

> With lowly spirit, lowered knee and head
> In fear I come; I offer Thee my dread.
> But once with Thee I seem to have no worth
> More than a little worm upon the earth.

O Fullness of the World, Infinity—
 What praise can come, if any can, from me?
Thy splendor is not contained by the hosts on high,
 And how much less capacity have I!
Infinite Thou, and infinite Thy ways;
 Therefore the soul expands to sing Thy praise.

It was the combination of Arabic literary techniques, a philosophical interpretation of Jewish religious traditions, and a warm, personal voice that made this new liturgical poetry the most treasured Hebrew devotional writing after the Psalms.

Moses Ibn Ezra (ca. 1055–ca. 1135) was a member of a large family of Jewish public functionaries in Granada. Of all the Golden Age poets, he is the one who most closely follows the model of the formal Arabic ode in his Hebrew poems. He also wrote two treatises in Arabic on the theory of poetry and poetic criticism. As a liturgical poet, he was famous for his many penitential poems. He also wrote many elegant trifles celebrating the pleasures of courtier life [fig. 12]:[6]

The garden wears a colored coat,
 The lawn has on embroidered robes,
The trees are wearing checkered shifts,
 They show their wonders to every eye,
And every bud renewed by spring
 Comes smiling forth to greet his lord.
See! Before them marches a rose,
 Kingly, his throne above them borne,
Freed of the leaves that had guarded him,
 No more to wear his prison clothes.
Who will refuse to toast him there?
 Such a man his sin will bear.

Judah Halevi, who came from the north of Spain to al-Andalus, was one of the most prolific and musical of the Hebrew poets. He is best known for his many poems written in connection with his startling decision to leave al-Andalus and go on pilgrimage to Palestine, abandoning his family, his successful medical practice and public career, and the world of the courtier-rabbis. Some of these poems are replies to critics, defending his resolve; others are poems of longing for the Holy Land; others express his ambivalence about the step; and others are religious meditations describing his ocean voyage:[7]

Trapped in the heart of the sea, I say to my terrified heart
As it beholds in fear the terrible toss of the waves,
"If you will trust in God, the God who created the sea,
The God whose name will endure till the end of time and beyond,
Have no fear of the sea when its breakers surge toward the sky;
The God who created the shore to contain the ocean is nigh."

Figure 12 *(opposite)*
Pyxis, Madīnat al-Zahra', ca. 950–75, The Metropolitan Museum of Art, New York, The Cloisters Collection 1970, ex. Collection J. Revertera-Salandra, Ernst Kofler, 1970.324.5 (cat. no. 87)

The theme of the garden appears often in Andalusi art and literature. This pyxis was created in one of the sophisticated workshops located within the precincts of the caliphal palace at Madīnat al-Zahra', near Córdoba.

Like all the great Golden Age poets, Halevi also composed liturgical poetry of simple beauty and great warmth.

A key factor in precipitating the Jews' new literary creativity was their knowledge of Arabic. This knowledge was not unique to the Jews of al-Andalus; as in the rest of the Islamic world, the Jews spoke the same Arabic as did their neighbors, and they were perfectly content to write Arabic as well, even when dealing with communal or religious subjects. A great Jewish literature in Arabic deriving from every part of the Islamic world, including Spain, is still extant. The Arabic of this literature is not the classical language of Arabic belles-lettres. Though the Jews adopted the general conception of *ʿarabiyya,* with its implied claim of cultural superiority, they substituted biblical Hebrew for classical Arabic as the model language. Therefore, when they wrote Arabic they generally wrote more or less as they spoke. Better-educated writers writing in a more formal vein would tone up their style and approximate classical grammar; but ordinary Jewish written Arabic is a register of the language known as Middle Arabic.

The Middle Arabic spoken and written by the Jews was not a specifically Jewish language that distinguished them from their Muslim neighbors. It differed mainly in its written form, employing Hebrew rather than Arabic script, probably because most writing was intended for use within the community, where the Hebrew alphabet was far better known. Hebrew words were ordinarily used in Judeo-Arabic to the extent that the writer needed to refer to aspects of Jewish religious culture.

The Jews in Arabic-speaking territories had no compunctions about using Arabic, even when writing on religious subjects. In the Middle Ages, Arabic-speaking rabbis wrote their *responsa* on religious law, their books on Jewish theology, and certainly all books dealing with pure philosophical and scientific subjects in Arabic. In Islamic Spain, only secular and religious poetry or ornate prose were written in Hebrew. The situation in Arabic-speaking lands was thus quite different from that in the Christian territories of Europe, where all writing pertaining to internal communal affairs or religious matters was in Hebrew, and where Jews almost never knew Latin and had no access to high culture.

Even in this literary Golden Age, when Arabic culture was at its height and when Jews had access to the best that it could offer, we should beware of imposing on it an idealized picture of *convivencia*. Officially the Jews were a tolerated minority, not equal citizens. They were subject to special legislation—not always strictly enforced—intended to segregate them from Muslims, and they were occasionally the victims of violence. Culturally they were dependent on the dominant Arabic culture; they were not an equal counterweight to that culture, but recipients of it. There is no evidence that Arabs showed any interest at all in learning from Jews about Hebrew culture; why should they have had such an interest, seeing that the Jews as a whole were considered a backward subject people, adherents of a despised religion? As far as we can tell, the entire Hebrew Golden Age and its extraordinary Hebrew poetry went completely unnoticed by contemporary Muslim intellectuals. If we had to reconstruct the history of Jewish culture in al-Andalus on the basis of documents written by Arabs, all we would know was that some Jews wrote Arabic poetry. The truly original work of the Hebrew Golden Age, the brilliant synthesis of Arabic and Hebrew language and culture, the new biblical exegesis—all would be completely unknown.

THE TRANSITIONAL PERIOD (1100–1300)

The Almoravid invasion of the 1090s had caused some disruption of the Jewish Golden Age, but the Almohad invasions of the 1140s effectively ended it. In line with their fanatical orthodoxy, the Almohads outlawed all religions other than Islam within their domains, both in northwest Africa and in al-Andalus; nearly three and a half centuries before Ferdinand and Isabella, they imposed on the Jews the choice of conversion or death, thereby creating a large group of crypto-Jews. This degree of intolerance may have been an isolated episode in the history of the Jews under Islam, but it had a permanent effect on the Jewish community.

Judah Halevi, the successful physician, poet, and bon vivant, turned pilgrim just before the invasion, apparently motivated more by personal religious convictions than by political prescience. At the same time, Abraham Ibn Ezra (1089-1164), poet, grammarian, philosopher, scientist, and Bible commentator, left to embark on a life of wandering. He carried Andalusi Jewish learning and literary taste to Christian Europe, with the result that French rabbis utterly ignorant of Arabic culture were soon attempting to employ the Arabic prosodic system in their synagogue poetry. Abraham Ibn Ezra reached England in his wanderings, where his mathematical works were eventually translated into Latin for the use of Christian scholars.

Other exiles settled in Provence where they, too, played a role in mediating the peculiar Andalusi Jewish intellectual life and style to a community unfamiliar with Arabic. Maimonides, still a boy, was taken by his father, a Jewish judge in Córdoba, to Morocco. Here this distinguished family may have pretended to profess Islam until they were able to leave for Palestine and then Egypt. Decades later, living in prosperity and honor as a physician in the Ayyubid court and head of the Jewish community of Egypt (*raʾīs al-yahūd*), Maimonides would write in his *Epistle to Yemen,* drawing on his personal experience, that no power had ever been more hostile to Judaism than Islam. Yet his pride in his Andalusi heritage is observable throughout his writings. In the variety of his public activities, in his combination of religious orthodoxy and philosophical-scientific orientation, in everything but his disdain for poetry, he remained the very model of the Andalusi rabbi.[8]

Some Jews actually did convert. One famous convert of the Almohad period was the courtier Ibrāhīm ibn Sahl of Seville (d. ca. 1259), an important Arabic poet whose poems are transmitted enthusiastically by Arabic sources.[9] The following verse of his is said to refer to his worldly loves; but it could just as well be about his religious life:

> I have moved on from the love of Moses to the love of Muḥammad.
> This is right guidance from God; but for Him I would have strayed.
> I did not change out of hatred, but simply because
> Moses' law has been replaced by Muḥammad's.

But a new Iberia was being prepared for the Jews by a movement geographically contrary to the two great waves of North African invasion: the *reconquista*. Muslim Toledo had fallen to Castile in 1085. For the next century and a half the Christian kings of Castile and Aragon would press inexorably southward, eventually to expel the Almohads and leave only Granada as Muslim territory. The Christian states afforded refuge to the Jews from Almohad persecution, for the Christian rulers also found the Arabic-trained Jewish courtiers and administrators useful managers for their new and unfamiliar territories. Many Jews fled to the Christian territories in the north, their relative estimation of Christianity and Islam now reversed in favor of Christianity. Here the members of the Jewish courtier class found new courts in which their skills were welcome, and where they could replicate the kind of life they and their ancestors had led in al-Andalus.

Not only were the Jewish courtiers experienced in government administration and diplomacy, but, as before, they were not contenders for ultimate power and were thus more trustworthy than Muslims. They were well informed about the territories that the Christian kings were bent on conquering, and they had good reason to be hostile to the Almohads. Their knowledge of the Arabic language was indispensable for dealing with the masses of Arabic-speakers who now came under Christian control, and for negotiations with Muslim rulers. As in other Christian lands, the Jews were outside the feudal system; they were completely dependent on the ruler to guarantee their rights and to protect them against the masses and the Church. Thus the Christian rulers found the Jewish elite both useful and reliable. Before long the Jewish courtier class had reconstituted itself, partly out of the same families. The Jewish communities were allowed considerable autonomy, and, as before, the officially recognized heads of the community were drawn from the courtier class.

The Jewish courtiers were desirable as the bearers and mediators of the culture of prestige among the far less sophisticated knights and clerics of the Christian kingdoms. Arabic retained its status in Christian Spain as the language of a higher culture until well into the thirteenth century, and during this period its tradition was maintained by Jews. The Jews thus found themselves in the anomalous position of being the respected bearers of Arabic culture, when the actual creators of that culture were subjugated. In this role the Jews were active participants in the work of translation into Latin of philosophical and scientific writings through which Arabic science began to reach Latin Christendom. Some of the translators were apostates like Petrus Alfonsi (b. 1062); others, like Abraham bar Hiyya (d. ca. 1136), remained Jewish. A doubtful case is Avendauth, who may be identical with the Jewish historian and philosopher Abraham Ibn Daʾūd (ca. 1110-80). In most cases the Jewish translator, who knew Arabic, worked together with a Christian scholar, who knew Latin.

Hebrew literature fell silent for about a generation, but toward the end of the twelfth century new poets and literary figures began to emerge. Nor did the influence of Arabic literature on Hebrew suddenly end. At the time of these dislocations, a new and distinctive genre of Hebrew writing appeared. This was the *maqāma,* a narrative in rhymed prose studded with short poems, the pattern of which was derived from Arabic. The first example of this kind of writing in Hebrew had appeared just before the Almohad cataclysm, at about the time that the Arabic *maqāmāt* of al-Ḥarīrī reached al-Andalus, where they were destined to become enormously popular. But the Hebrew narrative, which seems to have gotten its start in the *maqāma,* bloomed in Christian Spain as if Hebrew writers were still an integral part of Arabic literary life.[10]

For all their rhetorical similarity to the *maqāmāt* of the Arab East, however, most of the Hebrew fictions in rhymed prose are different from the Arabic models in ways that seem to link them to the nascent Romance literatures. One of the outstanding Hebrew fictions is *The Book of Delight* by Joseph Ibn Zabara of Barcelona (b. ca. 1140), which resembles the *maqāma* in its use of rhymed prose interspersed with poems, but whose narrative technique and stress on character recall the romance. Like the *maqāma,* the book describes the travels and adventures of the narrator, who plays the straight man, with a rogue, who beguiles the narrator into taking the journey. But in the *maqāma* the successive brief episodes are not related to each other, and though the characters may appear in many guises, they never grow or change. In *The Book of Delight,* the characters, and therefore the relationship between them, change in the course of an extended narrative, so that by the end, the narrator dominates the trickster and resolves to return home. Another hybrid narrative work is the collection of stories in rhymed prose by Jacob ben Eleazar (twelfth to thirteenth centuries). Some of these are philosophical allegories of a type attested in Hebrew in other Islamic countries at this time, whereas others seem more like the European vernacular romances of the period. The Andalusia Arabic *maqāmāt* have not yet been sufficiently studied to permit a rounded assessment of their cultural ties to the Hebrew *maqāma.* But at the present stage of research, and with the important exception of Judah al-Ḥarīzī, we may generalize that in form the Hebrew narrative prose of the period seems to look back to the symbiosis with the Arabic-speaking world, but in theme it looks forward to a potential new symbiosis with Christendom. Certainly such a shift seemed possible at the end of the twelfth century.

The Almohad persecution had cut Andalusi Jewish culture off at the root. The Jews of Iberia would retain their link with Arabic for at least another century, but signs of change were evident almost as soon as the new Hebrew literature emerged in the triumphant Christian kingdoms. One such sign was the abrupt cessation of Judeo-Arabic literature in Spain. From the mid-twelfth century on, Hebrew predominated as the language of Jewish writing in Spain and soon became the sole language for internal purposes. From this time dates a wave of translations of Judeo-Arabic works into Hebrew, both for the use of Jews in Christian Europe, as well as for Spanish Jews no longer familiar with Arabic. This trend is distinct from the stream of translations of philosophical and scientific works intended for the use of Christians.

This internal shift from Arabic to Hebrew reflects a significant change in the linguistic situation of the Jews. Throughout the Arabic-speaking world, the daily language of the Jews was merely a variety of the language that also served as the medium of high culture. While vernacular Arabic was not the same as learned Arabic, knowing the vernacular gave access to

Figure 13 *(opposite)*
Hanukkah Lamp, Northern Spain, 13th–14th century, Musée national du Moyen Age, Thermes de Cluny, Paris, Cl. 12248 (cat. no. 96)
During the High Middle Ages, Spain was increasingly influenced by intellectual, cultural and artistic trends from northern Europe, particularly France. The combination of rose windows and arcades appears often in the minor arts of medieval France and Germany.

the language of philosophical and scientific writings and provided a solid foundation for learning the language of fine literature; moving from one register of the language to the other was no more difficult for Arabic-speaking Jews than for their Muslim neighbors. The situation was completely different in Christian Europe, where the Latin vernaculars had diverged so radically from Latin that even knowing a Romance language did not provide access to higher literature. Furthermore, the Islamic world boasted a class of scholars who were not clergy, so that there was much that a non-Muslim could study without coming too intimately into contact with religious scholarship. In Christendom, scholarship was more tied to the Church and was almost exclusively in the hands of the clergy, so that it was much more difficult for a Jew to become learned in Christian high culture, even if he did manage to learn Latin. With the spread of Christianity throughout the Iberian peninsula, the linguistic, and therefore the cultural situation of Iberian Jewry became more like that of the Jews of the rest of Europe. But this process was gradual and did not affect everyone equally. Even as late as the fifteenth century we still encounter in Castile Jews who are learned in Arabic and Latin.

Catalonia had never been deeply Arabized and had close links to the south of France. Here the Andalusians soon lost their connection with Arabic and came under the influence of intellectual and cultural trends from beyond the Pyrenees [fig. 13]. By the thirteenth century the Jewish culture of Catalonia and of all Aragon (the former was absorbed by the latter in 1137) had largely lost its Arabic cast. While philosophy and science were still being studied (now from Hebrew rather than Arabic texts), and while Arabic-style secular poetry continued to be written by such poets as Meshulam da Piera (first half of the thirteenth century), the emphasis was now on such intrinsically Jewish subjects as Talmud, which was studied according to northern European methods, and kabbalah. Individual Jews continued to serve the Aragonese government as Arabic interpreters.

Castilian Jewry retained its ties to Arabic language and culture longer. Toledo had been a major center of Arabic civilization prior to its reconquest in 1085, and Arabic continued to be spoken there long after it was forgotten in Aragon. Jews in Castile continued to bear Arabic traditions: Meir Abulafia (d. 1244), a famous Toledan rabbi, wrote Hebrew secular poetry in Arabic forms, and even translated a short poem by the eleventh-century Sevillian prince al-Muᶜtamid ibn ᶜAbbād into Hebrew. Abraham Ibn al-Fakhkhār (d. 1240), a Jewish grandee and a patron of Hebrew poetry, wrote Arabic poetry considered good enough to be transmitted by Muslim sources; one is in praise of Alfonso VIII of Castile. Judah al-Ḥarīzī was a major Hebrew writer who was notably untouched by new Romance influences. Active as a translator, he rendered many Judeo-Arabic works into Hebrew, and he also per-

formed the tour de force of translating into Hebrew the *maqāmāt* of al-Harīrī, a notoriously difficult masterpiece of Arabic rhymed prose. He followed this achievement by composing his own collection of Hebrew *maqāmāt,* the *Taḥkemoni*. Here he reverted to the narrative type of the pure Arabic *maqāma,* showing little interest in the new type of narrative cultivated by writers like Ibn Zabara or by his fellow Toledan Jacob ben Eleazar. Al-Ḥarīzī left Spain and traveled, via Provence, to the Muslim East where he was probably culturally more at home.[11]

Under Alfonso X, the Wise (1252-84), Jewish activity in the field of translation took a new direction, for the king encouraged the development of Castilian, and under his patronage many works were translated into the vernacular.[12] Jews were prominent among the translators. This project, undertaken for the benefit of non-Jewish scholars, involved mainly scientific works, but Alfonso also sponsored the translation of Jewish and Islamic religious writings for the use of the Church. Hebrew literature also continued to flourish. Todros ben Judah Abulafia, a Jewish man of letters who was close to several of Alfonso's court Jews, left a huge *dīwān,* including some Hebrew verses addressed to the king. They were supposedly engraved on a goblet that Todros presented to Alfonso:[13]

> Truth beheld revenge on falsehood
> When Alfonso was crowned our king.
> To wait on you I come; a cup
> Engraved with Hebrew verse I bring.
> For thus the Lord bade: "Every pilgrim
> Must bear Me an offering."

His Hebrew poetry is mostly in forms derived from Arabic, but he experimented with verse forms derived from Romance, as in his Hebrew *canzone,* which is also dedicated to Alfonso. He also cultivated pattern verses, which became fashionable at this time. It is a sign of the times that the introduction to his *dīwān* and the headings to the poems describing the circumstances of their composition are in Hebrew rather than in Arabic. Particularly interesting is his love poetry, which includes, alongside salacious verse, poems that bespeak a more spiritual idea of the nature of love. In a radical break with the traditions of the Golden Age, he even has Love itself speak:

> I am Love; as long as I live I will dominate all creatures...
> The souls of the great-hearted are my lovers,
> The souls of the unworthy are my enemies.

CHRISTIAN PERIOD (ca. 1250–1492)

As the *reconquista* progressed into the mid-thirteenth century, the Christian rulers found themselves less in need of Jewish administrators and courtiers. With the development of local culture, Arabic declined in prestige, and as Christians acquired linguistic skills, administrative experience, and scientific training, the Jews gradually lost their role as indispensable administrators and mediators of Arabic culture. At the same time the anti-Jewish pressure from the masses and the Church mounted. By end of the century, Spain was far less hospitable to Jews than it had been at the beginning. Jewish fortunes rose and fell until 1391, when pogroms and mass conversions heralded the collapse of the Jewish community. But individual members of the Jewish elite maintained the Arabic scholarly tradition and the Hebrew literary culture that was so closely tied to it. Even in the fifteenth century we hear of Jews translating Arabic texts into Latin or Hebrew, and secular Hebrew poetry cast in Arabic meters and rhyme schemes was written in Spain right down to the expulsion in 1492.

A monument to the continuing prestige of Hebrew poetry within the Jewish community may be observed to this day in the Tránsito synagogue in Toledo (dedicated in 1357), where the dedicatory inscription is in Hebrew verse, employing the Arabic metrics of the Golden Age. The synagogue's founder was Samuel Halevi, a financier to Peter the Cruel (1350-69). The use of a poem to commemorate the founder of a synagogue is consistent with the practice of Spanish Jewish grandees since the time of Ḥasdai ibn Shaprūṭ, four centuries earlier, as we saw in the epistle of Menaḥem.

One of Samuel's contemporaries, Shemtov ben Ardutiel, known in Spanish as Santob de Carrión, exemplified a potentially new development in the literary history of Iberian Jewry. Shemtov was distinguished as a Hebrew writer: he was the author of a lengthy poem of confession for Yom Kippur that is still found in some prayer books, a kabbalistic treatise, and a charming Hebrew *maqāma* called *The Battle of the Pen and the Scissors*. He was also an expert Arabist who translated a halakhic work into Hebrew. But he achieved fame in the wider world for the *Proverbios Morales,* a work that he dedicated to Peter the Cruel. Written in Spanish just as the Tránsito synagogue was under construction, this collection of proverbs was an important and influential contribution to the nascent Spanish literature. Shemtov does not hesitate to call attention to his being Jewish: "Lord King, noble and high, hear this discourse, which Santob, the Jew from Carrión, carries forward to speak for the benefit of all, rhymed in the vulgar manner, and culled from the glosses taken from moral philosophy."[14]

As one who drew on both Hebrew and the Arabic literary traditions while writing in Spanish, Shemtov is a pivotal figure in Iberian literary history. Other writers of Jewish origin made contributions to Spanish literature in this period, but Shemtov is the only belletrist known to us who was active as a Jew both in Hebrew and in Spanish.

Toward the end of the fourteenth century a circle of poets appeared who revived the tradition of Hebrew literature in Spain. These poets were connected with the Caballeria family of Saragossa, an important Aragonese Jewish family of financiers and courtiers who were also devotees of Hebrew letters. Solomon da Piera, a descendant of Meshulam da Piera, served as Hebrew secretary to three successive heads of the family and exchanged poems with many of the distinguished Jewish leaders of the time. His literary circle included his disciple Vidal Benveniste, a member of the Caballeria family who became his patron; Joseph ben Lavi, and Solomon Bonafed. These poets were among the members of a kind of poets' club known as the "The Congregation of Singers" (*ʿAdat nogᵉnim*); they engaged in poetic competitions and addressed poems to each other. They were, however, destined to endure hard times for Spanish Jewry. The peninsula-wide pogroms and forced conversions of 1391 caused traumatic upheaval, which is reflected in the synagogue poetry of the period. Along with other leaders of the Jewish community, these poets were present at the fateful Tortosa Disputation in 1413-14, in the wake of which many Jewish grandees converted to Christianity. Among the converts were da Piera and Vidal Benveniste, while apparently Solomon Bonafed and Joseph ben Lavi remained Jewish. But their poetic relationship did not end; even after their conversion, several of them continued to exchange poems in Hebrew, with Bonafed using this medium for chastising the converts for their unfaithfulness. Thus among the oddities of Spanish Jewry's last century we find Christians writing poetry in Hebrew![15]

The poetry of this generation carries on many of the formal traditions of the Golden Age. The prosody remains completely in accordance with the Arabic practices adopted by Dunash four centuries earlier, and the poets frequently allude to poems of the classical period. Some of the genres cultivated by the earlier poets also remained intact. But there are new formal features, like the frequent practice of ending a poem by repeating or alluding to its opening words. This practice is not merely a technical device but a structural principle, for it lends many poems a closed, circular feeling that is different from the open-endedness inherited by the Golden Age poets from Arabic. Strophic Hebrew poetry on secular themes was now much less common in Spain, where it had originated, than in other Mediterranean lands, which had learned it from earlier Spanish Hebrew poets, or which were adopting new strophic forms from Italian. One has the impression that contemporary tendencies in Spanish literature left little mark on Hebrew poetry, but this topic has not been investigated by scholars familiar with both Hebrew and Spanish literature; remarkably, the poetry of the Saragossa circle has not been studied at all except for its documentary value. Traditional Hebrew scholars have been content to label it epigonic, thereby discouraging serious investigation of an important creative moment in Hebrew letters.[16]

In what was left of Islamic Spain, the Jewish community had been reduced by the Almohads to insignificance, never to recover. Jews returned to Granada after the establishment of the Nasrid dynasty in the thirteenth century, but we have little information about them. After the anti-Jewish riots and forced conversions that raged throughout Christian Spain in 1391, many *conversos* made their way to Muslim Granada where they could return to Judaism. The last Hebrew poet of Islamic Spain was a Granadan Jew, Saadia ibn Danan, who was among the Jewish exiles of 1492. He went to Morocco, where he wrote a treatise on the craft of poetry. Among the last Hebrew poets of Christian Spain was Judah Abravanel. In 1503 he wrote a long poem, still using the Arabic prosody first adapted for use in Hebrew by Spanish Jews four and a half centuries earlier, to describe his experiences at the time of the expulsion and the dislocation he experienced thereafter.[17] Under the name Leone Ebreo he became famous among Italian writers of the Renaissance as the author of a treatise on love. He is thus a bridge figure who represents a different *convivencia:* that of Jews and Italian culture. But that is another chapter in the colorful history of Hebrew letters.

NOTES

1. Several recent studies have demonstrated the existence of secular Hebrew poetry outside al-Andalus and before the age of Ḥasdai ibn Shaprūṭ. This is not the place for a detailed analysis of these texts. So far they remain isolated cases that do not change the overall picture given here of Iberian priority in the creation of a distinctive and coherent school of poets.

2. Hebrew text in Ḥayyim Schirmann, *Hashira haʿivrit bisefarad uveprovans,* 1st ed., 2 vols. (Jerusalem and Tel Aviv, 1954-56), 1:23-24.

3. Besides the *Kitāb al-muḥāḍara waʾl-mudhākara,* mentioned above, he wrote the *Maqālat al-ḥadīqa fī maʿnāʾl-majāz wal-ḥaqīqa* ("The Treatise of the Garden: On the Meaning of Figurative and Literal Speech"), which is still in manuscript.

4. See Raymond P. Scheindlin, "Rabbi Moshe Ibn Ezra on the Legitimacy of Poetry," *Medievalia et Humanistica,* n.s. 7 (1976): 101-15; Ross Brann, *The Compunctious Poet: Cultural Ambiguity and Hebrew Poetry in Muslim Spain* (Baltimore and London, 1991).

5. Translation from Raymond P. Scheindlin, *The Gazelle: Medieval Hebrew Poems on God, Israel, and the Soul* (Philadelphia, 1991), 177.

6. Hebrew text in Schirmann, *Hashira haʿivrit,* 1:505.

7. Translation from Raymond P. Scheindlin, *Wine, Women, and Death: Medieval Hebrew Poems on the Good Life* (Philadelphia, 1986), 35.

8. Recent studies by Joel Kraemer indicate that it may be necessary to revise the traditional view of Maimonides' negative attitude toward poetry.

9. Ibn Sahl has the distinction of being accorded, probably by inadvertence, two entries in the *Encyclopaedia Judaica.* The brief entry at 8:1193, is full of mistakes; the longer one at 8:1213, is somewhat better. There is no reason to assume that he was related to the Hebrew poets Joseph ibn Sahl and Solomon ibn Ṣaqbel as stated in the article on Joseph ibn Sahl, 8:1194.

10. For examples, see my translations in David Stern and Mark Mirsky, eds., *Rabbinic Fantasy* (Philadelphia, 1990), 253-311.

11. His *maqāmāt* were translated by V. E. Reichert, *The Taḥkemoni,* 2 vols. (Jerusalem, 1965-73).

12. Hebrew text in Schirmann, *Hashira haʿivrit,* 2:441-42.

13. For a survey of the translators and their activities, see Norman Roth, "Jewish Collaborators in Alfonso's Scientific Work," in *Emperor of Culture: Alfonso X The Learned of Castile and His Thirteenth-Century Renaissance,* ed. Robert I. Burns, S.J. (Philadelphia, 1990).

14. T. A. Perry, *The Moral Proverbs of Santob de Carrión* (Princeton, N.J., 1987), 17.

15. There is much confusion about the exact identity of several members of the Saragossa circle and which of them converted to Christianity. The preceding sketch is based on the reconstruction by Ḥayyim Schirmann in *Hashira haʿivrit,* 2:564-643.

16. Typical in this regard is Ezra Fleischer's *obiter dictum* "'The Gerona School' of Hebrew Poetry," in *Rabbi Moses Naḥmanides (Ramban): Explorations in his Religious and Literary Virtuosity,* ed. Isadore Twersky (Cambridge, Mass., and London), 37.

17. A translation of the poem by Raymond B. Scheindlin appears in "Judah Abravenel to His Son," *Judaism* 41 (1992): 190-99.

Social Perception and Literary Portrayal: Jews and Muslims in Medieval Spanish Literature

Dwayne E. Carpenter

The collective presence of Jews, Muslims, and Christians in the Iberian peninsula is very nearly a unique phenomenon in medieval European history. Only thirteenth-century Sicily can claim a similar mélange, but its tricultural society falls short of its Iberian counterpart in both intensity and permanence. Given that Jews, Muslims, and Christians shared Iberian soil for nearly seven centuries—Jewish-Christian relations go back even further, at least to the third century C.E.—it is not surprising to discover that each group sought to portray the other two in accordance with its own religious traditions and in response to contemporary political demands.[1]

Because literature both reflects and determines our perception of reality, it has often been pressed into dual service as witness and as propagandist. Literary depictions, whether of individuals or of groups, often reveal stereotypes, which in turn derive from myriad historical and cultural circumstances. Medieval polemicists, for instance, employed any means at their disposal to combat their opponents' errors, at the same time that they sought to fortify their coreligionists' faith. In these verbal conflicts, the most disparaging, uninformed, and one-sided depictions were considered legitimate means of exposing the foolishness of the enemy's beliefs and the intrinsic malevolence of his character.

The celebrated works of medieval Spanish literature date from the twelfth century onward and, consequently, our chronological net extends from this period through the fifteenth century, although somewhat greater weight is accorded texts composed during the thirteenth and fourteenth centuries. The focus will be on works in Castilian, with the notable exception of the *Cantigas de Santa Maria* (*Songs in Praise of Holy Mary*) of Alfonso X, the Wise, composed in Galician-Portuguese. Although the pieces selected for analysis fall, for the

Figure 14 *(opposite)*
Jewish quarter, Toledo

most part, under the rubric of belles-lettres, it is important to note that medieval writers did not make the rigid generic distinctions of which we today are so fond. As a result, works more commonly associated with jurisprudence and theology will also be considered.

Medieval Jewish, Muslim, and Christian authors bequeathed to later generations a rich legacy of reciprocal literary portrayals.[2] Christians, for example, generally depicted Jews as their inveterate theological enemies, while they often cast Muslims as a military menace. The Jewish-Christian conflict harks back to early rivalries between the two religions, which were already bitter at the time of the Council of Elvira (ca. 300), and became ever more acute as Christianity sought to extend its religious and political hegemony.[3] With regard to Muslim-Christian relations, Christians viewed the invasion in 711 under Tāriq ibn Ziyād as both a religious and a military threat; as a result, the *reconquista* often assumed the guise of a crusade to extirpate the Muslim usurper. For nearly seven centuries Iberian Christians strove to consolidate their authority over the Muslims—their military adversary—and the Jews—their theological foe—and the literature that Christians composed during this time bears witness to their efforts and their attitudes.

By the thirteenth century, Christian writers had amassed a substantial corpus of material on Jews and Judaism, much of it in Latin, but increasingly in the vernacular. Gonzalo de Berceo, one of the earliest Castilian authors, employed Latin sources for his rhymed saints' lives and collection of miracles in honor of the Virgin. Berceo composed his works for a largely unlettered audience, thus revealing the existence on a popular level of certain classic theological notions concerning Jews.[4] The Riojan poet echoes traditional anti-Jewish sentiment, for example, in his *Loores de Nuestra Señora* (*Praises of Our Lady*), when he asserts that Old Testament prophets foretold the Jews' loss of temporal power, or when he inveighs against the Jews for their obdurate rejection of Jesus as the messiah:

> Jacob and Daniel declared [in the Scriptures]
> That the Jews would forfeit scepter and anointing.
> O blind, deaf, and hard-hearted people!
> You deny the words of Scripture and ignore the voice of reason.[5]

By far the most common accusation that Christians leveled against Jews, however, was their alleged complicity in the death of Jesus. All other indictments, including sorcery, blasphemy, and usury, pale in comparison with the charge of deicide. This crime became the pretext of popes and the rallying cry of the rabble as they proclaimed the enduring antipathy of the Church toward the Synagogue. Reflecting this hostility, Berceo accuses the Jews of conniving with Judas, of participating in the scourging of Jesus, and finally, of partaking in the actual crucifixion:

> Guided by the wolf [Judas] the soldiers had taken with them,
> That treacherous crowd took hold of the Lamb.
> The false, unfaithful ones exercised great cruelty;
> They flogged Him with rough cords.
>
> And this unbelieving people did even more:
> They inflicted a large wound in His right side,
> From which flowed blood and water; health and life for us.[6]

Juan Ruiz, author of the fourteenth-century classic, the *Libro de buen amor* (*The Book of Good Love*), expresses similar sentiments, and adds that as a result of their heinous crime, the Jews are condemned to perpetual captivity:

> At the hour of terce
> Christ was judged;
> The people of the Torah judged Him,
> A foresworn tribe;
> For this reason it lives
> In appointed bondage
> From which it will never escape,
> Nor will it have a redeemer.[7]

The preeminent cultural patron of the Spanish Middle Ages, Alfonso the Wise (1252–84), repeats eleven times in his lavish *Cantigas de Santa Maria* the traditional Christian accusation of Jewish culpability for the death of Jesus. The following passage, taken from a story whose protagonist is a blaspheming Jewish gambler, is typical: "The cursed one refused to see how God became flesh of the Virgin and was later killed by the Jews; rather, he determined with all his heart and mind to vilify Holy Mary, by whom God became flesh."[8] The fact that the charge is made in passing, and hence at a tangent to the narrative thread, should not lead us to underestimate its significance. The ubiquitous occurrence of the indictment in medieval literature indicates that Jewish guilt for the death of Jesus was a given for Christians, an item so common in the repertoire of anti-Jewish expression that it required neither elaboration nor emphasis.

Despite the gravity of the Jews' crime, many medieval theologians entertained the hope that a remnant of them would ultimately be saved. Bernard of Clairvaux's attitude is typical:

> Under Christian princes they [the Jews] endure a hard captivity, but "they only wait for the time of their deliverance." Finally, we are told by the Apostle that when the time is ripe all Israel shall be saved.... If the Jews were utterly wiped out, what [would] become of our hope for their promised salvation, their eventual conversion?[9]

A second category of references to the Jews and crucifixion appears within the context of desecration of images. Although Jews were sometimes accused of profaning images of the Virgin, charges that they desecrated images of Jesus were more widespread and resulted in more dramatic protests on the part of Christians. Complaints of such desecration were primarily of two types: that Jews dishonored crucifixes, and that they manufactured waxen images of Jesus and then profaned them.[10]

The fifteenth-century *Libro de los exenplos por A.B.C.* (*The Alphabetical Book of Exemplary Tales*) contains an account typifying the first accusation. A certain Christian rents a house and attaches a crucifix to the wall. He ultimately vacates the house, but neglects to remove the crucifix. The new tenant, a Jew, invites a Jewish friend to dinner. Upon seeing the crucifix in his friend's home, the guest becomes angry and subsequently reports the fact to other Jews. The synagogue leaders go to the house and beat the first Jew unmercifully, after which they then take the crucifix and administer to it "as many insults and torments as their forefathers had done during the Passion of Jesus Christ." To complete their reenactment of the Crucifixion, the Jews plunge a lance into the side of the image.[11]

Frequent stories of sanguineous crucifixes coincided with and reinforced the popular belief that Jesus existed in images, just as he was present in the wine and wafer of the Eucharist. Indeed, it was widely held that Jews would obtain a wafer from a Christian, and then seek to recreate the Passion by grinding the wafer in a pestle, by trampling it, or by inflicting similar pains on the *Corpus Domini*. According to some accounts, blood would flow from the wafer, and the Jews participating in the sacrilege would be either converted or massacred, depending on the author's didactic aim.[12]

The second type of image desecration, that of waxen images of the crucifixion, is vividly described by Berceo in his *Milagros de Nuestra Señora* (*Miracles of Our Lady*) (miracle 18), and by Alfonso the Wise in his *Cantigas* (song 12). According to the narrative, the anguished voice of Mary interrupts services in her honor in the cathedral of Toledo. She excoriates the Jews for killing her son, and warns that even as she speaks they are reenacting the Crucifixion. Accompanied by the archbishop, the parishioners make their way to the Jewish quarter [fig. 14, p. 60], where they discover a large waxen image of the crucified Jesus, fastened by nails and displaying a wounded side. Rising up in righteous indignation, the mob slays all the assembled Jews.

Many of the charges leveled by medieval Christians against Jews were ultimately linked to the notion of the Jews as intimate allies of the Devil. It was by means of satanic inspiration, and often with diabolical aid, that Jews engaged in usury, ritual murder, and sorcery. Doubtless the best-known literary accounts of the Devil-Jew alliance are the widespread legends of Theophilus, forerunner of the popular figure of Faust. Medieval Spanish literature preserves the tradition in several works, including Berceo's *Milagros* (miracle 25), and Alfonso's *Cantigas* (song 3). Berceo describes the Jew, assisted by the Devil in his evil designs, as capable of any treachery. Perhaps most distressing to Berceo is the naive enthusiasm with which the common folk submit to the diabolical schemes of the artful Jew; indeed, they have come to adore him because of his wondrous powers:

> In that same bishopric where Theophilus resided,
> There lived a Jew in the Jewish quarter.
> He was learned in every evil deed and treachery,
> For with the ancient host [i.e. the dead] he had his confraternity.
>
> The wicked scoundrel was full of evil;
> He knew both enchantments and many spells,
> and devised magic circles and other schemes;
> Beelzebub guided him in all his deeds.
>
> He was well schooled in giving evil counsel;
> The false traitor killed many souls.
> Since the Jew was the vassal of a most wicked lord,
> Whatever evil the Devil commanded, he did with even greater skill.
>
> People thought that the Jew was guided by his intellect;
> They did not realize that Satan advised him in all he did.
> When by chance the Jew was successful in some deed,
> The foolish rabble nearly worshiped him.
>
> The Devil granted the Jew high standing;
> All came to him for advice.
> They did whatever he counseled them to do,
> For he was an adept deceiver.
>
> Everyone, young and old, considered him a prophet;
> All ran to him like pigs to acorns.
> They brought the sick to him on stretchers,
> And everyone said: "We will do whatever you command."[13]

The relationship between the Devil, the Jews, and sorcery is implicit in a fourteenth-century collection of sermon anecdotes, the *Espéculo de los legos* (*Moral Tales for the Laity*). In a doctrinal discourse on the importance of penance, the anonymous author recounts the words of Odo of Cheriton: "The Devil said to a sorcerer that he holds in his hand three groups of people: Moors, Jews, and wicked Christians. The first two cannot escape, but the third may be freed by means of penance."[14]

An important feature of the medieval portrayal of Jews is their relationship to the Virgin. The rise of the cult of Mary in the late Middle Ages coincided with a flourishing of literary accounts of the Virgin's power over non-Christians, including numerous incidents of Jews converted as a result of Mary's intervention on their behalf. In many of these narratives, the Virgin's mercy is juxtaposed to the Jews' malevolence. This amalgam of virtue and vice is patent in the following widely diffused story. A Jewish child, together with his Christian friends, partakes of communion on Easter Sunday. During the service, the Jew is transfixed by an image of the Virgin. Upon his return home, the child innocently informs his father that he has just participated in a Christian service. The irate father punishes his son by shoving him into an oven, but the boy is saved by the Virgin, who appears with him in the fiery furnace. Alerted by the mother's cries of despair, a crowd assembles and subsequently casts the father into the oven, where he is rapidly reduced to ashes.[15] Although at first glance it seems that the narrative is going to revolve around the young Jew's participation in the Mass—especially considering the frequent charges of desecration of the Host—the child's adoration of the image of the Virgin prepares the way for Mary's miraculous intervention. The story's outcome underscores the contrast between the Virgin's eagerness to protect those who honor her, and the terrible end awaiting those who maltreat her charges.

Figure 15 *(opposite)* Alfonso X El Sabio, *Cantigas de Santa María,* Cantiga 108, Spain, 13th century, Biblioteca de El Escorial, Madrid, T.I-I. The first two scenes of the story show Merlin in conversation with a Jew in his shop and Merlin praying to Mary (first scene illustrated here).

Alfonso the Wise records several instances of the Virgin's succor to the Jews [fig. 15]. On one occasion (*Cantigas,* song 89), the Virgin comes to the aid of a Jewess, pregnant but unable to deliver her child. The distressed woman calls upon the Virgin, even though other Jews label her a heretic and a renegade. Mary, in her new role as celestial midwife, assists the Jewess, who then gratefully converts to Christianity.

On another occasion (song 107), a Jewess, ostensibly guilty of adultery, is to be cast from a mountain pinnacle. Recalling that the Virgin had promised to help those in need, the woman vows to convert if rescued from her plight. Mary accedes to her pleas and gently conveys her to safety.[16]

Alfonso also records the tale of a Jew who is captured and viciously assaulted by Christian brigands (song 85). The Virgin rescues the Jew and, after reminding him of his generic guilt in the death of Jesus, shows him a vision of hell, where the souls of Jews are subjected to one hundred thousand types of suffering. The Jew then enjoys a vision of heaven, where all is peace and joy. Mary implores the Jew to desist from his sacrifices and embrace Christianity. To this he gladly assents, and straightaway enters a monastery.

The identification of Jews with wealth is a commonplace in medieval literature. The classic Spanish epic, the *Poema de mio Cid* (*Poem of the Cid*), contains a hotly debated passage in-

volving Jewish moneylending.[17] The Cid, having been exiled by King Alfonso VI, finds himself in desperate need of financial resources. By a clever ruse, he tricks two moneylenders, Raquel and Vidas (Hebrew Ḥayyim), into advancing him a substantial quantity of money in return for two coffers, allegedly filled with gold dinars and silver dirhems, but in reality containing only sand. While the anonymous author of the epic does not explicitly identify the two moneylenders as Jews, his portrayal of them as greedy clandestine businessmen leaves little doubt that he sought to depict stereotypical Jews in an equally stereotypical occupation. The resultant picture emphasizes the Jews' surreptitious and lucrative livelihood, and the implied conclusion is that their material success is the result of avarice and covert business dealings. The Cid's deception of the arch-deceivers is consequently not perceived to be immoral; he is merely beating the Jews at their own game. The medieval Christian audience probably even saw the episode as humorous, since they know something the secretive Jews will not discover for an entire year; namely, that their riches are nothing but sand.

The portrayal of Jews as moneylenders appears in other contexts, as well. According to one account, an impoverished Christian borrows money from a Jew, pledging that St. Nicholas will be his guarantor. On the day when the debt is to be repaid, the Christian hollows out a staff and puts in it gold equal to the amount of the loan. He then gives the staff to the Jew, who is unaware of its value. The Christian swears that he has repaid his debt, and then asks the Jew, who is still ignorant of the ruse, to return the staff to him. On his way home, the Christian falls asleep at an intersection, where a cart soon runs him over, killing him and shattering his staff. The Jew happens to pass by and sees the gold, finally realizing that he has been duped. He incongruously refuses, however, to collect the scattered gold until the Christian has been resurrected by St. Nicholas. The saint does his part, the revived Christian confesses his deception, and the Jew is baptized.[18] Although in this instance it is the Christian who is guilty of deceit, the picture of the Jew as moneylender remains constant. Furthermore, the Jew's conversion, here and in other narratives, requires supernatural intervention. The narrative thus not only demonstrates the Virgin's forbearance for non-Christians, but also evinces the recalcitrance of the Jews, who are capable of salvation solely by miraculous means.

Jews and their putative wealth at times appear in unlikely contexts. A sermon illustration tells of an extremely rich Jew who needs to pass through mountains infested with thieves. In order to assure the Jew's safety, the king provides him with a bodyguard. This protection proves illusory, however, when the bodyguard, impelled by greed, murders the Jew he is assigned to defend. When the king learns of the Jew's murder, he angrily orders the malefactor put to death.[19] Two points may be noted: first, the wealthy Jew enjoys royal protection, indicating the often close political and economic relationship between the central authority and "its" Jews. As *servi camerae regis* (serfs of the royal chamber), Jews were sometimes granted extensive privileges in return for services rendered to the crown. The narrative's primary message, however, is the importance of faithfulness to one's word, as indicated by the vernacular gloss: "Safety granted [by the king] / Must be extended *even* to Jews."

Another admonition concerning Jews is found in the fourteenth-century *Libro del Cavallero Zifar* (*The Book of the Knight Zifar*), where kings are warned not to retain Jews in their

Figure 16

Feudal Customs of Aragon, called "Vidal Mayor," Aragon, second half of the 13th century, Collection of the J. Paul Getty Museum, Malibu, 83.MQ.165 (Ms. Ludwig XIV 6), fol. 180r. (cat. no. 24)

The two scenes represent successive moments of action: first a Jew deceives a Christian customer by selling him a lightweight silver goblet; the Christian then uses the goblet as insufficient surety on a loan.

service. They are, according to the author, "most crafty in doing evil and enemies of our faith," "engaged in undoing the good counsel of princes," "devoid of all true affection," and "desirous of deceiving the servants of Jesus Christ."[20]

The Jew's alleged duplicity is exemplified in one of the most important legal texts of medieval Spain, the *Vidal Mayor* (ca. 1250) [fig. 16]. In one of the laws dealing with deception, the author cites a case in which a Jew pays his debt to a Christian with a fake silver goblet. The Christian resolves to deceive the Jew in the same way in which he has been deceived. Claiming to have been robbed, the Christian returns to the Jew and requests a loan. Once the Christian has the money in hand, he offers the same fake silver goblet to the Jew as collateral. The law code upholds the Christian's conduct, since he was only acting in response to the Jew's original deception.[21]

Sometime in the first half of the twelfth century, an anonymous writer composed the *Auto de los Reyes Magos* (*Drama of the Magi*), the only extant dramatic piece in Castilian until the fifteenth century.[22] Among the dramatis personae are two rabbis summoned by a distressed Herod to inform him whether the Scriptures herald the coming of a rival king. The response of the two rabbis accords with medieval portrayals of Jews concerning the messiah: the first claims ignorance of Old Testament prophecies, while the second implies that the Jews have intentionally concealed knowledge of such predictions. The rabbis' exasperated dialogue provides not only a comic interlude, but also theological information for the Christian audience.

Polemical writings are by their very nature confrontational, and religious polemics are an especially confrontational type of literature, in part because of the fervor with which sacrosanct beliefs and practices are attacked and defended. Religions are, for reasons of pride and survival, traditionally ill-disposed to admit to shared verities. Indeed, what invests dogmatic conflicts with particular urgency is the nonnegotiable character of religious truth. Even in those rare instances when Jews, Muslims, and Christians came together in a sort of intellectual community, each participant doubtless perceived his religious identity in absolute terms and was therefore fully cognizant of his learned colleagues' dogmatic errors.

Jewish-Christian polemics covered a broad spectrum of issues, including the Old Law versus the New, alleged blasphemies in the Talmud, transubstantiation, the Incarnation, the Trinity, and the nature and coming of the messiah. Many of the works dealing with these topics were written by converts to Christianity, some of whom display intimate acquaintance with Jewish texts, as well as the fervor begotten of a newfound faith. Most polemical treatises are no longer extant, since their purpose was more immediate, their public more local, and their language more plebeian than, for example, those of the grandiose disputations of Barcelona (1263) or Tortosa (1413–14).[23] However, a fragmentary work from the early thirteenth century, the "Disputa entre un cristiano y un judío" (*A Debate between a Christian and a Jew*), has been preserved in all its acerbic glory.[24] The Christian disputant berates his Jewish opponent for practising circumcision, transgressing the Sabbath, and ignoring the triune nature of God. The dialogue contains a smattering of words in Hebrew, thus suggesting that the author was a *converso*.

The charged character of polemical literature is also evident in a quadrilingual treatise, the *Libro de las tres creencias* (*Book of the Three Beliefs*), attributed to Abner of Burgos (also known as Alfonso of Valladolid after his conversion to Christianity around 1320).[25] Ostensibly a dispassionate examination of Judaism, Islam, and Christianity aimed at revealing the superior religion, the work is actually a vigorous apology of Christianity and a harsh indictment of Judaism. In the course of his exposition of key Christian dogmas, such as the Trinity, the sacraments, and Jesus' redemptive death, Abner disparages Jewish religious authorities and their reliance on the Talmud. Like generations of polemicists before him, Abner makes potent use of his lexical arsenal, labeling his opponents fools, blind, slaves, liars, and deceivers.[26]

This hostility toward Jews was exacerbated by the late medieval Spanish obsession with *limpieza de sangre* (purity of blood).[27] As a result of legislation enacted in Toledo in 1449, *conversos* were no longer permitted to hold public office or testify in court cases. Despite papal denunciations of these laws, both religious and secular organizations continued to require proof of blood purity. Even well-ensconced *converso* ecclesiastics justifiably worried about the Inquisition's indefatigable efforts to uncover evidence of crypto-Judaizing. Writers, most notably Fernando de Rojas, author of the hugely successful *La Celestina* (1499), often reflected in their works the uneasy climate for conversos.[28] This fixation with blood purity did not end with the expulsion; on the contrary, for centuries afterward, the Inquisition, at home and in the New World, continued its search for "tainted" Christians.

Polemics concerning Jewish practices and theology formed an integral part of fifteenth-century Spanish literature. The voluminous poetic compilations known as *cancioneros* are among the richest sources for such material. Many of the poets represented in these collections were of Jewish origin, a fact clearly evidenced by the polyglot nature of some of the poems, as well as by the disparaging references to the *converso* status of certain poets.[29] Some of the *cancionero* poetry mirrors theological issues earlier debated in more formal settings. Of particular interest are the efforts of *converso* poets to place Christian doctrines, such as the Trinity and the Incarnation, within a cabbalistic and Jewish philosophical framework.[30]

Although medieval Spanish literature generally portrays Jews in a negative light, there are a few notable exceptions. Don Juan Manuel (1283–1348), nephew of Alfonso the Wise, waxes eloquent on the competence of Jewish physicians: "When you are able to obtain a physician, I advise you that he be of the lineage of Don Çag [Isaac], who was my father's and my physician. And never give him up for another, for I tell you truly that to this day I have never found such competent and loyal physicians...."[31]

Despite the fact that Jews were not widely recognized for their military prowess, several authors mention their talents on the battlefield. Alfonso the Wise, for example, refers to their martial bravery in his influential law code, the *Siete partidas* (Seven Divisions): "And this name [*judío*] is derived from the tribe of Judah, which was more noble and valiant than any of the other tribes.... In addition, members of that tribe always struck the first blows in battle."[32] The *cancionero* poet Pero Ferrús likewise cites notable Jewish warriors, although his encomium contains an ironic twist:

> Joshua, and even Gideon,
> Leaders of the Jews;
> Judas with the Maccabees,
> King David and Absalom:
> You will note that, despite being Jews,
> They did not allow the cold to stop them
> From fighting in all seasons.[33]

According to these writers, the Jews' military valor is purely historical. Just as their theological standing has been eclipsed, so their battle prowess is a thing of the past.

Whereas Christians often viewed Jews through a religious lens, they tended to see Muslims both as infidels and as invaders. And although Christians could easily perceive the genetic relationship between Judaism and Christianity, they sometimes had difficulty appreciating the link with Islam. Even after some five and a half centuries of Christian-Muslim coexistence, and during a period when intellectual exchanges between the two cultures were at their apex, Alfonso the Wise was nonetheless capable of the following error-ridden definition of Muslims:

> Moors are a type of people who believe that Muḥammad was a prophet and messenger of God. And because his works and deeds do not demonstrate any great sanctity, such that he should be accorded so holy a status, their law is like an insult to God.... "Saracen" means Moor in both Latin and the vernacular. And this name is derived from "Sarah," who was the free wife of Abraham, although the Moors do not descend from her, but rather from Hagar, who was Abraham's servant. And there are two types of Moors: the first does not believe in either the Old Testament or the New; and the second accepts the five books of Moses [the Pentateuch], but rejects the prophets and refuses to believe them. And the latter are called Samaritans, because they originated in a city called Samaria, and the Gospel refers to them where it says that Jews and Samaritans should neither live together nor have any dealings with one another.[34]

Don Juan Manuel likewise adopts a hostile view of Islam:

> The religion of the Moors in so many ways is so foolish and unreasonable that any person of understanding can see that nobody could possibly achieve salvation by it. This is one argument. The other is that that religion was not given by God or by any of God's prophets, and so is no sort of faith, but an erroneous belief into which that evil man Muḥammad deceived them.[35]

While Christians generally expressed disdain for Islam, they nonetheless occasionally demonstrated an unusual degree of support for the infidel faith. In order to bolster their arguments in favor of the Immaculate Conception and the Virgin Birth, Christians declared that Muslims, despite all of their other doctrinal delusions, recognized the special nature of Mary. Abner of Burgos (Alfonso of Valladolid), for example, cites in garbled Arabic a passage presumably from the Qurʾān supporting his assertion that Mary was the mother of Jesus. He further argues that Muslims, in contrast to Jews, enjoy worldly glory and temporal power because they honor the Virgin.[36] Alfonso the Wise also claims that Muḥammad professed the Virgin birth (*Cantigas,* song 329), and, to show her gratitude, Mary goes so far as to help Muslim emigrants fend off an attack by Catalonian corsairs (song 379). Despite this exceptional acknowledgment of Muslim belief in the Virgin, Christians were nonetheless committed to converting their infidel enemy.

More often, however, Christians portrayed Muslims in negative ways. Alfonso frequently depicts them as dark-skinned unbelievers, ever ready to annihilate Christians and profane the symbols of their religion. In song 99 of his *Cantigas,* for instance, a Muslim horde seeks to wreak havoc on a Christian village and desecrate an image of the Virgin. Mary swiftly intervenes to prevent this sacrilege and the Muslims pay with their lives for their audacity. Later, in song 229, Mary blinds and cripples a band of Muslims who seek to destroy a church dedicated to her.[37]

The medieval Christian image of the Muslim as barbaric infidel appears alongside that of the Muslim as exotic sybarite. For Muslims, even death was but the doorway to a hedonistic existence, where the faithful disported themselves in luxurious surroundings, attended by obliging houris. Such notions were anathema to the self-denying ethos of Christianity, although the present and potential pleasures associated with Islam were enough of a temptation to Christians that conversion was a major concern for secular and religious authorities [fig. 17A]. The thirteenth-century *Estoria de España* (*History of Spain*) vividly describes, from a Christian perspective, the paradisiacal joys awaiting Muslims:

> He [Muhammad] even told them [his followers], and made them believe, that the man who kills his enemy, and he who is killed by his enemies, goes straight to paradise; and that paradise was a delightful place where one ate and drank well,

Figure 17A

"The Feast of Baltassar," Beatus' *Commentary on the Book of Revelations,* Monastery of San Salvador de Tabara, 940s, The Pierpont Morgan Library, New York, M644, fol. 255v (cat. no. 1)

As recorded in the Book of Daniel, "The Feast of Baltassar" was the occasion for the profanation of the Temple vessels. Here the event occurs beneath a horseshoe arch with alternating red and white stones, a symbol of the Mosque of Córdoba, whose presence transforms the illustration into an anti-Islamic statement.

> having three rivers, one of wine, one of honey, and one of milk; also that men in paradise would have virgin women, not of the kind that inhabit this world, but others of kinds here unknown; and that men would have to the full all those things they covet in their hearts.[38]

Christians, as well, recognized the powerful incentive that the promise of martyrdom on the battlefield could provide. In his effort to understand why Christians were forced to suffer at the hands of infidels, Don Juan Manuel saw a positive side to the incessant warfare between Christians and Muslims:

> Good Christian people think that the reason why God allowed the Christians to take such great harm from the Moors is so that they [the Christians] should be able to make war justly against them [the Moors], and so that those dying in such war, having obeyed the commandments of Holy Church, could be martyrs, their souls being absolved by such martyrdom of the sins they might have committed.[39]

The *Poema de mio Cid* contains numerous references to Muslims. In the course of his efforts to regain the honor unjustly taken from him, the Cid engages thundering Muslim throngs in fierce battle, invariably besting them, and often despite overwhelming odds. The more ferocious the antagonist, and the more evil the enemy, the greater the victory enjoyed by the Christian hero. Although the poet of the *Poema de mio Cid* generally depicts Muslims monochromatically as the military enemy of Christians, at least one Muslim, Abengalbón, appears as the Cid's friend and adviser.

It is the Muslims' valor on the battlefield that often elicits praise by Christian writers. The New Christian Mosén Diego de Valera, at the same time that he denounces Muḥammad's religious tenets, commends him for his military prowess:

> For if we wish to consider the nobility of the Muslims, who can be unaware of the many kings, princes, and noblemen who have arisen from among them? And if we wish to forget the others, let us at least recall some whose fame will endure forever. Who can ignore Muḥammad, that false prophet, by whose wisdom and skill on the field of battle he gave rise to that cursed sect, the Muslims? And although he was of lowly and poor lineage, he obtained the first crown of kingship among the Muslims and placed under his authority the entire African host, having already achieved great victories over the Romans.[40]

By the thirteenth century, two images of the Muslim had begun to merge in the Christian mind. Christians were very aware of the material and cultural superiority of many aspects of Islamic civilization, and consequently they attempted to adopt certain of these features. In addition, Christians had developed over the centuries of the *reconquista* a grudging admiration for the military expertise of their Muslim rivals. They recorded their enemy's exploits in chronicles ballads, and novels, and gradually there emerged an idealized, sentimental picture of the Muslim. The culmination of this process was the *novela morisca* (Moorish novel), most elegantly embodied in the romantic tale of the noble Abindarráez and the lovely Jarifa. The following is a description of the chivalrous knight:

> Looking closely, they could see a gallant Moor on a roan horse coming towards them. He was tall and handsome, and looked a fine figure as he rode. He wore a bright red jacket and a damask burnous of the same colour, all embroidered with gold and silver. He rode with his right arm bared and on his shirtsleeve there was worked the portrait of a beautiful lady. In his hand he held a thick and elegant two-edged lance. He carried a shield and a scimitar, and on his head wore a Tunisian turban which, wound many times round his head, served as both adornment and defence for his person. So dressed, the Moor rode along with a cheerful mien, singing a song he had composed in sweet celebration of his love, which went like this:
>
> Born in Granada,
> Raised in Cártama,
> Fell in love in Coín
> Not far from Alora.[41]

Medieval Spanish literature contains passages in which Jews and Muslims are treated together, if not equally. The thirteenth-century *Primera crónica* (*First Chronicle*), for example, accuses the Jews of plotting with the Muslims to invade Visigothic Spain, a notion subsequently—and uncritically—endorsed by many historians.[42] At the other end of our chronological spectrum, the late medieval *Dança de la muerte* (*Dance of Death*) includes in its catalogue of unwilling participants a rabbi and an *alfaquí,* the latter a Muslim specialist in religious law. Like their Christian counterparts, the rabbi and a*lfaquí* vainly attempt to persuade Death to exempt them from its stern decree and, like the others, they reluctantly join the macabre procession.[43]

The ambitious translation activity of the Spanish Middle Ages helped to disseminate a genre not always appreciated for its Semitic roots: gaming literature. Popular games, such as chess and backgammon, originated in the East, but were introduced to Western Europe through translations of Arabic treatises. One of the most important of these works, the *Libro de ajedrez, dados, e tablas* (*Book of Chess, Dice, and Backgammon*), translated at the behest of Alfonso the Wise, portrays in lavish illustrations the games' various devotees, including Christian nobles, nuns, Jews, and Muslims, often playing together in idyllic settings (Title page illustration).

There is evidence that gaming was not always the harmonious activity depicted in these miniatures. The *Ordenamiento de las tafurerías* (*Regulations concerning Gaming Establishments*)

Figure 17B *(opposite)*
Beatus' *Commentary on the Book of Revelations,* Monastery of San Salvador de Tabara, 940s, The Pierpont Morgan Library, New York, M644, fol. 142v (cat. no. 1)
The theme of the composite beast runs through the artistic and literary history of Spain during the Middle Ages. It appears in Beatus' Commentary in the tenth century and in the *Alborayque* of the late fifteenth century to describe Muslim and Jewish converts to Christianity.

super eas
ubi locuste
ledunt

reveals that Jews, Muslims, and Christians frequently gambled together. One of the issues raised is whether Christians, Jews, or Muslims can be pawned by players who find themselves short of funds. While the law initially prohibits the pawning of human beings on the grounds that Christians are unquestionably free, and most Jews and Muslims enjoy a similar status, it later declares that a player may pawn a captive Muslim or other slave. This and similar legislation points to the generally free status of Jews, as well as the servile condition of at least some Muslims.[44]

An especially evocative example of Christian literary portraiture of Jews and Muslims is the *Libro del Alborayque* (*Book of the Alborayque*), composed around 1488 and immediately prior to the expulsion of most of Iberian Jewry and the fall of the Islamic kingdom of Granada. This brief work derives its title from al-Burāq, the Arabic name of Muḥammad's mount. This fabulous beast, described by the anonymous author of the *Alborayque* as a bizarre combination of numerous animals, has the mouth of a wolf, the face of a horse, the eyes of a man, the tail of a serpent, and the body of an ox [fig. 17B]. *Alborayque,* as the author explains, was one of the names applied to converts from Judaism to Christianity. Just as Muḥammad's steed cannot be identified with a single animal, but rather is a corrupt composite of many creatures, so the *conversos* are said to be neither Jews, nor Christians, nor Muslims. The writer assigns moral qualities to each of the twenty physical attributes; thus, the *alboraycos,* i.e. the *conversos,* are, among other things, hypocrites, thieves, blasphemers, perpetrators of sodomy (which they taught to Muslims, who in turn instructed evil Christians in the practice), and Christ-killers.[45]

The sentiments expressed in the *Alborayque* go beyond the anti-Jewish harangues of Berceo, the hackneyed hostility of Alfonso the Wise, and the ad hominem accusations in the *cancioneros;* the *Alborayque* expresses an implacable contempt and suspicion for those Jews forced to abandon their ancestral faith. Some four years after the composition of the *Alborayque,* many Christians, from the anonymous author of this treatise to the Catholic Monarchs, doubtless believed that the twin events of the expulsion and the fall of Granada would solve their Jewish and Muslim problems. The subsequent preoccupation with *conversos* and *moriscos,* however, is compelling evidence that these concerns could not be dismissed so easily.[46]

This essay began with a reference to the collective presence of Jews, Muslims, and Christians in the Iberian peninsula, but it concludes with mention of *conversos, moriscos,* and Christians. In 1492, religious unity was ostensibly achieved by expelling the Jews and conquering the Muslims. Yet, although they no longer resided in Spain, the Jews endured for centuries in the Spanish obsession with purity of blood; and the Muslims, no more a military threat, lived on in the popular imagination as chivalrous knights. Even in their absence, Jews and Muslims could not fail to leave an indelible imprint on Spanish life and letters for centuries to come.

NOTES

1. On Jewish-Muslim-Christian relations in the Iberian peninsula, see Américo Castro, *The Spaniards: An Introduction to Their History,* trans. Willard F. King and Selma Margaretten (Berkeley, Calif., 1971); Eliyahu Ashtor, *The Jews of Moslem Spain,* trans. Aaron Klein and Jenny Machlowitz Klein, 3 vols. (Philadelphia, 1973-84); Yitzhak Baer, *A History of the Jews in Christian Spain,* trans. Louis Schoffman, 2 vols. (Philadelphia, 1961); and Thomas F. Glick, *Islamic and Christian Spain in the Early Middle Ages: Comparative Perspectives on Social and Cultural Formation* (Princeton, N.J., 1979).

2. Although scholars have examined specific aspects of Jews in Spanish literature, to date we lack a detailed study of the topic. See, however, Seymour Resnick, "The Jew as Portrayed in Early Spanish Literature," *Hispania* 34 (1951): 54-58; Kenneth R. Scholberg, "Minorities in Medieval Castilian Literature," ibid., 37 (1954): 203-9; Gilbert Smith, "Christian Attitudes toward the Jews in Spanish Literature," *Judaism* 19 (1970): 444-51; Charles F. Fraker, Jr., "Judaism in the *Cancionero de Baena,*" in *Studies on the "Cancionero de Baena"* (Chapel Hill, N.C., 1966), 9-62; and Cristina Arbós Ayuso, "Los judíos en la literatura medieval española (siglos XIII-XIV): los judíos y la economía; protecciones y privilegios," in *Actas de las Jornadas de Estudios Sefardíes, Universidad de Extremadura* (Cáceres, 1980), 141-50. The depiction of Muslims in medieval Spanish literature is studied by Harry Austin Deferrari, *The Sentimental Moor in Spanish Literature Before 1600* (Philadelphia, 1927); María Soledad Carrasco Urgoiti, *El moro de Granada en la literatura (del siglo XV al XX)* (Madrid, 1956); María Rosa Lida de Malkiel, "El moro en las letras castellanas," *Hispanic Review* 28 (1960): 350-58; and the magnificent collection of Spanish and Latin texts, complete with English translation, in Colin Smith, *Christians and Moors in Spain,* 2 vols. (Warminster, 1988-89).

3. José Vives, *Concilios visigóticos e hispano-romanos* (Barcelona, 1963), canons 16, 49, 50, 78.

4. Joël Saugnieux, *Berceo y las culturas del siglo XIII* (Logroño, 1982), 73-102.

5. *El duelo de la Virgen, Los himnos, Los loores de Nuestra Señora, Los signos del juicio final,* ed. Brian Dutton (London, 1975), *Loores,* st. 15. Unless otherwise noted, all translations are mine.

6. The first two passages are from the *Duelo de la Virgen,* sts. 16cd, 24ab; and the third is from the *Loores de la Virgen,* st. 77abc.

7. Translated by Raymond S. Willis in his edition of the *Libro de buen amor* (Princeton, N.J., 1972), st. 1053. Alfonso the Wise expresses a similar attitude in his massive legal compendium, the *Siete partidas* (*Seven Divisions*): "And the reason the Church, emperors, kings, and other princes permitted the Jews to reside among Christians is this: that they might live forever as in captivity and serve as a reminder to mankind that they are descended from those who crucified Our Lord Jesus Christ." Dwayne E. Carpenter, *Alfonso X and the Jews: An Edition of and Commentary on "Siete Partidas" 7.24 "De los judíos"* (Berkeley, Calif., 1986), 28.

8. Ed. Walter Mettmann, 4 vols. (Coimbra, 1959-72; repr., 2 vols., Vigo, 1981), *cantiga* 238.20-23. For an examination of the cultural milieu associated with Alfonso the Wise, see Robert I. Burns, ed., *Emperor of Culture: Alfonso X the Learned of Castile and His Thirteenth-Century Renaissance* (Philadelphia, 1990).

9. Cited in David Berger, "The Attitude of St. Bernard of Clairvaux Toward the Jews," *Proceedings of the American Academy for Jewish Research* 40 (1972): 91.

10. Note Alfonso the Wise's concern with ritual murder and waxen images; Carpenter, *Alfonso X and the Jews,* 64-65.

11. Clemente Sánchez de Vercial, *Libro de los exenplos por A.B.C.,* ed. John E. Keller (Madrid, 1961), no. 91.

12. Joshua Trachtenberg, *The Devil and the Jews: The Medieval Conception of the Jew and its Relation to Modern Antisemitism* (New Haven, Conn., 1943; repr. with introduction by Marc Saperstein, Philadelphia, 1983), 109-23; and Jacob R. Marcus, *The Jew in the Medieval World: A Source Book: 315-1791* (New York, 1979), 155-58.

13. *Los milagros de Nuestra Señora,* ed. Brian Dutton (London, 1971) sts. 721-26.

14. Ed. José M. Mohedano Hernández (Madrid, 1951), 353-54.

15. Gonzalo de Berceo, *Milagros de Nuestra Señora,* miracle 16; Alfonso the Wise, *Cantigas de Santa Maria,* song 4.

16. José Fradejas Lebrero, "La cantiga CVII o de Mari Saltos," *Fragmentos* 2 (1984): 20-32; and Anita Benaim de Lasry, "Marisaltos: Artificial Purification in Alfonso el Sabio's *Cantiga* 107," in *Studies on the "Cantigas de Santa Maria": Art, Music, and Poetry,* ed. Israel J. Katz et al. (Madison, Wis., 1987), 299-311.

17. The most recent analysis of this passage is Joseph J. Duggan, *The "Cantar de mio Cid": Poetic Creation in its Economic and Social Contexts* (Cambridge, 1989), 17-18. Note also Donald McGrady, "Did the Cid Repay the Jews? A Reconsideration," *Romania* 106 (1985): 518-27.

18. *Libro de los exenplos,* no. 234; and *Espéculo de los legos,* no. 459.

19. *Libro de los exenplos,* no. 167.

20. Edited by Cristina González (Madrid, 1983), 313-14.

21. *Vidal Mayor,* Facsimile Edition, with studies by A. Ubieto Arteta, J. Delgado Echeverría, J. Antonio Frago Gracia, and M. del Carmen Lacarra Ducay (Huesca, 1989), fol. 180r.

22. Ramón Menéndez Pidal, *Textos medievales españoles: ediciones críticas y estudios,* in *Obras completas,* vol. 12 (Madrid, 1976), 169-77.

23. Texts and analyses of these disputations are found in Hyam Maccoby, *Judaism on Trial: Jewish-Christian Disputations in the Middle Ages* (Rutherford, N.J., 1982).

24. Américo Castro, *Revista de Filología Española* 1 (1914): 173-80.

25. Dwayne E. Carpenter, "Abner de Burgos, *Libro de las tres creencias:* The Spanish Manuscripts," *Manuscripta* 31 (1987): 190-97.

26. Lucas Fernández employs equally aggressive terminology in his *Auto de la Pasión:* "falsos perros hebreos," "pueblo desconocido / luciferal Satanás / ingrato, desgradecido," "pueblo de traición, pueblo cruel" (noted in Humberto López Morales, *Tradición y creación en los orígenes del teatro castellano* (Madrid, 1968), 108.

27. The best work to date on the subject is Albert A. Sicroff, *Les Controverses des statuts de "pureté de sang" en Espagne du 15ᵉ au 17ᵉ siècle* (Paris, 1960).

28. Stephen Gilman, *The Art of "La Celestina"* (Madison, Wis., 1956); and *The Spain of Fernando de Rojas: The Intellectual and Social Landscape of "La Celestina"* (Princeto, N.J., 1972).

29. Francisco Cantera Burgos, "El *Cancionero de Baena:* judíos y conversos en él," *Sefarad* 27 (1967): 71-111; and Josep M. Sola-Solé and Stanley E. Rose, "Judíos y conversos en la poesía cortesana del siglo XV: el estilo polígloto de Fray Diego de Valencia," *Hispanic Review* 44 (1976): 371-85.

30. These issues are brilliantly studied in Fraker, "Judaism in the *Cancionero de Baena,*" 11-30.

31. *Libro enfenido,* ed. José Manuel Blecua, in *Obras completas,* 2 vols. (Madrid, 1982-83), 1:155.

32. Cited in Carpenter, *Alfonso X and the Jews,* 28.

33. *Cancionero de Baena,* facsimile edition (New York, 1926), fols. 106v-108r.

34. *Siete partidas,* 7.25.0, 1.

35. *Libro de los estados;* cited in Smith, *Christians and Moors,* 2:95. Useful analyses of medieval Christian attitudes toward Islam include R. W. Southern, *Western Views of Islam in the Middle Ages* (Cambridge, Mass., 1962); and Norman Daniel, *Islam and the West: The Making of an Image* (Edinburgh, 1960; repr. 1962).

36. *Libro de las tres creencias,* Biblioteca Nacional, Madrid, MS 9302, fol. 20r.

37. Albert I. Bagby, Jr., "Some Characterizations of the Moor in Alfonso X's *Cántigas,*" *South Central Bulletin* 30 (1970): 164-67; and Mercedes García-Arenal, "Los moros en las *Cantigas* de Alfonso X el Sabio," *Al-Qanṭara* 6 (1985): 133-51.

38. Cited in Smith, *Christians and Moors,* 1:5, 7.

39. *Libro de los estados,* cited ibid., 2:95.

40. Mosén Diego de Valera, *Espejo de verdadera nobleza,* in *Sociedad de Bibliófilos Españoles,* vol. 16 (Madrid, 1878), 212-13; cited in Scholberg, "Minorities in Medieval Castilian Literature," 206-7.

41. *El Abencerraje y la hermosa Jarifa,* cited in Smith, *Christians and Moors,* 2:121. The *moriscos* have received insightful analysis in Henry Charles Lea, *The Moriscos of Spain: Their Conversion and Expulsion* (London, 1901; repr. New York, 1968); Anwar G. Chejne, *Islam and the West: The Moriscos: A Cultural and Social History* (Albany, N.Y., 1983); and Francisco Márquez Villanueva, "El problema historiográfico de los moriscos," *Bulletin Hispanique* 86 (1984): 61-135.

42. The issue is thoroughly analyzed by Norman Roth, "The Jews and the Muslim Conquest of Spain," *Jewish Social Studies* 38 (1976): 145-58.

43. Josep M. Sola-Solé, "El rabí y el alfaquí en la *Dança general de la muerte,*" *Romance Philology* 18 (1965): 272-83; repr. in *Sobre árabes, judíos, y marranos y su impacto en la lengua y literatura españolas* (Barcelona, 1983), 145-62; L. P. Harvey, "The *Alfaquí* in *La dança general de la muerte,*" *Hispanic Review* 41 (1973): 498-510; and Alan D. Deyermond, "El ambiente social e intelectual de la *Danza de la Muerte,*" in *Actas del III Congreso Internacional de Hispanistas* (Mexico City, 1970), 267-76.

44. Dwayne E. Carpenter, "Fickle Fortune: Gambling in Medieval Spain," *Studies in Philology* 85 (1988): 276.

45. The *Libro del Alborayque* is edited in Nicolás López Martínez, *Los judaizantes castellanos y la Inquisición en tiempo de Isabel la Católica* (Burgos, 1954), 391-404. For a typology of the *converso,* see José Faur, *In the Shadow of History: Jews and Conversos at the Dawn of Modernity* (Albany, N.Y., 1992), 41-52.

46. See the fine study by John Edwards, "Mission and Inquisition Among *Conversos* and *Moriscos* in Spain, 1250-1550," in *Persecution and Toleration,* Studies in Church History, vol. 21, ed. W. J. Sheils (London, 1984), 139-51.

Science in Medieval Spain: The Jewish Contribution in the Context of *Convivencia*

Thomas F. Glick

The transmission of ancient science through translations from Arabic to Latin, involving the interaction of Muslims, Jews, and Christians, in medieval Spain has become a commonplace of the history of science.[1] Without this transmission, the assimilation of ancient science by Europeans would have been, at least, delayed. But the contents of the transmission also had a positive, if subtle, effect on European science: for example, the fact that the Arabs, particularly those of al-Andalus, stressed astronomy and astrology stimulated a far-reaching cycle of astronomical and cosmological renovation in Latin Europe that culminated in Copernicus and Galileo [fig. 18]. In the present essay, I will examine particular aspects of the scientific exchange among men of the three religions in medieval Spain in order to comment both on the content of that exchange and on its social and cultural meaning.

THE SCIENCE OF THE ARABS IN SPAIN

The early years of science in Islamic Spain, extending into the early tenth century, were marked by an idiosyncratic mixture of Latin and Visigothic traditions with other elements of science (and pseudoscience) of Eastern provenance. The Latin survival is observable in astrology, agronomy, medicine, and geography. In astrology, the ancestry of the Alfonsine *Libro de las Cruces* of the thirteenth century can be traced back to a Low Latin astrology manual used in Spain and North Africa before the Muslim invasion. The agricultural lore of the ancient agronomists, specifically Vindanios Anatolios whose treatise circulated in Syriac and Arabic translations, continued to have influence. In medicine, Muslim physicians of the ninth and early tenth centuries continued to write books of medical aphorisms following a Latin style based on the aphorisms of Hippocrates. In geography, Isidore of Seville's famous world map in the form of a T has survived with its legends written in Arabic evidently by an

Figure 22 *(opposite)* Astrolabe with Hebrew inscription, Europe, mid-16th century, The Adler Planetarium, History of Astronomy Collection, Chicago, M20 (cat. no. 102)

Arabic-speaking monk.[2] As a result of Abbasid influence, a new phase begins during the reign of ʿAbd al-Raḥmān II (822-852) when, according to an anonymous chronicler, the first Eastern astronomical tables (*zijāt;* singular *zīj*) arrived in al-Andalus.[3] Thus began the reception in the western Islamic world of the results of an extraordinarily intense period of astronomical activity in the East, which saw the translation of Greek texts, particularly those of Ptolemy, from Greek into Syriac and thence into Arabic and the contemporaneous reception in the Islamic East of the Indian astronomical tables known as the *Sindhind.*

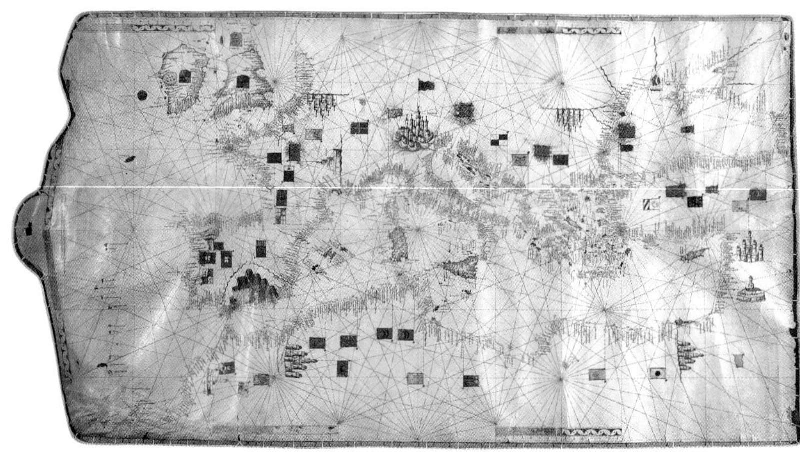

Figure 18
Petrus Roselli, Portolan Chart, Palma, 1456, The Newberry Library, Ayer Ms. Map 3
The increase in seafaring around 1300 led to a growing need for maps that charted coastal waters and harbors, the portolan maps.

This movement was the object of royal patronage in the reigns of the first two caliphs, ʿAbd al-Raḥmān III and al-Ḥakam II. In the 950s the Jewish chancellor Ḥasdai ibn Shaprūṭ promoted scientific interchange. First, he was involved in the famous episode of the *Materia Medica* of Dioscorides. According to the story recounted by Ibn Juljul, a Muslim physician, when the Byzantine emperor sent a Greek manuscript of this important pharmacological work to ʿAbd al-Raḥmān III, Ḥasdai secured from the emperor the services of a Greek monk, Nicholas, and also gathered together a group of Muslim scholars, including ʿAbd al-Raḥman ibn Ishāq ibn al-Haitham al-Qurṭubī, to work with Nicholas in order to translate into Arabic those plant names that the original Arabic translator, Istifan ibn Basil, had left untranslated. This project had the effect of stimulating most of the subsequent botanical and pharmacological work produced in al-Andalus, including treatises by Ibn Wāfid (who also wrote an agronomical work), Abūʾl Ṣalt (also a philosopher); Ibn al-Haitham himself, whose treatise on medical therapy circulated in a Hebrew version attributed, no doubt falsely, to Abraham ibn Ezra;[4] and Ibn Buklarish, a Jewish botanist in the service of al-Mustaʾin of Saragossa, author of a pharmacological treatise in the same tradition listing common plant names in a variety of languages. Ḥasdai also received an Eastern book on the construction of spherical astrolabes, probably that of the Jewish astronomer, Mashallah (the same work that Chaucer later translated into English).[5]

Toward the end of the tenth century, an astronomer and pedagogue named Maslama of Madrid adapted al-Khwārizmī's astronomical tables to al-Andalus and trained a great generation of astronomers including Ibn al-Ṣamh and Ibn al-Ṣaffār who, in the eleventh century, contributed important treatises on the construction and use of astrolabes. The greatest figure of Andalusi science of the eleventh century, however, was another astronomer, al-Zarqāl (the Azarquiel of Castilian treatises) of Toledo, author of the famous Toledan Tables based on his own observations. His description of the motion of the solar apogee was an important contribution to theoretical astronomy. Many of these same figures, notably Maslama, were involved in the diffusion of al-Khwārizmī's algebra and the use of Indian numerals, together with the concepts of position and the zero.

Virtually contemporaneous with the reception of Eastern science in al-Andalus was the transmission of this knowledge to Christian scholars, not only in Spain but over the rest of Latin Europe as well. Gerbert of Aurillac traveled to the Catalan monastery of Ripoll in the late tenth century to acquaint himself with the new mathematics and the early eleventh-century scientific miscellany (known as MS Ripoll 225), which Vernet has characterized as "the manual of study" of the monks of Ripoll,[6]—a veritable compendium of the new Arabic lore, particularly astronomical. In the twelfth century many Europeans were drawn to Spain by the new knowledge available there at the same time as a great generation of Jewish rabbis was discovering an interest in matters scientific. The creation of a scientific corpus in Hebrew marked a distinctive moment in Jewish intellectual history.[7] Jews were interested in science, particularly astronomy, not only because of the nature of their participation in Arabic culture generally, but for many of the same reasons that stimulated Christian interest: from the revival of ancient philosophy and its relation to theological issues to the practical needs of computation related to the religious calendar. In any case, the simultaneous interest of Jews and Christians in assimilating Arabic science created the immediate stimulus for the formation of interethnic teams of translators, in order to take maximum advantage of the linguistic skills of Jews and Christians. These teams became the standard means of transmitting Arabic science to Latin Europe. The same phenomenon continued in the thirteenth century, notably under the auspices of the scholarly king Alfonso X the Wise of Castile, only in this case both Jews and Christians trans-

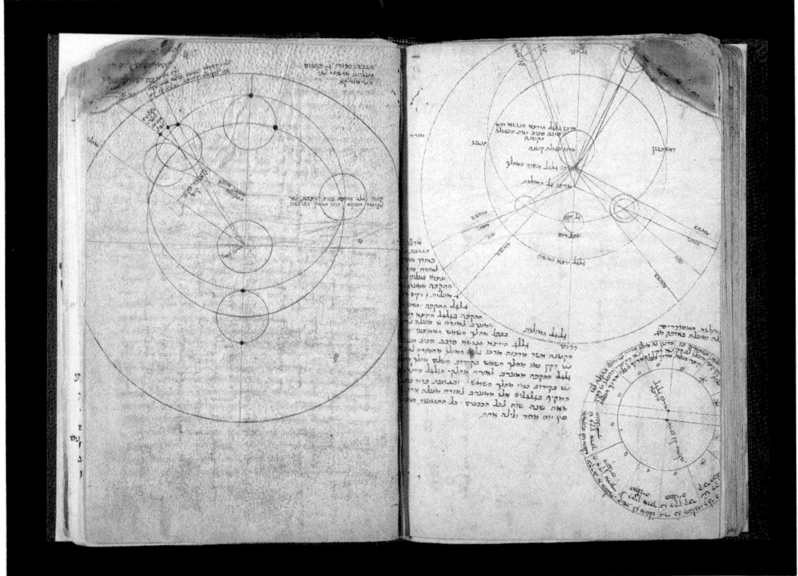

Figure 19

Abraham bar Ḥiyya (Savasorda), *Sefer Tsurat ha-Eretz,* Spain, 15th century, Courtesy of The Library of the Jewish Theological Seminary of America, New York, Mic. 2550, fols. 89v-90r (cat. no. 30)

This work is concerned with the shape of the earth.

lated into Castilian rather than Latin (although the former continued to compose scientific treatises in Hebrew as well).

In this close and complex interpenetration of ideas among scientists and philosophers of the three religions, three figures are particularly representative. The first is Abraham bar Ḥiyya, "Savasorda," who lived and worked in Barcelona in the first half of the twelfth century [fig. 19]. Bar Ḥiyya was an important figure in the transmission of Greek and Arabic mathematics (especially geometry) and astronomy to the West and the first great figure of Jewish science.[8] Abraham ibn Ezra (born ca. 1092 in Tudela; died 1167, possibly in Calahorra) was a polymath who wrote poetry and exegetical works in addition to acting as an intellectual intermediary in science and preparing astronomical tables.[9] Isaac ibn Sīd was the leading Jewish astronomer in the entourage of Alfonso the Wise of Castile whom he served in the 1260s and 1270s. He was both an observational and theoretical astronomer and left writings in both Hebrew and Castilian.[10]

THE TRANSMISSION OF ANCIENT ASTRONOMY

Astronomy was of immediate interest to medieval people because of the need to compose the religious calendar accurately, because of the belief in astrology, and for a variety of other reasons both practical (time reckoning, surveying) and "philosophical" (Aristotelian beliefs related to the nature of the heavens and celestial motion). Astronomy, as passed by the Arabs to medieval Europeans, consisted of three interrelated elements: instrumentation (the most important instrument being the astrolabe); astronomical tables (without which the instruments were of limited utility); and astronomical or cosmological theory, without which further refinements of the observational system could not take place.

Abraham ibn Ezra, in the preface to his Hebrew translation of Ibn al-Muthannā's commentary on the astronomical tables of al-Khwārizmī, gives an account of how Hindu astronomy was transmitted to the Arabs [fig. 20]. According to Ibn Ezra, an Arab king named al-Safah, desirous of learning about Indian science but fearing a religious backlash among Muslims for whom "profane sciences" were still unknown, sent for a Jew who knew both the Arabic and Indian languages. This Jew, who for the king translated *Kalīla wa-Dimna,* a book of Indian fables, later met a scholar named Kanka, whom he brought to the king and who subsequently

> taught the Arabs the basis of numbers, i.e., the nine numerals.
>
> Then from this scholar, with the Jew as an Arabic-Indian interpreter, a scholar named Jacob ben Sharah translated a book containing the tables of the seven plan-

ets, all the procedures for the earth, the rising times of the zodiac signs, the declination and the ascending degree of the ecliptic, the arrangement of the astrological houses, knowledge of the upper stars, and eclipses of the luminaries. But there is no mention in his book of the reasoning in all these matters; only facts are given as matters of tradition.[11]

Thus was astronomy introduced to the Arabs, among whom a great scholar named al-Khwārizmī then arose and who adjusted the values of the Indian tables to the geographical position of Persia. Khwārizmī, Ibn Ezra says, also introduced "Hindu reckoning" to later generations of Arab scholars. After him, al-Farghānī supplied the theoretical reasons for statements made by Khwārizmī (in his tables). Finally Ptolemy's book "about the constellations" (that is, the *Almagest*) was translated into Arabic. "No scholar can contradict his proofs, for they are taken from the science of measurement called *geometry* in Greek and *gematria* by the sages of Israel." Ptolemy's values in turn attracted Arab commentaries, one of which was that of Ibn al-Muthannā, the book that Ibn Ezra here presents in Hebrew translation.

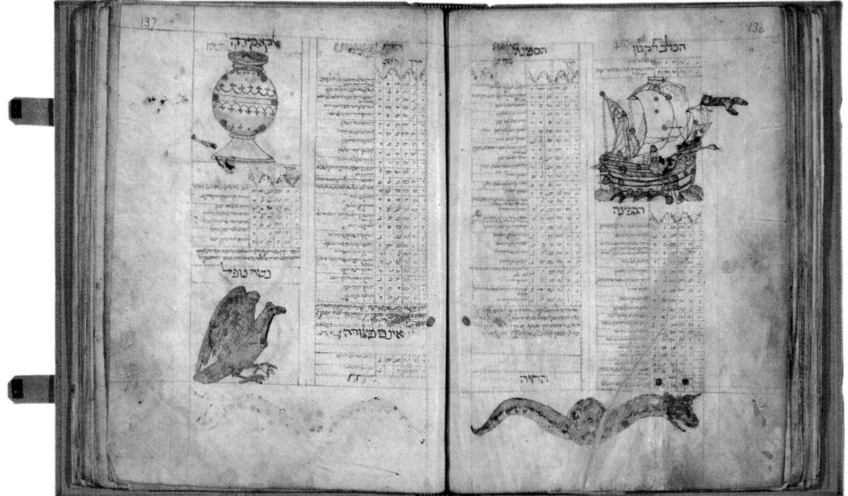

Figure 20

Astronomical Tables and Treatises on Astronomy, Spain, 1360-61, Carl Alexander Floersheim Trust for Art and Judaica, fols. 136v-137r (cat. no. 26)

An interesting aspect of the decoration of this manuscript is the constellation signs executed in gouache, gold paint, and inks.

Ibn Ezra's account of the reception of Indian mathematics and astronomy in the Arab-speaking world, although somewhat fictionalized, is in accord with an account given a century earlier by the astronomer al-Bīrūnī. According to al-Bīrūnī, Hindu astronomy was introduced with a translation of the Sanskrit tables called the *zīj al-Sindhind* made at the court of the Abbasid caliph al-Manṣūr in the 770s. Ibn Ezra's chronology diverges by only two decades from al-Bīrūnī's account. What is important is the fact that in astronomy only the raw data for various celestial observations were received; the rules by which those numerical values were derived were missing. Subsequently, Muslim scientists, beginning with al-Khwārizmī, were thus concerned both with making the observational data more accurate and with learning and refining the rules according to which the observations were to be made in the first place.[12]

It is, of course, understandable that a Spanish Jew, involved in making the results of Hindu/Arab astronomy available to both Jews and Latins, should be consciously playing out the role of scientific transmitter, one with deep and very pertinent historical roots.

THE ASTROLABE

The astrolabe was a composite astronomical instrument usually made of brass, with which a variety of observational operations could be performed [figs. 21A and B and 22, p. 82].[13] The most common form, the planispheric astrolabe, had on its front a depressed inner circle, called the "mother," into which was placed a removable disk (*ṣafīḥa* in Arabic; *azafea* in medieval Castilian) on which was portrayed a stereographic projection of the heavens for a particular latitude. In front of the *ṣafīḥa* was an engraved metal fitting called the "spider" that carried a stereographic projection of the fixed stars on the plane of the equator. The back of instrument was divided into four quadrants, upon which the altitude of the sun or a star could be read directly, to an accuracy of one degree, by rotating the sight or alidade. (The observer suspended the instrument from a peg, and then lined up the sights on the alidade with a star. As the alidade rotated, it moved along a scale of angles engraved on the edge of the astrolabe.) The instrument was particularly useful in navigation because the latitude of a place could be determined by the elevation of the sun, without the need to consult declination tables. The astrolabe served as a kind of computer, furnishing data for a wide variety of problems in spherical astronomy (calculating latitude, determining time) as well as for surveying and the casting of horoscopes.

Figure 21A
Astrolabe with Latin inscription, Spain, 1498, The Adler Planetarium, History of Astronomy Collection, Chicago, M28 (cat. no. 101)

The astrolabe was used by astronomers and astrologers of the three religions who mastered its construction and use from a set of related treatises written in Arabic, Hebrew, and Latin. The earliest such work was written in Arabic by an Iraqi Jew named Māshāʾallāh around 800 C.E. Ḥasdai ibn Shaprūṭ obtained a book on astrolabe construction, probably Māshāʾallāh's, from the East, and this was the basis of a family of such treatises written by Andalusi astronomers. Maslama of Madrid's eleventh-century treatise was translated into Latin in the early twelfth century by John of Seville, around the same time that Abraham ibn Ezra wrote his own treatise, *Keli ha-Neḥoshet* (*The Copper Instrument*) in Hebrew. Maslama's disciple al-Zarqāl (1029-87) had designed a "universal plate" (*lámina universal*), which avoided the inconvenience of having to change the *ṣafīḥa* for each latitude. Al-Zarqāl's description of the instrument was widely read in the thirteenth century in Castilian (in the Alfonsine *Libros del Saber de Astronomia, Libro de la Açafeha*), in Profeit ibn Tibbon's Hebrew translation, and in a Catalan version of the latter work.[14] Finally, at the end of the Middle Ages, Joseph Vecinho, a student of the great Jewish astronomer Abraham Zacuto, devised an improved astrolabe that the Portuguese used in the voyages of discovery.[15]

Figure 21B
Astrolabe with Arabic inscription, Spain, Smithsonian Institution, National Museum of American History, Washington DC, no. 3643 (cat. no. 93)

Despite the plethora of Hebrew treatises on the astrolabe, few medieval Hebrew instruments survive. Interestingly, the Smithsonian Institution has a hybrid astrolabe, made by an Arab instrument-maker in Valencia in 1090, with the star names on the spider in Hebrew, and the instrument's lettering in Arabic.[16]

Solomon Gandz has recovered an interesting rabbinical literature on the astrolabe, which became involved in a polemic between rationalists and conservatives when Abraham ibn Ezra identified the mysterious biblical *urim* and *thummin* (Exodus 27) as an astrolabe. In a *responsum,* Solomon ibn Adret of Barcelona authorized the use of astrolabes on the Sabbath because he deemed it the equivalent of consulting a scientific book.[17]

Knowledge of the astrolabe diffused to Latin Europe as early as the end of the tenth century. Elements of al-Khwārizmī's treatise turn up in the *Sententie astrolabii* included in MS Ripoll 225; other parts of this treatise were not translated from Arabic but rather written directly in Latin by a scholar conversant with Arab science who worked with an astrolabe in front of him. In the *Artem artium,* a twelfth-century astrological miscellany, the chapters on the astrolabe are taken from John of Seville's translation of a treatise attributed to Maslama of Madrid, while the following section, on astronomical tables, is derived from Abraham ibn

Ezra.[18] By the twelfth century, Jewish authors, writing in Hebrew or in Latin,[19] were becoming a vital agency for European access to Arabic science.

ASTRONOMICAL TABLES

Logically, elementary astronomical knowledge was diffused along with the astrolabe, which required astronomical tables in order to exploit it fully. Once an observer had determined the angle of an appropriate heavenly body, he could determine his latitude by consulting a table.

Abraham ibn Ezra, in the preface to his translation of Ibn al-Muthannā, noted that the tables in Ptolemy's *Almagest* were not usable in the form in which they were received (both for technical reasons and because of the passage of time). Nevertheless he follows Ptolemy's rules "as modified by the Arab *zīj*-writers whose observations were even more careful than those of Ptolemy."[20] Ibn Ezra followed his countryman al-Zarqāl on most points, while rejecting his computation of the solar apogee (which today we regard as al-Zarqāl's signal contribution to theoretical astronomy).[21] Ibn Ezra earned his living by wandering from town to town, adapting standard astronomical tables in the Arabic tradition to the meridians of different cities, mainly in Italy and France.[22]

As previously noted, al-Khwārizmī's tables were the first to be composed in the Arabic-speaking world and were strongly influenced by the *Sindhind.* [22] At the end of the ninth century the great Iraqi astronomer al-Battānī composed a set of tables based on Ptolemy's principles. Both of these *zijāt* were influential in medieval Spain, al-Khwārizmī's tables being translated into Latin by Adelard of Bath in 1126 and al-Battānī's somewhat later by Plato of Tivoli. Plato of Tivoli worked in partnership with Abraham bar Ḥiyya, whose tables, likewise based on those of al-Battānī, were the earliest Hebrew *zīj* (*luaḥ, luḥot,* in Hebrew). These compilations included tables of mean motions of the sun, the moon and the planets, tables of conjunction, and various calendrical tables. Each was accompanied by a set of rules, or canons, explaining their use.

Andalusi astronomy is best known for the famous Toledan Tables, the result of a collective project organized in the late eleventh century by the qadi Ṣāʿid of Toledo, a member of whose circle was al-Zarqāl, who wrote up the final version of the tables. The Arabic original has been lost, but on the basis of two Latin translations (one by Gerard of Cremona) we know that the tables drew upon both al-Khwārizmī's tables and the Ptolemaic stream embodied in those of al-Battānī,[24] as well as upon al-Zarqāl's own astronomical observations.

The Toledan Tables were the immediate antecedent of the even more famous Alfonsine Tables, produced at Alfonso the Wise's court by two Jewish astronomers, Isaac ibn Sīd and

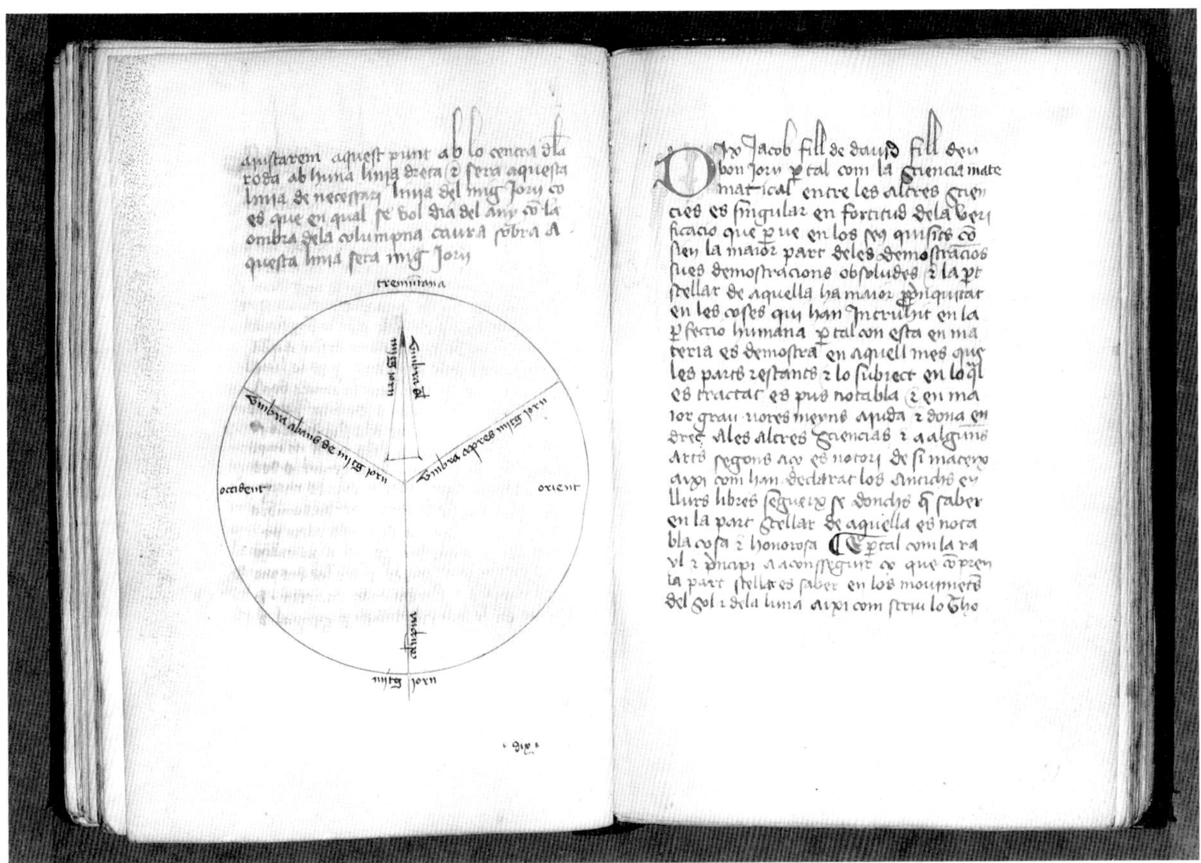

Figure 23
Jacob ben David Yomtob, *Astronomical Tables* (in Catalan), Spain, 15th century, The Newberry Library, Chicago, Ayer Ms. 746, fols. 50v.-51r. (cat. no. 31)

Jehuda ibn Mosca, between 1262 and 1272. These tables only became known outside Castile some fifty years after their composition, owing to the fact that they were written in Castilian, whereas the northern European universities used Latin. This also explains why the tables should have circulated in Europe, not with the original canons but with new Latin canons written by John of Saxony, a mid-fourteenth century writer. Thus did Alfonso's tables pass, according to J. D. North, "from relative Iberian obscurity to the rank of a great European institution," even though they were no longer Alfonsine in the strict sense.[25]

Jews continued to be active in the preparation of astronomical tables in the later Middle Ages: Jacob ben David Yomtob, or Bonjorn (as he was known in Catalan), a Jew of Perpignan (then in the Crown of Aragon) in the employ of Peter IV, the Ceremonious, composed a set of tables in 1361 of which Catalan, Latin, and Hebrew versions survive; and another set of tables was prepared for Peter by Yaᶜqob Carsono[26] [fig. 23]. In the same century, Joseph ibn al-Wakkar composed tables for Toledo in Judeo-Arabic, with a Hebrew translation.[27] Finally Abraham Zacuto (1452-ca. 1515) wrote a set of tables in Hebrew (*ha-Ḥibbur ha-Gadol*) for use at the University of Salamanca in 1473, about which he asserted he had "corrected all the books [containing the Alfonsine tables] in accordance with tables that I have prepared, and my tables circulate throughout all Christian and even Muslim lands." Vasco da Gama sought Zacuto's advice on navigational problems before he sailed for India and, as is well known, Columbus carried a copy of Zacuto's tables on his voyages. His tables were also used in sixteenth-century Egypt.[28]

Somewhat akin to astronomical tables were almanacs, works that provided planetary locations for a given year or planetary period. The origin of the term is most likely Arabic *manah,* "resting stage on a trip" in the sense of a "mansion," or region of the sky through which a constellation of the zodiac passes on its annual course around the sun.[29] The actual circumstances of the almanac's tranmission to the West is not clear, but the earliest reference in Latin appears in Abraham ibn Ezra's book on the foundations of astronomical tables.[30]

ASTRONOMICAL THEORY

The early phases of the renewal of astronomy in the Islamic world and its diffusion westward were marked by a practical cast, linked to the astrolabe and astronomical tables; theoretical treatises came somewhat later.[31]

Ibn Ezra observed that the *Sindhind* had arrived in the Arabic-speaking world shorn of its theoretical underpinnings. These were not known until al-Farghānī (d. after 861) diffused the rules and theories of Ptolemaic astronomy in his *Jawāmiᶜ* or *Elements,* later translated into Latin in Spain in two versions, by John of Seville (1137) and Gerard of Cremona. The latter also translated (ca. 1175) Ptolemy's *Almagest,* which was, of course, the single most influential astronomical treatise of the Middle Ages. By mastering Ptolemy, astronomers could learn how to construct geometric models to simulate the motion of celestial bodies in order to predict their positions. The numerical parameters of these models, in turn, could be established by instruments such as the astrolabe, and embodied in tables.[32]

Ptolemy's system, as is well known, proposed that anomalous prograde and retrograde motions of planetary orbits could be explained by supposing that although orbits were circular, as Aristotle had said, each planet in fact orbits an epicycle, whose center orbits the earth in a path called the deferent. Further observational anomalies were explained by supposing that the center of the deferent is not the center of the earth but at some remove from it, in which case the orbit is called an eccentric. The purpose of this complicated system was both to preserve the Aristotelian requirement that celestial motion be "perfect" or circular, and to explain observed celestial motions in order to predict them—a result that the system achieved with a high order of accuracy.[33] Ptolemaic theory was well known in medieval Spain, and two copies of the *Almagest* survive in Hebrew characters.[34]

Nevertheless a striking feature of Andalusi theoretical astronomy was the opposition of the dominant Aristotelian school to Ptolemy's system, which they attacked in an exaggerated defense of a pure kind of Aristotelianism.[35] Al-Biṭrūjī (fl. late twelfth century) wanted to replace Ptolemy's system by a nesting series of concentric spheres that would require no eccentrics or epicycles. Al-Biṭrūjī says he was inspired by Ibn Ṭufayl (d. 1185) and we know from Maimonides' account that Ibn Bājja (d. 1138) also rejected epicycles. Averroës (Ibn Rushd) takes the extreme position that pre-Ptolemaic astronomy, which rejected epicycles and eccentrics, had to be retrieved, "for it is the true astronomy that is possible from the standpoint of physical principles."[36] Maimonides, in the *Guide of the Perplexed,* takes a similar position, citing Ibn Bājja's rejection of epicycles and adding his doubts that Ibn Bājja would gain anything of value by preserving eccentrics.[37] Maimonides, of course, considered himself an "Andalusi" philosopher in the fullest sense of the word, even though he departed the country at the age of thirteen (recall that Avicenna had done all the reading for his *Shifāʾ* and *Qānūn* by age eighteen). He had also been in touch with the son of Jābir ibn Aflah whose *Correction of the Almagest* he had revised around 1185. Jābir also dwelt on Ptolemy's "errors" and was cited by al-Biṭrūjī.[38] It may be, as Sabra concludes, that these scholars, both Arab and Jewish, expressed a sense of Andalusi "national consciousness" through their philosophical views. Opposition to Ptolemy was not limited to philosophers, moreover. The historian Beaujouan, noting that many Andalusi astronomers preferred the *Sindhind*'s method of composing tables, concludes that this attitude may have reflected a generalized distrust of Ptolemy.[39] Al-Biṭrūjī influenced a number of Jewish scholars, notably Yahuda b. Salomon Kohen of Toledo (mid-thirteenth century) and Levi ben Gerson, but his ideas did not surface among Latin writers until the end of the fifteenth century.[40]

When this body of practical and theoretical astronomical knowledge reached the Christian West it was integrated into a religious worldview, in which natural knowledge still served the interests of revealed knowledge. Yet something had changed. Dominicus Gundissalinus, a Spanish canon deeply involved in the translation movement, gives the following reasons why astronomy was important: "To know the way in which the Most High God rules the world, to know the orders of spiritual angels, to know the laws according to which the heavenly spheres are ordered; this knowledge can only be attained if one knows astronomy, and none can acquire the science of astronomy without a knowledge of arithmetic and geometry." Inasmuch as angels moved the spheres, Christian theology was now linked to the new science—"an unfamiliar situation," as Jean Jolivet observes, "created by the translation of Arabic authors."[41]

The crowning achievement of medieval astronomy in Spain was the compilation commissioned by Alfonso the Wise entitled the *Libros del saber de astronomía* (*The Books of Astro-*

nomical Knowledge), comprising fifteen distinct treatises [figs. 24A and B]. These included the canons, or instructions, of the Alfonsine Tables; a star catalogue called the *Libro de las Estrellas Fijas;* a treatise on the armillary sphere and another on the quadrant, observational instruments that Isaac ibn Sīd had used; and an elementary astronomical treatise called the *Libro de la Alcora* (*Book of the Celestial Sphere*—a kind of spherical astrolabe), based on a ninth-century work by Qusṭā ibn Lūqā with introductory material, probably by Isaac ibn Sīd on how to construct the instrument and a final chapter by another Jew, "Don Moshe," on astrology.[42] The *Libros* represented, of course, more than a mere translation effort: in consonance with the Arab astronomical tradition, they also included the results of fresh observations. Isaac ibn Sīd, for example, had recorded his observations of the lunar eclipses of 1263, 1265, and 1266.[43]

INDIAN NUMERALS AND THE NEW MATHEMATICS

Ancient mathematics was not just rediscovered in the medieval Islamic world; its horizons were substantially enlarged. Indian numerals and the place system substantially enlarged the practical horizons of mathematics; the transmission of Euclidean geometry had repercussions throughout the cognitive worlds of the three religions; new disciplines like trigonometry, which was unknown to the ancients, were founded; and the urban environment of the medieval Mediterranean world, with its need for bookkeeping and other commercial calculations, proved a fecund medium for the diffusion of this reborn mathematics.

Once again Ibn Ezra has accurately described the reception of Indian reckoning (*ḥisāb al-hind*) in the Islamic East. The system consisted of the numbers 1 through 9 plus the zero (the origin of the English word, as well as the related term "cipher," is the Arabic *ṣifr*, which reached English through Spanish). The shapes of the individual numbers diffused at different rates (the written forms of our current 4, 5, 6, 7, 8, and 0 all evolved in medieval Spain), but the key to whether the Indian system with units, tens, hundreds and so forth was known was the presence or absence of the zero.[44] The key figure in the diffusion of Indian calculation was al-Khwārizmī whose book on the use of Hindu numerals survives only in the medieval Latin translation, *Algoritmi de numero indorum* (*Al-Khwārizmī on Indian Numerals*), the deformation of the author's name yielding "algorithm" in modern European languages. Adelard of Bath was the author of one version of this work, but John of Seville's translation was the more influential.

The Arabs called the new numbers *ghubār* or "dust numerals" because they were written in dust or on blackboards and were erasable. This introduced both flexibility and complexity

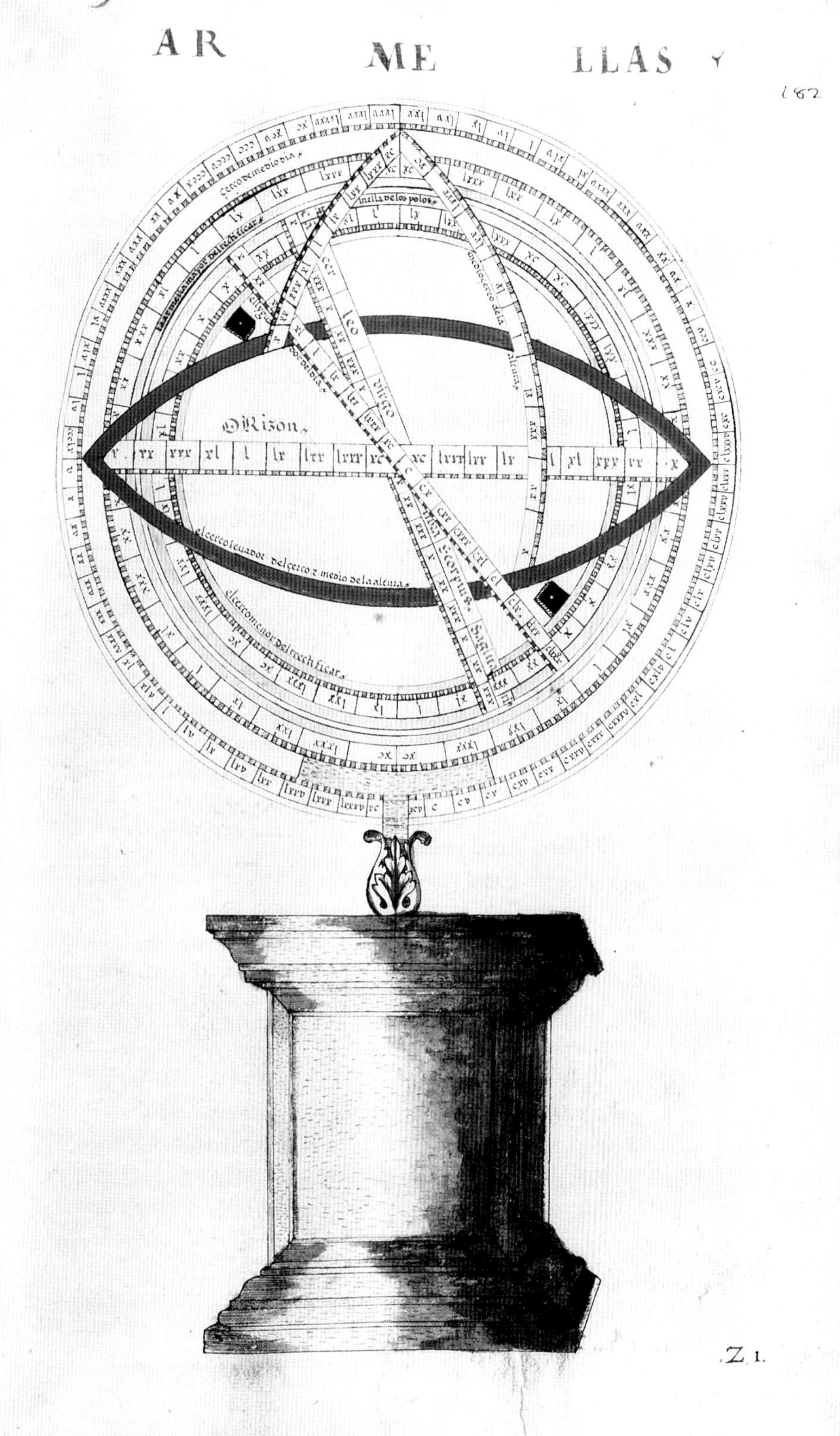

Figure 24A

Libros del Saber de Astronomía de Alfonso X, Spain, 16th century, Madrid, Biblioteca de El Escorial (Cod. h.I.1)

The *Libros del Saber de Astronomía* were a collection of various astronomical treatises composed in Castilian at the behest of Alfonso X the Wise by a multiethnic team of Muslims, Christians, and Jews. The texts served to create a scientific and technical vocabulary that made the Castilian language a medium for the expression of scientific knowledge (cat. no. 23).

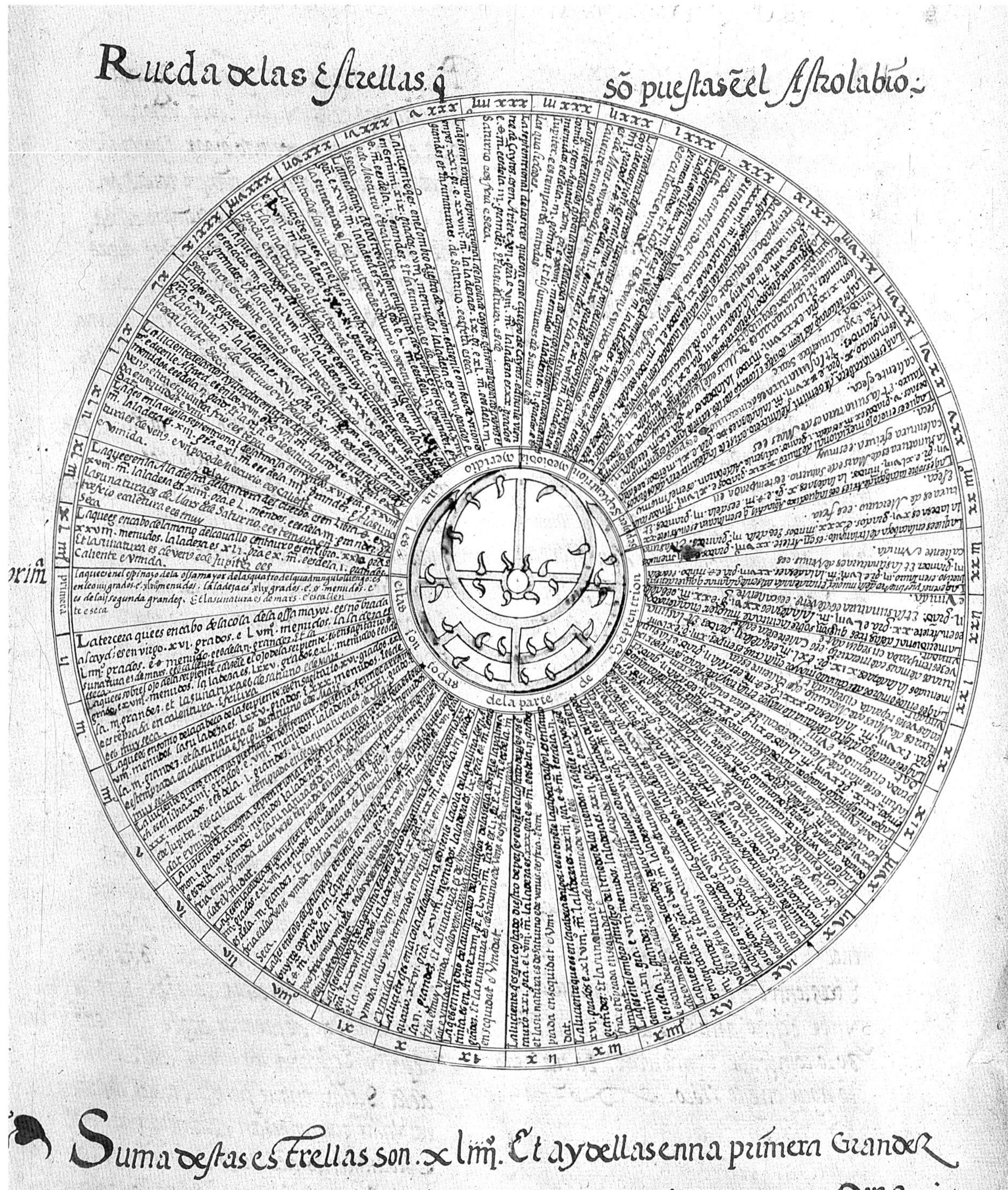

Suma destas estrellas son .xlviij. Et ay dellas enna primera Grandez
xij. et enna segunda .xviij. Et enna terçera .xiij. et enna quarta vna.

into arithmetic because the possibility of making successive corrections eased demands on memory for success in calculation.[45]

The system, once introduced, spread rapidly. The new numbers first appeared in Christian Spain in 9B6, in the so-called Albeldense Codex, in which the numerals from 1 through 9 appear, written from right to left. Around the same time, Gerbert of Aurillac (the future Pope Silvester II) appears to have learned the same incomplete system when he went to the monastery of Ripoll to learn the new Arabic science. His students used an abacus with nine columns, one for each Indian number, a system that was positional but that lacked the zero.[46] Indian calculation was widely discussed among Jewish scholars like Abraham ibn Ezra, who wrote three works on arithmetic and the theory of numbers. In his *Sefer ha-mispar* (*Book of the Number*) he "describes the decimal system for integers with place value of the numerals from right to left, and the zero is given as *qalqal* ('wheel' or 'circle') in the preface." In the body of the treatise, however, the numbers are represented by Hebrew letters.[47] In consonance with his deliberate use of biblical or rabbinical Hebrew terminology only, Ibn Ezra does not give a literal translation of the Arabic term for tens (*ʿuqūd,* "knots"), but adopts the traditional terms *peratim* (units) and *kelalim* (higher numbers) that, in the Talmud, "do not reflect the strict distinction between the units and the higher orders peculiar to the Hindu system." But since Ibn Ezra knew the Hindu system, he "adapted the Talmudic terminology to the Arabic *aḥad* (units) and *ʿuqūd*."

Al-Khwārizmī was even better known for his algebra text, the earliest written in Arabic. This, too, had Indian antecedents. But Greek tradition also figures in his account, which includes geometrical figures to illustrate equations, in the manner of Book II of Euclid's *Elements.*[49] In this way the diffusion of Al-Khwārizmī's algebra text prepared the ground for translations of the *Elements* themselves. By the end of the tenth century two complete Arabic translations were available, as well as a number of partial translations, some summaries (including one by Abūʾl-Ṣalt, a philosopher and astronomer in the court of the King of Denia in the early twelfth century), and a mass of commentaries. In Spain, there was a burst of interest in Euclid in the twelfth century when Gerard of Cremona translated the Arabic version of Isḥāq ibn Ḥunayn and Thābit ibn Qurra, the most literal of the Arabic versions, as well as al-Nayrizī's commentary on the *Elements;* another translation of the Arabic Euclid was made contemporaneously by Hermann of Carinthia. A more popular Latin version, however, was that of Adelard of Bath, who not only translated an Arabic text but also produced two commented versions of Euclid, in consonance with the medieval Western European interest in philosophical issues, such as the concepts of the infinite and the continuum, suggested by Euclid. The Arabized Latin version of Euclid replaced Boethius's pared-down version, in which propositions were given as self-evident and the method by

Figure 24B *(opposite)* *Libros del Saber de Astronomía de Alfonso X,* Spain, 16th century, Madrid, Biblioteca de El Escorial (Cod. h.I.1)

which they were arrived at was eliminated. For medieval philosophers, who saw Aristotle's demonstrative method, as elucidated in the *Posterior Analytics,* as the basis of all science, this was a major discovery. Euclid's *Elements* became the most important example of the demonstrative method, which was diffused along with Euclidean mathematics and became the basis of all other mathematical works.[50]

The point is well illustrated by the mathematical work of Abraham bar Ḥiyya. Bar Ḥiyya lived in Barcelona in the early twelfth century and not only played a key role in the creation of science in Hebrew, but also participated in the diffusion of Arabic science to Latin Europe through his partnership with the translator Plato of Tivoli. Bar Ḥiyya was best known for his treatise on geometry entitled *Ḥibbur ha-meshiḥah we-ha-tishboret.* Plato of Tivoli translated this book into Latin (as the *Liber embadorum*) in 1145, the first Hebrew science text translated into that language. The *Ḥibbur* is a treatise on practical geometry, whose novelty is its combination of Greek theory, derived mainly from Euclid, and practical mathematics, such as algebra and the new trigonometry devised by the Arabs. The *Liber embadorum* was the first trigonometry book in the West and may also have been the earliest Latin account of Arab algebra.[51] Bar Ḥiyya was also the author of a kind of mathematical encyclopedia, entitled *Yesode ha-tebunah u-migdal ha-emunah,* a veritable compendium elaborating on "the interdependence of the various divisions of mathematical science such as number theory, fundamental operations of calculation, commercial arithmetic (algebra), geometric definitions and practical geometry as in optics and music."[52] Bar Ḥiyya, interestingly, counted by tens but still did not use the zero, even though he was conversant with al-Khwārizmī's book on Indian calculation. Instead, he placed a mark above a numeral to indicate its order, the first such use of an indicator system in decimal calculation in medieval Europe.[53]

Modern elementary arithmetic is considered to have four basic operations, addition, subtraction, multiplication, and division. In the Middle Ages there was no such agreement on basic operations, or on the order of their importance. Thus Bar Ḥiyya and Abraham ibn Ezra give slightly differing accounts:[54]

Bar Hiyya	**Ibn Ezra**
multiplication	multiplication
division	division
subtraction	addition
fractions	subtraction
transformation of fractions	fractions
proportions	proportions
	square roots

This fluidity of classification reflected an intellectual world caught up in the assimilation and evaluation of new knowledge that resulted in a substantial reorganization of scientific disciplines.

THE REORGANIZATION OF THE QUADRIVIUM AND THE TRANSFORMATION OF SCIENCE

The "seven liberal arts" of medieval scholasticism included the trivium of grammar, logic, and rhetoric (broadly, the humanities) and the quadrivium of arithmetic, geometry, astronomy, and music (broadly, the sciences). Moreover, in consonance with Aristotelian norms, sciences were divided into the theoretical and practical, the former including physics, mathematics, and metaphysics, and the latter, politics, economics, and ethics. The two main classifications were conventional and flexible: different authors mixed both of them or used others such as Plato's, which did not distinguish the theoretical from the practical and whose three divisions were logic, physics, and ethics. The main markers of an Aristotelian classification were the inclusion of mathematics and the relegation of logic to the status of an auxiliary science.[55]

The Arabs acquired the Aristotelian classification of the sciences through John Philoponus's commentary on the *Isagogue* of Porphyry, on which al-Fārābī's scheme is based. The distinction between theoretical and practical sciences is omitted and replaced by a more empirical framework that includes religious and linguistic studies.[56] Spanish Jewish philosophers, building on al-Fārābī, nevertheless varied the structure according to personal predilection. Thus Abraham ibn Ezra lists seven sciences: logic, theology, the four quadrivium disciplines, and physics (including astrology). Baḥya ibn Paquda retains Aristotle's division of the theoretical and practical and places the quadrivium under the rubric of mathematics. And Judah Halevi, in the *Kuzari,* gives "snatches of classifications which seem to be torn out of an Aristotelian context." Maimonides, for whom al-Fārābī was a kind of personal hero, is closest to the Aristotelian scheme; he includes physics, mathematics, and metaphysics under the rubric of theoretical philosophy, and subdivides mathematics into the standard quadrivium disciplines.[57] There was much discussion among Jewish scholars of the subdivisions of mathematics, reflecting the variegated activity in that realm in the Arabic-speaking world. It was generally placed in a ranking of sciences, from lower to higher: for Baḥya and Judah Halevi, physics is lowest, then mathematics, and metaphysics is highest. But elsewhere, Halevi inverts the positions of mathematics and physics, as did Abraham ibn Daʾūd.[58] Mathematics itself includes arithmetic, musical measurement, and optical measurement for Halevi, whereas Shem-tob Falaquera places algebra and the theory of equations under the heading "technique." Maimonides follows al-Fārābī in considering the quadrivium to be the "roots" of mathematics while newer subjects are its "branches."[59]

By the time Christian scholars of the Latin West had worked through the new Arabic sciences, the traditional scheme of the seven arts had to be recast to accommodate a cognitive scene that had become substantially enlarged and that had different emphases than those of antiquity. Medicine and physics, for example, were nowhere encompassed in the ancient model. The Spanish translator Dominicus Gundissalinus therefore inserted medicine between the trivium and the quadrivium.[60] Astronomy, formerly a quadrivium science linked tightly to mathematics, had acquired not only a vastly complex technical literature but a sophisticated theoretical one as well. So Gundissalinus is constrained to adopt al-Fārābī's distinction between astronomy—the mathematical, rational, empirical part—and astrology—the practical part by which future events are predicted.[61] Nature, which had been mainly a source of edification for the Church fathers and early medieval thinkers, now had become the object of a new appreciation, more empirical and less abstract. According to Jolivet: "The ancient system of the Quadrivium symbolised and maintained a philosophy in which nature had no place; Arithmetic was an abstraction, and the other three mathematical arts provided no concrete ballast: Music was merely a consequence of Mathematics, Astronomy an application of spherical Geometry: Geometry itself juxtaposed speculation about abstract space with the most modest technical applications...." There was no alternative but to widen the classifications of science to reflect the transformed roster of disciplines.

THEORY AND PRACTICE OF TRANSLATION

Medieval scholars had rather carefully defined theories and conventions regarding the translation of scholarly or scientific texts. In all three religious groups there was debate over the merits of literal versus a freer style of translation. With reference to the translation of works of Greek philosophy into Arabic, al-Fārābī, whose influence on Andalusi Aristotelianism was so great, favored active translation (that is, translation accompanied by philosophical analysis of the concepts translated) over a passive one, to grasp the meaning (*maʿna*) rather than just the utterance (*lafẓ*).[63] Likewise Maimonides, so admiring of al-Fārābī in matters philosophical, strongly urged Samuel ibn Tibbon, who translated the *Guide of the Perplexed* from Arabic to Hebrew, "to first try to grasp the sense of the subject thoroughly, and then state the theme with perfect clarity in the other language. This, however, cannot be done without changing the order of words, putting many words for one word, or *vice versa,* and adding or taking away words, so that the subject be perfectly intelligible in the language into which he translates."[64]

In Hebrew translations made from the Arabic in medieval Spain literal translations (Hebrew: *ʾot be-ʾot*) seem to have been more common until the end of the thirteenth century. Afterward, the discussion over the two modes of translation disappears as the new philosophy and science become more acclimated to the structure of medieval Hebrew.[65] Translators into Hebrew had to overcome problems related to the interface between the two related Semitic languages. Shemtov Ardutiel of Carrión observed that three or four Hebrew words were required to translate one in Arabic, a language rich in synonyms; Judah al-Harīzī, on the other hand, said that for each difficult Arabic word he chose the appropriate among three or four Hebrew possibilities. Because of the self-imposed restraints of sticking to biblical or rabbinical Hebrew that many translators adopted, some still resorted to hebraizing foreign technical terms rather than adapting the later technical vocabulary of the Talmud. Thus Arabic weights and measures were retained because of the lack of Hebrew or Latin equivalents.[66] Many Christian translators from Arabic into Latin or Romance retained the traditional norm, laid down by Boethius, of translation *de verbo ad verbum* (word for word).

Here I wish to review a number of ways in which translation affected the nature of the languages of translation, both lexicographically and syntactically.

In arithmetic, for example, the Arabs had no term for multiplication (Latin, *multiplicare*): the terms they used were *ḍaraba,* "to strike," and *ḍaʿafa,* to fold or double.[67] Al-Khwārizmī introduced the term *daraba,* using *ḍaʿafa* only to explain the former term. Now, when Abraham bar Ḥiyya translated al-Khwārizmī's arithmetic into Hebrew, he used the verbs *kafal* (to fold or double, the equivalent of *ḍaʿafa*) and *manah* or *hashab* (to count, calculate). For stylistic reasons, he hesitated to translate *ḍaraba* with the Hebrew verb "to strike," *hikkah. Manah,* the word he preferred, is clearly the equivalent of Latin *ducere,* "to lead," which was used by Boethius in the sense "to multiply." Gandz suggests that Bar Ḥiyya adopted this term from his translating partner, Plato of Tivoli, who followed Boethius's use of *ducere* and used this word when he translated Abraham's geometry into Latin. After Bar Ḥiyya, these terms were discarded. Abraham ibn Ezra, a classical stylist, used *kafal* only, while others used *hikkah,* the literal translation into Hebrew of Arabic *ḍaraba,* as in Moses ibn Tibbon's Hebrew translation of Euclid from Arabic. The rich mixing of Arabic, Hebrew, and even Latin terms is a reflection of the ambience of scientific discussion and translation, when scholars with different linguistic skills debated the use of terms that were new to them. Also remarkable is the limitation of not departing from the biblical lexicon that a scholar like Ibn Ezra imposed upon himself, in science as well as in poetry.

The process of intellectual interaction that I have been describing required a high level of social interaction, in the form of teams of translators rendering Arabic texts into Latin (in the twelfth century) or Castilian (in the thirteenth). In the twelfth century such teams consisted of two men. An Arabic speaker read the original in Arabic and then translated aloud, word by word, into Castilian (or Catalan); his partner then wrote down the translation of each Romance word in Latin. The historian Charles Burnett paraphrases the Jew Ibn Daʾūd's account of translating Avicenna's *De anima* in partnership with Gundissalinus: Ibn Daʾūd took the text and pronounced the Arabic words one at a time as they were spoken by the people (*vulgariter*), while the Archdeacon Gundissalinus wrote down the Latin equivalent of these words as he heard them.[68] There is no doubt that Christian translators worked from the spoken, rather than the written, word. The oral nature of this process is illustrated by the kind of errors and slips that appear in the Latin products. In the same *De anima,* Gundissalinus confused the Arabic terms for "thing" and "cause" because in speaking Spanish, Ibn Daʾūd pronounced *causa* and *cosa* alike.[69] It is also clear that the translation process was not a simple linguistic exercise but that difficult terms and words were discussed by the two translators. Thus the Christian might confuse Arabic letters, such as the *qaf* and *kaf,* which sound similar when spoken aloud, leading to translation errors.[70] Because an interpretative discussion accompanied the act of translation, Christians normally worked with Jewish partners, whose academic culture was in general higher than that of Arabic-speaking Christians. Thus Michael Scot worked with Abuteus Levita and Plato of Tivoli with Bar Ḥiyya, although Gerard of Cremona, the most prolific of the twelfth-century translators working in Toledo, did in fact work with a Mozarab named Galip. Some translators, like Hugh of Santalla, worked directly from the Arabic text.

Teams preparing translations for Alfonso X a century later were similarly composed, although here the final product was generally in Castilian rather than Latin. Alfonso's "school" was truly international and interethnic and included five Jews, four Spanish Christians, four Italians, and a Muslim converted to Christianity. Among Alfonso's staff, Yehuda ben Mosca knew both Arabic and Latin, but he was an exceptional case. Alfonso's innovation was to turn translation into a kind of a colloquium that included not only translators (an Arabist, usually a Jew, and a Romanist) but technical editors called *emendadores* who verified, through discussion with the translators, the meanings of difficult technical terms, and secretaries (*glosadores*) who wrote the translations down.[71]

Under the impetus of the translation movement under Alfonso the Wise the scientific vocabulary of Castilian was substantially widened, as the language, in Georg Bossong's words, "developed the register of scientific prose."[72] Here we are talking, first, about technical terms, of which only 5 percent were Arabisms, while 30 percent were Latinisms with Arabized meanings (an example would be *cuerda* "sine," retaining its original metaphorical meaning of "bowstring," ultimately derived from Sanskrit), and 65 percent were calques, that is, literal translations of Arabic terms. But beyond the enlargement of lexicon, Bossong asserts that the inner form of the language also came to reflect Semitic influence in its "semantic, syntactic and stylistic make-up." To express a plethora of scientific and technical concepts, new abstract substantives were developed (using the endings *-iento, -ura, -eza,* and so forth). Forms of speech of great antiquity in Semitic culture, such as paranomasia (a sentence with a noun and a verb from the same root), were used, lending a distinctively Semitic tonality to this new literature Some of these effects were doubtless owing to the fact that the Jewish members of translation teams were unfamiliar with the rules of classical Latin syntax and therefore had to invent. When it first came face to face with Arabic science and philosophy, Castilian lacked the requisite syntactical resources to deal with concepts more complex than the spoken language could handle. One effect was to produce more complex subordinate clauses and subordinate clause chains of greater length, such as were required, for example, to convey the hierarchical relationship between different parts of mathematical equations (which had to be expressed in words before adequate mathematical notation was developed).

AN ARISTOTELIAN WORLD

It is one of the hallmarks of medieval civilization that Aristotelianism became the worldview of the scholarly community or, at least, a significant portion of it, in all three religious groups. In the Islamic world it is tempting to associate Aristotelianism with a group of cosmopolitan scholars, both Muslim and Jewish, who benefited from the intellectual stimulation that arose as a concomitant of the "Arab common market," extending from Spain to India, that was so fecund a medium for the diffusion of ideas and techniques. Here I wish to describe, in general terms, the Aristotelian component of the cosmopolitan worldview in the Islamic imperium and its somewhat less secular extension in Latin Christendom.

When the Arabs conquered Syria and Iraq, they came into contact with Syriac-speaking Christians who were familiar with the intellectual and scientific heritage of Greek antiquity, as we have noted with respect to the sciences. The Aristotelian corpus was translated into Arabic, mainly in Baghdad. First, some literal translations were made during the reign of the Abbasid Caliph al-Manṣūr. Then, under al-Maʾmūn (813-33), more refined versions were produced, especially by Ḥunayn ibn Isḥāq. Finally, early Arab Aristotelians like al-Fārābī (d. 950) were able to refine the corpus in consonance with the techniques of Aristotelian criticism they had acquired. By the middle of the eleventh century the translation movement was completed and all of Aristotle's important books with the exception of the *Politics* were available to Arabic-speaking scholars.[73] It should be noted that there was a high degree of congruence between Greek and Arabic (as a vehicle for its translation) in the area of philosophy owing to the latter's ability, because of its lexicographic richness and semantic structure, to express abstract ideas.[74] The Arabs did not stop with the translation of Aristotle's own works, but extended and completed the corpus with pseudepigrapha (that is, writings ascribed to Aristotle) in areas such as astrology that Aristotle had not touched. In philosophy itself, Neoplatonic concepts, at odds with the original spirit of Aristotle's thought, were assimilated into the corpus to supply wants in metaphysics and theology and to make certain points more congruent with Islamic theology: for example, Aristotelian "prime movers" were replaced by a theory of emanations.[75] As a result, Aristotelianism became a complete and general philosophical system and all-purpose worldview, and Aristotle (or "Pseudo-Aristotle") became all things to all people, not only philosopher and scientist, but alchemist, musician, and mineralogist as well.[76] Thus Ṣāʿid al-Andalusī described him as "the point of perfection of the philosophy of the Greeks" who had "redeemed the art of demonstration from dialectic and fixed it within syllogistic argumentation, whence it became the instrument of the mathematical sciences." Ibn Juljul, the physician, likewise styled him "*the* philosopher of the Greeks (*failasūf al-rūm*), their most learned and greatest scholar."[77] Aristotelianism in Arabic became, by antonomasia, philosophy: *falsafah*.

This worldview, in which philosophy became a method of textual criticism in theology and science, was linked to commerce through mathematics and to everyday life through astrology and medicine, surpassing the narrow bounds of academic learning. The connections of the scholarly class of Muslim *ulama* and Jewish intelligentsia with overseas trade and travel abroad for sake of study provided a social and economic context for the development of a tradition of learning that, while not secular in the modern sense, enjoyed partial autonomy with respect to religion.[78]

The Aristotelian corpus, together with its pseudepigraphic accretions, was transmitted to Hebrew and Latin readers in the form of commented texts, in particular those of Ibn Rushd (Averroës). Jewish Aristotelians like Shem-tob Falaquera embellished upon these, creating supercommentaries that commented on "the commentator" (Averroës) as well as on Aristotle.

By the end of the thirteenth century, the entire Arabic philosophical corpus (including works of Jewish authors, like Maimonides, who wrote in Arabic) had been translated into Hebrew, and according to Harry Wolfson, "Hebrew literature became also the repository of the whole Aristotelian heritage of Greek philosophy." This process stimulated a distinctive style of philosophical discourse among Jewish scholars, "an attitude of independence, of research and of criticism that, among those who continued to be opposed to philosophy, manifested itself in a change in the temper of their opposition, while among those who were aligned on the side of philosophy, it took the form of incisive, searching studies of older texts and problems."[79] The application of Aristotelian methodology followed Islamic norms: for Maimonides it was a necessary tool for theological speculation, it could explicate difficult passages in the Bible or Talmud. Aristotelianism, according to Maimonides, was the characteristic stance of Spanish Jewish philosophers: "As for the Andalusians among the people of our nation, all of them cling to the affirmations of the philosophers [that is, the Aristotelians] and incline to their opinions, insofar as these do not ruin the foundation of the Law. You will not find them in any way taking the paths of the *mutakallimun* [theologians]."[80] No doubt he meant to distinguish between the *mutakallimun*'s instrumentalist use of Aristotelian methodology for narrowly theological purposes, and a more authentic, secular tradition of Aristotelianism. Here he may be echoing the distinction that Arab commentators made between theology (*kalam*) as an Arab science and philosophy proper, which was counted as a foreign science. As F. E. Peters has observed, there is a thematic distinction between the two fields, but methodologically both were identical and, broadly speaking, rational.[81] Thus Moses ibn Ezra could describe his friend Abraham ibn Ezra as a *mutakallim,* intending the normative Islamic usage of that term to describe someone who applied the rational methods of Aristotelianism to theology.[82]

Interestingly enough, Jewish scholars were perceived by their Christian counterparts as prototypically Aristotelian: Peter the Venerable opined that Jewish philosophers in the Muslim world had been saved by rationalism from their own rabbis' "fables," while in the early thirteenth century William of Auvergne held the contrary opinion, that Aristotle had led the Jews into heresy.[83] In either version Jews were marked as peripatetics. The perception is accurate, for Aristotelian methods came to characterize scholarly discourse generally, and even the philosophical stance of Jewish anti-Aristotelians was articulated fully within the domain of Aristotelian discourse, as Wolfson noted. Thus the anti-Aristotelian Ḥasdai Crescas (b. Barcelona 1340; d. Zaragoza, 1410) "seems to have had the works of Aristotle on the tip of his tongue, and was always ready to use them at a moment's notice. He knew his Aristotle as he knew his Bible and Talmud."[84] There were entire families of Catalan Jews who became marked as Aristotelians, such as the Shem-tobs, two of whom, Isaac ben Shem-tob and his nephew Shem-tob ben Joseph, were vociferous opponents of Crescas.[85] The Ibn Tibbons, Spanish Jews who emigrated to Provence, were another family of participants in the Jewish "Aristotle industry."

I mentioned that according to Maimonides, Jewish philosophy in al-Andalus was noted for its Aristotelianism. Maimonides, of course, had studied with a disciple of Ibn Bājja and continued, long after his exile, to identify himself with the intellectual traditions of Islamic

Spain. This linking of Aristotelianism to a specifically Andalusi context reflects a similar trend among Arab Aristotelians of the Andalusi school. Indeed, A. I. Sabra links the exaggerated anti-Ptolemaic stance of the Andalusi Aristotelians to "an intellectual trend that prevailed in Andalusia under the Almohads among scholars working in such diverse fields as law, grammar, medicine, and philosophy," which he deems to be related to "often expressed Andalusian self-assertiveness vis-á-vis the rest of the Islamic world."[86] Sabra is careful to define this attitude, common to Arab and Jewish philosophers of al-Andalus, not as nationalism, but rather as "self-assertiveness" or "sense of identity." What interests me here is the fusing of the intellectual identities of Andalusi intellectuals with a cognitive world defined by Aristotelian methods and perspectives.

Although Western Christians had retained an Aristotelian corpus that Boethius had transmitted in stripped-down form, new translations from the Arabic made more works available in the twelfth century. In particular the *Posterior Analytics,* known in Arabic as the *Kitāb al-burhān* (Book of Demonstration), translated by Gerard of Cremona from the Arabic in Toledo in 1187, was to have most profound effects on western concepts of natural science. The "art of demonstration" that it expounded, and that medieval scholars held to be embodied in the work of Euclid, was not only employed in the field of mathematics. It provided an accessible and universal technique of reasoning that could be applied to all subjects and led to the belief, as articulated in the West by Adelard of Bath, for example, that reason was superior to the blind acceptance of authority. The method of reasoning, which was abstract, logical, and mathematical, and not empirical, was the one just described that Adelard had discovered among the Arabs.[87] When the Latin Averroists were condemned in Paris in the early thirteenth century, as Lynn White wisely has observed, philosophy was freed from theology, a liberation that had the most profound impact on the future of learning.

CONCLUSIONS

The science of medieval Spain constituted both a retrieval of ancient science plus a new stimulus to observation and theory construction. Its chief social characteristic was the high degree of interpenetration of the scholarly worlds of the three religions. The results of this active interchange of ideas were decisive for the future development of Western philosophy and science. Among these results were the systematic practice of science by Jewish scholars for the first time; the Aristotelianization of the medieval worldview; the development of vernacular language as a vehicle of scientific creation; significant inroads of empiricism in a cognitive world that preferred deduction, since the new ideas tended to weaken the magical worldview of earlier times and to substitute, as an unintended consequence of their pursuit, "a secular image for a religious one;"[88] and the rearrangment of the traditional classification of the sciences and the seating of all disciplines on a basis of logic, for which mathematics (particularly geometry) was the model. In this way, the Arabs and Jews introduced a new epistemology to the Latin West.

The nature of the scientific corpus received and developed in Islamic Spain strongly predetermined the nature of the Jewish approach to science and, because that corpus loomed so large in the birth of European science, the style of science cultivated in al-Andalus affected in turn what Europeans would stress. As Beaujouan puts it,

> The lack of interest in abstract mathematics, the predominance of astronomy and astrology in the early translations, the relatively late date of the Arabo-Latin versions of Aristotle's natural philosophy, the failure to use important works by eastern Arabic scholars: all are explained by the evolution of Arabic science in the Iberian peninsula, with its peculiarities of history and geography, its particularist pride within the Islamic world, its conditioning by the oppressive domination of the Malikite *fakihs*.[89]

Whatever selective factors may have been at play, the result was that, as Burnett points out, by the end of the twelfth century Europeans had at their disposal "an entirely new summa of scientific knowledge, based on sources which were almost completely unknown fifty years previously, but which were to remain standard text-books for many centuries to come."[90]

The Jewish role in this process was one of active participation in Islamic and Christian Spain, producing a scientific and philosophical corpus in Hebrew whose cumulative value increased over time. When, after the death of Averroës, philosophy went into permanent eclipse in the Islamic world and when Islamic Spain entered its death agony, the manuscript sources of Arabic philosophy and science dried up and the Hebrew Aristotelian and scientific corpus became the bank on which European science would continue to draw in the later Middle Ages.

NOTES

1. Among the many accounts, see Charles H. Haskins, "Translators from the Arabic in Spain," in his *Studies in the History of Mediaeval Science,* reprint ed. (New York, 1960), 3-19; Ramón Menéndez Pidal, "España y la introducción de la ciencia árabe en Occidente," in his *España, eslabón entre la cristiandad y el islam* (Madrid, 1956), 33-60; Richard Lemay, "Dans l'Espagne du XIIe siècle: Les traductions de l'Arabe au Latin," *Annales E.S.C.,* 18 (1963): 639-65; David C. Lindberg, "The Transmission of Greek and Arabic Learning to the West," in *Science in the Middle Ages,* ed. David C. Lindberg (Chicago, 1978), 52-90; Thomas F. Glick, *Islamic and Christian Spain in the Early Middle Ages* (Princeton, N.J., 1979), 248-276; Marie-Thérèse d'Alverny, "Translations and Translators," in *Renaissance and Renewal in the Twelfth Century,* ed. Robert L. Benson and Giles Constable (Cambridge, Mass, 1982), 421-62; and Ali A. al-Daffa and John J. Stroyls, "Transmission of Science and Technology Between East and West During the Period of the Crusades," in *Studies in the Exact Sciences in Medieval Islam* (New York, 1984), 1-18.

2. Following Juan Vernet and Julio Samsó, "Les developpements de la science arabe en Andalousie" (in press), Section 2, "La survivance de la culture isidorienne (711-850)."

3. Luis Molina, Una descripción anónomia de al-Andalus, 2 vols. (Madrid, 1983), 1:138.

4. Ibn Juljul's account is reproduced by Juan Vernet, "Los médicos andaluces en el 'Libro de las Generaciones de Médicos,' de ibn Yulyul," *Anuario de Estudios Medievales* (Barcelona) 5 (1968): 447-48. On Ibn al-Haitham al-Qurṭubī, see J. O. Leibowitz and S. Marcus, eds., *Sefer Hanisyonot: The Book of Medical Experiences attributed to Abraham ibn Ezra* (Jerusalem, 1984), 7, 33, 103; and Marcelino V. Amasuno, *La materia médica de Dioscorides en el Lapidario de Alfonso X el Sabio* (Madrid, 1987), 67.

5. Juan Vernet and M. A. Catalá, "Las obras matemáticas de Maslama de Madrid," *Al-Andalus* 30 (1965): 19.

6. Cited by Lindberg, "Transmission of Greek and Arabic Learning," 60.

7. See, on this account, Bernard R. Goldstein, "The Role of Science in the Jewish Community in Fourteenth-Century France," *Annals of the New York Academy of Sciences* 34 (1978): 39, and "The Survival of Arabic Astronomy in Hebrew," *Journal for the History of Arabic Science* 3 (1979): 31-39.

8. For biographical details, see Martin Levey, "Abraham bar Ḥiyya ha-Nasi," *Dictionary of Scientific Biography*, 1: 22-23. "Savasorda," *ṣāḥib al-shurṭa* in Arabic, denotes an urban magistracy, something like a police chief, common to medieval Islamic cities. In Bar Ḥiyya's case, however, the title was more likely honorific, the equivalent of Arabic *ḥakīm*, Hebrew *hakham*. See Reuben Levy, *The Social Structure of Islam* (Cambridge, 1962), 332-34, and Emile Tyan, *Histoire de l'organisation judiciaire en pays d'Islam* (Leiden, 1960), 606.

9. For biographical details, see W. Bacher, "Abraham ben Meir ibn Ezra," *The Jewish Encyclopedia*, 6: 520-24; and Martin Levey, "Abraham ben Meir ibn Ezra," *Dictionary of Scientific Biography*, 4: 502-3; *Encylcopedia Judaica*, 8: 1163-74.

10. For biographical details, see David Romano, "Le opere scientifiche di Alfonso X e l'intervenuto degli ebrei," *Accademia Nazionale dei Lincei: Atti dei Convegni* 13 (1971): 689-91.

11. Bernard R. Goldstein, *Ibn al-Muthannā's Commentary on the Astronomical Tables of al-Khwārizmī* (New Haven, Conn., 1967), 148 (translation).

12. Goldstein, *Ibn al-Muthannā's Commentary*, 4-5 (introduction).

13. On the operation of astrolabes, see Willy Hartner, "The Principle and Use of the Astrolabe," in *Oriens-Occidens*, 2 vols. (Hildesheim, 1968-84), 1:287-311; and Olaf Pedersen, "Astronomy," in Lindberg, *Science in the Middle Ages*, 309-11.

14. Roser Puig Aguilar, *Los tratados de la construcción y uso de la azafea de Azarquiel* (Madrid, 1987), 8-9. Jacob b. Makhir ibn Tibbon had translated Ibn al-Ṣaffār's treatise on the astrolabe into Hebrew; Solomon Gandz, "The Astrolabe in Jewish Literature," in *Studies in Hebrew Astronomy and Mathematics* (New York, 1970), 247.

15. Arthur Beer, "Astrolabe," *Encyclopaedia Judaica*, 788.

16. Bernard R. Goldstein and George Saliba, "A Hispano-Arabic Astrolabe with Hebrew Star Names," *Annali dell'Istituto e Museo di Storia della Scienza di Firenze* 8 (1983): 19-28. See also Goldstein, "The Hebrew Astrolabe in the Adler Planetarium, *Journal of Near Eastern Studies* 35 (1976): 251-60.

17. Gandz, *Studies*, 258; on *urim we-thummin*, see *The JPS Torah Commentary: Exodus* (Philadephia, 1991), 181-82. It is difficult to envision Ibn Ezra's interpretation from the context.

18. Paul Kunitzsch, "Al-Khwārizmī as a Source for the *Sententiae astrolabii*," *Annals of the New York Academy of Sciences* 55 (1987): 227-36; Charles F. S. Burnett, "A New Source for Dominicus Gundissalinus's Account of the Science of the Stars," *Annals of Science* 47 (1990): 363.

19. Abraham ibn Ezra wrote an original treatise in Latin on astronomical tables around 1160, the same period in which he translated Ibn al-Muthannā's commentary on al-Khwārizmī's tables into Hebrew. There is a debate over whether Ibn Ezra knew Latin well enough to have written a treatise on the astrolabe, ascribed to a "Magister Abraham," in that language. See J. M. Millás Vallicrosa, "Un nuevo tratado de astrolabio, de R. Abraham ibn Ezra," *Al-Andalus* 5 (1940): 1-29; Raphael Levy's rejoinder, "The Authorship of a Latin Treatise on the Astrolabe," *Speculum* 17 (1942) 566-69; and Millás, "El magisterio astronómico de Abraham ibn Ezra en la Europa Latina," in *Estudios sobre historia de la ciencia española* (Barcelona, 1949), 166, 167, 292, 339, 349.

20. Goldstein, *Ibn al-Muthannā's Commentary*, 150. It was, of course, fully recognized that ancient observations were rendered obsolete through the passage of time; see, in this regard, Ibn Khaldun, *The Muqaddimah*, 3 vols. (Princeton, 1958), 3: 134.

21. See Salo W. Baron, *A Social and Religious History of the Jews*, vol. 8, *Philosophy and Science*, 2nd ed. (New York, 1958), 173; and G. J. Toomer, "The Solar Theory of az-Zarqāl: A History of Errors," *Centaurus* 14 (1969): 316.

22. d'Alverny, "Translations and Translators," 443-44.

23. Thus Khwārizmī's tables include a number of parameters and procedures in the Indian style (e. g., there is no equant); Guy Beaujouan, "The Transformation of the Quadrivium," in Benson and Constable, *Renaissance and Renewal in the Twelfth Century,* 478.

24. Willy Hartner, "Al-Battānī," *Dictionary of Scientific Biography,* 507-16; Beaujouan, "Transformation of the Quadrivium," 479; Juan Vernet, "Al-Zarqālī," *Dictionary of Scientific Biography,* 14: 592-95.

25. J.D. North, "The Alfonsine Tables in England," in *Prismata: Naturwissenschaftsgeschichtliche Studien,* ed. Y. Maeyama and W. G. Saltzer, (Wiesbaden, 1977), 289.

26. José M. Millás Vallicrosa, "Una traducción catalana de las Tablas astronómicas (1361) de Jacob ben David Yomtob, de Perpiñán," *Sefarad* 19 (1959): 365-71; and "En torno de las Tablas astronómicas del rey Pedro IV de Aragón," in *Nuevos estudios sobre historia de la ciencia española* (Barcelona, 1960), 279-85.

27. Bernard R. Goldstein, "The Survival of Arabic Astronomy in Hebrew," *Journal for the History of Arabic Science* 3 (1979): 31-39.

28. "Abraham ben Samuel Zacuto," *Encyclopaedia Judaica,* 16: 904-6; Bernard R. Goldstein, "The Hebrew Astronomical Tradition: New Sources," *Isis* 72 (1981): 237-51.

29. According to Joan Corominas, *Diccionario crítico etimológico de la lengua castellana,* 4 vols. (Bern, 1954), 1: 142-43.

30. See the interesting discussion by Francis S. Benjamin, Jr., and G. J. Toomer, *Campanus of Novara and Medieval Planetary Theory* (Madison, Wis., 1971), 374-75.

31. See Beaujouan, "Transformation of the Quadrivium," 464.

32. Pedersen, "Astronomy," 314.

33. A very clear description of Ptolemy's system can found in Thomas S. Kuhn, *The Copernican Revolution* (Cambridge, Mass., 1977), chapter 2.

34. Goldstein, "Survival of Arabic Astronomy in Hebrew," 32.

35. See the important article by A. I. Sabra, "The Andalusian Revolt against Ptolemaic Astronomy: Averroes and al-Biṭrūjī," in *Transformation and Tradition in the Sciences,* ed. Everett Mendelsohn, (Cambridge, 1984), 133-53.

36. Ibid., 142.

37. Maimonides, *The Guide to the Perplexed* (Chicago, 1964), 322-27.

38. R. P. Lorch, "Jābir ibn Aflah," *Dictionary of Scientific Biography* 8: 37-39; Maimonides, *Guide to the Perplexed,* 268.

39. Beaujouan, "Transformation of the Quadrivium," 478.

40. Bernard R. Goldstein, *Al-Biṭrūjī: On the Principles of Astronomy,* 2 vols. (New Haven, Conn., 1971), 1: 40-43. On p. 43 he says that Isaac Israeli (fl. 1310) of Toledo mentions the author of a theory that shook the world and who lived until 1140, which Goldstein believes may refer to al-Biṭrūjī. It more likely refers to Ibn Bājja, who died ca. 1039. Biṭrūjī lived at the end of the twelfth century.

41. Jolivet, "The Arabic Inheritance," 137-38; also for the citation of Dominicus Gundissalinus.

42. For a survey of Alfonsine astronomy, see Julio Samsó, "La astronomía de Alfonso X," *Investigación y Ciencia,* December, 1984, 91-103.

43. Juan Vernet, *De ʿAbd al-Rahmān I a Isabel II* (Barcelona, 1989), 346. Isaac ibn Sīd was a very versatile scientist; he also left a manuscript in Judeo-Arabic in which he describes automatons (ibid., 304).

44. See discussion in Glick, *Islamic and Christian Spain,* 269-270.

45. See Beaujouan, "Transformation of the Quadrivium," 469.

46. Ibid., 467.

47. Martin Levey, "Abraham ben Meir ibn Ezra," *Dictionary of Scientific Biography,* 4: 502. According to Baron (*Social and Religious History,* 2: 150), Jews used *ghubār* numbers only when writing in Arabic and the Hebrew letter system when writing in Hebrew.

48. Solomon Gandz, "The Origin of the Ghubār Numerals or the Arabian Abacus and the Articuli," *Isis* 16 (1931): 421.

49. G. J. Toomer, "Al-Khwārizmī," *Dictionary of Scientific Biography,* 7: 360.

50. John Murdoch, "The Medieval Latin Euclid: The Arabic-Latin Phase," *Dictionary of Scientific Biography, s.v.* "Euclid," 4: 444-59; idem, "The Medieval Euclid: Salient Aspects of the Translations of the *Elements* by Adelard of Bath and Campanus of Novara," *Revue de Synthèse* 89 (1968): 67-94; Charles Burnett, "Scientific Speculations," in *A History of Twelfth-Century Western Philosophy,* ed. Peter Dronke (Cambridge, 1980), 151-76, esp. 158-60.

51. Martin Levey, "Abraham bar Ḥiyya ha-Nasi," *Dictionary of Scientific Biography,* 1: 22-23; idem, "The Encyclopedia of Abraham Savasorda: A Departure in Mathematical Methodology," *Isis* 43 (1952): 259; David Lindberg, "The Transmission of Greek and Arabic Learning to the West," in *Science in the Middle Ages,* 68; Millás Vallicrosa, *Estudios,* 260; Burnett, "Scientific Speculations," 161. Through the Liber Embadorum, Bar Ḥiyya influenced medieval Christian mathematicians like Leonardo Fibonacci; see Baron, *Social and Religious History,* 2: 158.

52. Levey, "The Encyclopedia of Abraham Savasorda," 257.

53. Martin Levey, "Abraham Savasorda and his Algorism: A Study in Early European Logistic," *Osiris* 11 (1954): 54; Kushayr ibn Labban, *Principle of Hindu Reckoning,* ed. Martin Levey and Martin Petruck (Madison, Wis., 1965), 5.

54. Ibid., 25.

55. Harry Austryn Wolfson, "The Classification of Sciences in Medieval Jewish Philosophy," *Hebrew Union College Jubilee Volume* (Cincinnati, 1925), 263-315, esp. 253-64.

56. Ibid., 264.

57. Ibid., 272-81.

58. Ibid., 285.

59. Ibid., 300-301.

60. Jean Jolivet, "The Arabic Inheritance," in Dronke, *A History of Twelfth-Century Western Philosophy,* 126.

61. Charles Burnett, "A New Source for Dominicus Gundissalinus' Account of the Science of the Stars," *Annals of Science* 47 (1990): 362-63. Gundissalinus was not the only Latin author to make this distinction. Curiously, he inverts the terms: he calls the theoretical part astrology, and the utilitarian, astronomy. I have used the conventional terms.

62. Jolivet, "The Arabic Inheritance," 127-28.

63. Shukri B. Abed, *Aristotelian Logic and the Arabic Language in Alfārābī* (Albany, N.Y., 1991), xix. Fārābī believed in universal "intertranslatability": inasmuch as languages are external expressions of universal mental concepts, they "can be adjusted in order to encompass ideas expressed in other languages." (ibid., xx).

64. Leon D. Stitskin, *Letters of Maimonides* (New York, 1977), 133.

65. Jean-Pierre Rothschild, "Motivations et méthodes des traductions en hébreu du milieu du XIIe a la fin du XVe siècle," in *Traductions et traducteurs au moyen age* (Paris, 1989), 297, 301.

66. Ibid., 198, 300.

67. This discussion follows Solomon Gandz, "The Terminology of Mathematics from Hebrew and Arabic Sources," in his *Studies in Hebrew Astronomy and Mathematics* (New York, 1970), 279-94.

68. Charles F. S. Burnett, "Some Comments on the Translating of Works from Arabic into Latin in the Mid-Twelfth Century," in *Orientalische Kultur und Europäisches Mittelalter* (Berlin, 1985), 166; paraphrase of the Latin "Habetis ergo librum, nobis [Ibn Daʾūd] praecipiente et singula verba vulgariter proferente, et Dominico Archidiacono singula in latinum convertente, ex arabico translatum."

69. Marie-Thérèse d'Alverny, "Les traductions à deux interprètes, d'arabe en langue vernaculaire et la langue vernaculaire en Latin," in *Traduction et traducteurs au Moyen Age* 197, n. 1.

70. Burnett, "Some Comments," 166, gives the example of Adelard of Bath's confusion between *mankus* (reversed) and *manqus* (diminished). He was not looking at the Arabic text but rather pondering a spoken word.

71. On the Alfonsine translators, see Norman Roth, "Jewish Collaborators in Alfonso's Scientific Work," in *Emperor of Culture: Alfonso X the Learned of Castile and his Thirteenth-Century Renaissance,* ed. Robert I. Burns (Philadelphia, 1990), 59-231; Romano, "Opere scientifiche," and José S. Gil, *La escuela de traductores de Toledo y sus colaboradores judíos* (Toledo, 1985).

72. The following remarks on the nature of the changes induced in Castilian by the translation movement of thirteenth century, I follow Georg Bossong, "Science in the Vernacular Languages: The Case of Alfonso X el Sabio," in *De Astronomia Alphonsi Regis* (Barcelona, 1987), 13-21; and José S. Gil, *La escuela de traductores de Toledo,* 89-199 (on Castilian scientific prose).

73. F. E. Peters, *Aristotle and the Arabs: The Aristotelian Tradition in Islam* (New York, 1968), 60-61.

74. Ibid., 34.

75. Ibid., 119; Fernand van Steenburghen, *Aristotle in the West: The Origins of Western Aristotelianism* (New York, 1970), 17. Two ancient Neo-platonic texts, the so-called "Theology of Aristotle" by Plotinus and the *Liber de causis* of Proclus, entered in the Aristotelian corpus via Arabic translations.

76. See Peters, *Aristotle and the Arabs,* 99.

77. Ṣāʿid al-Andalusī, *Kitab Tabakat al-Umam (Livre des Catégories des Nations),* ed. Régis Blachère (Paris, 1935), 63; Ibn Juljul, *Les générations des médicins et des sages (Tabaqat al-ʾatibba wal-hukama),* Fuʾad Sayyid, ed. (Cairo, 1955), 25.

78. See Norman Daniel, *The Arabs and Medieval Europe* (London, 1975), 296. On the relationship between commerce and learning, see Glick, *Islamic and Christian Spain,* 155, 175.

79. Harry Austryn Wolfson, *Crescas's Critique of Aristotle* (Cambridge, Mass., 1929 [1971]), ix.

80. Maimonides, *Guide of the Perplexed,* 177.

81. F. E. Peters, *Aristotle and the Arabs: The Aristotelian Tradition in Islam* (New York, 1968), 70, n. 2.

82. W. Bacher, "Abraham ben Meir ibn Ezra," *The Jewish Encyclopedia,* 5: 521.

83. Jeremy Cohen, *The Friars and the Jews: The Evolution of Medieval Anti-Semitism* (Ithaca, N.Y., 1982), 62, n. 20.

84. Wolfson, *Crescas' Critique of Aristotle,* 8.

85. Ibid.,. 31; José Chabas et al., "El problema de los antecedentes (Alfonso X, Levi ben Gerson) de las tablas astronómicas compuestas por Jacob ben David Bonjorn," in *De Astronomia Alphonsi Regis,* 97-104. Versions of the tables in Catalan and in Latin survive.

86. Sabra, "The Andalusian Revolt Against Ptolemaic Astronomy," 143.

87. Jolivet, "The Arabic Inheritance," 134.

88. Ibid., 128. See also Tina Stiefel, "The Heresy of Science: A Twelfth-Century Conceptual Revolution," *Isis* 68 (1977): 347-62, esp. 356.

89. Beaujouan, "Transformation of the Quadrivium," 465.

90. Charles Burnett, "Arabic into Latin in Twelfth Century Spain: the Works of Hermann of Carinthia," *Mittellateinisches Jahrbuch* 13 (1978): 133.

Mudejar Tradition and the Synagogues of Medieval Spain: Cultural Identity and Cultural Hegemony

Jerrilynn D. Dodds

Beginning in the eleventh and twelfth centuries, the Iberian peninsula underwent profound changes in rule and in the relationships among its three tensely poised religious groups: Muslims, Christians, and Jews. Important changes in political hegemony were taking place as Christian forces made major and often irreversible incursions into Muslim-ruled lands, a movement that resulted in the imposition of new Christian governments in cities that had for centuries been dominated by Islamic political and cultural traditions. The resulting transformations were complex, for though new Christian political structures could be rapidly devised to replace supplanted Islamic ones, the social and economic infrastructures of most cities were left intact, and the new Christian leadership penetrated the social and cultural fabric of cities with a good deal more trepidation than it did authoritative ruling bodies. In the realm of art and architecture, there developed a particularly vivid testimony to the complex interrelationships between cultures that resulted when Christian rulers presided over an artistic tradition that had been developed under Islamic rule: the arts called "Mudejar."

"Mudejar" and "Mozarabic," terms specific to the study of Spanish art, were conceived to resolve the problems of classifying the arts of a multicultural society in the Middle Ages. "Mozarabic" refers to the arts of Mozarabs, or Christians who lived under Islamic rule, but very early in their study an ambiguity developed in the term's use. Some employed it to designate patrons, and others, to refer to any arts made by Christians—inside or outside Islamic political frontiers—that reflected the influence of Islam. This last use constituted a significant and dangerous leap in meaning, for it implied that the only possible reaction of a subjected culture to the art of a dominant one was imitation. We know of course both in general, and in the case of the Mozarabs themselves, that oppressed groups often use their cultures as an important means of demonstrating defiance. They resist the dominant culture by reverting to an old vanquished tradition or by developing new forms in opposition to it.[1]

Figure 28 *(opposite)*
Interior of the Synagogue of Santa Maria la Blanca, Toledo, 13th century

The case with Mudejar artistic traditions is just as complex. The word refers literally to a subjected Muslim, and early artistic studies assumed Mudejar artisans to be the Muslim slaves of new Christian masters. Today however, it is understood that Christians, Muslims, and Jews alike worked on the buildings and objects we call Mudejar, though there is still some controversy as to the definition and limitations implied by the term. One scholarly opinion defines Mudejar as an artistic style and tradition of construction that was developed by the interaction of Muslim patrons and craftsmen, and then appropriated by new Christian rulers and patrons.[2] Another usage treats much the same group of buildings and objects simply as a chronological and geographical group gathered under the name Mudejar, which identifies any art created in Christian-ruled lands that had previously been under Muslim control, regardless of its stylistic features.

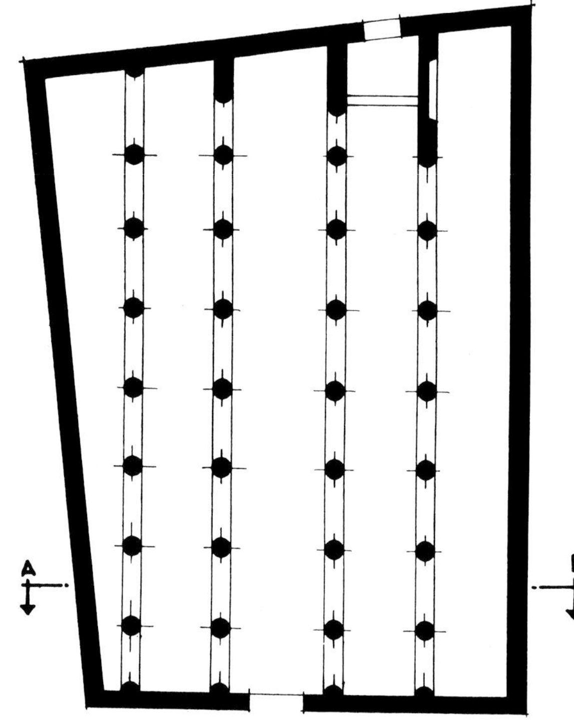

Figure 25
Plan of the Synagogue of Santa Maria la Blanca, Toledo, 13th century (after Cantera Burgos, *Sinagogas Españolas*)

It is significant that the terms of this debate eliminate the medieval Iberian peninsula's eternal other, the Jews, who were nevertheless significant patrons of Mudejar buildings. Because their participation in military and political power structures was limited, they are largely excluded, or treated as marginal, in contemporary scholarly discussions of Mudejar arts (a fact that ought to serve as a warning against the habit of establishing artistic classifications in culturally plural societies according to hegemonic categories).[3] Indeed, the synagogues of Spain are one of the key points of convergence of the rich cultural tensions that make Mudejar architecture unique and compelling.

There are four Sephardic synagogues from the medieval period on the Iberian peninsula, of which three are considered Mudejar by any definition: the congregational synagogue in Toledo (today the church of Santa Maria la Blanca), perhaps built by Joseph ben Meir ben Shoshan; the synagogue of Samuel Halevi in Toledo (El Tránsito); and the synagogue of Isaac Mehab in Córdoba. Another Mudejar synagogue, in Segovia, is known from paintings executed before its destruction in the nineteenth century. The fourth surviving synagogue is that of Tomar, from pre-expulsion Portugal, a building that presents particular problems of classification to which I will return. In reviewing their patronage, the historical conditions of their foundation, and the aesthetic language in which they are fashioned, I hope to demonstrate the way in which the synagogues of the Iberian peninsula can be seen as unique documents of three cultures that are both intertwined and divided.

Now a church dedicated to Santa Maria la Blanca, the earliest of Toledo's two surviving synagogues presents an unusual plan and disposition [fig. 25].[4] A simple trapezoidal building constructed of brick alternating with stone courses, it opens today on a short end to reveal an interior of five aisles of which the central aisle is slightly wider. The aisles are supported by twenty-four piers in octagonal section, and eight engaged piers where the arches meet the wall. The arches are elegant enclosed horseshoe arches that rest on high abacuses, cutting a cool sharp profile against the shadow of the aisle behind [fig. 26]. The stucco relief decoration that adorns the arch spandrels and upper walls of the arcades of Santa Maria la Blanca draws on architectural, vegetal, and geometric motifs. It has a restrained, linear quality, and is balanced by expanses of plain wall, which have been thought by some to be intended for inscriptions.[5] Only in the carved stucco capitals of the piers does the decoration erupt in what might be considered opulent and mannered fantasies of pinecones and interwoven bands in massive and deeply drilled forms [fig. 27].

Figure 26
Interior of the Synagogue of Santa Maria la Blanca, Toledo, 13th century, as depicted in a 19th-century lithograph.

We know nothing concerning the original orientation of the building, the placement of its *bimah,* or of its ark niche, or the disposition of its seating when it served as a synagogue. There are diverse opinions concerning the position of its women's gallery, roofs, and ceiling.[6] We also know very little for sure concerning its patronage, though a plausible connection has been proposed between this building and Joseph ben Meir ben Shoshan (also called Yusuf Abenxuxen), the finance minister of Alfonso VIII of Castile. Joseph ben Meir ben

Shoshan's epitaph records him as the patron of a synagogue, perhaps one he restored, since another inscription refers to a synagogue whose "ruins were raised up in the year 4940 [1180]."[7]

Figure 27
Pier capital from Santa Maria la Blanca, Toledo, 13th century

A synagogue clearly related in plan and formal tradition to the earliest of Toledo's synagogues was the congregational synagogue of Segovia, a building that subsequently became the church of Corpus Christi before its destruction by fire in 1899.[8] Like most Mudejar buildings throughout Spain, it was constructed of brick, and covered with both plain and carved stucco. Its arcades, which rested on eight massive piers, were identical with those of the Toledo synagogue, including sharp, enclosed horseshoe arches resting on abacuses, an arcade of blind arches in stucco relief at the clerestory level, and massive, plastic capitals with pinecones and foliage interlace [fig. 28, p. 112].

The existence of the Segovia synagogue forces us to put Toledo's earliest synagogue in its context. It is not a unique anomaly as has often been thought—an odd aisled type of synagogue that reflected, perhaps, a preexisting mosque plan. Instead, we have here a synagogue type codified in plan and elevation, which was fairly widely dispersed and perhaps issued from a single workshop. It was a lively paradigm as well, for the two surviving examples were constructed on a grand scale in two important cities of the medieval Iberian peninsula [figs. 29-30].

From where then, does this building type derive its particular character? The search for a close parallel in plan yields meager results. Aisled synagogues do exist in North Africa, in particular in Tunis, though their arcades do not run parallel to the long walls as in Toledo and Segovia, and the North African buildings are more recent.[9] Nevertheless, a western Islamic parallel might have some validity, for it is specifically in the artistic tradition of

Figure 29
Interior of the old Synagogue of Segovia. Watercolor by Ricardo Madrazo (1852-1917)

North Africa that we find the aesthetics and techniques that best recall these synagogue interiors.

The austerity and restraint of decoration on the interior of these aisled synagogues must derive from a tradition of building originating during the Almohad hegemony on the Iberian peninsula. The Almohads, who invaded the Iberian peninsula in 1125 in response to what they believed were the excess of the reigning Almoravid rule and the growing power of the Christian kingdoms to the north, harbored strict convictions concerning patronage of the arts. They themselves were responsible for the destruction and whitewashing of Almoravid mosques, which they considered too distracting and opulent in decoration, and their own constructions in Marrakesh, Tinmal, and Seville show planar relief carving that is confined to a rectangular frame, and sharply curved horseshoe and pointed arches that present cool white profiles against the shadows of the aisles behind [fig. 31].

In their fundamental principals and even certain basic components, then, the synagogues of Toledo and Segovia demonstrate strong links in spirit and design to the architecture of the Almohads. The use of Almohad architectural style is common in the Mudejar tradition, part of a strong craft that survived the fall of Almohad hegemony. One can imagine by extension that—at a certain point in the development of this synagogue type—a plan type evolved that might accommodate this use of freestanding piers, thus continuing within the Jewish community the development of the Almohad tradition of architectural construction and decoration.

The process outlined here is one that dissociates architectural style from religious belief and practice. Although the forerunners for the elevation, decoration, and possibly even plan of these two synagogues were probably mosques, the appropriation of these architectural forms took on stronger meanings disassociated with Islamic religion. Thus the architectural style begun under the Almohads had come to be part of a shared visual language of Jews and Muslims that lost its religious, and to some extent its political implications. This branch of Mudejar architecture reveals a deep cultural commonality that transcends the differences that separated Muslims and Jews. It also reminds us of the extent to which this style is oriented toward traditions developed under Muslim hegemony: the Jews in Spain would never exercise that level of cultural sympathy with the architectural traditions of the Christians however long they survived under their rule.

Figure 30
The Synagogue of Segovia after the fire of 1900

Why Spain's multicultural style should, in its essence, be derived from Islamic and not Christian artistic traditions is a complex issue that involves both practical and symbolic concerns. Clearly, Mudejar art evolved in cities that had been ruled for centuries by Muslims, who had patronized ateliers that promoted and responded to their cultural needs and tastes. After centuries of living side by side with the Muslims, indigenous Christians and Jews had become used to these crafts, and had to a greater or lesser extent made them their own. The styles therefore survived the demise of the ruling group that had introduced them. But there is more to the lively way in which Jewish patrons in particular embraced the Almohad-inspired Mudejar style. For the ability of the Jewish community—and for that matter, the Christian community—to identify with this austere, brick-based architecture with aniconic decoration is not related to the direct relationship of the Jewish community with Almohad rule. It derives instead from the generally high level of tolerance exercised by the first Muslim rulers

Figure 31
Tinmal Mosque, Morocco, 12th century

of al-Andalus, and the lasting cultural identification of one group with another's artistic forms.

It is generally understood that Jews fared better under Islamic rule than under the vigilance of Christian monarchs. Under Islamic rule, Christians and Jews were *dhimmis,* "protected people" or "People of the Book," whose autonomy as a group and freedom to worship and follow certain traditional ways of life were protected in return for obedience to Islamic rule and the payment of special taxes.[10] The Jews had fared badly under the Visigoths, and after the advent of Islam on the peninsula, the rights of Jews had varied wildly from laws that granted rights similar to those of Christians, to decrees that insisted on their inferior status, excluding them from normal social and economic life. While *dhimmi* legislation was somewhat variable in different parts of the Islamic world, one could largely count on a consistent treatment in any Muslim-ruled city on the Iberian peninsula during the years of the Umayyad caliphate and the reigns of the *taifa* kings. The result of this tolerance was that in the Tenth and Eleventh centuries Jews attained significant court positions and moved freely through each city, intermingling in its social and cultural life and presumably identifying with the visual world that was the setting for this urban society.[11]

When al-Andalus was invaded by the conservative North African dynasties, the Almoravids and Almohads, however, the traditional policy of tolerance was undercut. These Berbers were often herdsmen and soldiers whose entry to al-Andalus was sudden and shocking: they were largely intolerant, both of religious minorities and of the indigenous Muslims whom they regarded as soft and decadent. Under the Almoravids and Almohads there was intermittent persecution of Jews: the massacre of Jews in eleventh-century Granada is perhaps the most salient example, and it occurred significantly in response to controversy surrounding a powerful Jew, Joseph ibn Naghrila, chief minister for the Muslim king of Granada. Similarly, a number of intriguing limitations to the Jews' normal freedom of social behavior appears in twelfth-century legislation, which seem once again aimed at controlling the social and economic mobility of Jews in the Islamic polity. Thus, Ibn Abdun insisted that Jews be forced to wear distinctive dress, and Ibn Idhari recounts that the Almohad caliph al-Mansur insisted that Jews wear a prescribed costume, "with black burnouses and black caps," "because they had become so bold as to wear Muslim clothing and in their dress looked like the noblest among them, mingling with the Muslims in external affairs, without being distinguished from the servants of God."[12]

It seems clear that at least one motivation for the persecution of the Jews was their high degree of integration into Islamic society. In their important positions at court, in their wealth and social mobility, certain Jews provided a challenge to the Almohads' conviction that Muslims ought to enjoy a sequestered social ascendancy, an exclusivity the Umayyads never really insisted upon regarding Jews, perhaps because they were more secure in their own aristocratic identity.[13] Thus, though the Almoravids and Almohads were the least tolerant of masters, their rule reveals to us that already by the eleventh century, the Jews of al-Andalus had come to identify to a high degree with Islamic culture, not only speaking Arabic, but interacting socially with members of the Andalusi elite and adopting Islamic dress. These were surely cultural habits established during the Umayyad Caliphate and the period of the *taifas,* in which tolerance and fruitful interaction of Muslims and Jews provided fertile ground for the sharing of culture.

Thus the identification of the Jews of al-Andalus with Islamic culture was already deeply felt by the time of the Almohad incursions, and explains both the disassociation of Islamic style from the intolerant hegemony, and also the Almohads' rather defensive stance toward the Jews as a group.

Later synagogues provide an intriguing extension of this notion. Córdoba's only surviving synagogue was constructed in the first quarter of the fourteenth century and is of a different type than the twelfth or thirteenth-century synagogues of Toledo and Segovia.[14] It is composed of an open court, an entryway (restored) with a gallery above, and a tiny prayer hall of nearly square proportions: twenty-one feet wide by twenty-three feet long [fig. 32]. This single room has no supports, and is broken only by the lambrequin, or scalloped arched openings to the gallery, and the ark niche in the western wall, which is distinguished by an elegant polylobed arch [fig. 33]. The rest of the room's walls are covered by a skin of stucco decoration: in particular geometric patterns based on expanding stars, or the schematized form of interlace called *ataurique* (from the Arabic *alturig,* leafy design).

The synagogue's dedicatory inscription proclaims its patronage and sets the tone for its meaning in Christian Córdoba. It reads: "Isaac

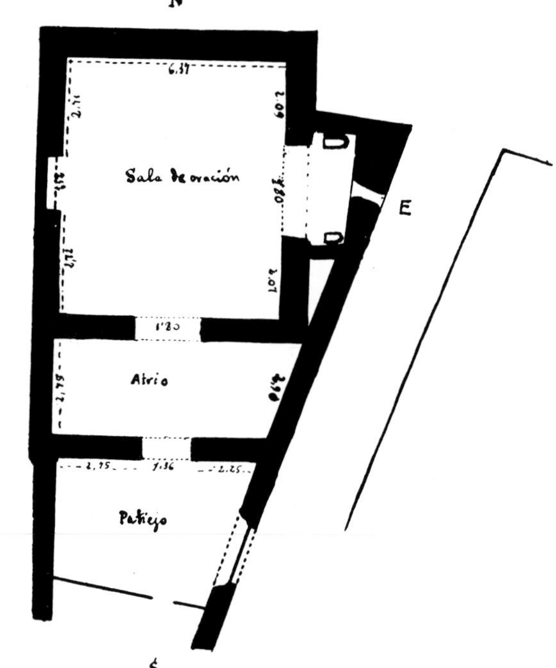

Figure 32
Plan of the Synagogue of Córdoba (see also cat. no. 56 a, b; after Cantera Burgos, *Sinagogas Españolas*)

Figure 33
Córdoba Synagogue, North Wall, Córdoba, 1314–15 (see also cat. no. 56 a, b)

Menhab, son of the honorable Ephraim, has completed this lesser sanctuary (*mikdash me'at*), and he built it in the year 75 [1314–15] as a temporary abode. Hasten, O God, to rebuild Jerusalem." Wischnitzer points out that the expression "lesser sanctuary" is common usage that alludes to the synagogue as a substitute for the Temple, until it is rebuilt in Jerusalem.[15] Though the inscription is a topos, it also evokes in many ways the recent history of the Jews of Córdoba. Córdoba fell to the Christians in 1235 when it was taken by Ferdinand III. By 1250, tensions between the new Christian rulers and the Jews had already surfaced. A pastoral letter of Pope Innocent IV records Christian resentment concerning the prominence of a new congregational synagogue:

> We have learned that, despite the prohibition of our dear son, the Archdeacon of the Chapter of Córdoba, the Jews of the province of Córdoba are rashly presuming to build a new synagogue of unnecessary height thereby scandalizing faithful Christians and causing much harm to the church of Córdoba, wherefore...we command [you]...to enforce the authority of your office against the Jews in this regard...."[16]

I wonder if the diminutive size of the Córdoba synagogue and the insistence of its inscription on the topos of a provisional structure and Jerusalem to come did not evoke for the Jews of Córdoba renewed restrictions on their right to build structures of monumental presence and rhetorical force. Wischnitzer has already suggested that the absence of windows on all but the south side of the synagogue might have been a response to further building constraints.[17] In any case, it is clear from Pope Innocent's letter, composed only sixty-five years before the construction of the small Córdoba synagogue, that it was built in an atmosphere of restricted artistic expression for Jews. It was this atmosphere that led to the renewal of the Jewish community's identification with cultural roots perceived as distinct from those of the conquering Christians.

The style of Córdoba's synagogue, like that of the earlier examples discussed, is consistently called Mudejar, though the synagogue's appearance and sources are quite divergent from the Toledo and Segovia examples. The closest parallels to its decoration can be found in the Islamic palace of the Alhambra in Granada, much of which is later, but whose decoration clearly reflects a Nasrid tradition begun in the thirteenth century [figs. 34-35]. Lambrequin arches in low relief, arabesques, or *ataurique,* and expanding star patterns in stucco all abound in the Nasrid palace, in a low relief style that recalls the stucco skin of the Cordovan synagogue.

The formal disposition of the Córdoba synagogue grows, then, not from an autonomous development out of earlier synagogue traditions, but from continual contact with new monumental developments in the Islamic world. This is not to say that the Mudejar tradition as it appears in the synagogue of Córdoba is a slavish copy of art according to Islamic rules, but that it is part of an artistic tradition that is alive and growing, and not in isolation but through its identification with an evolving Islamic tradition.

Figure 34
Mirador of Linda Raja, Alhambra, Granada, 14th century

An indication of the intensity of this identification and interchange can be found in the use of inscriptions in the Córdoba synagogue. While the dedicatory inscription

Figure 35
Detail of stucco from the Alhambra, Granada, 14th century

appears in a solid, legible block, other inscriptions occupy thin bands within the composition of the stucco decoration, much as Arabic inscriptions function in the Nasrid palace. The Hebrew inscriptions of the synagogue serve, on one level, as devotional texts, but they also function as part of the abstract design of the whole stucco composition, and imbue its complex *horror vacui* with meaning. This is not a copy of Islamic practice, but a deep understanding of its principles, one that regards writing both as holy and as a useful tool for the injection of meaning into an aniconic, abstract composition. In deciphering which fields are abstract design, and which are writing, the viewer becomes involved in an extended, meditative relationship with the work of art, in which writing becomes the elusive bearer of meaning.

This retention of the most basic principles of Islamic decoration is typical of synagogue construction in the Mudejar tradition, but quite different from Mudejar buildings constructed to serve the Christian cult. In Toledo, where these abound in a number of diverse permutations, the indigenous Islamic tradition of construction is especially evident in building exteriors. When the mosque of Bab al-Mardum, near the city walls, was converted into a church upon the conquest of the city in the late twelfth century, an apse was added in the same brick tradition in which the walls of the mosque had been constructed nearly two hundred years before: blind arcades of horseshoe and polylobed arches ornament the apse exterior in a planar decorative system based on the thickness of the brick itself. The exterior of this addition appears almost as a continuation of the mosque structure. The interior, however, is transformed, not only by a new axiality, but by the addition of figural wall paintings. These wall paintings and their sacred narrative become the primary means of communication with the Christian community, and their presence becomes a fertile evocation of the differences between Muslim and Christian worship and their opposing attitudes to images.

Figure 36
Fragment from an Arch, Convent of Las Dueñas, Córdoba, 14th Century, Museo Arqueológico Provincial, Córdoba, no. 579 (cat. no. 59)

Now it is clear that there existed Christian devotional buildings that utilized overall stucco decoration of a type similar to that used in the Cordovan synagogue: the convent of Las Dueñas [fig. 36], whose vestiges are now in the Archeological Museum of Córdoba, or even the vestiges of stucco from the monastery of Las Huelgas in Burgos. But in no Christian religious building do we see the absorption not only of a craft tradition and decorative style but also of principles of expressive meaning, such as we see in Mudejar synagogues. And in no synagogue is this principal more beautifully illustrated than that of Samuel Halevi Abulafia in Toledo, a synagogue known locally as El Tránsito.[18]

Constructed in 1360, El Tránsito is an open rectangular sanctuary of comparatively large proportions: about twenty-three by twelve meters in plan and nine-and-a-half meters high [fig. 37]. It possesses a spacious restored women's gallery on the north side, and on the east, three niches for Torah scrolls. The synagogue is covered with stucco relief of extraordinary quality in a unique state of preservation. It possesses the same geometric patterns and interlace we saw in the Cordovan synagogue, together with floral rinceau and cartouches,

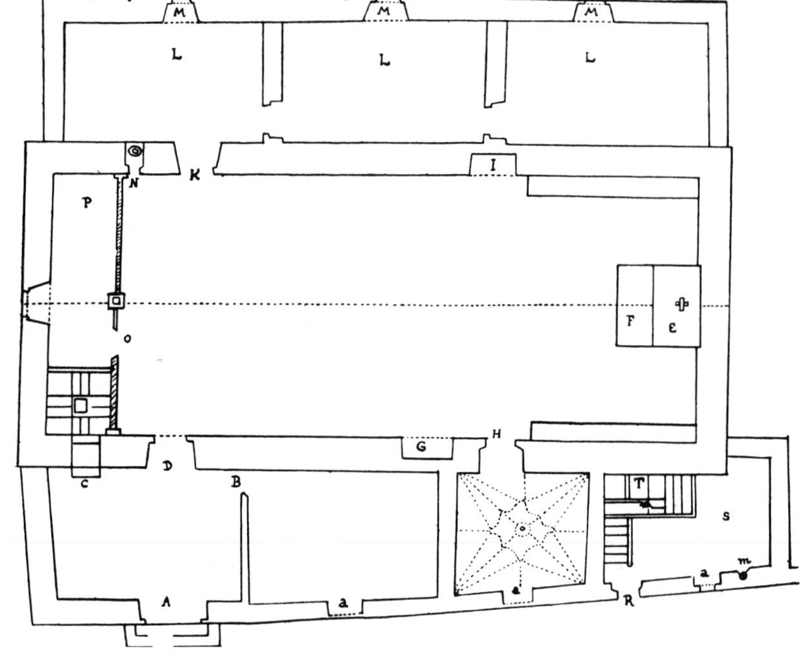

Figure 37
Plan of the Synagogue of El Tránsito, Toledo, 1357 (see also cat. no. 58 a, b, c; after Cantera Burgos, *Sinagogas Españolas*)

blind arcades, and heraldic shields [fig. 38].

The use of inscriptions in the overall design of the ornament is significant, for here we find not only Hebrew writing integrated into the complex stucco ornament, but Arabic writing as well, some of which includes texts from the Qurʾān. Various explanations have been offered for these last inscriptions. Wischnitzer contends that they are due to the use of Muslim craftsmen on the project. There is little doubt, of course, that Muslims were among those who worked on the synagogue. However, the idea of their quietly slipping long bands of Arabic writing into the design unbeknownst to Samuel Halevi, or that some carver added texts from the Qurʾān at his own whim without being in some way controlled by the patron, does not make any sense—in particular when we take into account the conscious nature of much of the rest of the program.

Instead, I believe we have here the analogue in literature to the connections we have traced in architectural style: the educated Jews of Toledo felt that much Islamic culture was their culture as well. The Jews of Toledo had spoken Arabic for hundreds of years, and they had long come to understand the literary and scholarly culture of Islam and considered it something that they shared.

Figure 38
Interior of the Synagogue of El Tránsito, Toledo, 1357 (see also cat. no. 58 a, b, c)

The stylistic use of the Arabic inscriptions and many of the motifs used in the opulent ornament of the *Transito* synagogue once again reveal a clear relationship to contemporary Nasrid ornament, suggesting a constantly renewed tradition of contact with Nasrid art. One aspect of the patronage of the synagogue of Abulafia relates directly to its use of contemporary Nasrid ornament, as well as its divergences from Córdoba's small temple. This first aspect derives from the patron's close association with a Christian court. Samuel Halevi Abulafia was treasurer and close adviser to King Peter I, the Cruel, of Castile, who was a close ally of the Nasrid monarch Muhammad V, one of the most active builders of the Alhambra. The frequent appearance of the arms of Castile, and the close relationship between the decoration of the synagogue and that of the Alhambra, have not only a general connection with the building as a monument of Mudejar tradition, but also a specific connection arising from Peter's political connections [fig. 39].

Figure 39
Detail of the Dedicatory Inscription with Coat of Arms of the Synagogue of El Tránsito, Toledo, 1357 (see also cat. no. 58 a, b, c)

Indeed, there are many ways in which this particular brand of Mudejar ornament, which combines Nasrid decoration with symbols of the kingdom of Castile, might be seen as part of a court style of Peter the Cruel. One is in his extraordinary additions to the palace of the Alcázar in Seville, a building that might be termed a Christian monarch's interpretation of an Islamic monarch's palace. In its labyrinthine plan, its Nasrid-style stucco carving, and even in its use of Arabic writing, it is proof of the extent to which Peter considered Islamic style appropriate to manifest royal dignity and power [fig. 40].

Clearly, at the court of Peter I, Islamic developments in stucco ornament and even certain building types were viewed as emblematic of high court culture, of a certain level of erudition and craftsmanship that were signs of strong kingship. We must remember also that the

Figure 40
Detail of Carved Stucco from the Synagogue of El Tránsito (see also cat. no. 58 a, b, c)

Alcázar of Seville was a preexisting Islamic palace appropriated by Peter, a symbol of his dominion over lands once under a powerful Islamic hegemony. For though the only Islamic state to survive on the Iberian peninsula was now the elegant but impotent Nasrid kingdom of Granada, the memory and myth of the time when Islam had dominated most of the peninsula was strong, and Christian monarchs had a strong sense of the antiquity and rootedness of the sophisticated culture that had preceded them in the southern part of the peninsula. For Peter, the adoption of Nasrid style was part of the appropriation of the mythic power of Islamic culture, which had come to mean wealth, power, refinement, and sophistication to all Spaniards.

But did the Nasrid style mean the same thing to Samuel Halevi Abulafia? His appropriation of it has, I think, a much more layered significance, as did his place in the social fabric of Christian Spain.

First, it has been noted that the dedicatory inscriptions in the Abulafia synagogue suggest pride on the part of the founder, and a generally more optimistic attitude than that presented in the humble synagogue of Córdoba:

> And the house which Samuel built
> And the wooden tower for the reading of the written law
> And the scrolls of the Law and the crowns thereto
> And its lavers and lamps for lighting
> And its windows like the windows of Ariel
>
> And its courts for them that cherish the perfect law
> And seats, too, for all who sit in the shade of God
> So that those who saw it almost said, "This semblance

Is as the semblance of the work which Bezalel wrought."
Go now, ye peoples, and come into my gates
And seek the Lord, for it is a house of God even as Bethel.[19]

Other inscriptions praise king Peter I, and hail Abulafia himself as "prince among the princes of the tribe of Levi."[20] In general, the synagogue of Abulafia is a monument in the court style of Peter I, bearing the king's coat of arms and appropriately unctuous evocations of his greatness. But it also creates a kind of "micro-court" for Samuel Halevi himself, setting him at the pinnacle of his own minority society, that of the Jews of Toledo. Indeed this largest and most opulent of all of the synagogues that survived on the Iberian peninsula was not a public prayer hall at all, but the private temple of Samuel Halevi, with a private entrance from his (now destroyed) house.[21]

Samuel Halevi Abulafia had built a kind of "palatine chapel" for himself, a grand private oratory of the type that Christian kings often built for their private worship and that of their courts. Abulafia's wealth and importance within and outside the Jewish community was both affirmed and augmented by his synagogue, which made its point in a number of diverse formal languages. First, it identified Abulafia as part of a Jewish community that had long seen its cultural identification in terms of Islamic architectural style, including a profound understanding of the importance and use of calligraphy—both in Arabic and Hebrew. Second, there is conscious reference to the particular permutation of that Islamic style at Samuel Halevi's synagogue, for he had adopted the Castilian court style, which superimposed signs of Peter I's hegemony on the latest Nasrid ornament. In this way he identifies himself with his king. Finally, in his inscriptions and in the construction of a private oratory, he gives himself an authoritative position within the Jewish community, one reinforced with architectural signs borrowed from the Christian monarch's architectural idiom.

Thus we see that for Jews and Christians, Mudejar architecture could take on divergent and layered meanings. For Peter I, the use of Nasrid style meant his appropriation of an Islamic image of kingship with its attendant implications of a powerful and old culture. For Samuel Halevi, adaptation of an Islamic style was part of his reaffirmation of the cultural traditions of Jews on the Iberian peninsula, traditions associated with Islamic style for hundreds of years. It was in his use of Christian forms, those associated with Peter I and his position in a Christian court, that Abulafia expressed *his* desire for power and authority.

That expression of power was not lost on Peter the Cruel. Abulafia's downfall followed closely upon the completion of the architectural expression of his wealth and power. Peter I "The Cruel" imprisoned him, and sent him to Seville where he was tortured and executed, because he failed to reveal the supposed hiding place of his mythical store or treasure.

Each Mudejar building on the Iberian peninsula encases multiple levels of meaning associated with its craft and style. Some of those attitudes are subconscious, and involve the way in which a community sees itself among others; the way it fashions an identity for itself. Others are conscious appropriations of some meaning that can be associated with architectural form. The Jews of the Iberian peninsula consistently used Islamic form because it became part of the way they defined their place on the cultural landscape of the peninsula: architectural style had nothing to do with religion per se, but had become instead part of their own cultural world.

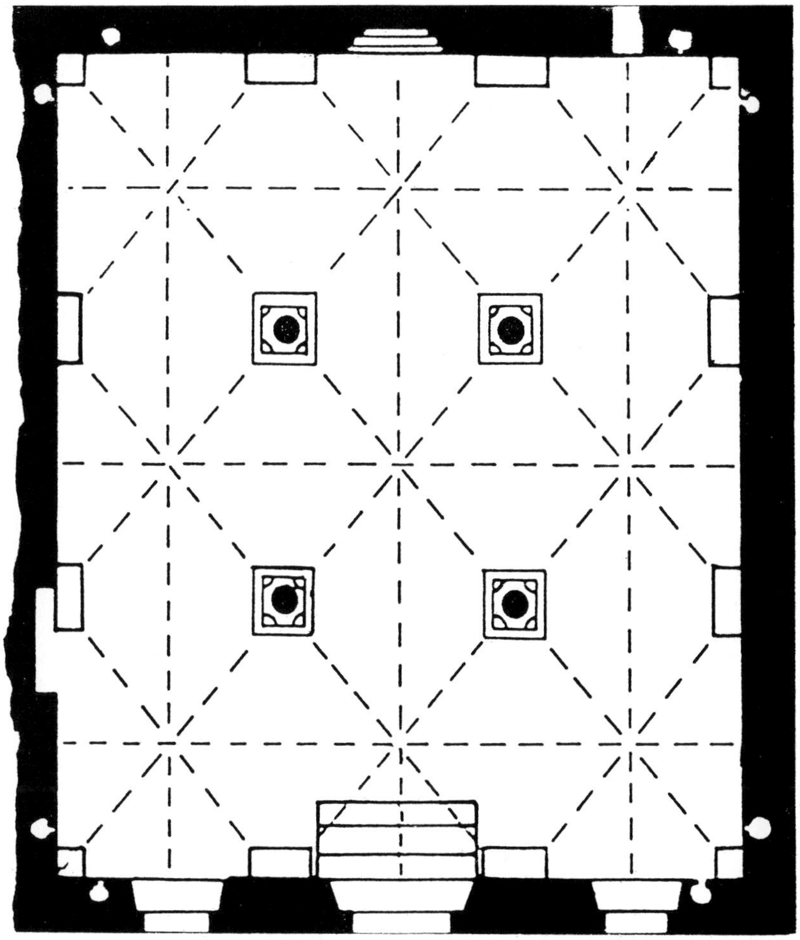

Though the synagogue of Tomar, in Portugal, is not linked by craft tradition or visual sympathy to the Mudejar synagogues described above, it presents an interesting analogy to them.[22] A nearly square prayer hall 9.5 by 8.2 meters, it is centrally planned around a square bay, enframed by four elegant stone columns with simple, abstract capitals. The building is vaulted by nine groin vaults that define nine bays in the building's interior [fig. 41].

Figure 41
Plan of the Synagogue of Tomar, Portugal, ca. 1460 (after Carol Krinsky, *Synagogues of Europe*)

Tomar is often dated to the fifteenth century, a unique monument of pre-expulsion Portugal. Though most scholarly efforts attempt to link it with Islamic craft traditions, its stone columns and capitals and its interior space and austere ornamental expression in stone point to a workshop steeped rather in the Christian tradition. What is extraordinary, then, is the fact that this Christian-oriented workshop built a synagogue in a plan typical of neighborhood mosques in Islam. The nine-bay plan is the standard type for a mosque built by a single individual to serve a small district; it is a plan known from Spain to Iran.[23] The open and dispersed space evokes the traditional prayer hall of a mosque more than any other building type that might have served as a model[24] [fig. 42].

It is moving to imagine that this elegant sanctuary might have been built on the eve of the expulsion by a people who saw their own artistic identity enmeshed with that of the Muslims who had for so long dominated the peninsula. The idea that the builders of Tomar might have wished to retain a connection with an Islamic building type, though craftsmen who might reproduce it were not available, is a tempting one. For it would pinpoint for us the extent to which Islamic architectural style—not just the inheritance of a craft tradition—had become part and parcel of Jewish identity on the Iberian peninsula.

Figure 42
Interior of the Synagogue of Tomar, Portugal, ca. 1460

NOTES

1. See Jerrilynn D. Dodds, *Architecture and Ideology in Medieval Spain* (University Park, Pa., and London, 1991), chapter 3.

2. G.M. Borras Gualis, *Arte mudéjar aragonés* (Zaragoza, 1978), 20.

3. Thomas F. Glick, *Islamic and Christian Spain in the Early Middle Ages* (Princeton, N.J., 1979); Glick and Oriol Pi-Sunyer, "Acculturation as an Explanatory Concept in Spanish History," *Comparative Studies in Society and History* 11 (1969): 136-54.

4. See J. Camarasa, "La sinagoga de Santa Maria la Blanca debe ser declarada monumento nacional," *Toledo, Revista de Arte,* 14 (1926): 2022-27; Rodrigo Amador de los Ríos, *Toledo,* (Madrid, 1905), 269-85.

5. C.H. Krinsky, *Synagogues of Europe: Architecture, History, Meaning* (New York and Cambridge, 1985), 332.

6. O. Czekelius, "Antiquas sinagogas de España," *Arquitectura* 13, no. 150 (October 1931), 327-41; R. Wischnitzer, *The Architecture of the European Synagogue* (Philadelphia, 1964), 24-25.

7. Krinsky, *Synagogues of Europe,* 334.

8. See Francisco Cantera Burgos, *Sinagogas españolas,* 2d ed. (Madrid, 1984), 290; C. de Lecea, *La iglesia del Corpus Christi de Segovia, antigua sinagoga* (Segovia, 1900); Rodrigo Amador de los Ríos, *Toledo* (Madrid, 1905), 273-77; Dan Halperin, *Ancient Synagogues of the Iberian Peninsula* (Gainesville, Fl., 1969), 43-46.

9. Krinsky, *Synagogues of Europe,* 333; see also J. Pinkerfield, *The Synagogues of North Africa* (Jerusalem, 1974), 5-8 (Hebrew).

10. Antoine Fattal, *Le statut legal des non-Musulmans en pays d'Islam* (Beirut, 1958), 69, 174-211; A.B. Tritton, *The Caliphs and their Non-Muslim Subjects* (London, 1930), 5-17; C.E. Bosworth, "The Concept of *Dhimma* in Early Islam," in *Christians and Jews in the Ottoman Empire,* ed. Benjamin Braude and Bernard Lewis, 2 vols. (New York, 1982), 1: 46-47.

11. Joseph F. O'Callaghan, *A History of Medieval Spain* (Ithaca, N.Y., 1975), 177. See also the essay by Raymond Scheindlin in this volume.

12. See O'Callaghan, *History of Medieval Spain,* 286, citing Ibnᶜdhariv, *Al-Bayan al-Mughrib,* Book 1: 204.

13. The Umayyads did insist on this visual separation in clothing with the Mozarabs, or Christians. See Dodds, *Architecture and Ideology,* chapter 3.

14. See Cantera Burgos, *Sinagogas españolas,* 1-32.

15. Wischnitzer, *The Architecture of the European Synagogue,* 28.

16. Ibid., 30.

17. Ibid.

18. After the Jews were expelled from Spain in 1492, the synagogue became a Christian church and then an oratory dedicated to Nuestra Señora del Transito. See Cantera Burgos, *Sinagogas españolas,* 65-151; J. Krohn, "La Sinagoga del Transito," *Toledo;* 1928; B. Maldonado, "Un problema arquelógico en la sinagoga de El Transito," *Sefarad* 26 (1976): 141-44.

19. See Wischnitzer, *The Architecture of the European Synagogue,* 34.

20. Ibid., 35.

21. Ibid., 31.

22. See Krinsky, *Synagogues of Europe,* 339-40; Halperin, *Ancient Synagogues,* 33; F.A. García Teizeira, *A antiga sinagoga de Tomar* (Lisbon, 1925); J.M. Santos Simões, *Tomar e a sua juderia* (Tomar, 1943).

23. See L. Golombek, "Abbasid Mosque at Balkh," *Oriental Art* 15 (1969): 173-89, esp. pp. 188-89; L. Golvin, *Essai sur l'architecture religieuse musulmane, 3. L'architecture des "Grands Abbasides": La mosquée de ibn Tulun, L'architecture religieuse des Aghlabides* (Paris, 1974), 210-212; T. Allen, "Early Nine-Bay Mosques" (unpublished manuscript). See also Oleg Grabar, "The Earliest Islamic Commemorative Structures: Notes and Documents," *Ars Orientalis* 6 (1966): 10-11.

24. It diverges in possessing a slightly larger central bay, a characteristic that tends to remind one of Byzantine cross plans. However, this aspect of the plan is mitigated by the fact that the tall columns and high vaults emphasize the dispersed nature of the interior, rather than any centralizing quality.

איש הישר בעיניו יעשה

ויהי

איש אחד
מן הרמתים צופים
מהר אפרים ושמו
אלקנה בן ירחם בן אליהוא
בן תחו בן צוף אפרתי ולו שתי
נשים שם אחת חנה ושם השנית
פננה ויהי לפננה ילדים ולחנה אין
ילדים ועלה האיש
ההוא מעירו
מימים
ימימה להשתחות ולזבח ליהוה
צבאות בשלה ושם שני בני עלי חפני ופנחס
כהנים ליהוה ויהי היום ויזבח אלקנה ונתן לפננה
אשתו ולכל בניה ובנותיה מנות ולחנה יתן מנה אחת
אפים כי את חנה אהב ויהוה סגר רחמה וכעסתה צרתה
גם כעס בעבור הרעמה כי סגר יהוה בעד רחמה וכן יעשה
שנה בשנה מדי עלתה בית יהוה כן תכעסנה ותבכה ולא

תאכל ויאמר לה אלקנה
אישה חנה למה תבכי
ולמה לא תאכלי ולמה
ירע לבבך הלא אנכי טוב
לך מעשרה בנים ותקם חנה
אחרי אכלה בשלה ואחרי
שתה ועלי הכהן ישב על
הכסא על מזוזת היכל יהוה
והיא מרת נפש ותתפלל
על יהוה ובכה תבכה ותדר
נדר ותאמר יהוה צבאות
אם ראה תראה בעני אמתך
וזכרתני ולא תשכח את
אמתך ונתתה לאמתך זרע
אנשים ונתתיו ליהוה כל ימי
חייו ומורה לא יעלה על
ראשו והיה כי הרבתה
להתפלל לפני יהוה ועלי
שמר את פיה וחנה היא
מדברת על לבה רק שפתיה
נעות וקולה לא ישמע
ויחשבה עלי לשכרה
ויאמר אליה עלי עד מתי
תשתכרין הסירי את יינך
מעליך ותען חנה ותאמר
לא אדני אשה קשת רוח
אנכי ויין ושכר לא שתיתי
ואשפך את נפשי לפני יהוה
אל תתן את אמתך לפני בת
בליעל כי מרב שיחי וכעסי

Hebrew Illuminated Manuscripts from the Iberian Peninsula

Gabrielle Sed-Rajna

The flourishing civilization of the Jewish communities of the Iberian peninsula is one of the most glorious chapters in the history of the European diaspora. The beginnings, in the first centuries of our era, are only sporadically documented. The next ten centuries saw an ever-increasing cultural activity, in some periods accompanied by high social status and appreciable economic well-being. Until the last century preceding the expulsion, Jewish statesmen, scientists, physicians, philosophers, poets, and artists were respected members of society. The civilization of Sephardic Jewry was a tree in full bloom that was uprooted by the decree of 1492.

Little survives from almost ten centuries of cultural activity. One of the few witnesses that, although decimated through loss and destructions, still gives a faithful image of the wide range of cultural works that were produced is manuscripts, that is, handwritten books.

In the life of Jewish communities, the book had a special status. It was the only vehicle for safeguarding and transmitting the revealed Word, the Law, that throughout Jewish history has set the rules for devotion, moral behavior, and social and family life [fig. 43].[1] The book ensured the survival of the sacred language, the only language in the world that has survived for almost two thousand years without being protected by a state or belonging to a defined geographical area. Books also created links among communities of people scattered in far-off places, living in societies that were more or less hostile to the Jews. Produced at a moderate cost and easy to carry, the book was also the only piece of culture, the only witness to a golden age, that was taken into exile when the time came to leave. Of the many Hebrew manuscripts produced in Spain that have survived, almost none is at present to be found in the peninsula. The book was the unfailing companion that could not be left behind.

Figure 43 *(opposite)*
Hebrew Bible, Castile (?), late 15th century, The Royal Library, Copenhagen, Cod. Heb. V, fol. 91r (cat. no. 12)

Manuscripts also offered a preeminent field for meeting aesthetic needs. Profeit Duran, physician, philosopher, and astrologer at the court of John I of Aragon at the beginning of the fourteenth century, wrote in a grammatical treatise entitled *Ma'aseh Efod*:

> ...study should always be in beautiful and pleasant books, containing harmonious script written on fine vellum, and with luxurious bindings, and should be carried on in pleasant buildings; for the beholding and study of beautiful forms with delicate drawing and fine painting is one of those things that please the soul, urges on and strengthens its powers. It has therefore been to the perfection of our nation that the wealthy and prominent in every generation have always exerted an effort in the production of beautiful codices (author's translation).

In the ornamentation of Hebrew manuscripts, the most important element is the script itself. The carefully drawn strokes, the harmonious shape of the letters, the juxtaposition of scripts of different dimensions constitute the multiple facets of an ever-varying decoration [fig. 44]. Minute script, known as micrography, was used to outline various ornamental motifs or to fill entire pages with abstract figures, making them similar to painted carpets—hence their name, "carpet pages" [fig. 45]. Titles and chapter headings were written in large letters, the strokes of which were adorned with animal and human forms, zoomorphic motifs, or scrolls; the strokes were often surrounded by floral outlines or filigree penwork. As no capitals are used in Hebrew script, it was the entire first word, or first line, that was enhanced by one or the other of these techniques. Besides having an aesthetic function, this method of decoration was also a way to emphasize the intellectual articulations of the text through visual means.

Figure 44
Prayer Book for Daily Use and Festivals, Spain, 15th century, Courtesy of The Library of the Jewish Theological Seminary of America, New York, Mic. 4366, fols. 41v-42r (cat. no. 18)

Ornamental script was not, however, the only way in which the text was embellished. Illumination, besides its aesthetic function, also expounded the symbolic meaning of a text, or gave visual form to the stories of the Bible, or helped elucidate a scientific treatise. By the fourteenth and fifteenth centuries, Hebrew manuscript painting encompassed a wide range of productions that by their quality, if not by their quantity in the absence of state or church patronage, had their well-established place in the artistic life of the peninsula. These works of art also bear witness to exchange and actual collaboration between Jewish and Christian

Figure 45

Abravanel Pentateuch, Castile (?), 1480, The Bodleian Library, University of Oxford, Oxford, Opp. Add. 4°26, fol. 238v (cat. no. 11)

artists, even during periods when political forces tried to create—and finally succeeded in creating—deep antagonisms between communities.

THE THIRTEENTH CENTURY: CASTILE

The earliest Hebrew manuscripts copied and illuminated in Spain were produced in Toledo, the political and cultural center of the Castilian kingdom. Already in the reign of Ferdinand II (1217-52), and above all during that of Alfonso X, the Wise (1252-85), Jews played an important role in the administration of the kingdom and the settlement of reconquered territories. They also participated in the cultural activities of Toledo, where scholars were involved in the translation of scientific and philosophical works from Arabic into Latin, Castilian, and Hebrew. The city was one of the most important centers for the transmission of the intellectual heritage of late classical times to the medieval Latin West. It can be assumed that among the texts imported from the East were also Hebrew biblical manuscripts and philosophical as well as ritual works, which were used as models for local production, starting at the end of the twelfth century.

The majority of the earliest codices were Bibles executed for home use to the order of wealthy patrons. Bibles from Toledo have specific features that appear at every level of production: the composition of the quires, the layout of the text, and even the adoption of the Palestinian system of *sedarim* for weekly readings, instead of the *parshiyot* used in most Western centers since the twelfth century. The only decoration of these early Bibles is provided by the beauty of the script. Illumination appears about the middle of the thirteenth century.

The first codex adorned in color is a four-volume Bible copied by the scribe Isaac ben Israel. The first volume, containing the Pentateuch, is at present lost. The three other volumes, separated in the course of time, arrived at an unknown date in Marseille (the Former Prophets and the Hagiographa: Municipal Library, Ms. 1626, II and III), and in St. Petersburg (Latter Prophets: Public Library, Ms. II 53).[2] The volume of the Former Prophets includes a precious historical record that allows us to follow the history of this Bible up to the sixteenth century. In an inscription on fol. 2v, Moses Cordovero, the renowned theologian and kabbalist, at that time president of the *bēt dīn* (rabbinical court) of Safed, discusses a will dividing the contents of a library between two brothers. The four-volume Bible copied by Isaac ben Israel—which at that date (1562) seems to have been still complete—is one of the items mentioned in the will.

Isaac ben Israel was a member of a family of scribes that is known to have been active for at least three generations. Besides manuscripts copied and signed by different members of the family, archival documents are extant that mention their names between the years 1236 and 1292.[3] A tombstone, dated 1303, mentions the name of "Israel the scribe." These documents show that in Jewish society the craft of copying was a family tradition, handed down from father to son.

The illumination of Isaac ben Israel's Bible consists of carpet pages placed at the beginning and end of the volumes; they function as an inner binding, protecting the text. The paintings are composed of symmetrical scrolls bearing palmetto leaves or floral buds outlined by a gold fillet and by lines of micrography set off against a light colored ground.

Style and composition clearly show Islamic features [fig. 46]. The basic pattern of symmetrical scrolls bearing palmetto leaves is widely used

Figure 46
Hebrew Bible, Castile (?), late 15th century, The Royal Library, Copenhagen, Cod. Heb. VII, fol. 65 (cat. no. 13)

Figure 47
Hebrew Bible, Perpignan (?), Kingdom of Majorca, 1301, The Royal Library, Copenhagen, Cod. Heb. II, fol. 12r (cat. no. 5)

in different media in Islamic art.[4] It appears on the carved wood panels of the Aqsa mosque in Jerusalem (705-15), among the mosaics adorning the Ummayyad mosque of Damascus, and on stucco panels of the al-Qaṣr al-Ḥayr al-Gharbī in Syria (724-27). Following the route of the Arab conquest of North Africa, the pattern appears on the carved marble panels of the *miḥrāb* of Kairouan from the ninth century, and arrives with the Umayyad conquest on the Iberian peninsula. Isaac ben Israel's Bible is the only example of a pictorial use of this pattern. It is, however, probable that the transfer of the pattern to a two-dimensional rendering had already taken place in the model used by the makers of the Toledo Bible, which may have been imported from the Middle East along with other manuscripts. The Toledo Bible itself served as a model for some other Hebrew manuscripts: a Bible copied in Burgos in 1260 (Jerusalem, Jewish National and University Library, Ms. Heb. 4°790), and a codex of which only two leaves have been preserved in a late fifteenth-century manuscript (Copenhagen, Royal Library, Cod. Hebr. IX).

The Oriental origins of Jewish decorative traditions in Spain are also perceptible in another group of Castilian Bibles from Toledo. The earliest of them, dated 1277, is signed by one Hayyim ben Israel, a member of the same family of professional scribes discussed above (Parma, Biblioteca palatina, Ms. Parm. 2668). An illumination on two opposite pages preceding the biblical text depicts the Temple implements: the menorah, the shewbread table, the altar of burnt offerings, and the incense altar, as well as smaller objects: jars, cups, and trumpets. Their shapes follow as closely as possible the descriptions in Exodus 25-30. Names are inscribed next to each object. This depiction has a symbolic meaning: it reminds the viewer that since the destruction of the sanctuary, scripture has been the only vehicle of tradition, the living witness to the revealed Word and the substitute for the lost Temple. The style as well as the composition of the paintings present purely Islamic features. The flat representation of objects, the avoidance of all devices that would create an illusion of space or volume, the geometrical division of the page, and the use of gold as the sole color against a plain parchment ground are among the most characteristic elements of book illumination in the Middle East.

The double-page composition of Temple implements became an often repeated element in Hebrew Bibles produced in Castile and Catalonia for almost two hundred years. The Islamic stylistic features, still prevailing at the end of the thirteenth century, were later superseded by a pictorial language adopted from contemporary Gothic art. The change is attested to for the first time in a Bible copied in 1301 at Perpignan, at that time part of the Kingdom of Aragon (Copenhagen, Royal Library, Cod. Hebr. II) [fig. 47]. Its composition follows the model of the Toledo Bibles, with the one difference that the parchment background is replaced by a red and blue chequered ground, according to the scheme of Gothic paintings. Adaptation to contemporary fashion went on for several decades, but only the style was updated, the symbolic composition and its message were carefully preserved. The Perpignan Bible of Copenhagen is a rare and precious record: it is witness to the turning point when Jewish iconography, which employed Islamic means of representation, starts a process of acclimatization to a new cultural environment. The process itself is a frequent phenomenon in the history of art; it is less frequent, indeed even exceptional, that a single work of art should embody its precise beginning.

THE FOURTEENTH CENTURY: ARAGON, NAVARRE, CATALONIA

The art of Hebrew manuscript illumination on the Iberian peninsula attained its fullest development around the forties to sixties of the fourteenth century. The works reflect an openness toward local culture, contact with Christian artists, an enlarged repertoire, and new inspiration from surrounding works of art. For example, in his Bibles the scribe-artist Joshua ibn Gaon used ornamentation borrowed from buildings in Tudela where he had once worked.[5] Some of his arcaded pages are exquisite pictorial transpositions of the lace-like decoration of the *taifa* castle Aljaferiya in Saragossa.

Jewish scribes became more than simple craftsmen entrusted with the material realization of a codex. The same Joshua ibn Gaon appended to one of the Bibles he copied a visual docu-

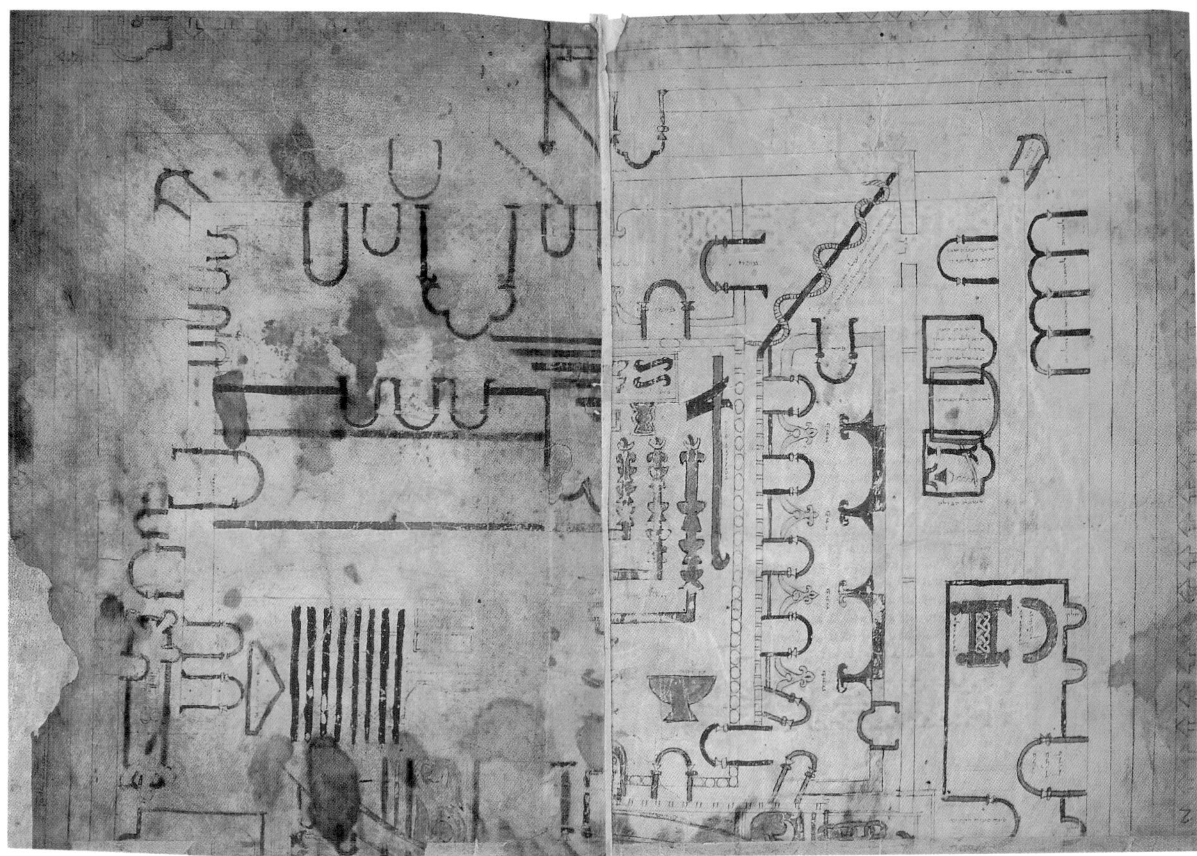

Figure 48
The plan of the Temple, Second Kennicott Bible, Soria, Old Castile, 1306, The Bodleian Library, University of Oxford, Oxford, Bodl. Ms. Kenn. 2, fols. 1v-2r (cat. no. 6)

ment expounding the Temple as described in the tractate *Middot* of the Mishna (Oxford, Bodleian Library, Ms. Kennicott 2) [fig. 48]. His brother, Shem Tov ibn Gaon, a professional scribe himself who copied a Bible called the *Keter Shem Tov* in 1312 (Carl Alexander Floersheim Trust for Art and Judaica) [fig. 49], is also known as the author of a learned commentary, *Migdal ᶜOz*, based on Nahmanides' commentary on the Torah, and a commentary on Maimonides' *Mishneh Torah*.

Around the middle of the century, workshops producing both Latin and Hebrew manuscripts existed in Barcelona. The most renowned of them, the workshop of the "Master of San Marco," was identified by Millard Meiss. In a famous study, Meiss analyzed the works attributed to the shop including the retable, the painting behind the altar, devoted to Saint Mark from the cathedral of Manresa, which gave its name to the workshop.[6] Among its productions are important Latin manuscripts such as the Anglo-Catalan Psalter (Paris, Bibliothèque Nationale, lat. 8846), a legal work from Barcelona called the *Llibre Verd* (Barcelona, Archivo Historico) and, as Francis Wormald pointed out many years ago, the famous illustrated copy of Maimonides' *Guide of the Perplexed* (Copenhagen, Royal Library,

Cod. Hebr. XXXVII) [fig. 50].[7] This last codex was copied by Levi ben Isaac Hiyo Caro of Salamanca for the learned physician Menaḥem Bezalel of Barcelona in 1348. It is the only dated manuscript of the group.

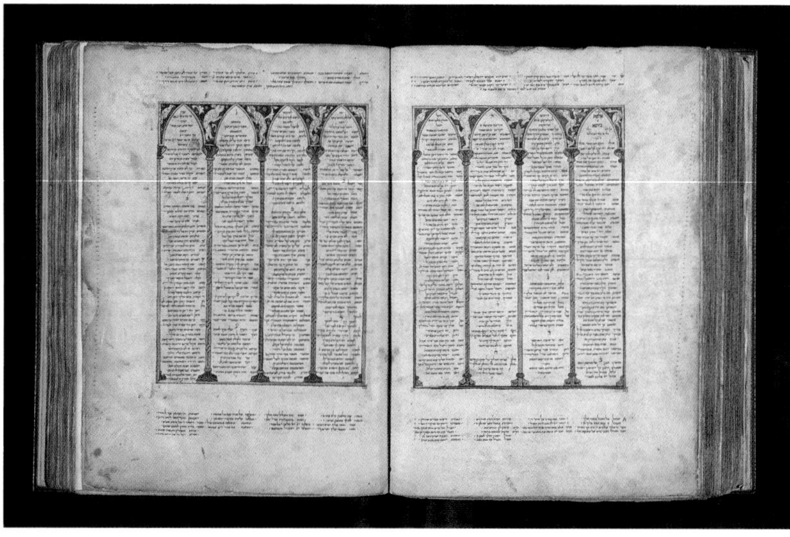

Figure 49 *(above)* *Keter Shem Tov,* Soria, Old Castile, 1312, fols. 502v–503r, Carl Alexander Floersheim Trust for Art and Judaica (cat. no. 7)

Besides floral ornaments within the text, the Maimonides codex has four full-page miniatures. The first two are at present almost entirely faded. The second part of the book, Maimonides' teachings on cosmology, is preceded by a miniature representing a lecture on astrology. Part three, Maimonides' metaphysics, is introduced by the symbols of the four *ḥayot* (beasts) of Ezekiel's vision (Ezek. 1) [fig. 51]. The style of these paintings is closely related to that of the Anglo-Catalan Psalter and the Barcelona *Llibre Verd* and attests to the strong Sienese influence present in all the works of the shop. This influence is attributed to the painter Ferrer Bassa who, along with his son Arnau, was the leading artist of the atelier.[8] The colophon of the Hebrew codex, however, does not mention the name of the artist. The full harmony between the content of the work and the subjects of its miniatures may indicate that the artist planning them was fully aware of the text and that he may have been Jewish. Several other Hebrew manuscripts are related to the output of the workshop, among them another copy of Maimonides' *Guide*[9] and a compendium of Galen's medical treatises (Paris, Bibliothèque Nationale, hébreu 1203).[10] The scrolls and thistle leaves enlivened by gold dots and birds of various species that are the typical ornaments of these codices also decorate a Bible from Barcelona, copied around 1360 to 1380, the Foa Bible.[11]

During the fourteenth century, the increasing production of Hebrew manuscripts offered new possibilities and stimulation to the art of miniature painting. Collections of *piyyutim* (liturgical poems), prayer books, and medical treatises were all produced with technically flawless ornament; scientific treatises were presented with diagrams that allowed a better understanding of the text. It is also during the fourteenth century that the most revolutionary innovation in the art of Hebrew manuscript illumination appeared: the emergence of narrative art.

Figure 50 *(opposite)* A Scientist teaching with an astrolabe, Maimonides, *Guide to the Perplexed,* Barcelona, 1348, The Royal Library, Copenhagen, Cod. Heb. XXXVII, fol. 114r (cat. no. 25)

The first attempts to create text illustrations appear in Joshua ibn Gaon's Bible of 1300.[12] The artist dismantled the traditional composition of Temple implements and juxtaposed the individual elements to the passages of Exodus where they are described. At the same time he enriched the repertoire with some new subjects, carefully avoiding the representation of human protagonists. Events are hinted at by signs and symbols, rather than really illustrated by full narrative scenes. Yet, however discreet this first attempt may have been, the intention to illustrate was clearly indicated. A further and decisive stimulus appeared around the middle of the thirteenth century with the production of a new type of manuscript, the prayer book for the Passover seder, the Haggadah.

Figure 51
The Four Beasts, Maimonides, *Guide to the Perplexed,* Barcelona, 1348, The Royal Library, Copenhagen, Cod. Heb. XXXVII, fol. 202r (cat. no. 25)

The text of the Haggadah is composed of prayers, liturgical poems, hymns of praise, and didactical parables, some of which were composed as early as the second or third centuries C.E. It was only in the eighth century, however, that a normative text was established in the Babylonian academies at Sura and Pumbedita. During the tenth and eleventh centuries, this text spread all over the European diaspora where, except for minor regional variations, an authoritative version came to be used.

Once the text was established, the tendency was to copy it as an autonomous book, and this book was an attractive field for decoration. Destined for home use only as part of a festive ceremony that was also meant for the instruction of children, not very voluminous and hence not too expensive to produce, the illustrated Haggadah soon became a popular work. The program of decoration and illustration is different in Sephardic and Ashkenazic Haggadoth, at least as far as the coordination of the images is concerned. Spanish Haggadoth are provided with two different types of illustrations. Images illustrating the ritual of the seder [fig.

Figure 52 *(above)*
Seder scene, Prato Haggadah, Spain, ca. 1300, Courtesy of The Library of The Jewish Theological Seminary of America, New York, Mic. 9478, fols. 35v-36r (cat. no. 20)

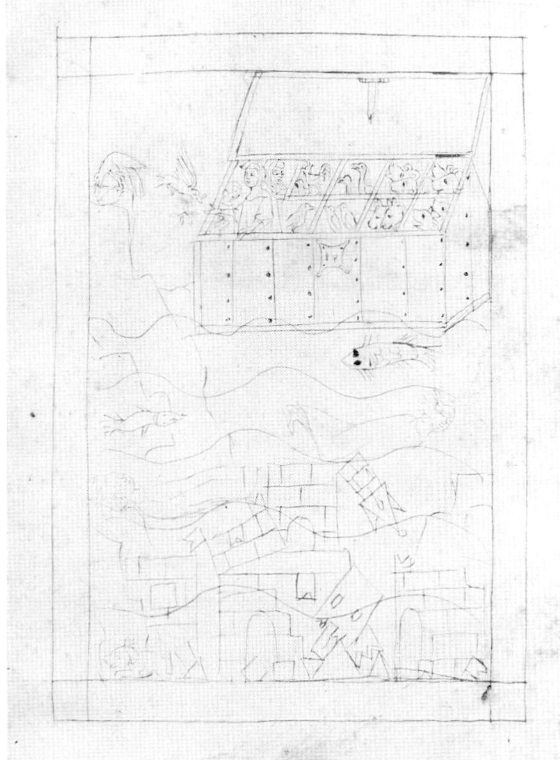

Figure 53 *(right)*
The Flood: the dove landing on dry land, Prato Haggadah, Spain, ca. 1300. Courtesy of The Library of the Jewish Theological Seminary of America, New York, Mic. 9478, fol. 84r (cat. no. 20)

52], or the didactic parables of the text, or the portraits of rabbis whose sayings are quoted, are placed within the text column or in the margin next to the relevant account. The basic feature of these images is their direct relationship to the text they illustrate. The close interdependence between the written account and the visual commentary clearly indicates that this iconography was created ad hoc, for the very purpose of illustrating this text. In the course of time a steady program evolved that was copied from manuscript to manuscript with only minor variants. The role of this imagery was not merely to enchant the eye of the reader, but also served correctly to transmit rites and gestures. For later generations these genre scenes provide precious visual records of the life and customs of Jews in the Middle Ages.

The illustrations of the second type, those to which the Sephardic Haggadoth owe their fame, are biblical images appended to the service book. Painted on independent quires, on two opposite pages (as only the flesh side of the parchment was fit to be used for paintings), the biblical cycles display episodes of sacred history in consecutive sets. Some of them start with the creation of the world or of man and follow the course of the story up to the crossing of the Red Sea [fig. 53]. In one case, the Sarajevo Haggadah,[13] the visual narrative continues up to the end of the Pentateuch. Other examples have an abridged version, from Moses' birth to the departure from Egypt. In contrast to the first type of images, which are basically visual commentaries on the text, the striking feature of this second type of illustrations is the total lack of relationship to the text or the Passover ritual. The episodes depicted are ignored in the text; the names of the protagonists—Noah, Lot, and Joseph, among others—are not even mentioned, their life stories are not even alluded to. Considering the criteria established by Kurt Weitzmann to investigate the "archaeology of the image,"[14] this absence of relation between the illustrations and the Haggadah in which they appear leads to the unavoidable conclusion that these biblical illustrations were created for another text and transferred to the Haggadoth at the time when these luxurious books were produced.

The origins of these biblical images have caused many debates and the issue is still open. It has been proposed that medieval Psalters, often provided with an introductory set of biblical images, were models for the Haggadoth. There is little doubt that the fashionable private Psalters produced in the thirteenth century offered an attractive pattern for the organization of the book [fig. 54]. But these Latin manuscripts provided the model only for the framework. The selection of the episodes and even their iconography is quite different in the Psalters and in the Hebrew codices. The latter have a much wider range of images and reflect a different approach. Latin Psalter illustrations single out episodes considered as the highlights of the story of salvation and Old Testament scenes are chosen only for their possible typological interpretations. In contrast to this theologically oriented selection, Haggadah illustrations depict episodes in a chronological order, ignoring all doctrinal implications. It is plain narration that runs like a comic strip without any differentiation, each episode having equal status. It might have been expected that the Exo-

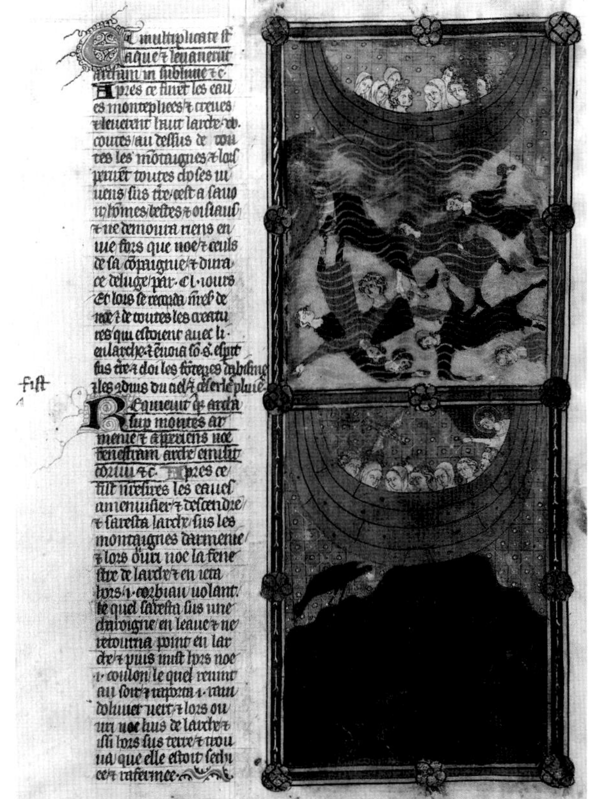

Figure 54
Flood scenes, *Bible Historiée et Vies des Saints,* ca. 1300, France, Spencer Collection, The New York Public Library, Astor, Lenox, and Tilden Foundations, New York, Ms. 22, fol. 11v (cat. no. 8)

dus cycles, at least, would be composed in a way that underscored the relationship between images and text since the Passover ritual refers to the same text. This, however, is not the case. Whereas the ritual evokes the history of the Exodus only by allusion, by means of mnemonic formulae, or in a symbolic language, the pictures give a full account of Moses' life and follow the story episode by episode, clinging faithfully to the biblical narrative. The Exodus cycles, like the Genesis cycles, reflect a mentality to which the doctrinally influenced Psalter illustrations, as well as the poetic and symbolic language of the Passover ritual, are alien.

Only a few Passover Haggadoth with biblical illustrations survive. All of them except two differ in style and none can be considered as having been the model of another, the selection of episodes being different in each cycle. Among the manuscripts that have Genesis and Exodus cycles are the Golden Haggadah from about 1310-20 [fig. 55],[15] the Catalan Haggadah produced around 1330,[16] and the Sarajevo Haggadah, which may date from about 1340.[17]

Figure 55
From right to left, top to bottom: Moses before the burning bush; Moses taking his family back to Egypt and meeting with Aaron; Moses and Aaron before the Elders of Israel; and Moses and Aaron before Pharaoh. Golden *Haggadah,* Barcelona, ca. 1320. By permission of The British Library, London, Add. 27210, fol. 10v

Three manuscripts have Exodus cycles only: the Kaufmann Haggadah, the main parts of which were executed probably not earlier than 1360-70;[18] the Rylands Haggadah [fig. 56],[19] and Or. Ms. 1404 of the British Library,[20] both around 1340-50. (The latter two manuscripts are stylistically related.) All of these manuscripts were probably produced in Catalonia, although their exact provenance cannot be given with any precision.

The manuscripts are the work of different artists, all differ in style, and no two present an identical selection of episodes. The most conspicuous common feature is the presence of episodes referring not to the biblical text but to legendary episodes found in midrashic compilations and in the Aramaic Targum, mainly the version known as the Targum of Pseudo-Jonathan. Many of these midrashic and targumic additions coincide in the different manuscripts, or at least in part of them. The abundant literature devoted to these midrashic illustrations allows us to mention only the most famous ones: Abraham thrown into the fiery furnace, the raven sent out by Noah resting on the drowned corpses, Joseph's coffin lowered into the Nile, and Moses rescued from the river by Pharaoh's daughter.[21] Further common features are iconographic formulae: Adam in paradise naming the animals, Eve emerging from Adam's side (instead of being created from a rib), which is based on a textual variant, and Potiphar's wife in bed attempting to seduce Joseph. A special reading of the Hebrew version is behind the representation of the fourth plague of Egypt as one of wild beasts instead of flies as in the Greek translation, the Septuagint. Besides these common iconographical formulae, from which only a few examples have been given, there are also some technical devices that appear in most of the cycles such as the separation of juxtaposed episodes by a tree, or the conflation of two or more episodes into a single representation, for example, the temptation of Adam and Eve.

Figure 56

Top: Moses before the burning bush; bottom: Moses and the serpent. Rylands Haggadah, Catalonia, mid-14th century, John Rylands Library, Manchester, Heb. 6, fol. 13v

Despite these common features, the fact that the selection of subjects, and in many cases the iconography as well, differ from one cycle to the other obliges one to exclude the possibility that any of the extant manuscripts is the copy of another. The common features can only hark back to common models—probably not one, but several parallel recensions—that were available in fourteenth-century Catalonia.

It necessarily follows from this analysis that any attempt to understand the origins of the Haggadah illustrations has to focus on the nature of these models. Three main questions that they raise are: where were they created, at what period, and for what purpose?

It should be stressed from the start that the investigation of the origins of these illustrations does not involve a search for the earliest evidence of a single biblical representation as it appeared in early synagogues, catacombs, or churches. The aim of the search is to identify when and where, and in what surroundings, narrative sequences illustrating biblical stories were conceived and materialized in cyclical images.

Since the discovery of the Dura Europos synagogue,[22] irrefutable evidence, owed to the almost miraculous survival of its wall paintings, proves that as early as the third century C.E. biblical illustrations were available and used in the cult building of a Jewish community [fig. 57]. But the paintings themselves were already a second or third stage in the history of biblical illustrations. The prayer hall of the synagogue displays a complex doctrinal program[23] destined to recall basic topics of Jewish theology, as well as interpretations of Scripture inspired by current concerns. It is a mosaic of elements assembled according to an elaborate underlying conceptual program, which means that the components chosen for the compositions were already extant. It must also be supposed that the repertoire from which these components were selected was far more extensive than what was actually used for the frescoes. Kurt Weitzmann's internal analysis of the frescoes has convincingly demonstrated that the most likely form in which such a repertoire of images may have first existed was text illustration. Evidence known from the Hellenistic period and from later Christian manuscripts shows that the genesis of narrative art is intimately linked to the intention to visualize a written account as faithfully as possible, and usually these visual elements are situated physically close to the text they illustrate. Whether the paintings of the Dura synagogue were planned with the help of such text illustrations, or whether they copy another major composition in which the transfer from text illustration has already been achieved, cannot be known. In either case they provide proof of the existence of biblical narrative illustrations at the beginning of the third, and possibly the end of the second, century.

Figure 57
Interior of Dura Europos Synagogue, North east corner (as rebuilt in the Damascus Museum), before 256 C.E.

Scholars are unanimous in considering it improbable that a provincial city like Dura, on a remote frontier of the Roman Empire, would have been the place of origin of such a far-reaching creation. Among the major cultural centers that have been considered are Alexandria, Antioch, and Palestine.[24] Each was a flourishing cultural center during the first centuries of the common era; in each there was a highly active Jewish community living on fairly good terms, for a while at least, with the Christian community; and in all three, Hellenistic culture with its strong inclination toward the visual arts was solidly implanted. There are only theories and sporadic archaeological evidence to support any of the propositions. The answer to this question—supposing that there is one, and only one—is intimately linked to what is the very heart of the problem: what were the texts that were first produced in illustrated editions? It goes without saying that the possibility of an illustrated Torah scroll has to be ruled out from the start; halakhic prescriptions prohibit the slightest ornament, even the use of gold ink for the script. But the Greek version of the Bible, the Septuagint, which was used by Alexandrian Jews from the third century B.C.E. on, and later became the authoritative text for Christians, was not included in this prohibition. This is one of the reasons why Kurt Weitzmann long favored Alexandria as the center where biblical iconography could have started. The Septuagint, however, was not the only noncanonical version of biblical texts. Long before an authoritative Hebrew recension was established, literary works based on the Bible, but enlarged by legendary material, were transmitted orally for an undetermined period and may have been written down during the last centuries B.C.E. to the first centuries of our era. They were compiled as historiated Bibles (*Bibles historiales*), containing some parts of Scripture with abundant secondary material integrated into the narrative. Many of these texts are still preserved, though not in their original form but mostly in Greek or Latin versions. Called the "biblical pseudepigrapha," most are considered to be of Jewish origin. They may have been written down in Palestine, perhaps in Hebrew or Aramaic. The Targum itself, especially the version known as the Targum of Pseudo-Jonathan, belongs to this literary genre and there is a strong probability that some of the midrashic compilations known today through late redactions were originally a similar type of literature. For the question of the origins of biblical iconography these texts are of major interest. Much of the legendary material integrated into these writings found its way into images. The relation between text and image is straightforward. Moreover, the specific narrative trend so conspicuous in this literature is also reflected in the images of Dura and in the later biblical cycles. The Targum, the *Pirqe Rabbi Eliezer* (or rather the sources used in this late compilation), the Apocalypse of Baruch, the Fourth Book of Esdras, and the Book of Jubilees, all contain elements that allow a clearer approach to the Dura paintings.[25] Perhaps none of the known texts was the one used for the iconography, but surely this is the literature in which it was rooted. And this literature also left its mark on the biblical illustrations of the Haggadoth.

The lack of archaeological evidence tends to turn any attempt to establish a link between the biblical cycles of the Haggadoth and the Dura paintings, or rather their sources, into a daring abstract elaboration. The eleven centuries that separate them are, on the Jewish side, totally devoid of any document that could at least partly fill the gap. But there is important evidence in Christian art that bears witness to the transmission of narrative art, and these works provide the missing links and allow one to trace the route along which this iconography spread to the West. Studies devoted to the Cotton Genesis, the Vienna Genesis, the Christian Iconography of Cosmas Indicopleustes, the Octateuchs, and the Salerno Ivories[26] have brought overwhelming arguments for a direct connection between the illustrations of these works and Jewish sources, and, for some of them, a relationship to the paintings of the Dura synagogue.[27] These works of art also help to understand the history of the biblical images of the Haggadoth.

I have demonstrated elsewhere that complex relations can be traced between the iconography of individual scenes of the Haggadah cycles and illustrations in Late Antique Christian manuscripts.[28] The Christian works of art belong to two great recensions, the Cotton Genesis tradition and that of the Octateuchs. The Haggadoth do not belong clearly to either, but include elements of both. Some of the manuscripts have a preponderant affinity to one or the other recension. For example, the Sarajevo Haggadah is mainly related to the tradition of the Octateuchs. Yet, some of its illustrations are similar in iconography to the pen drawings of the twelfth-century Millstatt Genesis, which belong to the Cotton Genesis recension.[29] Other images of the Sarajevo Haggadah reflect a tradition that may predate the crystallization in parallel recensions. An example of the latter is Jacob's dream, which is represented in a similar way in the eleventh-century Octateuch (Vatican Library, gr. 747, fol. 50r), on the Salerno ivory plaques, and in the Millstatt Genesis.[30] This iconography appears already in the Dura synagogue and it is also used in the Via Latina Catacomb.[31] It seems, therefore, that some elements of the Haggadah cycle descend from models that derive directly from a now lost archetype.

The analysis of the Catalan Haggadah leads to a similar conclusion. Although this manuscript reflects mainly the Cotton Genesis recension, relationships to the Octateuch illustrations (e.g. Creation of Eve) or to the Salerno Ivories (Noah building the ark) can also be traced.[32] The supposition that the painters who were in charge of the Haggadah illustrations knew these Christian works of art is quite improbable. The only hypothesis that would offer a plausible answer to the complex problems raised by the Jewish picture cycles is the presence in fourteenth-century Spain of an iconographic tradition of Bible illustrations that derived from an archetype preceding the differentiation into parallel recensions.

The presence, several centuries before the creation of the Haggadah cycles, of specific traditions of biblical imagery on the peninsula is attested to by works such as the seventh-century Ashburnham Pentateuch[33] or the León Bible of 960, which is supposed to be a copy of an earlier, lost prototype.[34] In both of these manuscripts iconography and style reflect Near Eastern models. This hypothesis would also account for the unusual, midrash-influenced illustrations of the twelfth-century Pamplona Bibles.[35]

The route along which this tradition spread was probably through southern Italy, Sicily and/or North Africa to the southern part of the peninsula and, after the Reconquest, to the northern kingdoms. Whether a specific Jewish tradition, transmitted within the Jewish communities of the southern European centers, did exist has to remain an open question. The possibility cannot be ruled out, as the influence of these traditions is sporadically attested to also in northern European Ashkenazic manuscripts.[36]

None of the extant Haggadah manuscripts was produced later than the 1360s. Whether the evidence at hand is a mere accident of history or production was abandoned cannot be determined. It is, however, certain that the Jewish community flourished for several more decades. Physicians, scientists, scribes, and cartographers were respected members of society. One of the most famous maps of the world, now in the collection of the Bibliothèque Nationale in Paris (Ms. esp. 30) is the work of Abraham Crescas, cartographer at the court of John I, and the map may be the one offered by John to the king of France in 1375.[37] Another member of the Crescas family copied and decorated the famous Farhi Bible, formerly in the collection of the late David Sassoon (Ms. 368).[38]

THE FIFTEENTH CENTURY; CATALONIA, CASTILE, LEON, ASTURIAS, PORTUGAL

It is only in the fifteenth century that the increasing pressure of political troubles came to weigh heavily on cultural life. Yet, there are some outstanding works produced during the fifteenth century. Among these, the so-called *Biblia de Alba* deserves special attention.[39] Commissioned by the grand master of the Order of Calatrava, Don Luis Guzmán, the manuscript offers an improved translation into Castilian of the Hebrew Bible. The translation was entrusted to Rabbi Moses Arragel who worked under the supervision of a Franciscan friar. A long introduction, written by the learned rabbi, gives an account of the negotiations that preceded the execution of the work, and the hesitations of the rabbi, who

Figure 58 *(opposite)*
First Kennicott Bible, La Coruña, 1476, The Bodleian Library, University of Oxford, Oxford, Bodl. Kenn. I, fol. 120v

was for a long time reluctant to take on the responsibility. Moses Arragel accompanied the biblical text with commentaries and illustrations. The commentaries are a compendium of Jewish and Christian exegetical teachings commented on by the rabbi himself. This part of the work is the most astonishing, attesting to the vast culture of the author as well as the freedom he took to discuss delicate doctrinal issues, insisting on the differences between Jewish and Christian interpretations. The more than three hundred illustrations were not executed by Moses Arragel himself, but apparently he took part in their planning as the illustrations of the Pentateuch are often based on midrashic elements.[40]

Figure 59
Carpet Page, Lisbon Bible, Lisbon, 1482, By permission of The British Library, London, Or. 2626-2628, vol. III, fol. 185r

Delicately ornamented prayer books and lavishly decorated biblical manuscripts were still produced in the fifteenth century. Technically, manuscript illumination was at its zenith, but as far as Jewish manuscripts are concerned, creativity declined. A typical work exemplifying this dichotomy between technical skill and genuine creativity is the famous Kennicott Bible in the Bodleian Library (Ms. Kennicott 1) [fig. 58].[41] The copy, dated 1476, was executed by Moses ibn Zabarah in La Coruña. The decoration was entrusted to Joseph ibn Ḥayyim who created a work of exceptional scope. His ornaments, executed with the precision of a goldsmith's engravings, appear on almost every page of the voluminous codex. But his figure style is archaic and, owing to his heterogeneous sources, the work lacks a personal character. Besides playing cards and Qurʾān carpet pages, Ibn Ḥayyim copied the illustrations of a Bible made in 1300 in Cervera that happens to have been preserved.[42] He even included a painting displaying the Temple implements that, transformed into an assemblage of unidentifiable motifs, shows that the real meaning of the genuine Jewish symbolic composition was lost.

The Lisbon School[43] was the last chapter in the history of Hebrew manuscript painting on the Iberian Peninsula. It flourished from about 1460 to the very year of the expulsion from Portugal in 1496, a period that coincides with the final years of manuscript illumination in general, as also of Jewish civilization on the peninsula. The books produced by this workshop reflect the traditional culture of the community for which they were commissioned. They include luxurious Bibles, for example the Lisbon Bible of the British Library [fig. 59],[44] the Bible of the Bibliothèque Nationale (Ms. hébreu 15), and that of the Hispanic Society in New York (Ms. B 241); prayer books like the Paris Siddur (Bibliothèque Nationale Ms. hébreu 592); Psalters, two of which are now in the Vatican Library (Cod. ebr. 463 and 473), and another in a private collection (Carl Alexander Floersheim Trust for Art and Judaica); as well as other works. Moreover, for the first time in the history of Hebrew manuscripts, a real workshop seems to have existed. Whether in a luxury edition or in a more modest codex, all the manuscripts follow a similar program down to the smallest detail. Floral borders, filigree decoration, burnished gold letters are shaped according to identical patterns even though the execution was entrusted to several draftsmen. The way these manuscripts were manufactured is the ultimate stage of the craft before it was superseded by the industrial production of the printed book. More than a final episode, the Lisbon School was a transitional phase that marked the shift toward a new epoch in the history of European culture, that of the diffusion of printing. Indeed, some of the scribes belonging to the Lisbon School are known to have been among the first Hebrew printers.

The sumptuous Bible now in the Bibliothèque Nationale was started in Lisbon (Ms. hébreu 15). The text and two of its decorated pages were still executed there. Then the work was interrupted. It was resumed and finished some decades later in Florence. It is a symbol of the abrupt end that was forced on a Jewish culture in its full strength. The copying of manuscripts and the production of printed books was resumed in North Africa, in Italy, and in the Ottoman Empire, wherever the refugees found shelter. The art of the book continued for many centuries to bear the marks of the civilization that the Sephardic Jews brought with them. The richness of this culture, however, was never again equaled.

NOTES

1. As is well known, only scrolls prepared and copied according to precise rules were used liturgically.

2. See Gabrielle Sed-Rajna, "Toledo or Burgos?" *Journal of Jewish Art* 2 (1975): 6–21.

3. Pilar Léon Tello, *Los Judíos de Toledo,* (Madrid, 1979), vol. 2, nos. 147, 187, 211, 212, 240, and 258.

4. Sed-Rajna, "Toledo or Burgos?" 18–21.

5. G. Sed-Rajna, "Hebrew Manuscripts from Toledo and Tudela: Creation or Transmission?" in *Abraham ibn Ezra and his Age,* ed. F. Diáz Esteban (Madrid, 1990), 301–307.

6. Millard Meiss, "Italian Style in Catalonia and a Fourteenth-Century Catalan Workshop," *Journal of the Walters Art Gallery* 4 (1941): 45–87.

7. Francis Wormald, "Afterthoughts on the Stockholm Exhibition," *Kunsthistorisk Tidskrift* 23 (1953): 74–78.

8. N. de Dalmases and Jose I. Pitarch, *Historia de l'art catalan,* vol. 3 (Barcelona, 1984), 152–62.

9. London, British Library, Or. Ms. 14061. (See Toledo, Sinagoga del Tránsito, *La Vida Judía en Sefarad,* exhibition catalogue, 1991–92, no. 126.)

10. See G. Sed-Rajna, "Ateliers de manuscrits hébreux dans l'Occident médiéval," in *Artists, artisans et production artistique au moyen âge,* ed. X. Barral y Altet, vol. 1 (Paris, 1986), 359–382.

11. See M. Garel, "The Foa Bible," *Journal of Jewish Art* 6 (1979): 78–85.

12. See B. Narkiss and G. Sed-Rajna, "La première Bible de Josuè ibn Gaon," *Revue des Etudes Juives* 130 (1974): 4–15.

13. Cecil Roth, *The Sarajevo Haggadah* (New York, n.d.); Sarajevo, National Museum, *Sarajevska Hagada, A Study with the Facsimile Edition,* introduction by E. Werber (Belgrade and Sarajevo, 1983).

14. Kurt Weitzmann, *The Illustrations in Roll and Codex: A Study of the Origin and Method of Text Illustration* (Princeton, 1947, 2nd ed., 1970).

15. London, British Library, Add. Ms. 27210. See Bezalel Narkiss, *The Golden Haggadah* (London, 1970).

16. London, British Library, Or. Ms. 2884. See Bezalel Narkiss, *Hebrew Illuminated Manuscripts in the British Isles* (Jerusalem and London, 1982), no. 12.

17. See above, note 13.

18. Budapest, Academy of Sciences, Kaufmann Collection, Ms. A 422. *The Kaufmann Haggadah,* facsimile edition with an introduction by Gabrielle Sed-Rajna (Budapest, 1990).

19. Manchester, John Rylands Library, Ms. Heb. 6. *The Rylands Haggadah: A Medieval Manuscript in Facsimile,* facsimile edition with an introduction by R. Loewe (London, 1988); Narkiss, *British Isles,* no. 15.

20. Narkiss, *British Isles,* no. 16.

21. Joseph Gutmann, "Abraham in the Fire of the Chaldeans: a Jewish Legend in Jewish, Christian and Islamic Art," *Frühmittelalterliche Studien* 7 (1973): 342–52; idem, "Noah's Raven in Early Christian and Byzantine Art," *Cahiers Archéologiques* 26 (1977): 63–71; Gabrielle Sed-Rajna, *The Hebrew Bible in Illuminated Manuscripts* (Fribourg and New York, 1987), 75; Joseph Gutmann, "The Haggadic Motif in Jewish Iconography," *Eretz Israel* 6 (1960): 17*–21*.

22. C. H. Kraeling, *The Excavations at Dura Europos: Final Report. VIII. The Synagogue* (New Haven, Conn., 1956).

23. See Kurt Weitzmann and Herbert L. Kessler, *The Frescoes of the Dura Synagogue and Christian Art* (Washington, D.C., 1990), 151ff.

24. Kurt Weitzmann, "Die Illustration der Septuaginta," *Münchener Jahrbuch der Bildenden Kunst,* 3d. ser. 3–4 (1952–53): 96ff.; Weitzmann and Kessler, *Dura Synagogue,* 146ff.; Sed-Rajna, *The Hebrew Bible,* 156.

25. Herbert L. Kessler, "Prophetic Portraits in the Dura Synagogue," *Jahrbuch für Antike und Christentum* 30 (1987): 149–55.

26. See Weitzmann, "Die Illustration der Septuaginta," 96ff; O. Mazal, *Kommentar zür Wiener Genesis. Faksimile Ausgabe des Codex theol. 31 der Österreichischen Nationale Bibliothek in Wien* (Frankfurt, 1980); Robert Bergman, *The Salerno Ivories: Ars Sacra in Medieval Amalfi,* (Cambridge and London, 1980).

27. Weitzmann and Kessler, *Dura Synagogue,* 146ff.

28. Sed-Rajna, *The Hebrew Bible,* 75.

29. See A. Kracher, "Millstätter Genesis und Physiologus-Handschrift," introd. to facsimile edition of the Codex Klagenfurt, Museum Rudolfinum, Cod. VI, 19 (Graz, 1967).

30. Cf. Weitzmann and Kessler, *Dura Synagogue,* fig. 12.; ibid., fig. 17; ibid., fig. 15.

31. Ibid., fig. 14.

32. Narkiss, *British Isles,* fig. 156; Sed-Rajna, *The Hebrew Bible,* 25.

33. Paris, Bibliothèque Nationale, Ms. lat. 2334. Cf. Bezalel Narkiss, "Towards a Further Study of the Ashburnham Pentateuch," *Cahiers Archéologiques* 19 (1969): 15–60.

34. Cf. J. Williams, "A Castilian Tradition of Bible Illustration: The Romanesque Bible from San Millan," *Journal of the Warburg and Courtauld Institutes* 28 1965): 66–85.

35. François Bucher, *The Pamplona Bibles* (London and New Haven, Conn., 1970).

36. Gabrielle Sed-Rajna, "Further Thoughts on an Early Illustrated Pentateuch," *Journal of Jewish Art* 10 (1984): 29–31.

37. The identification of this map with that offered to the king of France is still controversial. Cf. François Avril et al., *Manuscrits enluminés de la péninsule ibérique* (Paris, 1982), 98; Washington, The National Gallery, *ca. 1492,* ed. Jay Levinson, exhibition catalogue, 1991, see Jean Michel Massing, "Catalan Atlas," cat. no. 1.

38. Bezalel Narkiss, *Hebrew Illuminated Manuscripts* (Jerusalem, 1969), 72.

39. S. Fellous, "Une Bible à la rencontre des cultures," in *Le Livre au moyen âge* (Paris, 1989), 148–54.

40. Carl O. Nordström, *The Duke of Alba's Castilian Bible* (Uppsala, 1967).

41. *The Kennicott Bible,* facsimile editon with an introduction by Bezalel Narkiss and Aliza Cohen-Mushlin (London, 1985).

42. Lisbon, Biblioteca Nacional, Ms. 72. Narkiss, *Hebrew Illuminated Manuscripts,* 52.

43. Gabrielle Sed-Rajna, *Manuscrits hébreux de Lisbonne* (Paris, 1970).

44. Or. Ms. 2626–28. *The Lisbon Bible,* facsimile edition with an introduction by Gabrielle Sed-Rajna (London and Jerusalem, 1988); see also Washington, National Gallery, *ca. 1492,* Jay A. Levinson, "Lisbon Bible," cat. no. 29.

Material Culture in Medieval Spain

Juan Zozaya

Until recently, very little was known about the material culture of medieval Spain, although the great monuments and a few exceptional objects have of course been described in a general way.[1] Medieval Spain presents many problems of analysis, partly because large tracts of its territory were occupied for more than seven centuries by a culture foreign to that of Europe. Furthermore, there was no "central" government to counterattack the Muslims, but rather a motley group of small Christian kingdoms that eventually grew, attacked, and defeated their enemy, and finally united themselves through political means.[2]

Over the past fifteen years, however, developments in archeology have allowed a truer image to emerge. It is now possible to delineate two major phases in the material culture of medieval Spain.[3] One, prior to the early thirteenth century, may be defined as a period of great development in the material culture of al-Andalus. The second phase speaks more of the development of the material culture of the Christian kingdoms, once conditions were favorable for improved economies, social development, and the acquisition of technical capabilities.

The entry of the Muslims into the Iberian peninsula meant the establishment of a cultural syncretism made up of Byzantine, late Roman, and diverse Hispanic elements, as well as of Arab, Berber, Syro-Palestinian, and Islamic Mesopotamian elements, to which others would be added from the beginning of the tenth century onward, especially Chinese and Persian.[4]

Figure 60 *(opposite)*
Interior of the Mosque of Córdoba, begun in the 8th century

The pre-Islamic tradition was quite strong in church and palace architecture, as may be seen from buildings like the church at Melque (Toledo),[5] the palace at Reccopolis (Guadalajara),[6] and the villa at Plà del Nadal (Valencia),[7] influenced by Armenian techniques. The same may be said of military architecture, such as the late Visigothic walls at Condeixa-a-Velha (Portugal),[8] Talavera de la Reina (Toledo),[9] and possibly those at Vascos (Toledo).[10] More domestic elements like house architecture,[11] seem to have been extremely modest and derived from as yet unknown prototypes related to typical pre-Islamic farmhouses.

Metalwork seems to be by far the best product stemming from this period. Steel was of very good quality and was used both in agricultural tools and in weapons, following Germanic patterns in swords and throwable axes (*franciscae*).[12] Bronzework was of high quality, as may be appreciated from scabbards, as well as liturgical items like jugs, patens, and crosses, and belt buckles, and above all *fibulae* or pins.[13]

Jewelry, especially in gold, was rather common and highly specialized, with plentiful examples of earrings, pectoral decorations, and votive crowns like those at Guarrazar (Toledo) or Torredonjimeno (Jaén).[14] Ceramics, on the other hand, were poorly represented in Visigothic craftsmanship,[15] and therefore most other artifacts, such as mosaic work, glass, ivory, and bone-work, were of Roman origin and already debased in relation to those of the empire.

The arrival of the Muslim peoples in the Iberian peninsula led to the introduction of many different cultural elements, mainly Near-Eastern and North African,[16] and, most important of all, a continuing relationship with the East, based mainly on political links and religious connections to the cosmopolitan religious center of Mecca.[17] Both were essential in the formation of al-Andalus, whose history may be divided, from the perspective of material culture, into two main periods. One, the Umayyad, prior to the fall of the *taifa* kings, may be considered to end in 1086. The second period, the North African, runs from 1086 to 1492 and the aftermath of the fall of Granada. There are different phases, and the development of material culture differs in each period, as we shall presently see.

Some of the remnants of the Christian Visigothic government were sheltered in Asturias, protected by the Cantabrian mountains and by the Bay of Biscay, across which links with northern Europe continued. Other Christian elements took refuge in the Pyrenees, eventually establishing contacts with the Carolingian Empire. In both cases, the idea of legitimate derivation from the preconquest Visigothic kingdom is essential in understanding the process of winning back territory from the Muslims, commonly known as the Reconquest (*reconquista*).[18]

On the Islamic side a pre-Andalusi phase (711-756) characterizes the arrival of the first Muslims. This phase cannot be said to have produced many innovations, which do not, in fact, appear until the turn of the century. One is the construction of fortifications, in the form of large numbers of watchtowers, throughout the newly settled territories as a bulwark against the Christian kingdoms.[19] The other is the common cemeteries for Muslims and Christians and the sharing of churches, which is associated with the introduction of new coinage, with inscriptions at first in Latin, then in Latin and Arabic, and finally, at a slightly later date, in Arabic only.[20]

An Early Umayyad phase lasting from 825 to 925 was marked by two interesting technological innovations. The horizontal loom appeared, together with the use, well in advance of Christian Europe, of silk thread, as in the shroud of Oña, Burgos (dateable to sometime around 925),[21] and glazed pottery came into use, with the appearance of the first Eastern forms, as well as pottery with different colors on the same piece. The implications are clear: the horizontal loom was already in use in al-Andalus at least three centuries before the rest of Europe, giving rise to a weaving industry there. Polychrome textiles seem to arrive at the same time as polychrome pottery with which it shared both colors and decorative motifs. Cosmopolitan trends were beginning to become commonplace in tenth-century al-Andalus.

The other important development is that Andalusis (not only Muslims, but also Christians and Jews) used a new type of pottery, unknown in Christian Spain and, in fact, in the rest of Europe. They must therefore have had access at low cost to the production of the acids necessary for making glazed pottery.[22] Lead glazing was thus a common feature of material culture in a society that had started to enlarge its economic frontiers, with new industries on the coast, as at Pechina, new developments in irrigation with techniques imported from the East, and a general advance in communications, based on the reconstruction and maintenance of the preexisting Roman road network that allowed a steady development of the hinterlands.[23]

During the same phase a massive network of fortifications was built in the mountains north of the Duero river, though it was partly destroyed sometime around 920-25. A remnant of these fortifications may be seen in the castle of Gormaz (Soria). The network protected roads and communications, as well as the expansion of agriculture. The countryside was repopulated, new cities were founded, and probably a *commendatus* system of colonization was put into effect. The sites now under archeological investigation at Qalᶜat Abd al-Salām (present-day Alcalá de Henares), Qalᶜat Khalīfa (Villaviciosa de Odón), Qalᶜat Rabāḥ (Calatrava la Vieja), Qalᶜat ᶜAyyūb (Calatayud)—all with names compounded on the Arabic *qalᶜa,* fortress—and Madīnat Sālim (Medinaceli) were established.

This military policy created a very wide distribution of wealth, which must have affected the whole population including the rural elements, especially during the full Umayyad phase extending from 944 to 1000. At this time, there must have been few differences in material well-being between the cities and the countryside.

Fortifications were very well built, comprising structures with different levels of protection. Watchtowers, country military buildings, castles, and fortified towns were all part of the network[24] that attained its zenith during this period. They were all built according to plan, with common techniques and formulas to allow full adaptability to the terrain. This meant that there were certain types of walls, towers, gates, posterns, and so forth, that could be articulated and organized according to different tactical and topographical requirements.[25]

Most probably handbooks of military engineering were already in existence, as a great homogeneity of construction techniques may be observed in town walls and castles built between 820 and 860.[26] Standardized construction modules were used to "compose" each fortification using construction modules; in addition standard materials were employed, with variations depending on the character of each fortification. Building of fortifications was accomplished quickly thanks to the widespread use of rammed-earth construction, which could easily be carried out by unskilled labor. It is known from archeological evidence that mule trains provided the builders with stone, sand, lime, and water, and that several teams worked on a single building simultaneously.[27] This system was also used for city fortifications, as in the cases of Mérida or Córdoba.

More than thirty principal forms of pottery are known, among them oil lamps, pots (including pressure cookers), bottles and bowls of Chinese design, bowls of Iraqi inspiration, inkwells copying Persian glass ones, and Syrian-style cups.[28] All this says a great deal about the cosmopolitan world of al-Andalus, blending with elements of Berber and Hispano-Roman origin. Practically every household could have access to these wares, as far as can be seen from archeological finds.

Simple polychrome and *cuerda seca* or cloisonné polychrome-decorated pottery had already become common in al-Andalus. The decoration was rich and varied, with bird, animal, and vegetable motifs used to create patterns that were not only beautiful, but also had powerful religious meaning that was acceptable to people of different religions. It is difficult therefore to identify a specific pottery that may be ascribed to each of the three religious groups living in al-Andalus. Chinese motifs like the hare, the siren or the phoenix bird in the shape of a peacock with a displayed tail, or Indian motifs like the lotus blossom, as well as other decorative elements of Eastern origin, were in widespread use during this period.[29]

As for the variety of pottery utensils, vessels for use at high temperature, as well as pressure cookers complete with safety valves, were already known. So also were distillation equipment, both in glass and earthenware, pots for water wheels, feeding bottles for babies and sick people, and small portable burners for cooking. In sum, pottery bears witness to a very sophisticated material culture.[30]

Imports were quite scarce, as far as material culture is concerned, but Iraqi Abbasid and Egyptian luster pottery found its way to such places as the palace of Madīnat al-Zahrā᾽, Medinaceli, and Tiermes.[31] Fatimid rock crystal in the form of kohl bottles reached many places in al-Andalus, some finding their way to church treasures: there were chess sets, like the ones in Lugo or Les Avellanes, and textiles made their way to Christian monasteries where they were reused as linings for small boxes.[32] These items were probably brought by sailors and pilgrims to Mecca who were trading on the side.

Metalwork seems to have been less common, except for bronze, brass, and iron, with Fatimid influence much in fashion. The area occupied by al-Andalus had been a producer of copper and tin as well as iron since prehistoric times. All these metals were mined and worked in Umayyad times,[33] as may be seen from the great quantity of objects of daily use, such as belt buckles, bowls, balances, oil lamps, and luxury and palace items like the deer fountain from Madīnat al-Zahra᾽, all made of bronze.

A great many such objects have survived, and give a general idea of the importance of bronze wares in al-Andalus. Some of them were signed: and a certain Rāshiq must have been important, as many thimbles and lamps from the first half of the tenth century bear his name. Another bronze artist, named Salomon, apparently a Christian, worked about the same time in Córdoba, making lamps based on oriental models but with a distinctive Andalusi flavor.[34]

The mining of iron and the manufacture of steel were important, although unfortunately not much is known about them. However, the quantity of agricultural and mining tools made of these metals, such as hoes, picks, sickles, chains, ploughshares, hammers, and stonecutters' chisels, found in Lietor (Albacete) and Madīnat al-Zahrā᾽ enlarges the scope of our technical knowledge about how they were made and used. Steel was of high quality, judging by the number of well-preserved objects such as hammers and balances that have survived, and whose steel still has a beautiful glint. Steel was also used for bits, stirrups, and weapons, imitating Chinese and Parthian styles, as well as Visigothic and Viking styles.[35] This was truly a cosmopolitan moment when the formation of a distinctive Andalusi Umayyad culture flourished, leading to what may be termed the "full Umayyad" phase, between 944 and 1000.

Ivory was introduced, as far as we can now tell, by the court workshops at Madīnat al-Zahrā᾽, sometimes using the full diameter of elephant tusks to produce marvelous pyxides like the ones at the Victoria and Albert Museum, the Louvre, or the National Archeological Museum in Madrid, or the ivory caskets from Madīnat al-Zahrāʾ.[36] These objects obviously became part of court art and were limited to the noble classes. Less-valuable objects were made in a substitute medium, bone, of which little has survived.

Jewelry must have been rather commonplace, with the routine use of silver and gold. Not many gems have been found adorning it, though river pearls were used, as well as coins. The techniques employed were not very innovative, but they show a definite taste peculiar to al-Andalus. Filigree was the most common technique used for high-quality objects, and the more ordinary pieces were cast, as may be seen from the molds at the National Archeological Museum. The use of coins as jewelry decoration may be inferred from the perforations on many coins, which have allowed the dating of the hoard at Charrilla and the later one from Lorca (Murcia). Fatimid influence is present, lingering on until the thirteenth century. The Gerona casket is a good example of sheet jewelry in silver, its uniqueness lying in the fact that it is the only known object of its type.[37]

Houses consisting of a common room and bedrooms were installed surrounding a courtyard. In urban sites a latrine was included. In large towns dedicated to mining like Vascos (Toledo province), the normal arrangement of surviving early Islamic houses (probably of Visigothic origin) seems to be a simple common room and one private room (perhaps a bedroom) with a courtyard with sheds for animals and tools. Houses of the rich, palaces, and official buildings seem to have had living quarters leading to a patio with a central oblong common room and two private rooms, probably bedrooms, on the sides, following the system of the eastern house (*bayt*).[38]

Palace architecture is little known, except for Madīnat al-Zahrāʾ, the palace city founded by ʿAbd al-Raḥmān III on the outskirts of Córdoba in the first half of the tenth century. It is walled and divided into three main sectors, one of them devoted to agriculture and gardening, the others to administration.[39] In general the structure shows the influence of Abbasid royal cities, but there are also clear decorative references to the late eastern Umayyad world.

For both practical and political reasons, mosques seem to have inherited from churches the practice of directional orientation and their generally T-shaped ground plan. Roman *spoliae* were used purposefully in a symbolic manner as references to Damascus and Jerusalem in the main mosque at Córdoba [fig. 60, p. 156], and to reinforce this, mosaics were also installed in the *miḥrab*.[40] Less important mosques, such as the Cristo de la Luz mosque in Toledo, tended to repeat this pattern.[41]

In urban settings, baths and latrines were built near the mosques of the Muslim quarters.[42] Synagogues and churches existed in the quarters occupied by Jews and Christians although we know little about their interior decoration, which was probably painted. These quarters were walled and could be locked for security purposes. Streets were sinuous, with dead ends in residential quarters. Country villas were common for the rich. Permanent markets (*sūqs*) were established in the large towns, where different types of wares could be acquired, some brought from overseas by sailors and travelers to Mecca.

Cemeteries were normally located on the outskirts of towns.[43] Some residences were also established on the outskirts, normally in association with mills, pottery kilns, tanneries, and other polluting industries.[44] Weekly markets were held in these areas, in the vicinity of the city gates, where peasants would come to sell their products to city dwellers.

Land communications, based on the Roman highway pattern, were well established.[45] Road maintenance was particularly easy because vehicular traffic was avoided and much trade was carried on with the help of mule trains. As for bridges, those from the Roman period were either preserved, as in Mérida, or reconstructed, as in Córdoba or Gormaz; and new ones were built when necessary, as at Pino Puente. Large cities were no more than eighty kilometers apart, and an inn or post could be found within every seven or eight kilometers, where rest or refreshment was available.

Sea communications were encouraged by the building of arsenals, like those at the ports of Almería, Málaga, or Lisbon,[47] and links were established with trade routes heading for North Africa and hence to Egypt and Syria, where contact was made with the silk route to the Far East. These routes were secured by a navy, with an admiral at its head, protecting the shores and the minor industries based on them from pirate attacks by Norsemen or Fatimids.

Internal strife had been latent in al-Andalus since the second half of the ninth century, the most important uprising being that of ʿUmar ibn Ḥafṣūn. Commonplace tribal uprisings, however, did not impede the flourishing of material culture. The phase of civil war, or *fitna* (1000-1035), may be considered as post-Umayyad. Besides the products of official Amirid art, examples of which are the marble ablution basins made for al-Manṣūr in the National Archeological Museum of Madrid or the one dedicated to his son ʿAbd al-Malik at the Moulay Youssef madrasa in Marrakesh, local and popular workshops started producing wares that were luxurious but not innovative. Some details give a small idea of the material culture of this period. Decoration seems to focus on anecdotal rather than official elements, as in the bottle from the Plaza de San Cayetano, today in the Córdoba Archeological Museum. The practice of science continued unabated throughout the period of civil strife. The stone sundials from Córdoba, dating from around 1000, and the astrolabe of 1002 at the Naval Museum in Madrid demonstrate this fact [fig. 61].[48]

A kind of appendix phase, which I call epi-Umayyad (1000-1035), corresponds to the time of the *taifa* kings. Not much is known about the material culture of this period, except that there was a general impoverishment and localized styles appeared in pottery decoration.[49] Among the governing classes, purity of form in ceramics and glass gives way to a kind of preciosity, as in the marble decoration of Toledo and Denia, based respectively on Visigothic and late eastern Umayyad patterns, or the eastern Umayyad ideas of a desert castle coming back to life in the Aljafería (Saragossa),[50] or in local, everyday products like pottery, whose origins can be determined quite easily.

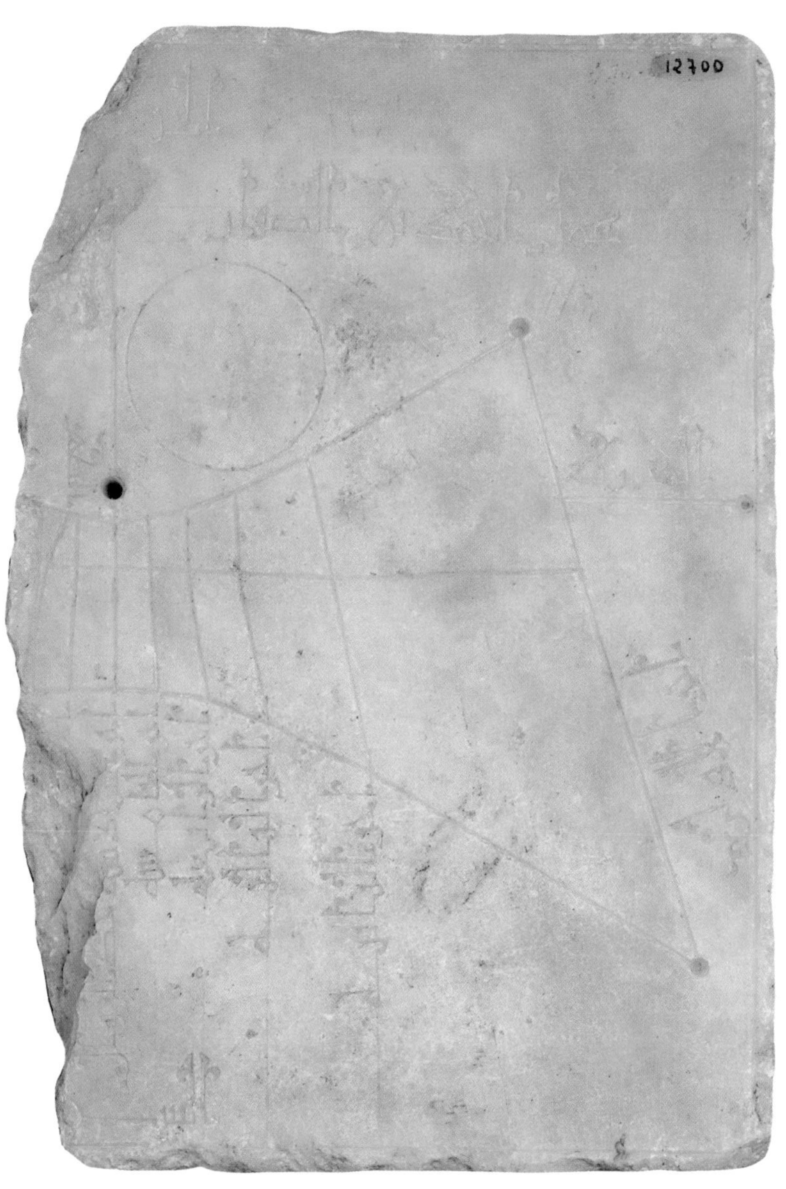

Literature and science, however, were the most important cultural products of this period. Therefore a characteristic element of material culture are the brass astrolabes from the workshop of Ibn Ṣāʿid al-Sahli, who worked in Toledo around the middle of the eleventh century and was probably a member of the mathematical and astronomical circle of Maslama of Madrid. The most famous examples are the plane astrolabes of Madrid and Oxford dated 1067 and 1068, respectively.[51]

Figure 61
Fragment of a Sundial, Córdoba, ca. 1000, Museo Arqueológico Provincial, Córdoba, no. 12700 (cat. no. 103)

What was the situation in the Christian kingdoms during the same period? Material culture there seems to have been very backward. Glazing was introduced in the kingdom of León only in the second half of the tenth century, and then not with the highly developed techniques of al-Andalus. Courtly objects were certainly made, as early as the first half of the eleventh century, like the ivory Christ of Don Fernando and Doña Sancha, and the silver boxes from León, decorated with Arabic inscriptions in niello technique.[52] But this was, of course, courtly art. Otherwise common pottery seems to have been more related to patterns coming from northern Europe, especially France and Britain, either by sea or by the land routes through the Pyrenees.[53]

Variations on this theme may be found in monasteries, but very little is known of the material conditions of the normal civilian population, which presumably lived in very poor conditions. This did not change until sometime around the eleventh century, when the Christian kingdoms were more powerful, not only from a military but also from an economic standpoint. A small urban middle class arose, and there is an eleventh-century mention of Jewish bankers in Burgos lending money to El Cid that may be taken as one of the first references to a flow of money that could somehow stimulate a higher level of material culture. Although some Christians could already afford a better life, it must be assumed that objects like the Oña shroud were more likely booty seized from the Islamic south than the result of trade or local production.

The transition from the Umayyad to the North African period is significant because the entire structure of society was altered. A new social dynamic came into being when Alfonso VI captured Toledo in 1085: it became a Christian city with large Muslim and Jewish subject populations. Islamic territories had already been greatly reduced by 1085, with the result that Andalusi cities like Seville, Córdoba, and Murcia started to swell to two, three, or even four times their original size. The balance between urban and rural sectors tipped to the benefit of cities. Migrations occurred not only for political reasons, but also for economic ones, stimulating technological transfer to the Christian kingdoms. Migrations were imposed on Christians and Jews by the Almoravids (1085-1171), with these minorities emigrating in ever larger numbers to the northern Christian kingdoms, especially under the Almohads (1171-1248).

Life in the cities must have been quite similar, in some cases, to that in parts of present-day Morocco. An urban quarter recently excavated in Cieza (Murcia) suggests a refined society, albeit a modest one in accordance with austere religious principles, with houses having more than one bedroom, more than one living room to make life comfortable during harsh winters and summers, and latrines as well as Almohad-style plaster decoration.[59]

Pottery in general followed Turkic and North African patterns, both in shape and decoration, and was still characterized by a great range of forms.[55] Interesting elements like jug stands appear, but household furnishings are, in general, more primitive, or perhaps less sophisticated, than during the previous Umayyad period; and the same is true of metalwork.[56] Ivory is worked in the shape of sheets or pieces inlaid into wood (*tarsiya*),[57] implying difficulty in obtaining materials and restrictions on upper-class assertion of status through ostentatious objects offensive to the norms of modesty.

By 1212, the Christians had already reached the Guadiana Valley, and the conquest of Valencia, the Balearic Islands, Seville, and Córdoba quickly followed. The Muslims left behind now took their place in Christian society as Mudejars, earning their livelihood as farmers, shepherds, potters, carpenters, and masons. Indeed, the best example of surviving Almohad art left in Spain, besides the Giralda minaret in Seville, is the Santa María la Blanca synagogue built by Mudejars in Toledo.

During the thirteenth century a great many Jewish communities sprang up in Castile, especially in the zones around Burgos, Logroño, Soria, Segovia, and Toledo. In some cases their adaptability to Christian surroundings produced synagogues that from the outside resembled churches, as at Agreda.[58] Other important works built in Mudejar style in the following century are the Tránsito synagogue in Toledo, and those in Segovia and Córdoba, where the Islamicizing decorative style is not different from what may be found in Christian palaces, churches, or monasteries.

During this period not many innovations occurred in what was left of al-Andalus, except for luster pottery, which was produced in Calatrava la Vieja and Málaga, and presumably in other places as well. Ottoman influence was introduced in the Nasrid kingdom of Granada (1223-1492), and can be detected in art motifs, weapons, and hydraulic works such as oval-shaped dams. Whatever small remnants of Jewish material culture are left betray strong assimilation to the immediate cultural surroundings, as in the brass tefillin cover in the cathedral of Toledo, with its late Romanesque decoration and Hebrew inscriptions or, later, jewelry from Teruel, which reflects contemporary Islamic patterns [fig. 62].

Figure 62
Silver Rings, Teruel, 13th-14th century, Museo de Teruel, Teruel, I. G. 593/ I.G. 5.354
This jewelry was discovered during excavations of the former *judería* (Jewish quarter) of Teruel.

The Nasrid kingdom of Granada was certainly a case of contrasts. Heir to the Almohad empire in the Iberian peninsula, it was the last stronghold of Islam in Spain. Its contacts with Christians probably helped it survive for more than two centuries when presumably the power of the Muslims was exhausted. The kingdom's survival must be understood in light of the access that Nasrids had to African gold through their relatives the Marinids of Morocco, and their trade in two basic products, silk and luster pottery. The latter was made in Málaga, and the trade was controlled by the Genoese who had a quarter of their own near the city walls.

Little is known of town life in the Nasrid kingdom. It may be assumed that the Alhambra was a model of affluence for the rest of the towns. Of course, not all of the Alhambra consisted of royal palaces, because as a palace-city it also contained elements found in a normal town. The prevailing house floor plan was that of a central courtyard with rooms around it. The houses were rather small, had a second story, and were built of brick. Running water was commonplace.

Figure 63
Deep Dish (*Brasero*), Valencia (Manises), 1420-30, The Metropolitan Museum of Art, New York, The Cloisters Collection, 1956, 56.171.127 (cat. no. 78)

There were three grades of pottery. "Rich" pottery, basically the luster wares derived from Almohad techniques and styles, was probably fired in Málaga and imitated after the end of the thirteenth century in Manises (Valencia) [fig. 63].[59] The average grade of pottery was glazed in turquoise blue and black decoration, with clear influence of Seljuk and Ottoman types, although some decorative elements were clearly local, like the bowl with a couple dressed in Gothic robes at the Alhambra Museum.[60] Finally, the "popular" wares, used in the kitchen and for domestic storage purposes, were based on the Berber wares of the preceding Almohad period.[61]

Surprisingly, parts of the Nasrid kingdom were impoverished, if the excavations at Los Guájares are indicative of how people in the countryside lived.[62] All power seems to have resided in the main cities, like Granada, Málaga, Antequera, and Ronda.[63] Emigration to North Africa was rather common, as was that of Muslims from other parts of the peninsula to Granada. This, at least, is what may be deduced from the surviving inscriptions of the Nasrid kingdom.

If we look at the social conditions left to the conquerors in 1492 the economic situation of the Muslim peasants and shepherds seems hardly ideal. The Christians coveted their fields and pastures, but not their social status. The Christian occupation generated popular uprisings of Muslims, and discontent lingered on among the Moriscos until their eventual expulsion.

Christian Spain, meanwhile, had developed into a wealthy society of the urban type, with kilns producing a great variety of pottery ranging from lusterware to commonplace pots. The influence of Islamic progress and development in agriculture and diverse crafts meant a more varied diet for the Christian population, which up to then had been restricted to a typical, cereal-based country diet still found in fourteenth-century Castile.[64] This certainly influenced the amount of pottery forms available to the population, according to their required specialization. Couscous seems to have been a very popular meal in the Christian kingdoms of this period. The kilns at Paterna and Manises produced special pots to make it.

The result was the flourishing of kilns making lusterware in Manises, Muel, and Reus; green and white products in Manresa, Paterna, and Teruel.[65] There were many other kilns, such as those now under study in Alcalá de Henares, Valladolid, Zamora, and other places, all of them most likely in the hands of Mudejars [fig. 64].

Figure 64
Earthen Bowl, Teruel, 15th century, Museo de Teruel, Teruel, I.G. 7.146 (cat. no. 82)

Figure 65 *(above)*
Hanukkah Lamp (fragment), Teruel, 15th century, Museo de Teruel, Teruel, I. G. 7.167 (cat. no. 79)
Only two lights of the original lamp remain; the rest have been restored to give a sense of the lamp's original appearance.

Figure 66 *(left)*
Passover Plate, Probably Valencia, Spain, ca. 1480, The Israel Museum, Jerusalem

Figure 67
Nasrid Textile with Star Pattern, Spain, 15th century, The Metropolitan Museum of Art, New York, Fletcher Fund, 1946, 46.156.16 (cat. no. 110)

The standard of living seems was quite high for the period. Pisan[67] and Genoese merchants busied themselves in trade between the Christian kingdoms of Europe (Spain included) and al-Andalus, thus making many objects available to Christian Spain. A flourishing middle class was established with access to better and more varied objects, including ones specific to their cultural or religious needs, like the Hanukkah lamp from Teruel [fig. 65], a Passover plate, probably from Valencia [fig. 66], or the jewels with Hebrew inscriptions from Teruel, Monteagudo (Soria), and Barcelona.[68]

Living conditions amongst city dwellers must have been very good, considering what life must have been like during the thirteenth, fourteenth, and fifteenth centuries. Certainly in the last two centuries the urban standard of living compared favorably with that of other

European cities, excepting Genoa, Venice, and Pisa. Silk and leather clothing must have been common [fig. 67]. Houses were by then rather luxurious and housing in general quite good, judging from the houses in Agreda, Córdoba, Toledo, and Segovia, with two or three stories and central courtyards.

People lived on the floor *a la morisca* (that is, in "Moorish" style), sitting on cushions, with separate quarters for women (although without imposing any harem rule). This fashion in seating reached the upper classes, and Queen Isabella seems to have adhered to it, as may be surmised from her will: her furniture consisted mainly of chests and cushions to be strewn on the floor, and standard European furniture pieces are surprisingly absent.

As may be seen through this survey, al-Andalus gave birth to a flourishing and unique civilization, reaching a high level of development in the eleventh and twelfth centuries when the two opposing cultures became practically equal in their material development. Not only was the level of material culture the highest in western Europe up to that time, but it was, in general, accessible to most of the population.

It is only when Islamic society became more "Africanized" and less "Oriental" that we see isolation creeping in and richness and advancement curtailed even as Islamic territory was reduced. Nevertheless we can also see a transfer of ethnic and cultural coexistence from one society to another the moment that crisis appeared in the first one. Medieval Spain varied in its capacity for tolerance, subject to the vagaries of royal patronage, whether Muslim or Christian, and subject, of course, to the total victory of one side or the other. This in fact was to occur in 1492, with the expulsion of the Jews and the conflicts with the Moriscos, who would also have to face conversion or exile in 1609. North Africa was a common destination for the Muslim remnant, as it had been for the Jews before them. Although the principle of coexistence was similar in North Africa, neither the social system nor the development of material culture achieved the same level as it had in al-Andalus.

NOTES

1. As an example, see Manuel Gómez Moreno, "El arte árabe español hasta los almohades: Arte mozárabe," *Ars Hispaniae,* vol. 3 (Madrid, 1951); Leopoldo Torres Balbás, "Arte Hispanomusulmán hasta la caída del Califato de Córdoba," in *Historia de España,* ed. Ramón Menéndez Pidal, vol. 5 (Madrid, 1957), 333-788.

2. For the politics of this period, see Derek W. Lomax, *The Reconquest of Spain* (London, 1978).

3. Manuel Retuerce and Juan Zozaya, "Variantes y constantes en la cerámica andalusí," in *V Congreso de Cerámica Medieval del Mediterráneo Occidental* (Mertola, 1991), 315-22.

4. Juan Zozaya, "Essai de chronologie pour certains types de céramique caliphale andalouse," in *I Congrès Internationale de Céramique Médiévale dans le Méditerranée Occidentale* (Paris, 1980), 311-20.

5. L. Caballero and J. Latorre, *La iglesia y el monasterio visigodo de Santa María de Melque (Toledo), San Juan de la Mata (Toledo) y Santa Comba de Bande (Orense)* (Madrid, 1979).

6. Lauro Olmo, "Arquitectura religiosa y organización litúrgica en época visigoda: La basílica de Recópolis," *Archivo Español de Arqueología* 61 (1988): 157-78.

7. Empar Juan and Ignacio Pastor, "Los visigodos en Valencia, Plá de Nadal: ¿Una villa áulica?" *Boletín de Arqueología Medieval* 3 (1989): 137-93.

8. See Juan Zozaya, "Fortification Building in al-Andalus," in *Spanien und der Orient* (Berlin, forthcoming).

9. Sergio Martínez Lillo, "Algunos aspectos inéditos en la fortificación musulmana de Talavera la Reina," in *II Congreso de Arqueología Medieval Española,* 3 vols. (Madrid, 1986), 2: 200-205.

10. R. Izquierdo, "Excavaciones en la ciudad hispano-musulmana de Vascos," in *Noticiario Arqueológico Hispánico* 7 (1979): 249-392; idem, "La ciudad hispano-musulmana de Vascos (Navalmoralejo, Toledo). Campañas 1979-1980," ibid., 16 (1982): 291-380; idem, "Los baños árabes de Vascos (Navalmoralejo, Toledo), ibid., 28 (1986): 193-242. For a reference to Armenian construction styles, see Juan Zozaya, "Las influencias visigóticas en al-Andalus," in *XIV Corso di Cultura e Arte Revennatico e Bizantina* (1987), pp. 395-425.

11. F. Colmenarejo, *Arqueología medieval de Colmenar Viejo* (Colmenar Viejo, 1987).

12. For examples of Visigothic metalwork, see Pere Palol and M. Hirmer, *L'Art en Espagne du Royaume Wisigoth à la fin de l'epoque romane* (Paris, 1967). For weapons, see Viscount Bernard Law Montgomery of Alamein, *A History of Warfare* (Cleveland, Ohio, 1968).

13. On bronze work, see Pere de Palol, *Bronces hispano-visigodos de origen mediterráneo. I. Jarritos y patenas litúrgicos* (Barcelona, 1950); and H. Zeiss, *Die Grabfunde aus dem Spanischen Westgotenreich* (Berlin and Leipzig, 1934). An update may be found in G. Ripoll, "La necrópolis visigoda de El Carpio de Tajo (Toledo)," in *Excavaciones Arqueolígicas en España* 142 (1985).

14. For examples and studies on Visigothic jewelry, see Palol and Hirmer, *Spanien Kunst des frühen Mittelalters vom Westgotenriech bis zum Ende der Romanik* (Munich, 1965).

15. For Visigothic pottery and the transitional period, see various authors, "Cerámicas de época visigoda en la Península Ibérica, precedentes y perduraciones," *Boletín de Arqueología Medieval* 3 (1989): 9-135.

16. For the intrusion of other peoples, see Pierre Guichard, *Al-Andalus: Estructura antropológica de una sociedad islámica en Occidente* (Barcelona, 1976). For a survey of Islamic elements, see W. Montgomery Watt, *A History of Islamic Spain* (Edinburgh, 1965). For an analysis of the impact of culture contact, see Thomas F. Glick, *Islamic and Christian Spain in the Early Middle Ages* (Princeton, N.J., 1979), and the revised Spanish edition: *Cristianos y musulmanes en le España medieval* (Madrid, 1991).

17. For ideas on the transitional period, see ibid. See also, for the archeological data, Zozaya, "Influjos visigóticos en al-Andalus." For a brief outline of the same pertaining to eastern influences, see idem, "Influjos orientales en al-Andalus," in *O legado cultural de Jueus e Mouros* (Lisbon, 1991), 103-15.

18. The historiographical debates about this subject are well summarized for the English-speaking reader in Glick, *Islamic and Christian Spain,* 3-15.

19. For this subject, see L. Caballero and A. Mateo, "El grupo de atalayas de la sierra de Madrid," in *Madrid del siglo IX al XI* (Madrid, 1990), 65-77; Juan Zozaya, "El Islam de la región madrileña," ibid., 195-203.

20. For a discussion of this aspect, see Juan Zozaya, "Recientes estudios sobre la arqueología andalusí: la Frontera Media," in *Aragon en la Edad Media* 19 (Zaragoza, 1991), 371-87. On monetary problems, see A. Balaguer, *Las emisiones transicionales árabe-musulmanas de Hispania* (Barcelona, 1976).

21. For the horizontal loom, see Manuel Returece, "El templén: ¿Primer testimonio del telar horizontal en Europa?" *Boletín de Arqueología Medieval* 1 (1987): 71-77. The Oña shroud is not widely known and was exhibited publicly only once, in 1979. Allegedly found in the tomb of Count Sancho (fl. 1017) at the monastery of Oña, it is embroidered in yellow, black, green, and white, the same colors that are characteristic of caliphal pottery. A reference is to be found in the catalogue of the exhibition *Silos y su época* (Madrid, 1974), 49, n. 126, though it must be earlier and dated to 925-950.

22. In spite of occasional flare-ups against the Jews and Christians, sharing the same space was normal and structured by norms governing intergroup relations; see Glick, *Cristianos y musulmanes,* 220-34. For distilling pots using polychrome glazing and Chinese coloring techniques, see Carmen Bosch Ferro and Marina Chinchilla Gómez, "Formas cerámicas auxiliares: anafes, arcaduces y otras," in *II Congreso de Arqueología Medieval Española,* 2: 491-500. On Pechina, see Francisco Castillo Galdeano, Rafael Martínez Madrid, and Manuel Acien Almansa, "Urbanismo e industria en Bayyana: Pechina (Almería)," ibid., 540-48. For irrigation and agricultural innovations, see Glick, *Cristianos y musulmanes,* pp. 88-101. On Roman roads, see José Manuel Roldán Hervas, *Itineraria Hispana: Fuentes para el estudio de las vías romanas en la Península Ibérica* (Valladolid, 1975); Juan Zozaya, "Notas sobre las comunicaciones en al-Andalus omeya," in *II Congreso Español de Arqueología Medieval,* 1: 220-27.

24. Zozaya, "Fortification Building in al-Andalus."

25. See the following articles by Zozaya: "Islamic Fortifications in Spain: Some Aspects," *British Archeological Reports (International Series)* 193 (1984), 636-73; "Fortification Building in al-Andalus"; "El proceso de islamización en la provincia de Soria," in *I Simposio de Arqueología Soriana* (Soria, 1984), 483-95; "Recientes estudios sobre la arqueología andalusí."

26. A. Soler and J. Zozaya, "Castillos omeyas de planta cuadrangular: su relación funcional," in *III Congreso de Arqueología Medieval Española* (Orviedo, 1992), 265-74.

27. Zozaya, "Recientes estudios sobre la arqueología andalusí."

28. Manuel Retuerce and Juan Zozaya, "Variantes geográficas de la cerámica omeya andalusí: los temas decorativos," in *Atti dello III Congresso sulla Ceramica medievale nel Mediterraneo Occidentale* (Florence, 1986), 69-128; Manuel Retuerce, "Cerámica islámica en la Comunidad de Madrid," in *Madrid del siglo IX al XI,* 145-63.

28. Zozaya, "Essai de chronologie," 311-15. For oriental influence on decorative motifs, see A. Turina, "Algunos elementos orientales en la cerámica omeya," in *II Congreso Internacional de Cerámica Medieval en el Mediterráneo Occidental* (Madrid, 1986), 455-59.

29. Zozaya, "Influjos orientales"; Turina, "Algunos elementos orientales."

30. G. Rosselló Bordoy, *El nombre de las cosas: Una propuesta de terminología cerámica* (Palma de Mallorca, 1991).

31. For examples of lusterware imported from the East, see Richard Ettinghausen, "Notes on the Lustreware of Spain," *Ars Orientalis* 1 (1954): 133-56; M. Gómez Moreno, "El arte árabe español hasta los almohades," 320; J. R. Mélida, "Ocilis. Medinaceli," *Memorias de la Junta Superior de Excavaciones y Antigüedades,* 82; Museo Numantino, *Guia del Museo* (Soria, 1990), 96.

32. Gómez Moreno,"El arte árabe español," 341-44; Manuel Casamar, "Flascó de perfums," in *Thesaurus: Estudis. L'art als bisbats de Catalunya 1000/1800* (Barcelona, 1986), 21; Manuel Casamar, "Peces d'escacs," ibid., 19-20.

33. For the metal trade, see Maurice Lombard, *Les métaux dans l'ancien monde du Ve au XIe siècle* (Paris, 1974).

34. Gómez Moreno, "El arte árabe español," 335.

35. A. Soler, "El armamento en época omeya," in *Madrid del siglo IX al XI,* 171-87.

36. For a general survey of Andalusi ivories, see Ernst Kühnel, *Die Islamischen Elfenbeinskulpturen des VIII-XIII. Jahrhunderts,* 2 vols. (Berlin, 1971).

37. Juan Zozaya, "Joyería altomedieval española," in *Un siglo de joyería y bisutería española: 1890-1990* (Palma de Mallorca, 1991), 15-16. For the Gerona casket, see Manuel Casamar, "Arqueta de Hixem II," in *Exposición de arte, tecnología y literatura hispano-musulmanas, Teruel, 1988* (Madrid, 1988), 74-75.

38. R. Izquierdo, "Excavaciones en la ciudad hispanomusulmana de Vascos." For a general survey of problems pertaining to Andalusi houses, see *La casa hispano-musulmana: Aportaciones de la arqueología* (Granada, 1990).

39. Serafín López-Cuervo, *Medina az-Zahra'. Ingeniería y formas* (Madrid, 1985), 36-40.

40. Christian Ewert, *Forschungen zur almohadischen Moschee. Lieferung a: Vorstufen* (Mainz, 1981); H. Stern, *Les mosaïques de la Grande Mosquée de Cordoue* (Berlin, 1976).

41. Christian Ewert, "Die Moschee am Bab al-Mardum in Toledo—Ein 'Kopie' der Moschee von Córdoba," *Madrider Mitteilungen* 18 (1977): 287-354.

42. A good, coherent study of baths in the region of Valencia may be found in the collective volume, *Baños árabes en el País Valenciano* (Valencia, 1989). A convenient reference to the role of Jewish baths in urban settings is Pedro J. Lavado, "Los baños árabes y judíos en la España medieval," ibid., 47-78; Clara Delgado Valero, *Toledo islámico: ciudad, arte e historia* (Toledo, 1987); Juan Zozaya, "Acerca del urbanismo andalusí: algunas observaciones," forthcoming.

43. For a general survey on Islamic cemeteries, see G. Rosselló Bordoy, "Almacabras, ritos funerarios y organización social en al-Andalus," in *III Congreso de Arqueología Medieval Española* (Oviedo, 1989), 1:153-68.

44. Leopoldo Torres Balbás, *Ciudades Hispanomusulmanas,* 2 vols. (Madrid, n.d); and Zozaya, "Acerca del urbanismo andalusí."

45. Roldán, *Itineraria Hispana;* Zozaya, "Notas sobre las comunicaciones."

46. Juan Zozaya, "Esquemas de poblamiento en al-Andalus: algunas observaciones," in *Les Illes Orientals d'al-Andalus* (Palma de Mallorca, 1987), 395-403.

47. Leopoldo Torres Balbás, "Atarazanas hispanomusulmanas," *Al-Andalus* 11 (1946): 175-209.

48. On astronomical instruments, see *Instrumentos astronómicos en la España medieval. Su influencia en Europa* (Santa Cruz de la Palma, 1985). Regarding the general evolution of science in al-Andalus, see Juan Vernet, *La cultura hispanoárabe en Oriente y Occidente* (Barcelona: Ariel, 1978), and the essay by Thomas F. Glick in this volume.

49. Juan Zozaya, "Aproximación a la cronología de algunas formas cerámicas de época taifa," in *Actas de las I Jornadas de Cultura Arabe e Islámica* (Madrid: 1978), 277-85; Retuerce and Zozaya, "Variantes geográficas."

50. Christian Ewert, "Tradiciones omeyas en la arquitectura palatina de época de los taifas: La Aljafería de Zaragoza," in *XXIII Congreso Internacional de Historia del Arte* (Granada, 1976), 2: 64-75.

51. See Vernet, *Cultura hispanoárabe.*

52. Manuel Gómez Moreno, "El Cristo de Don Fernando y Doña Sancha," *Cuadernos del Instituto Central de Restauraciones* 1 (1966); idem., "El arte árabe español hasta los almohades."

53. For Christian pottery, see "Ceràmica grisa i terrisa popular de la Catalunya medieval," *Acta Medievalia,* Annex 2 (Barcelona, 1984). For the north and northwest parts of the peninsula, see the collective volume *La cerámica medieval en noroeste de la Península Ibérica. Aproximación a su estudio* (León, 1989). An interesting study of the pottery sequence based on population and depopulation of sites may be found in M. Urteaga, "Metodología del estudio sobre cerámica medieval de la comarca vallisoletana de Tierra de Campos," in *Atti dello III Congresso sulla Ceramica Medievale,* 147-61.

54. Julio Navarro Palazón, "La casa andalusí en Siyasa: ensayo para una clasificación tipológica," in *La casa hispanomusulmana,* 177-98.

55. Retuerce and Zozaya, "Variantes y constantes."

56. Julio Navarro, *La cerámica islámica en Murcia* (Murcia, 1986); idem, *Una casa islámica en Murcia* (Murcia, 1991). Leopoldo Torres Balbás, "Arte almohade. Arte Nazarí," in *Ars Hispaniae* 4 (Madrid, 1949).

57. For examples, see J. Ferrandis, *Marfiles Hispano-Musulmanes,* 2 vols. (Madrid, 1940), vol. 2.

58. Francisco Cantera Burgos, *Sinagogas españolas* (Madrid, 1955).

59. On problems relating to the origins of Málaga ware, see Manuel Gómez Moreno, "La loza primitiva dorada de Málaga," *Al-Andalus* 5 (1940): 383-98; Ettinghausen, "Notes on the Lustreware of Spain"; H. Blake, "La ceramica medievale spagnola e la Liguria," in *Atti del V Convegno Internazionale della Ceramica* (Albisola, 1972), 55-97. For more recent approaches, see also M. Jenkins, "Medieval Maghribi Luster-painted Pottery," in *I Congrès sur la Céramique Médiévale,* 335-42; Pedro López Elum, "Orígen y evolución de dos grandes centros cerámicos," in *III Congresso Internazionale sulla Ceramica Medievale,* 163-81. The Málaga wares are the subject of recent studies by I. Flores, "Estudio preliminar sobre loza azul y dorada nazarí de la Alhambra," *Cuadernos de Arte e Arqueología* 4 (1988); and M. Muñoz and M. Dominguez, *Cerámica hispanomusulmana en Almería: loza dorada y azul* (Almería, 1989).

60. See Luis M. Llubiá, *Cerámica medieval española* (Barcelona, 1967), 81.

61. For examples, see Juan Zozaya, "Aperçu générale sur la céramique espagnole (X^e^-XVe siècles)," in *I Congrès Internationale sur la Céramique Médiévale,* 265-315. For decorative examples, see Llubiá, *Cerámica medieval española.*

62. Patrice Cressier, Antonio Malpica Cuello, and Guillermo Rosselló Bordoy, "Análisis del poblamiento medieval de la costa de Granada: el yacimiento de 'El Castillejo' y el valle del río de La Toba (Las Guájares)," in *II Congreso de Arqueología Medieval Española,* 150-60.

63. Manuel Acién Almansa, *Ronda y su Serranía en tiempo de los Reyes Católicos,* 3 vols. (Málaga, 1979).

64. P. Banks et al, "Excavaciones en la Ermita de San Baudelio de Berlanga," *Excavaciones Arqueolígicas en España* 16 (1983): 382-41, which relates to continuity in the diet of Castilian villages from the Middle Ages up to around twenty years ago.

65. M. González Martí, *Cerámica del Levante Español,* 3 vols. (Barcelona, 1944-52); M. Almagro and L. Llubiá, "Aragón-Muel," in *C.E.R.A.M.I.C.A.* (Barcelona, 1952). A more recent appraisal is I. Alvaro, *Cerámica aragonesa* (Zaragoza, 1976); J. Ainaud de Lasarte, "Cerámica y vidrio," in *Ars Hispaniae,* X (Madrid, 1952); F. Riera i Vilar and J. Cabestany i Fort, *Ceràmica de Manresa: Segle XIV* (Barcelona, 1980); J. Pascual and X. Martí, *La cerámica verde-manganeso de Paterna* (Valencia, 1987); M. Almagro and L. Llubiá, *La cerámica de Teruel* (Teruel, 1962). For a later appraisal, see Alvaro, *Cerámica aragonesa.*

66. A. Turina, "Cerámicas medievales cristianas de Alcalá de Henares," in *I Congreso de Arqueología Medieval Española* (Huesca, 1986), 5: 649-661; M. Urteaga, "La cerámica roja de Valladolid," in *Actas do V Congresso de Ceramica Medieval,* 263-72.

67. A good example of the involvement of these merchants is the detailed story given by a witness to the surrender of Mallorca to James I of Aragon in the *Liber Maiolichinus de gestis Pisanorum illustribus,* trans. Mireia Mulet Más (Palma de Mallorca, 1991).

68. J. Casanovas and O. Ripoll, "Catálogo de los materiales aparecidos en la necrópolis judáica de Deza (Soria), *Celtiberia* 65, 135-48.

Convivencia

Catalogue

CONTRIBUTORS TO THE CATALOGUE

JD	Jerrilynn Dodds
EFP	Eduardo Fresneda Padilla
TG	Thomas Glick
AMLA	Ana María López Alvarez
VBM	Vivian B. Mann
PMS	Purificacíon Marinetto Sánchez
CN	Claudia Nahson
RS	Raymond Scheindlin
GSR	Gabrielle Sed-Rajna
MSF	María Paz Soler Ferrer
JVR	Jaime Vicente Redón

Biblical Manuscripts

1 **Commentary of Beatus of Liébana on the Apocalypse**

Scribe and illuminator: Maius

Monastery of San Salvador de Tabara, 940s

Ink and gouache on parchment

15¼ x 11¼ in. (38.7 x 28.5 cm), 300 folios

New York, The Pierpont Morgan Library, M644

Beatus was a Spanish monk who lived in the eighth century. His Commentary on the Apocalypse was extremely popular during the tenth and eleventh centuries due to widespread dread of catastrophes predicted to occur around the year 1000. Manuscripts with the Beatus text were often paired with Jerome's Commentary on the Book of Daniel, which records similar millennial events; this is the case here. The text is written in a Visigothic script that was used in Spain until the twelfth century, long after it had been replaced by the Carolingian uncial elsewhere in Europe. One part of the decoration consists of embellishments of the script, display texts, and ornamental initials.

In addition, there are full-page miniatures executed in bright tones of red, green, yellow, and blue, along with black outlining and white highlights. The effect of the simplified repetitive forms and bright saturated colors is to transform narrative events into strong visual patterns. Occasionally, the miniatures refer to contemporary political events, as in the depiction of Baltazzar's Feast on fol. 255v, where the setting for this scene of profanation occurs within a horseshoe arch formed of red and white voussoirs, a hallmark of the Mosque of Córdoba.

BIBLIOGRAPHY John Williams and Barbara Shailor, *A Spanish Apocalypse: The Morgan Beatus Manuscript* (New York, 1991), which gives the older literature.

—*VBM*

2 **First Cambridge Castilian Bible**

Castile, third quarter of the thirteenth century

Ink, tempera, and gold on vellum

13⅜ x 11¼ in. (33.8 x 28.5 cm), 246 folios

Syndics of Cambridge University Library, Ms. Add. 465

This codex is among the earliest preserved Hebrew Bibles originating on the Iberian peninsula. Although the colophon has been erased, a Castilian provenance is suggested by characteristic features of the script and decoration. The elegant, carefully shaped square script, and the artistic layout and sobriety of the decoration (which includes only geometric shapes and abstract motifs) are found in most manuscripts produced in Toledo and Burgos, the two earliest centers that have been identified.

In the early Hebrew Bibles, text has absolute primacy. Decoration is admitted only to enhance the script, emphasize its divisions, and draw the reader's eyes to the beginning of new sections. Liberty was allowed only in the minute script of the Masoretic notes in the margins, which were copied in ornamental shapes rendering the notes themselves rather difficult to decipher.

The decoration of the Cambridge Bible follows this general pattern. The main ornaments are micrographic notes that frame prominent passages of the text such as the Songs of Moses in Exodus (fol. 20r) and in Deuteronomy (fol. 58v). The candelabrum motif of the latter page may be a later addition. Some of the ornaments enhancing the letters indicating the beginning of the pericopes may be part of the original decoration; others, executed in brush gold, may be later additions. The space-filling ornament at the end of the Prophets, composed of interlaced fillets on a ground painted in red, blue, and violet compartments, shows stylistic affinities to the ornamental initial letters of tenth- and eleventh-century Visigothic manuscripts from Castile.

The manuscript was in Poland in the eighteenth century, where a decorated title page was added to it. It was acquired by the Cambridge University in Cracow from M. Lipschutz in 1869.

BIBLIOGRAPHY H. Loewe, *Handlist of the Hebrew Manuscripts in the University Library of Cambridge* (n.d.), no. 22; B. Narkiss, *Hebrew Illuminated Manuscripts in the British Isles* (Jerusalem and London, 1982), cat. no. 1; G. Sed-Rajna, "Toledo or Burgos," *Journal of Jewish Art* 2 (1975): 6–21; S. M. Schiller-Szinessy, *Catalogue of the Hebrew Manuscripts Preserved in the University Library of Cambridge* (Cambridge, 1876), 1, no. 13.

—*GSR*

3 Latin Bible

Probably Spain, ca. 1300

Ink and colored inks on parchment

5⅛ x 3⅜ in. (13.0 x 8.4 cm), 309 folios

Chicago, The Newberry Library, Ms. 22

This thirteenth-century Bible contains all the books of the Hebrew Bible and the New Testament with the exception of Psalms. The choice of prologues and the use of typical Spanish line endings may indicate that this small-sized manuscript was created in Spain, as was suggested by Saenger.[1] Its decoration, mostly in the margins, consists of flourishes in red and blue and feather-like motifs. The manuscript has fine calligraphy, with its chapter headings marked with red ink in the same script as the text, and red initials with blue decoration alternating with blue initials with red decoration. It has a red-brown morocco Spanish binding on wooden boards, from the fifteenth century.

In the fifteenth century, the manuscript belonged to the Carthusian monastery of Paular, as is indicated by the inscription "Este libro es del monastiro [sic] de Santa María al Paular." It later passed into the collection of Henry Probasco and was then acquired by The Newberry Library.[2]

NOTES 1) P. Saenger, *A Catalogue of the Pre-1500 Western Manuscript Books at The Newberry Library* (Chicago, 1989), 38. Henry Probasco, who in 1890 sold the manuscript to The Newberry Library, believed that this Bible had been copied by a German scribe [*Catalogue of the Collection of Books, Manuscripts and Works of Art Belonging to Mr. Henry Probasco,* Cincinnati, Ohio, (Oakwood, Clifton) (1873), 374, no. 5.]. 2) Saenger, *A Catalogue of the pre-1500 Western Manuscript Books at The Newberry Library,* 38.

BIBLIOGRAPHY H. Probasco, *Catalogue of the Collection of Books, Manuscripts and Works of Art Belonging to Mr. Henry Probasco,* Cincinnati, Ohio, (Oakwood, Clifton) (1873), 374, no. 5; S. De Ricci, *Census of Medieval and Renaissance Manuscripts in the United States and Canada* (New York, 1935), 1:523; P. Saenger, *A Catalogue of the Pre-1500 Western Manuscript Books at The Newberry Library* (Chicago, 1989), 38–39.

—*CN*

4 Leaf from a Qurʾān

North Africa, ca. 1300

Ink on parchment

6½ x 6 in. (16.5 x 15.2 cm)

New York, Lent by The Metropolitan Museum of Art, Rogers Fund, 1921, 21.28

This page from an illuminated Qurʾān features verses from *Sura* 5. Here, as in most manuscripts from North Africa and Spain, the script used is *Maghribi* or western script. It is an elegant script, with attenuated letters joined in a fluid continuity.

Everywhere on the page, writing is treated both as the bearer of the sacred words of ʾAllah, and as a beautiful abstract design that is worthy of contemplation in its own right. In this way the page conveys both the content of the text and the sense of its sacredness and importance.

The combination of elaborate geometric decoration and opulent arabesque and vine scrolls, such as that found in the medallion of the chapter heading, reminds one of the combination of motifs found on the Iberian peninsula under the Nasrids, and in North Africa during the

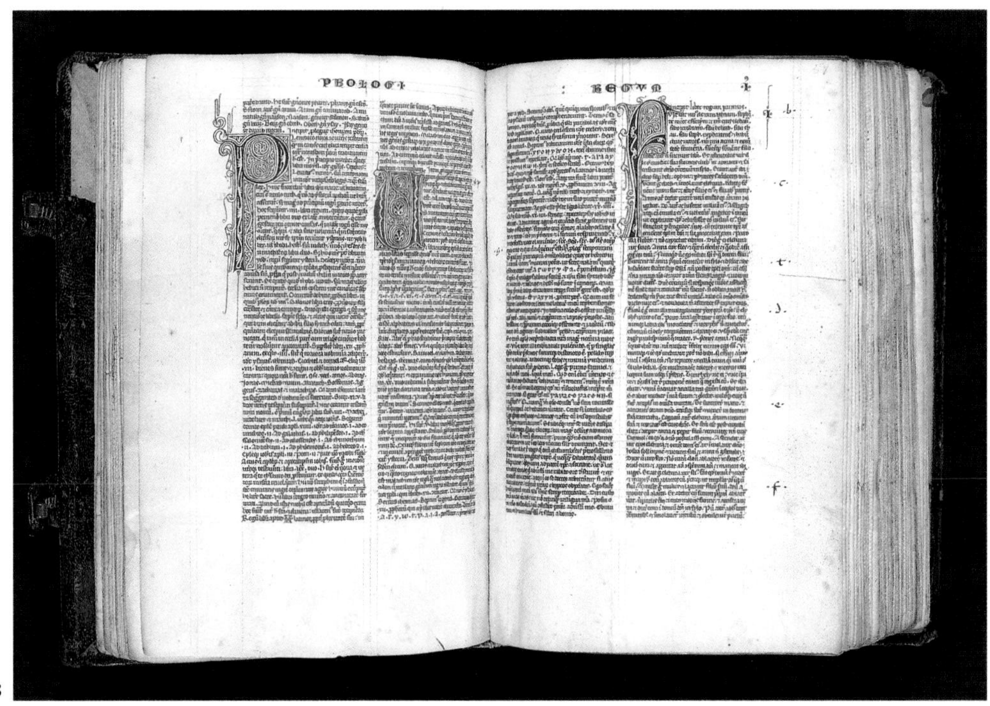

3

Merenid dynasty. Although this page comes from a North African Qurʾān, it is similar to contemporary Spanish Qurʾāns. The fourteenth century was no longer a time of common rule between the two continents, as was the case under the Almohad and the Almoravid dynasties, but strong links still existed between their artistic traditions.

—JD

5 Hebrew Bible

Perpignan (?), Kingdom of Majorca, 1301

Ink, gouache, and gold on vellum

12½ x 9¼ in. (31.9 x 23.5 cm), 523 folios

Copenhagen, The Royal Library, Cod. Heb. II

Although the name of the scribe has been erased in the colophon (fol. 521r), there is little doubt that this sumptuous Bible was copied and decorated in the same workshop as the Perpignan Bible copied in 1299 (Paris, Bibliothèque Nationale, ms. Hébreu 7), only two years before the Copenhagen Bible. Both manuscripts have the same layout and similar decoration, and both contain double-page paintings of the Temple implements.

The symbolic display of the objects and implements of the Tabernacle, as described in Exodus chapters 25 to 30, with additional implements of Solomon's Temple, was a tradition of Hebrew Bibles from Spain from the end of the thirteenth to the end of the fifteenth century. The earliest known example is a Toledo Bible dated 1277. Both Perpignan Bibles contain a faithful copy of the Toledo prototype, executed in a much more refined technique. The Temple implements in the Copenhagen codex (fols. 11v–12r) are painted in brush gold on a checkered blue and red ground, attesting to the gradual acceptance by Jewish artists of the norms of local Gothic art.

The influence of contemporary Gothic painting is also present in the organization of the opening pages containing Masoretic treatises. These texts are copied in columns and surrounded by Gothic or trilobed arches (fols. 2v–9r). The influence of Gothic art is also present in the grotesque and animal figures filling the spandrels, the most elaborate of which is a griffin on folio 8r.

The carpet pages (fols. 10v–11r), decorated with geometric patterns outlined in micrography, are characteristic of Hebrew manuscripts from the Iberian peninsula. Also typical of Spanish manuscripts are the filigree ornaments that enhance several pages and frame the colophon (fol. 521r). On almost every page the Masoretic notes in the lower margin are written in ornamental shapes.

This Bible was acquired by the Royal Library of Copenhagen in 1732 from the collection of Count Christian Danneskjold-Samsoe, whose ex libris appears on the binding.

BIBLIOGRAPHY A.E. Mehren and A.A. Wolff, *Codices Orientales Bibliothecae Regiae Hafniensis*, Hafniae, 2 (1857), 5; C. Roth, "Jewish Antecedents of Christian Art," *Journal of the Warburg and Courtauld Institutes* 16 (1953): 24–44, pl. 6; Amsterdam, Joods, Historisch Museum, *Joodse verluchte handschriften*, exhibition catalogue (Amsterdam, 1961), no. 7; R. Edelman, *Hebraica from Denmark—Manuscripts and Printed Books in the Collection of the Royal Library, Copenhagen*,([New York], 1969), no. 5; Frankfurt am Main, Historisches Museum, *Synagoga*, exhibition catalogue (Frankfurt, 1961), no. 78, fig. 43; C.O. Nordstom, "Some Miniatures in Hebrew Bibles," *Synthronon* 2 (1968): 89–105; T. Metzger, "Les objets du culte, le sanctuaire du désert et le Temple de Jérusalem dans les Bibles hébraïques médiévales en Orient et en Espagne," *Bulletin of the John Rylands Library* 53 (1970–71): 175–85; New York, The Jewish Museum, *Kings and Citizens: The History of the Jews in Denmark 1622-1983*, 2 vols. (New York, 1983), vol. 2, exhibition catalogue, essay and description by Ulf Haxen, no. 7; Berlin, Berliner Festspiele, *Jüdische Lebenswelten: Katalog*, exhibition catalogue, ed. A. Nachama and G. Sievernich, (Berlin, 1992), no. 20: 1/11.

—*GSR*

6 Second Kennicott Bible

Soria, Old Castile, 1306

Scribe and artist: Joshua ben Abraham ibn Gaon

Ink, gouache, and gold on vellum

12⅛ x 8⅞ in. (30.8 x 22.5 cm), 428 folios

By permission of the Curators of The Bodleian Library, Oxford, Bodl. Kenn. 2

Like his brother Shem Tov (see no. 7), Joshua ben Abraham ibn Gaon was not only a professional scribe, but also a scholar and even an artist. As he indicates in his colophons, he was responsible for both copying and decorating his manuscripts. He was an imaginative artist and prolific scribe: four manuscripts bear his signature and two more can be attributed to him by the style of the ornaments.

This Bible, copied in Soria in 1306, is profusely decorated with arcaded pages, full-page interlaced carpet pages, painted pericope signs, painted frames for Masoretic annotations at the end of the books, and the ornamental Masora in the lower margins. The style of these ornaments, where Mudejar motifs such as horseshoe and polylobed arches are combined with Gothic grotesque figures filling the spandrels, are similar to that of Joshua's Bibles copied in Tudela in 1300 (Paris, Bibliothèque Nationale, ms. Hébreu 20) and in Soria a few years after the Kennicott codex (Paris, Bibliothèque Nationale, ms. Hébreu 21). However, the codex exhibited here, which seems to have been the second Bible produced by Joshua ibn Gaon, includes an additional element of special interest: a visual commentary to Mishnah *Middot* describing the Second Temple.

The study of the Second Temple, based on the Mishnah *Middot* was pursued by Jewish scholars including Rashi, Maimonides, and many others. Joshua ibn Gaon's visual explanation follows the text of the Mishnah accurately, adding some elements from Maimonides' commentary, and endeavors to show the plan of the building including the placement of the implements. This attempt to visualize the rather complex description of *Middot* required a profound knowledge of the text, as well as the skill of the artist. The Temple plan of Joshua ibn Gaon is essentially different from all representations of the Tabernacle or the Temple known from synagogue pavements or symbolical representations in manuscripts, inasmuch as it constitutes an accurate scholarly commentary carrying a symbolic message. The two leaves of the plan, unfortunately not completely preserved, are precious witnesses to an age when intellectual ability and artistic skill were both focused on the study of tradition.

The Bible has a seventeenth-century Turkish brown calf binding on wooden boards, with red and gold decorated applied leather pieces.

An inscription indicates the sale of the volume in 1519 with the price paid in Damascene coins.

BIBLIOGRAPHY B. Narkiss and G. Sed-Rajna, "La première Bible de Josué ben Abraham Ibn Gaon," *Revue des Études Juives* 130 (1972): 255–69; B. Narkiss, *Hebrew Illuminated Manuscripts in the British Isles* (Jerusalem and London, 1982), cat. no. 3; A. Neubauer, *A Catalogue of Hebrew Manuscripts in the Bodleian Library and the College Libraries of Oxford* (Oxford, 1906, repr. 1986), no. 2323.

—*GSR*

7 *Keter Shem Tov*

Soria, Old Castile, 1312

Scribe: Shem Tov ibn Gaon

Ink, gouache, and gold on parchment

13½ x 9⅞ in. (34.5 x 25.2 cm), 384 folios

Carl Alexander Floersheim Trust for Art and Judaica

Named after the copyist Shem Tov ben Abraham ibn Gaon, the *Keter Shem Tov* is one of the most important and precious Bibles of the Sephardic legacy. As was true of many Jewish scribes, Shem Tov ibn Gaon was not simply a copyist; he was also a learned man and scholar. He was the author of several halakhic and kabbalistic works, the best known of which are his commentary on Maimonides' *Mishneh Torah* called *Migdal ʿOz,* and a kabbalistic work, *Badey ha-aron.* The Ibn Gaon family lived in Soria (see also no. 6), and it was there that Shem Tov copied this Bible in 1312. Shortly after completing the copy, Shem Tov left Spain for the Holy Land and spent the rest of his days in Safed.

When copying the Bible, Shem Tov ibn Gaon made use of all the authoritative documents at hand in order to provide an accurate text. Among his sources listed on folios 251–53 are Talmudic authorities, as well as contemporary sages like Moses Nahmanides, his teacher David Kimḥi, and even Rashi. He refers also to the Codex Hilleli, a famous model codex mentioned in several thirteenth-century Spanish Bibles, which, however, has not been preserved.

Shem Tov ibn Gaon's Bible is also profusely decorated with illuminated pericope signs and arcades surrounding the Masoretic lists and the Masoretic notes at the end of the books. The ornaments attest to the permanence of Mudejar motifs such as horseshoe arches decorated by scrolls bearing palmetto leaves, as well as to the growing influence of Gothic art seen in spandrels and half-acanthus leaves coiled around the straight stems that frame the page.

BIBLIOGRAPHY D. S. Sassoon, *Ohel David: A Descriptive Catalogue of the Hebrew and Samaritan Manuscripts in the Sassoon Library* (London, 1932), 1:2, no. 82; D. S. Loewinger, *R. Shem Tov b. Abraham Ibn Gaon: Sefunot–Sefer Zefat* (Jerusalem, 1964) 9–39; Sotheby's, *A Further Ninety-Seven Highly Important Hebrew Manuscripts From the Collection Formed by the Late David Sassoon,* sales catalogue, December 4, 1984, no. 97; Berlin, Berliner Festspiele, *Jüdische Lebenswelten: Katalog,* exhibition catalogue, ed. A. Nachama and G. Sievernich, (Berlin, 1992), no. 20: 12/6.

—*GSR*

8 *Bible Historiée et Vies des Saints (Historiated Bible and Lives of the Saints)*

Northern France, ca. 1300

Ink, gouache, silver, and gold leaf on parchment

12¼ x 8⅞ in. (31.2 x 22.5 cm), 154 folios

New York, Spencer Collection, The New York Public Library, Astor, Lenox, and Tilden Foundations, Ms. 22

In 1194, King Sancho el Fuerte of Navarre (1194–1234) commissioned an illustrated Bible (Amiens, Bibliothèque Communale, ms. Latin 108) that originally included 635 scenes from the Hebrew Bible and 105 scenes from the New Testament, as well as pictures of saints and illustrations of the Apocalypse.[1] A few years later a copy was made (Harburg, ms. 1,2, lat. 4, 15) presumably intended as a gift from King Sancho to one of his female relatives.[2] Today, portions are missing from both Bibles, but together they reveal an extensive cycle of biblical images. The production of such a richly illustrated work was an innovation in thirteenth-century Iberia; no similar cycle is known to have existed prior to King Sancho's commission. In the early fourteenth century, the Amiens Bible was copied in a workshop in northern France, probably in Troyes; it is now in The New York Public Library.

Audiens aute iacob / q alimenta uenderent / in egypto / dixit filius suis &c.
Iacob / qui demouroit en la terre de chanaan / ou la famine aussi estoit
grant / oi dire / que len uendoit bles / & uiures en egypte / lors il appela ses enfans /
& leur dist / pour quoy estes uous si pereceus / alez uous en en la t're degypte / &
nous pourchaces des uiures / & achetez des blez / p quoi / nous puissions estre sou
stenu / & eschaper ceste pourete / & ceste famine.

Descendentes igit · x · fratres ioseph / in egyptu / &c. Lors se departiret les · x
fils / de leur pere iacob / & li laissieret beniamin / le meinsne deuls / pour li tenir
compaignie / du comandement du pere / qui lamoit mlt / & se doubtoit quil neust a sou
frir / ou uoiage / auec euls / & sen alerent en egypte / a tout leurs chamels / charges de
sacs / & dautres necessites

8

Sancho el Fuerte was extremely tolerant toward the Muslims and Mudejars resident in his realm. He forged alliances with the caliph of Granada and against his fellow Christian rulers, for which he was excommunicated; he may even have married a Muslim princess. This tolerant attitude extended to the Jews of Navarre as well; they served in the army and were assigned guard duty over important castles.[3] François Bucher has suggested that the king's closeness to his Jewish subjects may lie behind the clear understanding of Old Testament iconography in the original Bible.[4] A comparison of the imagery of the Sancho Bibles and the biblical cycles of fourteenth-century Haggadot indicates that some of the influences were reciprocal.

NOTES 1) F. Bucher, *The Pamplona Bibles,* 2 vols. (New Haven and London, 1970), 1:19. 2) Ibid., 6. 3) Ibid., 38-40. 4) Ibid., 10.

BIBLIOGRAPHY F. Bucher, *The Pamplona Bibles,* 2 vols. (New Haven and London, 1970), 1:63–75, figs. 12-32 (also for the older literature).

—*VBM*

9 Torah Scroll

Spain, fifteenth century
Ink on leather
H 23¾ in. (60.32 cm)
New York, The Library of The Jewish Theological Seminary of America

The Jewish tradition of writing the Hebrew Bible on a scroll for synagogue use continued even after this ancient book form fell into disuse with the general population during the fourth century of this era. Even earlier, by the first century, Jews had begun the practice of reading from the Torah scroll in the synagogue on a regular basis, a practice that still continues today.

Unpublished

—*VBM*

10 The Floersheim Psalter

Lisbon (?), last quarter of the fifteenth century
Ink, gouache, and gold on parchment
3⅞ x 2¾ in. (10 x 7 cm), 196 folios
Carl Alexander Floersheim Trust for Art and Judaica

At the end of the fifteenth century and mainly in the Lisbon workshop, many small Psalters and prayerbooks were copied for private devotion. This Psalter, which in the sixteenth century was owned by the Norsa family, is one of the most delicate examples of this type of manuscript.

The 149 psalms (listed on fols. 2v–8v) are decorated by filigree pen-work panels surrounding the burnished gold initial words, in the characteristic style of a Lisbon workshop. The beginning of each of the five books of the Psalter (Ps. 1, 42, 73, 90, 107) is decorated by an elaborate double-page frontispiece: on the left side the burnished gold initial word and the first lines of the text are framed by gold interlace on blue and red painted ground or by fleshy acanthus leaves. On the facing page, the motif of the frame is developed as a full-page ornament. Some delicately drawn animals and scrolls enhance the margins.

The manuscript, most probably produced in Lisbon, was brought to Italy by Spanish refugees after the expulsion. In 1519 it was acquired by the well-known Ferrarese banker Isaac ben Immanuel from Norcia (1485–1560) as is attested by the sale inscription (fol. 1r). It was probably after Isaac's death that the Psalter came into the possession of his son Jacob, who had it rebound, adding a bifolium to the manuscript with his family coat of arms (fol. 10r), which appears also on the binding. The book has a red velvet binding with niello medallions on each cover: on the front cover King David playing the harp, on the back cover the coat of arms of the Norsa family. It later came into the collection of M. De Bry, Paris. It was then acquired by Jacob Michael, New York, in 1970 and later by the Carl Alexander Floersheim Trust for Art and Judaica.

BIBLIOGRAPHY P. Norsa, *Una famiglia di banchieri—La famiglia Norsa (1350–1950)* (Naples, 1953–59); C. Roth, "The De Bry Psalter and the Norsa Family," *Revue des Études Juives* 125 (1966): 401–5; G. Sed-Rajna, *Manuscrits*

10

hébreux de Lisbonne (Paris, 1970), no. 23; Amsterdam, Jewish Historical Museum, *The Image of the World-Jewish Tradition in Manuscripts and Printed Books,* exhibition catalogue (Amsterdam and Leuven, 1990), no. 19, figs. 36–37; Berlin, Berliner Festspiele, *Jüdische Lebenswelten: Katalog,* exhibition catalogue, ed. A. Nachama and G. Sievernich, (Berlin, 1992), no. 20: 1/14.

—*GSR*

11 **Abravanel Pentateuch**

Castile (?), 1480

Ink on vellum

9 x 6⅝ in.
(22.9 x 17 cm),
240 folios

By permission of The Curators of the Bodleian Library, Oxford, Opp. Add. 4°26

This compound text of the Pentateuch, followed by the readings of the Prophets (*haftarot*), the *Five Megillot,* and the apocryphal *Megillat Antiochus,* was produced during the last years of the Jewish communities in Spain. It was probably the effect of the growing political pressure that in manuscripts of this final period micrography was the only ornament. This decoration was usually executed by the scribe himself, or by the copyist of the Masora, and hence there was no need to have recourse to other craftsmen or workshops specializing in painted ornaments.

Moses ben Jacob the Sephardi, son of Moses ibn Qalif, the scribe of this manuscript, is also known from another Bible, now in the Biblioteca Palatina of Parma (ms. Parm. 2809), completed in 1473. A few other manuscripts, where his signature does not appear, may also be attributed to him on the basis of the style of the script and of the characteristic ornaments in micrography.

The ornaments in micrography, besides enhancing the aesthetic effects of the layout, also emphasize the articulations of the text. The main divisions are separated by carpet pages of interlaced outlined fillets; the lists of Masoretic annotations preceding or following the biblical text are surrounded by ornamental frames; more elaborate frames emphasize especially solemn passages in the text, such as the two Songs of Moses, and the colophon. Finally, the marginal Masoretic notes accompanying the biblical text are also copied in ornamental shapes. These ornaments are symmetrical and more elaborate on the first and the last page of each quire in order to ensure the correct order of the quires at the binding.

This Pentateuch is a precious historical document. Its first owner was Don Samuel Abravanel who, after having left his native city, Lisbon, for Castile in 1483, became the Chief Rabbi of Naples during the years 1496–1541. It was later the property of Elisha Finzi (1491).

BIBLIOGRAPHY B. Narkiss, *Hebrew Illuminated Manuscripts in the British Isles* (Jerusalem and London, 1982), cat. no. 55; A. Neubauer, *Catalogue of Hebrew Manuscripts in the Bodleian Library and the College Libraries of Oxford,* (Oxford, 1886, 1906), no. 30.

—*GSR*

12 Hebrew Bible

Castile (?), late fifteenth century

Colored inks on vellum

10¾ x 9⅛ in. (27.2 x 23.3 cm), 363 folios

Copenhagen, The Royal Library, Heb. V

Written in a beautiful square Sephardic script, this Bible is lavishly decorated with micrography and filigree pen work in color, in the traditional style of late fifteenth-century Castilian book illumination. The filigree ornaments, executed in red ink, enhance the opening pages of the Bible, surrounding the gold initial words placed within a panel painted in red or dark blue. Red pen drawn scrolls enlivened by blue flowers and vine leaves run along the text column in some of the vertical margins.

The Masoretic notes, copied in micrography in the outer and the lower margins, form stylized acanthus leaves rising from the coiled stems, often enclosing flower buds. In layout as well as in design, the ornaments outlined in micrography attest to a highly refined technique. Pen-work ornaments of scrolls in red, green, or blue decorate the three letters indicating the beginning of the weekly pericopes. Similar ornaments enhance the numbers of part of the Psalms and the Masoretic notes at the end of the books.

Both script and decoration are characteristic of late fifteenth-century Hebrew manuscript illumination in Castile. Yet at some moment in the history of the codex, an attempt was made to falsify its date; after having erased some passages, a later hand inscribed on several pages (e.g. fols. 121v, 154r, 334v, etc.) the date of 4506 after the Creation (746 C.E.), which is not consistent with either the script or the decoration.

The Bible was acquired for King Frederick V and brought to Denmark by Carsten Niebuhr in 1766. It has a brown morocco binding on cardboard with blind-tooled decoration of scrolls framing a central amphora. On the front is the monogram of King Christian VII.

BIBLIOGRAPHY B. Kennicott, *Dissertatio Generalis in Vetus Testamentum Hebraicum cum Variis Lectionibus ex Codicibus Manuscriptiis* (Brunovici, 1783), 172; A. E. Mehren and A. A. Wolff, *Codices Orientales Bibliothecae Regiae Hafniensis,* Hafniae, vol. 2 (1857), 11–12; Amsterdam, Joods Historisch Museum, *Joodse verluchte handschriften,* exhibition catalogue (Amsterdam, 1961), no. 16; Frankfurt am Main, Historisches Museum, *Synagoga,* exhibition catalogue (Frankfurt, 1961), no. 87; R. Edelman, *Hebraica from Denmark—Manuscripts and Printed Books in the Collection of the Royal Library, Copenhagen,* ([New York], 1969), no. 3; L. Avrin, *Hebrew Micrography: One Thousand years of Art in Script* (Jerusalem, 1981), pl. 29; New York, The Jewish Museum, *Kings and Citizens: The History of the Jews in Denmark 1622-1983,* vol. 2, exhibition catalogue, essay and description by Ulf Haxen (New York, 1983), no. 8; Copenhagen, Royal Library, *Carsten Niebuhr und die arabische Reise 1761-1767,* exhibition catalogue (Copenhagen, November 1986 - February 1987), no. 63.

—*GSR*

13 **Hebrew Bible**

Castile (?), late fifteenth century

Ink, gouache, and gold on vellum

12½ x 9¼ in. (31.9 x 23.5 cm), 93 folios

Copenhagen, The Royal Library, Cod. Heb. VII

This volume is the first part of a complete Bible now divided into three volumes, but originally planned to be bound as a single manuscript. On fol. 4r, a legal document relates that the Bible was given as a present by Joseph ben Judah ben Hanin to his son, along with some other manuscripts, in Tunis, on 4 Adar, 5252 (February 2, 1492). This inscription suggests that the Bible was brought to Tunis by a Spanish refugee.

Among the full-page ornaments in micrography (fols. 1r, 2r, 92v–93v) are some based on a motif traditionally used in Castile in the thirteenth century. Double palmetto leaves placed symmetrically within a rectangular frame are outlined in micrography on a ground colored red, green, ochre, and magenta. The entire page is surrounded by an inscription in large display script placed between two lines of minute script. This layout is reminiscent of thirteenth-century Hebrew book illumination of which this codex presents a late variant in a considerably finer technique. The carpet page with the symmetrical palmetto leaves may also have been executed earlier and reused in this Bible.

Masoretic notes are copied in minute script in the vertical and horizontal margins. The lines of micrography form ornamental shapes, stylized flowers, scrolls, and knots. Masoretic treatises preceding the biblical text are placed within horseshoe arches outlined in micrography (fols. 2v–3v). Micrography is also used to frame the Masoretic notes at the end of the books of the Bible.

The Bible has a brown morocco binding on cardboard with blind-tooled decoration, gold tooled amphoras in the corners, and the monogram of King Christian VII in the center of the front cover. The Bible was acquired in the Middle East by Christian Van Haven and brought to Denmark by Carsten Niebuhr in 1766.

BIBLIOGRAPHY B. Kennicott, *Dissertatio Generalis in Vetus Testamentum Hebraicum cum Variis Lectionibus ex Codicibus Manuscriptiis* (Brunovici, 1783), no. 171; A. E. Mehren and A. A. Wolff, *Codices Orientales Bibliothecae Regiae Hafniensis,* Hafniae, 2 (1857), pp. 11–12; Amsterdam, Joods Historisch Museum, *Joodse verluchte handschriften,* exhibition catalogue (Amsterdam, 1961), no. 15; Frankfurt am Main, Historisches Museum, *Synagoga,* exhibition catalogue (Frankfurt, 1961), no. 86; R. Edelman, *Hebraica from Denmark—Manuscripts and Printed Books in the Collection of the Royal Library, Copenhagen* (New York, 1969), no. 2; G. Sed-Rajna, "Toledo or Burgos," *Journal of Jewish Art* 2(1975): 17, fig. 14; L. Avrin, *Hebrew Micrography: One Thousand years of Art in Script* (Jerusalem, 1981), pl. 34; New York, The Jewish Museum, *Kings and Citizens: The History of the Jews in Denmark 1622–1983,* vol. 2, exhibition catalogue, essay and description by Ulf Haxen, (New York, 1983), no. 7; Copenhagen, Det Konigelige Bibliotek, *Carsten Niebuhr und die arabische Reise 1761-1767,* exhibition catalogue (Copenhagen, November 1986–February 1987), no. 64.

—*GSR*

14 **First Hispano-Portuguese Bible**

Castile (?), late fifteenth century

Ink, colored inks, and gold on vellum

7¼ x 5⅛ in. (18.0 x 13.0 cm), 578 folios

The Master and Fellows, Trinity College, Cambridge, F 12.106

As in many biblical manuscripts of the final period of Jewry in Spain, micrography is the only ornament of this codex. There is little doubt that the restriction of the decoration to the sole element that could have been executed by the scribe, or by a specially trained copyist, reflects the degradation of social life and was the consequence of the isolation of Jewish craftsmen from workshops led by Christian artists.

Yet, by the end of the fifteenth century the art of book decoration in general, and that of micrographic ornament in particular, attained their fullest development, and each of the manuscripts is a masterpiece of layout. Full-page ornaments, consisting of interlacing patterns in varying colors of ink and painted space fillers surrounded by motifs reminiscent of Mudejar ornament or by inscriptions in Hebrew display script, provide the most harmonious, abstract compositions. Within the text the *massorah magna* (in the horizontal margins) and the *massorah*

14

parva (in the outer vertical margins), are copied in different shapes, among them interlaced knots, and undulating fillets twisted around straight stems ending in stylized flower buds. The symmetry of the ornamental Masora on the last page of one quire and the first page of the next indicates that the scribes used these ornaments as a means of ensuring the correct sequence of the quires for the binding.

Some special passages of the biblical text were to be enhanced, as usual, by frames, also executed in micrography. Only one of these frames has been completed (fol. 569r, end of Neḥemiah). On other pages (Song of Moses, the last pages of the Pentateuch, Former and Latter Prophets, Chronicles) the space planned for the frame was left empty. No doubt, as in many other manuscripts, the decoration had to be interrupted under the pressure of hostile circumstances.

In the nineteenth century, the manuscript was owned by the Segre family of Italy. Later it was owned by William Wright whose inscription appears on the flyleaf: "William Aldis Wright, Trinity College, 13 December 1906." In 1912, Wright, who was vice master of Trinity, gave the manuscript to the college.

BIBLIOGRAPHY B. Narkiss, ed., *Hebrew Illuminated Manuscripts in the British Isles* (Jerusalem and London, 1982), no. 57; H. Loewe, *Handlist of Hebrew Manuscripts in the University Library of Cambridge*, (n.p., n.d.), no. 21.

—GSR

15 **Hebrew Psalter**

Lisbon, 1495

Ink and gouache on parchment

3⅜ x 4½ in. (8.6 x 11.5 cm), 134 folios

Vatican City, Biblioteca Apostolica Vaticana, Cod. Ebr. 473

This small Psalter, copied in Lisbon by Moses ben Isaac (colophon on fol. 134v) only one year before the expulsion of the Jews from Portugal, is written in a semicursive Hebrew script that was also used for Hebrew texts printed on the earliest Portuguese presses. The space left around the initial words (written in square script), may suggest that originally these were planned to be decorated by filigree ornaments as in most Lisbon manuscripts. However, the decoration was not completed, either under the pressure of constraining circumstances, or because of the withdrawal of the person who commissioned the work, whose name was erased from the colophon. Still, the elegant script and careful execution are typical features of manuscripts produced in Lisbon at the end of the fifteenth century.

A sale inscription on fol. 2r records the name of an earlier owner, Isaac Tsarfati, son of Solomon Tsarfati "Yarhi." This specification may indicate that the family originated from Lunel in Southern France. However, the manuscript was bought for one zecchino, a coin that was used in Venice, and hence the sale probably took place in Italy.

The Psalter has a brown morocco binding on cardboard with blind-tooled decoration and gilt edges. In the center of each cover is a medallion with the name ISAC (front cover) TEDESCO (lower cover), probably the name of an earlier owner.

BIBLIOGRAPHY B. Kennicott, *Dissertatio Generalis in Vetus Testamentum Hebraicum cum Variis Lectionibus ex Codicibus Manuscriptiis* (Brunovici, 1783), no. 509; A. Mai, *Catalogum Codicum Biblothecae Vaticanae...Hebraicorum* (Rome, 1831), vol. 2, p. 86; G. Sed-Rajna, *Manuscrits hébreux de Lisbonne* (Paris, 1970), no. 10. T. Metzger, *Les manuscrits hébreux copiés et décorés à Lisbonne dans les dernières décennies du XVe siècle* (Paris, 1977), no. 10.

—GSR

16 **Hebrew Psalter**

Lisbon, last decade of the fifteenth century

Ink and gouache on parchment

4⅝ x 6¼ in. (11.7 x 15.7 cm), 218 folios

Vatican City, Biblioteca Apostolica Vaticana, Cod. Ebr. 463

Although no colophon has been conserved, the Lisbon origin of this small Psalter is almost certain. The delicate filigree ornaments surrounding the letters numbering the psalms are typical of manuscripts produced in Lisbon. Some of these ornaments are executed in the characteristic violet of the Lisbon school, and others are in different shades of red, blue, or brown, with feathery scrolls issuing from them.

In the course of time, the first leaves of the Psalter were lost; the original manuscript starts on fol. 9. Other lacunae are between fol. 210v and 211r. The manuscript has a red morocco binding with gold tooled decoration.

BIBLIOGRAPHY A. Mai, *Catalogum Codicum Bibliothecae Vaticanae...Hebraicorum* (Rome, 1831), vol. 2, 84; T. Metzger, *Les manuscrits hébreux copiés et décorés à Lisbonne dans les dernières décennies du XVe siècle* (Paris, 1977), no. 20; G. Sed-Rajna, *Manuscrits hébreux de Lisbonne* (Paris, 1970), no. 20.

—GSR

Prayer Books

17 **Hamilton *Siddur***

Southwest France (Languedoc), end of the thirteenth century

Ink and gouache on parchment

8¼ x 6½ in. (21 x 16.4 cm), 106 folios

Berlin, Staatsbibliothek zu Berlin Preussischer Kulturbesitz, Orientabteilung, Ms. Ham. 288

This manuscript, containing prayers for the feasts of Passover and Sukkoth, belongs to a group of small-sized books probably copied in southwest France (Languedoc) in the thirteenth century, as some transliterated terms occurring in the text reflect the French dialect of this area. All the manuscripts of the group share the same style of script—a large Sephardic square script—and of decoration.

The typical ornaments of these manuscripts are display letters of initial words formed by anthropomorphic and zoomorphic elements painted in yellow, violet, and red. The ornamental letters of the Hamilton *Siddur* are the most elaborate of the group. They end in caricatures of human profiles, or two-legged anthropomorphic hybrids; others are shaped entirely as grotesque animals. Some initial words are placed within the panels painted in red and blue compartments.

The text of the Haggadah is accompanied by the traditional illustrations of the *matzah* and the *maror* (bitter herbs), represented here, as in all other manuscripts of the group, in a stylized, abstract manner.

The *Siddur* was previously in the collection of the Duke of Hamilton, and was then acquired by the State Library of Berlin.

BIBLIOGRAPHY M. Italianer, *Die Darmstadter Pesach Haggadah* (Leipzig, 1927), 25, 272–74; Frankfurt am Main, Historisches Museum, *Synagoga,* exhibition catalogue (Frankfurt, 1961), no. 91, fig. 37B; B. Narkiss, *Hebrew Illuminated Manuscripts* (Jerusalem, 1969), 54; M. Metzger, *La Haggada enluminée* (Leiden, 1973), index s.v.; The New York Public Library, *A Sign and a Witness: Two Thousand Years of Hebrew Books and Illuminated Manuscripts,* exhibition catalogue, ed. L. S. Gold (New York and Oxford, 1988), no. 55; Madrid, Ministerio de Cultura, *La vida judía en Sefarad,* exhibition catalogue (Sinagoga del Tránsito, Toledo, 1991–92), no. 12; Berlin, Berliner Festspiele, *Jüdische Lebenswelten: Katalog,* exhibition catalogue, ed. A. Nachama and G. Sievernich, (Berlin, 1992), no. 20: 12/8.

—GSR

18 **Prayer Book for Daily Use and Festivals**

Spain, fifteenth century

Ink, colored inks, silver, and gold leaf on vellum

Volume II: 6¾ x 5 in. (17.1 x 12.7 cm), 95 folios

New York, The Library of The Jewish Theological Seminary of America, Mic. 4366

Most of the decoration of this manuscript consists of elaborate colored scroll and vegetal forms surrounding word panels with gold letters. On fol. 47r and 51v are two human heads blowing horns, the only instances of anthropomorphic decoration. Another interesting feature is the shields with "heraldic" decoration that appear throughout.

BIBLIOGRAPHY New York, The Jewish Museum, *The Book and its Cover: Manuscripts and Bindings of the Twelfth through the Eighteenth Centuries,* exhibition brochure by V. B. Mann (New York, 1981), no. 6.

—VBM

זה המטה כמה שנאמר ואת
המטה הזה תקח בידך אשר
תעשה בו את האותות:
זה הדם כמה שנאמר ונתתי
מופתים בשמים ובארץ דם

17

19 *Siddur*

Lisbon, Portugal, last quarter of the fifteenth century

Ink, gouache, and gold on parchment

3¼ x 2¼ in. (8.3 x 5.7 cm), 140 folios

Carl Alexander Floersheim Trust for Art and Judaica

This small-sized prayer book is a typical product of the Lisbon workshop that flourished in the last decades of the fifteenth century until the expulsion of the Jews from Portugal in 1496. As with all manuscripts produced by this school, the script and the decoration display a highly refined technique and an exquisite delicacy. The manuscript contains hymns and supplications followed by the morning prayers (fol. 11r), and the prayers for the Sabbath (fol. 126).

All initial words are written in burnished gold within panels decorated by violet filigree pen work. Each page is framed by a gold fillet with tiny pen-drawn scrolls enlivened by red and blue buds in the margins. The beginnings of the main sections have more elaborate decorations of large borders with interlaced gold fillets on painted grounds. Perfection of execution and refinement of taste are the hallmarks of the Lisbon school. Thérèse Metzger identified a manuscript of The Library of The Jewish Theological Seminary of America, New York, as having been originally part of this *Siddur* (Mic. 8235).

BIBLIOGRAPHY D. S. Sassoon, *Ohel David: A Descriptive Catalogue of the Hebrew and Samaritan Manuscripts in the Sassoon Library,* vol. 1 (London, 1932), 298, no. 59; ; G. Sed-Rajna, *Manuscrits hébreux de Lisbonne* (Paris, 1970), 88; Zurich, Sotheby & Co. A.G., *Thirty-eight Highly Important Hebrew and Samaritan Manuscripts from the Collection formed by the Late David Solomon Sassoon,* sales catalogue, November 5, 1975, no. 25; T. Metzger, *Les manuscrits hébreux copiés et décorés à Lisbonne dans les dernières décennies du XVe siècle* (Paris, 1977), 154-57; M. Schmelzer, *Ethics of the Fathers,* introduction to the facsimile edition of ms. Mic. 8235 of the Library of The Jewish Theological Seminary of America (New York, 1987); Amsterdam, Jewish Historical Museum, *The Image of the World-Jewish Tradition in Manuscripts and Printed Books,* exhibition catalogue (Amsterdam and Leuven), 1990, no. 50, figs. 34-5; Berlin, Berliner Festspiele, *Jüdische Lebenswelten: Katalog,* exhibition catalogue, ed. A. Nachama and G. Sievernich, (Berlin, 1992), no. 12/11.

—GSR

20 **Prato Haggadah**

Spain, ca. 1300

Ink, gouache, and gold leaf on vellum

8⅜ x 5⁵⁄₁₆ in. (21.3 x 13.5 cm), 85 folios

New York, The Library of The Jewish Theological Seminary of America, Mic. 9478

The decorative program planned for this Haggadah was quite extensive and included illuminated word panels, borders of vegetal ornament, grotesques and drolleries, text illustrations such as Rabbi Gamliel teaching his disciples, genre illustrations (the family at the seder) and biblical illustrations. Unfortunately, much was not completed; only outlines of two biblical scenes hint at what was intended to be a rich iconographic cycle.

Still, the unfinished nature of the manuscript allows a glimpse into the working methods of the atelier that produced it. The scenes and decoration were first drawn in pencil, then colored washes were used to block out large areas of one hue. Bole (clay) was applied to hold gold-leaf highlights; finally, different-colored gouaches were applied to define the forms.

Tom Freudenheim drew attention to the stylized, heraldic treatment of the illuminated *matzah* in this and related Haggadot. Their designs relate to similar elaborated roundels on contemporaneous textiles of Mudejar origin that were prized *objets de luxe* in medieval Spain (see cat. no. 108).

This manuscript passed to Italy where a few leaves of Ashkenazi rite were added. A censor's note, written in Italian, was added to the last page in 1617.

BIBLIOGRAPHY New York, The Jewish Museum, *Illuminated Hebrew Manuscripts from the Library of the Jewish Theological Seminary of America,* exhibition catalogue, introduction by T. L. Freudenheim (New York, 1965), no. 31; M. Metzger, *La Haggada Enluminée* (Leiden, 1973), 18, n. 1, 398 (App. 234, n. 1), 405 (App. 383, n. 4).

—VBM

20

21 Mocatta Haggadah

Castile (?), early fourteenth century

Ink, gouache, and silver leaf on vellum

9½ x 7⅜ in. (24.2 x 18.8 cm), 58 folios

London, The Library, University College London, Ms. 1

The decoration of this Haggadah encompasses various types of Hebrew manuscript decoration of the late thirteenth to the early fourteenth century, probably due to the use of several models, each of different origin. One of the models belonged to the group of ritual books decorated by zoomorphic letters (see no. 17). Letters of this type, painted in blue, violet, and red within red outlines, appear on folio 19r. Many other pages probably had similar ornamental letters that at a later stage of the decoration were overpainted in gold, keeping only the shape of zoomorphic letters but not specific motifs (e.g. fols. 36r, 40r–42r, etc.).

The painted grounds with fine scroll or stylized foliage decoration divided into irregular compartments have the most decorative effect. The numerous grotesque figures within the panels or extending from the corners point to a model of French origin, while the micrographic ornaments, filled with color, that run along the script in the outer margins occur in biblical manuscripts of Aragón and southwestern France or Languedoc. On some pages these micrographic bands form a candelabrum, a motif that was mainly used in fourteenth-century Catalan Bibles. Finally, Catalan influence is also discernible in the only illustration of the manuscript, the full-page representation of the *matzah* (fol. 43r). The ornamental disc, with gold fillet interlaces and painted color fillings, became a typical ornament of the fourteenth-century Haggadot of Catalonia.

The decoration of the Mocatta Haggadah is highly effective, although not very refined. The program lacks a unified design, either because of the use of heterogeneous models or because it was executed in several phases. It is a production of early fourteenth-century Jewish folk art, created at the crossroads of the main stylistic trends of Hebrew book illumination in Spain.

BIBLIOGRAPHY R. A. Rye, *Catalogue of the Printed Books and Manuscripts Forming the Library of Frederic David Mocatta* (London, 1904), 424; B. Narkiss, *Hebrew Illuminated Manuscripts in the British Isles* (Jerusalem and London, 1982), cat. no. 10.

—*GSR*

22 **Cambridge Catalan Haggadah**

Catalonia, end of the fourteenth century (?)

Ink, tempera, gold, and silver on vellum

8¹⁄₁₆ x 6¼ in. (20.5 x 16 cm), 164 folios

Syndics of Cambridge University Library, Add. 1203

This delicately decorated ritual book contains *piyyutim* for the festivals and special sabbaths, and the text of the Haggadah, written in square Sephardic script with initials in larger letters, and gold for the title (fol. 31r) and the first words of the Haggadah (fol. 60v). The manuscript contains only two illuminations: the ornamental disc representing *matzah* (fol. 66v), and a bunch of green leaves depicting the *maror* (fol. 67r). These two illustrations belong to the most ancient traditions of Haggadah illustrations, as is attested by eleventh-century Genizah fragments.

Except for the two initial words written in gold on painted blue grounds, all sections start with the first word written in large ink letters, set in panels decorated by red or violet filigree pen work. The style of the filigree ornaments, shaped like palmetto leaves enclosed in drop-like curves, as well as the feathery and nonetheless naturalistic *maror* leaves, shows affinities with the decoration of late fourteenth-century manuscripts of the southwestern provinces of France (Comtat Venaissin), among them the so-called Wolf Haggadah copied at the end of the fourteenth century in Avignon. This combination of Sephardic and Provençal influences is also present in the style of the script.

The Haggadah shows several owner's inscriptions: Moses b. Maimon (fifteenth century), Abraham son of Moses b. Maimon (fifteenth century), Yoseph Shwaki ben Israel Shwaki (eighteenth century?), and Eliahu Ashwaki ben Israel (nineteenth century). It was purchased by the University of Cambridge from F. Hirsch in 1875.

BIBLIOGRAPHY M. Garel, "The Rediscovery of the Wolf Haggadah," *Journal of Jewish Art* 2 (1975): 22–27; B. Narkiss, *Hebrew Illuminated Manuscripts in the British Isles* (Jerusalem and London, 1982), no. 18; H. Loewe, *Handlist of Hebrew Manuscripts in the University Library at Cambridge,* (n.d.), no. 480.

—*GSR*

Science, Law, and Philosophy

23 *Libros del Saber de Astronomía de Alfonso X*

Spain, sixteenth century

Ink on paper

16⅞ x 11¼ in. (42.8 x 28.5 cm), 257 folios (70 folios missing)

Madrid, Biblioteca de El Escorial (Cod. h.I.1)

The *Libros del Saber de Astronomía* were a collection of various astronomical treatises composed in Castilian at the behest of Alfonso X the Wise of Castile by a multiethnic team composed of a Muslim converted to Christianity, five Spanish Christians, four Italian Christians, and five Jews. Among the Jews were two observational astronomers, Isaac ibn Sid and Yehudah ibn Mosca.

Among the astronomical treatises were the *Book of the Fixed Stars,* a star catalogue based on Arabic sources; a Castilian version of the canons, or instructions, of the Alfonsine Tables (the most famous astronomical tables of medieval Europe), a treatise on the armillary sphere, and another, by Isaac ibn Sid, on the observational quadrant.

The *Libros del Saber* served to create a scientific and technical vocabulary that made the Castilian language a medium for the expression of scientific knowledge. The king himself reviewed the drafts of the treatises to ensure that the texts were readable, accurate, and stylistically acceptable.

The original manuscript is presently in the library of the Central University of Madrid. This later illustrated copy on paper was commissioned by King Philip II for Prince Charles in 1562.

BIBLIOGRAPHY Toledo, Museo de Santa Cruz, *Alfonso X,* exhibition catalogue (Toledo, June–September 1984), p. 184, (no. 219); Madrid, Ministerio de Cultura, *La vida judía en Sefarad,* exhibition catalogue (Sinagoga del Tránsito, Toledo, 1991-92), no. 148.

—TG

24 *In Excelsis Dei Thesauris* **(called *Vidal Mayor*)**

Aragon, second half of the thirteenth century

Maker: Michael Lupi de Çandiu

Ink, gouache, and gold leaf on vellum

14¼ x 9½ in. (36.3 x 24.3 cm), 277 folios

Collection of the J. Paul Getty Museum, Malibu, California, Ms. Ludwig XIV 6, 83.MQ.165

In 1247, King James I of Aragón commissioned the bishop of Huesca, Vidal de Canellas, to create a new and systematic code of law. The bishop wrote two compilations in Latin, one called the "major," and the other the "minor." The *Vidal Mayor,* or major code, was subsequently translated from Latin into Navarro-Aragonese. It is the translated version that survives in this manuscript.

The decoration consists of small framed scenes, historiated initials, as well as those that are embellished with only abstract and floral ornaments, and drolleries. Of the 156 miniatures in the manuscript, four include figures of Jews, and two depict Muslims. The Jews are shown as craftsmen, as merchants of metalwork or cloth, as pawnbrokers (fols. 114r, 180r, 243v), or as litigants before the king (fol. 175v). They are distinguished by their pointed headdresses and their long beards. Muslims, depicted as having dark brown skin and Negroid features, are seen converting to Christianity (fol. 242v) or as slaves (fol. 244r). The king's law is thus shown to be applicable to all three religious groups within his domains, as well as to various classes within Christian society.

24

The facial types, the slender figures, and the minimal settings offset by gold backgrounds are all traits found in French manuscript painting of the thirteenth century.[1]

NOTE 1) Malibu, J. Paul Getty Museum, *The Vidal Mayor: Feudal Customs of Aragon,* brochure (Malibu, Calif., 1990), 1.

BIBLIOGRAPHY A. Ubieto Arteta, J. Delgado Echeverría, J. A. Frago Gracía, and M. del C. Lacarra Ducay, *Vidal Mayor: Estudios* (Huesca, 1984) (gives the older literature); Malibu, J. Paul Getty Museum, *The Vidal Mayor: Feudal Customs of Aragon,* brochure (Malibu, Calif., 1990).

—VBM

25 **Maimonides,** ***Guide to the Perplexed***

Barcelona, 1348

Scribe: Levi ben Isaac ben Caro

Ink and gouache on vellum

7⅝ x 5⅛ in. (19.5 x 13 cm), 352 folios

Copenhagen, The Royal Library, Heb. XXXVII

Maimonides' great philosophical compendium, translated into Hebrew from the Arabic original by Samuel ben Judah ibn Tibbon, was, and still is, one of the most-studied works of Jewish philosophy. The manuscript of the Royal Library of Copenhagen was copied by Levi ben Isaac son of Caro of Salamanca, for the physician Menaḥem Bezalel of Barcelona, in the year 1348. The codex owes its fame to its lavishly decorated pages and to the painted frontispieces introducing each of the three books of the *Guide*.

An astronomer explaining the astrolabe to his disciples on fol. 114r introduces Book II, devoted to cosmology. Book III, where Maimonides expounds his teachings on metaphysics, is preceded by a representation of the four "living creatures," the *ḥayot* of Ezekiel's vision, as described in chapter 1.

By their style the paintings of the Hebrew codex are related to the works of the Catalan artists Ferrar and Arnau Bassa whose paintings are characterized by the influence of Sienese art. Francis Wormald identified the Copenhagen Maimonides codex as belonging to the group of manuscripts attributed to their workshop, although the question whether Ferrar Bassa himself was responsible for the four paintings of the *Guide* is still open. As the only dated manuscript of the group, the Maimonides codex is a highly important document for the history of fourteenth-century book illumination in Catalonia. It is also a precious witness to *convivencia,* bearing testimony to the close collaboration of Christian and Jewish artists and craftsmen.

In the seventeenth century, this codex was acquired by the Danish theologian Hans Bartholin, who presented it to Frederic Rostgaard (1671–1745). It entered the collection of Count Christian Danneskjold-Samsoe. After his death, in 1732, it was purchased by the Royal Library.

BIBLIOGRAPHY Millard Meiss, "Italian Style in Catalonia and a Fourteenth-Century Catalan Workshop," *Journal of the Walters Art Gallery* 4 (1941): 45–87; F. Wormald, "Afterthoughts on the Stockholm Exhibition," *Konsthistorisk Tidskrift* 22 (1953): 75-84; Amsterdam, Joods Historisch Museum, *Joodse verluchte handschriften,* exhibition catalogue (Amsterdam, 1961), no. 53; Frankfurt am Main, Historisches Museum, *Synagoga,* exhibition catalogue (Frankfurt, 1962), no. 148M; R. Edelman, *Hebraica from Denmark—Manuscripts and Printed Books in the Collection of the Royal Library, Copenhagen* (New York, 1969), no. 1; B. Narkiss, *Hebrew Illuminated Manuscripts* (Jerusalem, 1969), 76; New York, The Jewish Museum, *Kings and Citizens: The History of the Jews in Denmark 1622–1983,* vol. 2, exhibition catalogue, essay and description by Ulf Haxen (New York, 1983), no. 6; The New York Public Library, *A Sign and a Witness: Two Thousand Years of Hebrew Books and Illuminated Manuscripts,* exhibition catalogue, ed. L. S. Gold (New York and Oxford, 1988), no. 70; Berlin, Berliner Festspiele, *Jüdische Lebenswelten: Katalog,* exhibition catalogue, ed. A. Nachama and G. Sievernich (Berlin, 1992), no. 20: 1/75; G. Sed-Rajna, "Hebrew Manuscripts of Fourteenth Century Catalonia and the Workshop of the Master of Saint Marc," *Jewish Art* 18 (1992).

—GSR

26 Jacob ben David ben Yomtob and Other Authors

Astronomical Tables and Treatises on Astronomy

Spain, 1360–61

Ink and gouache on vellum

$10^{15}/_{16}$ x $8\frac{1}{4}$ in. (27.8 x 21 cm), 228 folios

Carl Alexander Floersheim Trust for Art and Judaica

This work is a fourteenth-century Hebrew scientific miscellany from Catalonia that includes the astronomical tables (*luḥot*) of Jacob ben David Yomtob or Bonjorn (see no. 31), an astronomer in the employ of King Peter the Ceremonious of Aragón. Besides the tables, this manuscript includes a number of short treatises on Ptolemaic and Indian astronomy. Because of the king's interest in astrology, the tables contain an almanac of oppositions and conjunctions of the sun and the moon, as well as tables predicting lunar and solar eclipses.

BIBLIOGRAPHY M. Steinschneider, *Hebräische Übersetzung des Mittelalters* (Berlin, 1893), 614-16; D. S. Sassoon, *Ohel David: A Descriptive Catalogue of the Hebrew and Samaritan Manuscripts in the Sassoon Library,* vol. 2 (London, 1932), 1041–43, pl. 32; Zurich, Sotheby & Co. A. G., *Thirty-Eight Highly Important Hebrew and Samaritan Manuscripts from the Collection Formed by The Late David Solomon Sassoon,* sales catalogue, November 5, 1975, no. 15; Amsterdam, Jewish Historical Museum, *The Image of the World: Jewish Tradition in Manuscripts and Printed Books,* exhibition catalogue (Amsterdam and Leuven, 1990), no. 94, fig. 17; Berlin, Berliner Festspiele, *Jüdische Lebenswelten: Katalog,* exhibition catalogue, ed. by A. Nachama and G. Sievernich (Berlin, 1992), no. 20:1/83.

—TG

27 Nathan ben Joel Falaquera, *Tsarei ha-guf*

Spain, fourteenth century

Ink on vellum

$10\frac{5}{8}$ x $8^{1}/_{16}$ in. (27 x 20.5 cm)

New York, The Library of The Jewish Theological Seminary of America, Mic. 2736

Nothing is known of the life of Falaquera, who wrote in the second half of the thirteenth century. The *Tsarei ha-guf* (*Balsam for the Body*) is a compilation of medical aphorisms derived from Arabic sources that recapitulates the medical lore of both antiquity and medieval Arab physicians. The first twenty-eight chapters are devoted to medical theory; a second part on clinical practice and hygiene (seventeen chapters) follows; then an account of diseases and their cures, following Avicenna's head-to-foot organization (twelve chapters); and a final section on drugs. In keeping with the prevailing linguistic norms of purism, Falaquera rendered technical medical terms in biblical or Talmudic Hebrew, providing Arabic or vernacular expressions where no Hebrew equivalent existed.

Unpublished

—TG

28 **Avicenna, *The Canon***

Spain, fourteenth century and 1468

Ink, colored inks, and gold on vellum

9 5/16 x 7 3/16 in. (23.6 x 18.3 cm), 361 folios

New York, The Library of The Jewish Theological Seminary of America, Mic. 8184

The *Qanun,* or *Canon,* of the Persian philosopher and physician Ibn Sina (980–1037), known as Avicenna in the Latin West, was arguably the most influential medical text of the Middle Ages. An immense work of more than one million words, it was divided into five parts: (1) a book of generalities (*al-Kulliyat*), really a complete medical text in itself; (2) a *materia medica,* listing drugs alphabetically; (3) an account of human diseases proceeding from the head to the toes; (4) general diseases not limited to single organs, like fevers; and (5) a book on compound drugs.

The *Canon* was used widely by medieval Jewish physicians. Those of Spain who cited, commented on, or translated medical works of Avicenna from Arabic into Hebrew include Aaron ben Isaac of Córdoba, Solomon ben Joseph ibn Ayyub of Granada (mid-thirteenth century), Isaiah ben Isaac of Córdoba (mid-fourteenth century), Zeraḥiah ben Isaac Gracian of Barcelona, Joseph al-Lorqui, and Abraham Zacuto, to name only a few.

The decoration consists largely of beautifully executed word panels in colored inks and gold leaf.

BIBLIOGRAPHY New York, The Jewish Museum, *Illuminated Hebrew Manuscripts from the Library of the Jewish Theological Seminary of America,* exhibition catalogue, introduction by T. L. Freudenheim (New York, 1965), no. 51.

—*TG*

29 **Portolan Chart**

Palma, 1456

Maker: Petrus Roselli

Ink and gouache on vellum

27⅜ x 14½ in. (69.5 x 36.7 cm)

Chicago, The Newberry Library, Ayer Ms. Map 3

Pere Rosell (in Latin, Petrus Roselli) was a Christian cartographer from Mallorca who drew maps and portolans between 1447 and 1468. Little is known of his life except that Rosell was a name common among Catalan *conversos* of the period.

Portolan charts (meaning handy or portable) became standard equipment for ship captains in the fourteenth century. Their distinctive feature was a network of overlapping lines representing directions of the compass course. Distances along well-explored coasts, like those of the Mediterranean, were marked in nautical miles. This map is noted for the angular decorative moldings along the mile scale.

Rosell's chart was drawn in 1456 on the island of Mallorca, the leading center of nautical cartography in the late Middle Ages whose leading figures were the Jewish cartographer Abraham Cresques and his son Yahuda (later converted to Christianity with the name Jaume Ribes).

This map is a characteristic representation of the late medieval world, showing the Mediterranean and the Black seas and the European coast as far north as Denmark and the British Isles. Only the northwestern coast of Africa is shown, but Spanish and Portuguese exploration and colonization of the Atlantic islands (the Canaries, Madeira, and the Azores) are reflected. No mountains are depicted except a pyramid-shaped mass in southern Spain representing the Sierra Nevada, a detail that Rosell borrowed from Baptista Becharius, a cartographer with whom he was in touch.

BIBLIOGRAPHY H. Winter, "Petrus Roselli," *Imago Mundi: A Review of Early Cartography Edited by Leo Bagrow* 9 (1952): 1–11.

—*TG*

30 **Abraham bar Ḥiyya (Savasorda), *Sefer Tsurat ha-Eretz***

Spain, fifteenth century

Ink on parchment

7⅜ x 5⅛ in.
(18.7 x 13 cm),
107 folios

New York, The Library of The Jewish Theological Seminary of America, Mic. 2550

Abraham bar Ḥiyya of Barcelona was the founding father of medieval Jewish science, and his contributions to mathematics were particularly noteworthy. The *Tsurat ha-Eretz* (*Form of the Earth*), however, is a general treatise on astronomy and cosmography designed as a manual for use by French Jews.

The treatise is divided into ten sections covering the various kinds of observed celestial movements, including planetary and lunar orbits, the nature of eclipse, the retrograde motion of the planets, and the size of the earth. The work is highly dependent on that of the Arab astronomer al-Farghānī, with some parameters derived from al-Battānī.

BIBLIOGRAPHY A. Marx, "The Scientific Work of Some Outstanding Jewish Scholars," *Essays and Studies in Memory of Linda R. Miller* (New York, 1938), 131–35; New York, The Jewish Museum, *Illuminated Hebrew Manuscripts from the Library of the Jewish Theological Seminary of America,* exhibition catalogue, introduction by T. L. Freudenheim (New York, 1965), no. 46; Berlin, Berliner Festspiele, *Jüdische Lebenswelten: Katalog,* exhibition catalogue, ed. A. Nachama and G. Sievernich (Berlin, 1992), no. 20:12/19.

—TG

31 **Jacob ben David ben Yomtob, *Astronomical Tables* (in Catalan)**

Spain, fifteenth century

7⅛ x 4¾ in.
(18 x 12 cm)

Ink on parchment

Chicago, The Newberry Library, Ayer Ms. 746

Jacob ben David Yomtob (Bonjorn in Catalan) was a Jewish astronomer in the service of Peter the Ceremonious of Aragón, a king who was well known for his interest in astronomy and astrology. For Peter, Bonjorn composed some astronomical tables in 1361 for the latitude of Perpignan, where he lived.

Versions of Bonjorn's tables are extant in Hebrew (see no. 26), Catalan, Latin, and even Greek. This manuscript is an astronomical miscellany that begins with a treatise on the use and construction of the astrolabe, based on an Islamic model (it specifies directions for locating the *qibla,* or direction of Mecca). There follow brief instructions for constructing an equatorial sundial for the latitude of Barcelona. Next is a manuscript of Bonjorn's tables preceded by some canons, or instructions on their use. The canons begin with a prologue in praise of mathematics.

Bonjorn also acknowledges his debt to certain illustrious antecedents, including Ptolemy, Jabir ibn Aflah, Maimonides, Abraham bar Ḥiyya, Levi ben Gerson, and "the opinion of the illustrious king Don Alfonso in his tables." The tables themselves are a kind of perpetual calendar for predicting solar and lunar eclipses, some of the parameters of which are taken directly from the Alfonsine tables.

BIBLIOGRAPHY M. D. Johnston, "A Catalan Astronomical Manuscript of the Fifteenth Century: Newberry Library Ayer Ms. 746," *Proceedings of the Illinois Medieval Association,* ed. Roberta Bux Bosse (Macomb, Ill., 1984), 76–101.

—TG

32 **Benjamin of Tudela, *Masaʾot* (*Travels*)**

Constantinople, 1543

Ink on paper

5½ x 3¾ in. (14 x 9.5 cm),
32 folios

New York, The Library of The Jewish Theological Seminary of America, Mic. 5721

Benjamin of Tudela traveled through continental Europe to Constantinople, then by sea to Syria and overland to Iraq and Egypt between approximately 1159 and 1173. The *Masaʾot* appear to be a log recorded during his travels, written in a formal Hebrew in which many Arabisms appear, suggesting that Arabic was his native language although he lived in Tudela, in the Christian kingdom of Navarre.

Besides providing notices of numerous aspects of secular life, such as the fortifications of a city or the commercial goods on sale there, he was also interested in Jewish communities, their size, number of synagogues, their leadership, and the approach to the Talmud and other local aspects of religious practice. Places of biblical interest or significance are carefully noted.

His information about the places he actually visited is precise, but his notices of the further reaches of Egypt are the usual medieval mix of fact and fantasy (such as the griffins of the Indian Ocean). He was the first European to mention China, even though his notices are extremely vague.

BIBLIOGRAPHY New York, The Jewish Museum, *A Tale of Two Cities,* exhibition catalogue by V. B. Mann (New York, 1982), cat. no. 138; Berlin, Berliner Festspiele, *Jüdische Lebenswelten: Katalog,* exhibition catalogue, ed. A. Nachama and G. Sievernich (Berlin, 1992), no. 20:12/26.

—TG

33 **Averroës, *De generatione et corruptione,* translated by Kalonymos ben Kalonymos; *De anima* and *Parva naturalia,* translated by Moses ibn Tibbon**

Spain, fifteenth century

Ink on parchment

8½ x 5 15/16 in. (21.6 x 15.1 cm)

New York, The Library of The Jewish Theological Seminary of America, Mic. 2302

This is a manuscript containing Hebrew translations of the commentaries of Averroës (ibn Rushd, 1126–98) on three different treatises of Aristotle (generally known by their Latin names): the *De generatione et corruptione* (a physical treatise dealing with the nature of substance); the *De anima* (*On the soul*), which was Aristotle's basic statement on epistemology; and the *Parva naturalia,* a grouping of short treatises on memory, dreams, and predicting on the basis of dreams, but which was read for its bearing on the soul or, rather, the distinction between mind and body. Averroës' epitome, or short commentary, on the *Parva naturalia* was especially popular among medieval Jewish scholars; at least twenty-five different Hebrew manuscripts of it survive.

As a set, these three treatises convey notions of Aristotelian epistemology that were the heart of medieval "rationalism." The first treatise was translated into Hebrew by Kalonymos ben Kalonymos, the remaining two by Moses ibn Tibbon, two Provençal Jews whose entire careers were devoted, broadly speaking, to the translation or explication of Aristotelian texts.

Unpublished

—TG

34 **Compendium including Abraham ibn Ezra's** (1089-1164) ***Keli ha-Neḥoshet***

Constantinople, eighteenth century

Ink on parchment

8⅝ x 6⅝ in. (22 x 16.9 cm), 74 leaves

New York, The Library of The Jewish Theological Seminary of America, Mic. 2631

The *Keli ha-Neḥoshet* (*The Copper Instrument*) was Ibn Ezra's manual on the use of the astrolabe that follows the Arabic format of such treatises, explaining the construction and use of the instrument and giving instructions on how to use it to determine the hour, and the direction and altitude of the sun, moon, and planets. He explains, on the basis of such observations, how to determine the latitude of the point of observation. Also included are indications concerning practical uses of the astrolabe, for example, for the casting of horoscopes, or for use as a surveying instrument (finding angles of topographical elevation and depression).

Unpublished

—TG

Poetry Manuscripts

35 Isaac ben Abraham ibn Ezra, *Diwan* (Collection of Poems)

Cizre (Turkey), 1142

Ink on paper

8⅜ x 5⅝ in.
(21.3 x 14.3 cm)

New York, The Library of The Jewish Theological Seminary of America, Mic. 8386. Purchased by the Harry G. Friedman Memorial Fund

This collection of poems or *Diwan* consists largely of poems by the twelfth-century Hebrew poet Isaac ibn Ezra, son of the prominent Spanish poet, grammarian, biblical commentator, philosopher, astronomer, and physician, Abraham ibn Ezra (1089–1164).

Probably born in Spain, Isaac ibn Ezra spent most of his life in the Near East. In Baghdad, he became court poet and secretary to the philosopher and physician Abu al-Barakat Hibat ʾAllah and he seems to have followed his master's example when Abu al-Barakat converted from Judaism to Islam (after 1143).[1]

This manuscript also includes compositions by other members of the illustrious Ibn Ezra family; Moses ibn Ezra, one of the most prolific poets of the Spanish school (ca. 1055 - after 1135), and Abraham ibn Ezra (Isaac's father), as well as poems by one of the latter's closest friend, and his travel companion, the Spanish Hebrew poet and philosopher Judah Halevi (before 1075–1141).

NOTES 1) *Encyclopedia Judaica,* 8:461–62, 1170.

BIBLIOGRAPHY New York, The Jewish Museum, *The Book and Its Cover: Manuscripts and Bindings of the Twelfth through the Eighteenth Centuries,* exhibition brochure by V. B. Mann (New York, 1981), no. 1.

—CN

36 Judah Halevi (1075-1141), *The Ages of Man (Ben adama yizkor bemoladto)*

Egypt (?), thirteenth century

Ink on paper

5–5⅛ x 3¼–3⅜ in.
(12.7–13 x 8.2–8.6 cm)
4 folios

Byram, Collection of Daniel Friedenberg

This poem is recited in Sephardic synagogues as a spur to repentance. The opening lines, which serve as a refrain, read:

> Let every son of earth bethink, while yet alive on earth,
> that one day soon he must return to her who gave him birth.

The following stanzas depict a person at each of the ages of life: the five-year-old, who clings to his mother's lap and rides on his father's shoulders; the ten-year-old who can hardly be controlled; the twenty-year-old, who thinks mostly of love; the thirty-year-old, burdened by family cares; the forty-year old, who is resigned to his lot, whatever it may be; the fifty-year old, who lives in fear of death; the sixty-year-old whose strength is gone; the seventy-year-old, who is nothing but a burden to "his friends, himself, and his staff"; and the eighty-year-old, who has lost his faculties. The poem concludes with the observation that the only happy person is one who always bears in mind the brevity of life and the need to prepare for the life to come after death.

Traditionally attributed to Abraham ibn Ezra, the poem is now thought to be by his older contemporary and fellow Tudelan, Judah Halevi.[1] This copy was found in the Cairo Genizah and passed into the collection of Elkan N. Adler. It was then acquired by Charles E. Feinberg before being purchased by its present owner.

NOTE 1) H. Schirmann, *Shirim hadashim min hageniza* (Jerusalem, 1965), p. 235, n. 4. For a similar poem by Samuel the Nagid, see R. Scheindlin, *Wine, Women and Death* (Philadelphia, 1986[3]), p. 165.

BIBLIOGRAPHY New York, Parke-Bernet Galleries, Inc., *The Charles E. Feinberg Collection of Valuable Judaica,* sales catalogue, November 30, 1967, lot no. 208.

-*RS*

37 **Ibn Sahal, *Diwan* (Collection of Poems)**

Spain (?), late twelfth or early thirteenth century

Ink on paper

8½ x 6½ in. (21.5 x 16.5 cm), 64 folios

Madrid, Biblioteca de El Escorial, no. 379

Ibn Sahl al-Israʾili (1212/3–1251) was a Jewish convert to Islam who lived in Muslim Seville until it was conquered by Ferdinand III of Castile. He was also an Arabic poet of first rank, who wrote mostly love poems, many of them in *muwashshah* form. We do not know what kind of Jewish education he had as a youth or whether he wrote poetry in Hebrew before his conversion, but from a statement attributed to him he seems to have known the Bible. Opinions are divided as to whether his conversion occurred early or late in his career and whether or not it was sincere. When he drowned in the Mediterranean, the ruler of Tunisia said, "The pearl has returned to the sea."

Ibn Sahl's love for a youth named Musa was the subject of many of his poems and eventually became legendary. According to a folk tale of the Jews of Algiers, Ibn Sahl was a grocer. Too shy to proclaim his love to Musa, he wrote love poems on the grocery paper in which he would wrap the boy's purchases; in this way his love became known.

BIBLIOGRAPHY H. Derenbourg, *Les manuscrits arabes de l'Escorial* (Paris, 1884), vol. 1, no. 379.

—*RS*

38 **Judah al-Harīzī, *Sefer Taḥkemoni* and *Makamat***

Sephardic hand, fourteenth century

Ink on paper

6½ x 4½ in. (16.5 x 11.4 cm), 294 folios

New York, The Library of The Jewish Theological Seminary of America, Mic. 1506

Born in Spain, the Hebrew poet and translator Judah ben Solomon al-Harīzī (1170–1235) spent most of his life traveling through the Orient.[1] This manuscript includes al-Harīzī's most important translation, his Hebrew rendering of the *Makamat,* or *Sessions,* a work written by the Arabic poet al-Harīrī, which popularized the literary form called *makama*. In the *makama*, the narrator serves as a foil to the hero who is a learned scoundrel and rhymester able to meet all difficulties.[2] This form was introduced to Spain (ca. 1108) by the Andalusian poet Yusuf b. Ali-Kudai who had studied under al-Harīrī.

After translating the *Makamat,* al-Harīzī decided to use the *makama* form in his major original work, the *Sefer Taḥkemoni* (*The Wise One*) (completed after 1220), a copy of which is also preserved in the present manuscript. Al-Harīzī, who was among the first authors to introduce the *makama* genre in Hebrew literature, composed the *Taḥkemoni* during his travels, introducing into the text valuable information about the Jewish communities he visited.

Following al-Harīrī's model, the *Taḥkemoni* has two characters: the narrator Heman the Ezrahite, and the bohemian hero Heber the Kenite, who speaks in rhymed prose. Although al-Harīzī borrowed the main literary form from his Arabic predecessor, the author achieves an original composition, with skillfully interwoven biblical references, that gives a distinct Hebrew flavor to a typically Arabic form.[3]

NOTES 1) *Encyclopaedia Judaica,* 2: 627; *The Jewish Encyclopedia,* 1: 390. 2) E.J. Brill's *First Encyclopaedia of Islam 1913–1936* (repr. 1987), 5:161–64; *Encyclopaedia of Islam* (new edition), 3: 221–22. 3) *First Encyclopaedia of Islam 1913–1936,* (repr. 1987), 5: 164; *Encyclopaedia Judaica,* 2: 627–28.

Unpublished

—*CN*

39 **Abu'l Walid al-Himyarī (1026-48),** ***Poems on Spring***

Spain (?), fourteenth century

Ink on paper

9⅞ x 5 11/16 in. (24 x 13.5 cm), 78 folios

Madrid, Biblioteca de El Escorial, no. 353

Abu'l Walid al-Himyarī was the author of *al-Badi 'fi wasf al-rabi'* (*The Wonderful Book of Descriptions of Spring*), the earliest extant anthology of Arabic poetry from Spain. He lived in the first half of the eleventh century, during the period when Muslim Spain had broken up into a number of small principalities. Al-Himyarī was a courtier of al-Muᶜtaḍid, the king of Seville, which had been an independent state since 1013. Like most Muslim princes, al-Muᶜtaḍid was a devotee of poetry; it was for him that the anthology was composed.

Al-Himyarī 's anthology is devoted to one of the most popular subjects of Andalusian poetry, descriptions of flowers, gardens, and spring. It contains selections, mostly short pieces and fragments of longer ones, by forty-nine Sevillian poets, including al-Himyarī himself. The book includes a programmatic introduction in which the author explains that one of his reasons for composing the book was to display the independence and superiority of Andalusi poets vis-à-vis the Arabic poets of the East. It was in fact during this period, that of the *taifa* kingdoms, that Andalusi poetry flourished most brilliantly.

BIBLIOGRAPHY H. Derenbourg, *Les manuscrits arabes de l'Escurial,* vol. 1 (Paris, 1884), no. 353.

—*RS*

40 ***Piyyutim***

Spain, fourteenth-fifteenth century

Ink on vellum

7⅜ x 3⅜ in. (18.8 x 13.6 cm), 242 folios

Copenhagen, The Royal Library, Cod. Hebr. XXX

A *piyyut* is a liturgical poem that enhances prayer or a religious ceremony. This form became popular in Spain from the middle of the tenth century onwards.[1] Among the most prominent Spanish *paytanim* (authors of *piyyutim*) are Solomon ibn Gabirol (ca. 1020–ca. 1057), Judah Halevi (before 1075–1141) and Abraham ibn Ezra (1089–1164) all of whose compositions are compiled in this manuscript.

Solomon ibn Gabirol is considered to be the major representative of liturgical poetry in Spain. Many of Gabirol's poems, which seem to have been commissioned by Jewish communities or synagogues, humbly express the author's yearnings for the redemption of Israel and his understanding of the insignificance of man confronting God.[2] Among his successors are Abraham ibn Ezra, whose religious poems express a devout Jew's longing for God as well as the tension between human sin and divine mercy, and Judah Halevi, whose poems reflect a strong identification with the sufferings of the Jewish people.[3]

Although this manuscript is a liturgical compilation, its last poem (in fol. 241v–242r) is a secular composition rendered in the Arabic literary form called *muwashshah*, an ode meant to be sung. The invention of this form is attributed to Mukaddam ibn Muʾafa, a poet of the court of the Cordoban caliph AbdʾAllah ibn Muḥammad (ruled 888–912).[4]

This manuscript, written on vellum by an unknown Spanish hand, has fine calligraphy enhanced by abstract decoration in red ink. From Spain, this book was taken to Italy where it passed papal censorship by Dominico Irosolymitano in 1595 and again in 1617, by Giovanni

Dominico Coretto, both times in the city of Mantua. In Italy, the manuscript was later purchased by the Danish collector Count Otto Thott (1703–85) who bequeathed it to the Royal Library of Copenhagen.[5]

NOTES 1) *Encyclopaedia Judaica,* 13:573-602; 2) Ibid., 7:235–46; E. Ashtor, *The Jews of Muslim Spain,* 3 vols. vol. 3 (Philadelphia, 1984), 29–51. 3) *Encyclopaedia Judaica,* 8:1165–66; ibid., 10:355–66. See also entry no. 34 in this catalogue. 4) E. J. Brill's *First Encyclopaedia of Islam 1913–1936* (repr. 1987), 6:795–97. 5) R. Edelman, *Hebraica from Denmark: Manuscripts and Printed Books in the Collection of the Royal Library, Copenhagen* ([New York], 1969), no. 4; New York, The Jewish Museum, *Kings and Citizens: The History of the Jews in Denmark 1622–1983,* vol. 2, exhibition catalogue, essay and description by Ulf Haxen, (New York, 1983), no. 9.

BIBLIOGRAPHY R. Edelman, *Hebraica from Denmark: Manuscripts and Printed Books in the Collection of the Royal Library, Copenhagen* ([New York], 1969); New York, The Jewish Museum, *Kings and Citizens: The History of the Jews in Denmark 1622–1983,* vol. 2, exhibition catalogue, essay and description by Ulf Haxen (New York, 1983), no. 9.

—*CN*

Documents

41 **Gregory IX urges King Ferdinand III of Castile to Confiscate Copies of the Talmud**

St. John Lateran, Rome, June 18, 1239

Ink on parchment; lead seal missing

8¾ x 10½ in. (22.3 x 26.7 cm)

Madrid, Archivo Histórico Nacional, Clero, Carpeta 3019, no. 19

In this Latin document, Gregory IX (Pope 1227–41) informs the king of Castile and León, Ferdinand III (ruled 1217–1252), that he has been informed that the Jews follow not only the Mosaic law, but also the Talmud.[1] Gregory IX warns the king against the Talmud on the grounds that it contains numerous errors and is the main cause of the Jews' "perfidious obstinacy" in their beliefs. He also advises Ferdinand III to have volumes of the Talmud collected and given to the priests on the first Saturday of Lent, while the Jews are congregated in their synagogues.[2]

Under the influence of Nicholas Donin, a French Jewish apostate who, along with other converts, compiled a list of thirty-five accusations against the Talmud, Pope Gregory ordered the confiscation and burning of the Talmud.[3] Among other measures taken by Gregory against Jews were his bulls insisting on the use of a distinctive badge in Portugal and Castile (1231) and later in the Kingdom of Navarre (1234), as well as his prohibition of the appointment of Jews to public offices.

NOTES 1) The complete Latin text is published in P. León Tello, *Judíos de Toledo,* 2 vols. 1 (Madrid, 1979), 375–76, document no. 7. León Tello mentions an identical bull issued by Gregory IX, on the same date, addressed to the archbishops of Aragón, Portugal, Castile, and León (ibid., 2: 37). A similar bull issued by Gregory on June 9, 1239, and addressed to the archbishops of France is published in both Latin and English in S. Grayzel, *The Church and the Jews in the 13th century* (Philadelphia, 1933), 241. 2) The first Saturday of Lent was on March 3, 1240, ibid.; see also *Encyclopaedia Judaica,* 6:167. 3) Ibid., 167-68, 7:919-20.

BIBLIOGRAPHY S. Grayzel, *The Church and the Jews in the 13th century* (Philadelphia, 1933), 241; P. León Tello, *Judíos de Toledo,* (Madrid, 1979), 1:375–76, no. 7, 2:37, no. 121.

—*CN*

42 **Sale of a Property**

Astorga (Province of León), November 1262

Ink on parchment

9⅞ x 4½ in. (25 x 11.5 cm)

Astorga, Archivo Diocesano

In this document, the Astorgan Jew Abraham Pardal and his wife sell their property in Santibañez de la Isla to Juan Miguel Rodríguez. The sale was executed in the presence of a notary of the Council of Astorga, Juan Gil, who authorized it with his emblem at the bottom of the document. The text of the document is written in Castilian but the seller's signature is in Hebrew.[1]

Jews lived in the fortified area of Astorga as early as the eleventh century. The Astorgan chronicler Matías Rodríguez López mentions the existence of a synagogue and two Jewish quarters or *juderías.* One of these *juderías,* called "Castro," was in the area of the church of San Bartolomé, and the other, called "Fuego de Cañas," was located in the western part of the city, in the area of the church of Santa Marta.[2] Despite forced conversions in 1230–31 and persecutions in 1412, a Jewish community existed in Astorga until the expulsion of 1492.[3]

NOTES 1) *Las Edades del Hombre: Libros y documentos de la Iglesia de Castilla y León,* exhibition catalogue (Burgos, 1990), no. 384; 2) M. Rodríguez López, *Historia de…la ciudad de Astorga* (Astorga, 1907), 794 (quoted in F. Cantera Burgos, *Sinagogas Españolas* [Madrid, 1955], 166). 3) *Encyclopaedia Judaica,* 3:785.

BIBLIOGRAPHY *Las Edades del Hombre: Libros y Documentos en la Iglesia de Castilla y León,* exhibition catalogue, (Burgos, 1990), 379–381, no. 384.

—CN

43 **Bequest of Property**

Toledo (Castile), March 13, 1280

Ink on parchment

10¾ x 9½ in. (27.3 x 24.2 cm)

Madrid, Archivo Histórico Nacional, Clero, Carpeta 3014, no. 15

In this document, a Jewish widow named Chamila bequeaths all of her fortune, composed of both immovable and movable property, to her granddaughter Palomba (?). The widow also decides to cover her head to avoid any suitor and thereby any claims on her bequest.[1]

In the text, Chamila is identified as the daughter of Judah Halevi ben R. Todros ben Al-Levi, which might indicate that she was related to the distinguished contemporary poet Todros ben Judah Halevi. In 1280–81, during Prince Sancho's revolt against his father Alfonso X, the poet was taken prisoner along with other prominent Jews until the Jewish community paid Alfonso a special tax. Judah Halevi appealed to the members of the community who repented and committed themselves to abstain from relations with non-Jewish women and to conduct their businesses with the utmost honesty.[2]

The document is written in Arabic with a few Hebrew words. The Jews were the only population that knew all three languages of medieval Spain: Castilian, Hebrew, and Arabic. The various documents extant show that the Jews conducted business in all three languages.

NOTES 1) The complete text of the document is published in A. González Palencia, *Los mozárabes de Toledo en los siglos XII y XIII,* 4 vols., vol. 3 (Madrid, 1928), 584–85, no. 1145. 2) *Encyclopaedia Judaica,* 15:1202; J. L. Lacave, *Sefarad, Sefarad: La España judía,* Comisión Quinto Centenario, Sefarad 92 (Barcelona and Madrid, 1987), 204; J. F. O'Callaghan, *A History of Medieval Spain* (Ithaca, N.Y., and London, 1975), 519.

BIBLIOGRAPHY A. González Palencia, *Los mozárabes de Toledo en los siglos XII y XIII,* vol. 3 (Madrid, 1928), 584–85; no. 1145. P. León Tello, *Judíos de Toledo,* vol 2 (Madrid, 1979), 59–60, no. 202.

—CN

44 **Decorated Jewish Marriage Contract (*Ketubbah*)**

Tudela, 2 Elul, 5060 (August 19, 1300)

Ink and watercolors on parchment

11 x 22 in. (28 x 56 cm)

Gobierno de Navarra, Departamento de Educación, Cultura y Deporte, Archivo Real y General, Pamplona, Cámara de Comptos, Caja 192, no. 2

This contract was written for the marriage of Solomon, son of Yomtov Alfarga, to Shuli, daughter of Ḥayyim ben K'laf. It is the earliest extant contract from Navarre and the only one with zoomorphic decoration. The decoration consists largely of geometric and abstract elements, but also includes two birds in triangular frames that fill the space between the first five lines of text and the geometric border.

The careful placement of the decoration is significant in the light of discussions among Spanish rabbis concerned with preventing tampering with the text. Rabbi Simeon ben Ẓemah Duran of Mallorca (1361–1444) recommended adding decoration to the empty spaces on the parchment to avoid the possibility of clauses being added or altered on the marriage contract.[1] He mentioned the use of biblical verses and pictorial decoration for this purpose. The three decorated Navarrese contracts include rectangular elements that fill the empty spaces above the text.

NOTES 1) I. Epstein, *The Responsa of Rabbi Simon b. Ẓemah Duran* (London, 1930), 83–84.

44

BIBLIOGRAPHY F. Cantera-Burgos, "La *'ketuba' de* D. Davidovitch y las *ketubbot* españolas," *Sefarad* 33 (1973): 378–79; S. Sabar, "The Beginnings and Flourishing of *Ketubbah* Illustration in Italy: A Study in Popular Imagery and Jewish Patronage During the Seventeenth and Eighteenth Centuries," (Dissertation, University of California, Los Angeles, 1987), 40; idem., "The Beginnings of Ketubbah Decoration in Italy: Venice in the Late Sixteenth to the Early Seventeenth Centuries," *Jewish Art* 12-13 (1987), 102, n. 50, fig. 6; idem., *Ketubbah: Jewish Marriage Contracts of the Hebrew Union College Skirball Museum and Klau Library* (Philadelphia and New York, 1990), 9; Madrid, Ministerio de Cultura, *La vida judía en Sefarad,* exhibition catalogue, Sinagoga del Tránsito, Toledo, 1991-92, no. 98.

—VBM

45 **Decorated Jewish Marriage Contract (*Ketubbah*)**

Milagro (Navarre), 5 Sivan, 5069 (May 15, 1309)

Ink and watercolor on parchment

11⅜ x 22 in. (29 x 56 cm)

Gobierno de Navarra, Departamento de Educación, Cultura y Deporte, Archivo Real y General, Cámara de Comptos, Caja 192, no. 54

The groom was Samuel, son of Yomtov Zuri; the bride was Jamila, daughter of Isaac ben Bibach. As with the other example here, the decoration is unsophisticated, but carefully placed in relation to the text (see no. 44).

BIBLIOGRAPHY F. Cantera-Burgos, "La *'ketuba' de* D. Davidovitch y las *ketubbot* españolas," *Sefarad* 33 (1973): 375-86; J. L. Lacave, *Sefarad Sefarad: La España Judía* (Barcelona and Madrid, 1987), fig. 211; Shalom Sabar, "The Beginnings and Flourishing of Ketubbah Illustration in Italy," (Dissertation, University of California, Los Angeles, 1987), 40 and n. 123; idem, "The Beginnings of *Ketubbah* Decoration in Italy: Venice in the Late Sixteenth to the Early Seventeenth Centuries," *Jewish Art* 12–13 (1987): 102-3, n. 50; Madrid, Ministerio de Cultura, *La vida judía en Sefarad,* exhibition catalogue, Sinagoga del Tránsito, Toledo, 1991-92, no. 99.

—VBM

46 Sale of Houses to a Jewish Woman

Avila (Castile), 1400

Ink on parchment

18¾ x 10⅜ in. (47.5 x 26.3 cm)

Avila, Parroquia de San Juan Bautista

In this document the clerics of the Cabildo of San Benito sell several houses to an Avilan Jewish woman named Ayha. The text defines the property as bordering the houses of a certain Baru Aliahen and a Moorish property, which indicates that Jews lived near Muslims. The price to be paid by the buyer was forty-five maravedis and two hens. Although the document is not dated, it can be deduced from the form of payment—the hens and the first part of the amount for the coming Christmas, and the second payment for the feast of St. John in June 1401—that it was issued in the year 1400.[1]

Jewish presence in Avila is mentioned as early as the year 1085. Jews later formed one of the most prominent communities of Castile. There were two synagogues in Avila, and in 1303 the property book of the cathedral mentions about forty Jewish homes on the cathedral's lands.[2] While most of the Jews were shopkeepers or artisans, some also cultivated their own lands and owned sheep or cattle.[3] In 1295, the community was swept with a messianic fervor after a seer, the so-called "Prophet of Avila," declared that he had experienced mystical visions.[4]

The community continued to flourish until the Catholic Monarchs imposed several restrictive measures against the Jews, and in 1480 ordered their confinement in a separate quarter of the city. In 1490, an inquisitional tribunal was established in Avila and in 1491 the "La Guardia trial," one of the most inflammatory trials of the time, took place there. The Jew Jucé Franco and several members of his family were burned at the stake after being falsely accused of the ritual murder of "the child of La Guardia."[5] After the 1492 expulsion, the two synagogues of Avila were sold and the Jewish cemetery was given to a monastery.

NOTES 1) *Las Edades del Hombre: Libros y Documentos de la Iglesia de Castilla y León,* exhibition catalogue (Burgos, 1990), no. 387. 2) F. Cantera Burgos, *Sinagogas Españolas* (Madrid, 1955), 168–69. 3) Y. Baer, *A History of the Jews in Christian Spain* (Philadelphia, 1961), 192, 198. 4) Ibid., 277–78; *Encyclopedia Judaica,* 3:970. 5) L. Suárez Fernández, *Documentos acerca de la expulsión de los judíos* (Valladolid, 1964), 44.

BIBLIOGRAPHY *Las Edades del Hombre: Libros y Documentos en la Iglesia de Castilla y León,* exhibition catalogue (Burgos, 1990), no. 387.

—CN

47 Edict of Expulsion of the Jews from Spain

Granada, March 31, 1492

Ink on paper

12½ x 8¹³⁄₁₆ in. (31.7 x 22.4 cm)

Avila, Exmo. Ayuntamiento de Avila, Archivo Histórico Provincial de Avila, 1/77

Several factors led to the 1492 Edict of Expulsion.[1] First was a drive toward the political and religious unification of Spain in which the marriage of Isabella and Ferdinand in 1469 and the association of the two kingdoms in 1479 were first steps.

The protective attitude that most Christian rulers had adopted toward Jews since the beginning of the Reconquest became an obstacle toward this goal, provoking anti-Jewish sentiment among municipal authorities and the general populace. In response, the monarchs instituted severe measures against Jews, whose presence in a Christian state was regarded as dangerous to national security.

Despite increasing numbers of *conversos,* the Church felt that many were not true Christians and that their contacts with Jewish relatives undermined religious unification. To confront this problem, the monarchs agreed in 1480 to the institution of the Inquisition. Although appointed to investigate *conversos* and not Jews, the Inquisition deeply affected Jewish communities that maintained close ties with the *conversos.*

The expulsion of 1492 was preceded, in 1483, by the expulsion of the Jews from Andalusia, an area considered by the Inquisition as the most dangerous due to the high concentration of

Jews in its cities.[2] The time that elapsed between these two expulsions was used by the monarchs to gather Jewish support for the prolonged and expensive war against Granada, the last Muslim stronghold on the Iberian peninsula, which fell on January 2, 1492. Once political unity, for which Jewish economic and military support were valuable, was accomplished, the drive for religious unity increased.

In the text of the edict, the monarchs explain that the only way to prevent Jews from inflicting further injuries upon the Christian faith is to expel them. The monarchs ordered "that all Jews leave the kingdoms ... by the end of July. ..." If Jews were found in the kingdoms after that date "they are to be put to death and all their property confiscated."

Although the edict was signed on January 31, it did not become public until the end of April. In the intervening period, prominent Jewish officials like Isaac Abravanel and Don Abraham Seneor, Chief Rabbi of Castile, tried to obtain its repeal.[3] The only way to avoid expulsion was through conversion, and a considerable number of Jews, including Don Abraham Seneor himself, chose this option even though they became a target for the Inquisition. Those leaving were obliged to sell their property at extremely low prices and were often victims of abuse despite efforts by the Crown to carry out the expulsion in a quiet manner. Many exiled Jews found temporary refuge in Portugal, where they remained until 1496 when they were again forced to choose between conversion and expulsion. Other Jews fled to Navarre, where they remained until 1498, the date of the final expulsion from the Iberian peninsula.[4]

NOTES 1) The complete text of the edict preserved in the Avila Archives was published by F. Fita, "Edicto de los Reyes Católicos (31 de Marzo de 1492) desterrando de sus estados a todos los judíos," *Boletín de la Real Academia de la Historia* 11 (1887): 512–20. See also F. Baer, *Die Juden im christlichen Spanien,* vol. 2 (Berlin, 1936), 404–8, no. 378. Two other copies of the Edict of Expulsion are preserved. The first is in the Archive of Simancas (Patronato Real, leg. 28, fol. 6) and was published by L. Suárez Fernández in *Documentos acerca de la expulsión de los judíos* (Valladolid, 1964), 389–95, no. 177. The second copy is part of the collection of the Archivo de la Corona de Aragón and it was published by A. de la Torre in *Documentos sobre las relaciones internacionales de los Reyes Católicos,* vol. 4 (Barcelona, 1962), 27–31. 2) A document mentioning the expulsion of the Jews from Seville in Andalusia, is preserved in Simancas (Suárez Fernández, *Documentos acerca de la expulsión de los judíos,* 224–26, no. 69. 3) See J. S. Minkin, *Abravanel and the Expulsion of the Jews from Spain* (New York, 1938). 4) On the subject of the expulsion of the Jews from kingdom of Navarre see B. Gampel, *The Last Jews on Iberian Soil* (Berkeley, Calif., Los Angeles, and Oxford, 1989).

BIBLIOGRAPHY F. Fita, "Edicto de los Reyes Católicos (31 de Marzo de 1492) desterrando de sus estados a todos los judíos," *Boletín de la Real Academia de la Historia* 11 (1887): 512–20; L. Suárez Fernández, *Documentos acerca de la expulsión de los judíos* (Valladolid, 1964); Y. Baer, *A History of the Jews in Christian Spain,* vol. 2 (Philadelphia, 1966), 431-43; *Encyclopaedia Judaica,* 15:239–41.

—CN

48 Compilation of Documents: The Jews of Cervera React Against the Expulsion

Cervera (Catalonia), August 20, 1492

Ink on paper

12¾ x 8¾ in. (32.4 x 22.2 cm), 54 folios

New York, The Library of The Jewish Theological Seminary of America, Ms. Spanish 6

This manuscript provides a unique perspective on the expulsion of the Jews from Spain. It is a compilation of documents in Latin and Catalan that was prepared by the notary public of Cervera for the use of the bailiff on August 20, 1492, a few weeks after the expulsion. In these documents the Jews mention several privileges they were granted by former rulers in the fourteenth century and strongly protest against the edict of Expulsion.[1] Although we know of the work of prominent Jewish officials to obtain the repeal of the edict (see no. 47), documentation attesting to an entire community's reaction against the expulsion is quite rare.

The Jewish community of Cervera was established in the late thirteenth or early fourteenth century and lived in two residential quarters,[2] an older one called the "Call de Agrimontell," and a newer one, the "Call Nuevo," where a house also functioned as a synagogue. Apparently this was without permission from the ecclesiastical authorities, who ultimately obtained a royal order to confiscate the building.[3]

The Jewish quarters were looted and set on fire during the years of the Black Death (1348–49), but the community seems to have recovered shortly afterward. Despite anti-Jewish riots in 1391, and the municipal authorities' attempt to expel the Jews in 1392, the community of Cervera managed to survive and even flourish during the fifteenth century, until its expulsion in 1492.

NOTES 1) A. Marx, *Bibliographical Studies and Notes on Rare Books and Manuscripts in The Library of The Jewish Theological Seminary of America,* (New York, 1977), 133–34 (68–69). 2) Y. Baer, *A History of the Jews in Christian Spain,* vol. 1 (Philadelphia, 1961), 112. 3) The confiscation was ordered by King Peter IV on March 29, 1348. Only in 1384, by order of the Infanta Violante, could the Jews of Cervera build a new synagogue. See F. Cantera Burgos, *Sinagogas españolas* (Madrid, 1955), 194–95.

BIBLIOGRAPHY A. Marx, *Bibliographical Studies and Notes on Rare Books and Manuscripts in The Library of The Jewish Theological Seminary of America,* (New York, 1977), 133–34 (68–69).

—CN

Printed Books

49 **Abraham Zacuto,** ***Astronomical Tables***

Leiria, 1473

Ink on paper: printed

8⅛ x 5⅞ in.
(21.5 x 15 cm)

New York, The Library of The Jewish Theological Seminary of America, Z 14

Zacuto's tables (*Ḥibbur ha-Gadol*) were composed between 1473 and 1478. Subsequently a commission of King John II of Portugal drew up a simplified version designed for use by seamen. By using a cross-staff or an astrolabe, a navigator found the meridian altitude of the sun and compared that value to that of the sun's declination as given in Zacuto's quadrennial tables in order to establish his latitude at sea. Zacuto's tables were used by the first generation of Spanish and Portuguese explorers, most notably by Columbus and Vasco da Gama. They circulated widely in Latin translation and in an Arabic version, were used routinely in sixteenth-century Egypt.

BIBLIOGRAPHY F. R. Goff, ed., *Incunabula in American Libraries* (New York, 1964), no. Z14.

—*TG*

50 **Rashi,** ***Commentary on the Pentateuch***

Published by Samuel ben Musa

Zamora, 1487

Ink on paper: printed

10⅜ x 8 in.
(26.3 x 20.3 cm)

New York, The Library of The Jewish Theological Seminary of America, H94b

This is one of the earliest Hebrew printed books. After the expulsion, Jewish printers carried their technical knowledge with them and established the first printing press in the Ottoman Empire. Samuel ben Musa is known to have published three works; this is the only extant copy of any of them. It reproduces the extensive commentary on the Hebrew Bible written by Rabbi Solomon ben Isaac, known as Rashi (1040–1105).

According to notes in the book, it was sold in Italy in 1523 by Jacob Israel of Forli to Isaac ben Obadiah of Mestre. In 1854, it came into the collection of the Breslau Theological Seminary and subsequently passed into private ownership in Holland from whence it was brought to the United States.

BIBLIOGRAPHY M. Steinschneider, *Catalogus Librorum Hebraeorum,* 4 vols. (Berlin, 1852-60), vol. 3, col. 2342, no. 6927, 4; C. Haebler, *Bibliografia Iberica del Siglo XV* (The Hague and Leipzig, 1904), no. 568; Aaron Freimann, *Otzer le-Melekhet ha-Defus ha-Ivri ha-Rishonah be-Meah ha-Ḥamesh Esreh* (Jerusalem, 1968), 257–59.

—*VBM*

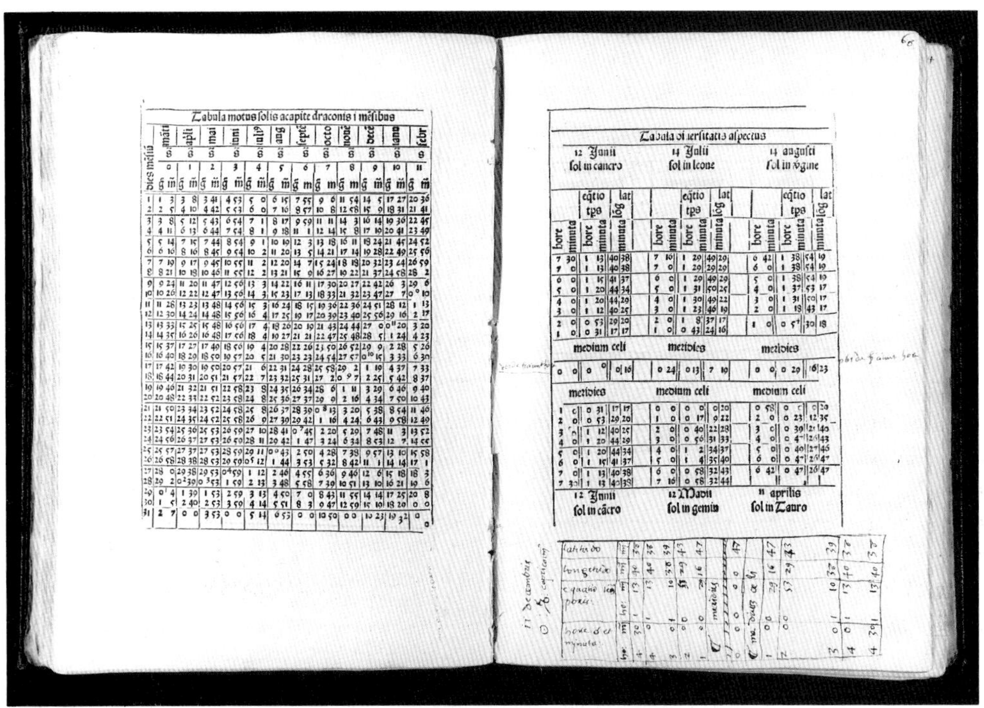

Tabula motus solis a capite draconis i mensibus

Tabula diversitatis aspectus

49

אלו נתן לנו את ה

ולא קרבנו לפני הר סיני

אלו קרבנו לפני הר סיני

ולא נתן לנו את התורה דיינו

אלו נתן לנו את התורה

ולא הכניסנו לארץ ישראל דיינו

אלו הכניסנו לארץ ישראל

ולא בנה לנו את בית המקדש דיינו

על אחת כמה וכמה טובה כפולה ומכפלת למקום עלינו הוציאנו

51

51 **Leaves from the Oldest Illustrated Printed Haggadah**

Spain or Portugal, late fifteenth century

Ink on paper: printed

7⅜ x 4¾ in. (18.8 x 12.1 cm)

New York, The Library of The Jewish Theological Seminary of America, Very Rare Collection 5637

These two leaves, together with a third in the same collection, are among the oldest illustrations for printed Haggadot. Over a period of years an additional six leaves were found in the Genizah Collection at Cambridge University by Abraham Haberman and Alexander Scheiber. In all, nine leaves are extant. Of these, eight are different and one is a duplicate. One Cambridge leaf bears the second and third plagues of Egypt on one side and the sixth and seventh on the other, which suggests that the leaf is a trial proof rather than an illustration from a completed book.

Most experts agree that the typography and the texts accompanying the illustrations indicate an origin in Spain or Portugal prior to the expulsions of the late fifteenth century. There is the additional possibility that the plates and type were set on the Iberian peninsula and then taken to Constantinople by Jewish refugees and printed there. Other instances of this occurrence are known. In any case, these haggadah illustrations represent a unique enterprise since no other Hebrew printed book from Spain, Portugal, or sixteenth-century Constantinople was illustrated. The leaves are an interesting example of cultural creativity during the last years of Jewry on the peninsula.

BIBLIOGRAPHY Soncino Gesellschaft, *Haggadah: Das Fragment der ältesten mit Illustrationen gedruckten Haggadah* (Berlin, 1927); A. Yaari, *Bibliography of the Passover-Haggadah from the Earliest Printed Edition to 1960 with Twenty Five Reproductions from Rare Editions and a Facsimile of a Unique Copy of the First Printed Haggadah in the Jewish National and University Library, Jerusalem* (Jerusalem, 1960), no. 5 (Hebrew); A. M. Habermann, "An Unknown leaf of the Haggadah, Constantinople? 1515?," *Kirjath Sefer* 38 (1963): 273; A. Scheiber, "New Pages from the First Printed Illustrated Hagaddah," *Studies in Bibliography and Booklore* 7 (1965): 26-36; Yosef Hayim Yerushalmi, *Leaves from the Oldest Illustrated Printed Haggadah* (Philadelphia, 1974); New York, The Jewish Museum, *A Tale of Two Cities: Jewish Life in Frankfurt and Istanbul 1750–1870,* by Vivian B. Mann, exhibition catalogue (New York, 1982), no. 24.

—*VBM*

Architectural Elements

52 **Fragment of the Altar Screen from San Miguel de Escalada**

San Miguel de Escalada, León, tenth century

Limestone

Monastery of San Miguel de Escalada, Province of León

52

This plaque, covered with low-relief carving, was part of a low altar barrier in the church of San Miguel. The monastery was built by Mozarabic monks, who had lived under Islamic rule. This particular monastery moved en masse from Córdoba to a site near the capital of the Christian kingdom of León in the north, to begin a new life on lands donated by King Alfonso III. It was long thought that the Mozarabs were the unwitting bearers of an overwhelmingly Islamic style to the Christian north, but they seem instead to have held tenaciously to the memory of their ancient Christian artistic traditions, inherited from the Hispano-Romans living under Visigothic rule, before the advent of Islam on the peninsula. This can be seen in the use of a high altar screen at San Miguel, in conjunction with this low barrier.

This fragment also reveals close connections with the older style in its decoration. Plants and animals in vine scrolls abound in churches of the Visigothic period: San Pedro de la Nave and Quintanilla de las Viñas are two examples. But there is also evidence of a shared language of forms with the Islamic south. The palmetts within vine scrolls are reminiscent of stucco motifs brought to Córdoba along with the stucco-carving traditions of the fertile crescent, as part of Islamic patronage. This new motif is adopted here by Christians working within the framework of an older, indigenous tradition. These same forms also appear in caliphal sculpture, and in much later Hebrew manuscripts produced on the peninsula. They became part of a peninsular art of abstract ornamentation.

BIBLIOGRAPHY M. Gómez-Moreno, *Iglesias Mozárabes* (Madrid, 1919), 141–62. P. Palol and M. Hirmer, *L'Art en Espagne du Royaume Wisigoth à la fin de l'epoque romane* (Paris, 1967) 40–41, figs. 31–35, 155, plates 42–45.

—*JD*

53 **Volute with Hidden Birds**

Alamiria (Córdoba), tenth century

Marble

6¼ x 4¾ in (16 x 12 cm)

Córdoba, Museo Arqueológico Provincial, no. 9523

53

This volute originally graced a capital from the palace of Alamiria, a late tenth-century country residence of al-Mansur, built outside of Córdoba. Al-Mansur was technically only chamberlain to the youthful Caliph Hisham, but he actually ruled as a potent dictator. When al-Mansur built the country palaces of Alamiria and Madīnat al-Zahira outside of Córdoba, he was imitating the courtly patronage of the great Umayyad caliphs of Córdoba, like ʿAbd al-Raḥmān III, builder of the legendary palace city of Madīnat al-Zahrāʾ.

The volute was found in excavations conducted by Ricardo Velázquez Bosco in 1910. Through his work and from chronicles, we know that a good deal of the sculpture of Alamiria was of marble, while the walls of the palace were covered with painted stucco. The fine carving and complexity of the volute speak for a high level of craftsmanship at Alamiria.

As is typical of capitals of the caliphal period on the Iberian peninsula, the different surfaces of the volute are squared off into separate planes. Though any one of the individual motifs might be found in the Christian arts of Spain from the period before the advent of Islam, they are combined here in a dense composition that makes their naturalistic components seem nearly abstract. The whole seems at first glance to be a jumble of vine scrolls and other vegetal motifs, but upon closer scrutiny, we see a lion's head poised to devour the rinceau of the volute's outer profile, and tiny birds hidden in the jungle of the volute's broad face. This interplay of figures in an apparently vegetal composition is a kind of delightful puzzle for the viewer, who constantly seeks the hidden animals in the *horror vacui* of vines and leaves. Such complex and minute compositions, as well as the interplay of figures and vegetal designs, are very similar to contemporary ivory carving, and all are part of the opulence characteristic of caliphal patronage in tenth-century Spain.

The vegetal motifs on one level are also an evocation of Alamiria's gardens, which chroniclers praised at length. Since the time of the first Umayyad emir on the Iberian peninsula, ʿAbd al-Raḥmān I, the building of country palaces with gardens was part of the creation of the image of a great ruler, an image al-Mansur was eager to create for himself.

BIBLIOGRAPHY R. Castejon, "Alamiria," *Boletín de la Real Academia de Córdoba,* 25, no. 70 (1954): 150–55.

—*JD*

54 **Capital**

Toledo, second half of the eleventh century

Marble: carved

13⅞ x 11¾ x 10¼ in. (35.5 x 30 x 26 cm)

Toledo, Museo Taller del Moro, no. 1270. Depósito del Cabildo de Párrocos

54

This capital, found in the Convento de la Reina in Toledo, dates from the period of the *taifa* rulers. These rulers of small kingdoms had little of the military power of the caliphate that had preceded them, but continued the caliphal tradition of patronizing the arts as a means of establishing their own visual identity in a religiously and ethnically diverse peninsula.

This capital may date from the period of the ruler al Maʾmun, a great *taifa* patron of Toledo. It is an example of a formal development in Toledo characteristic of the *taifa* period, the composed capital or *capitel compuesto,* which has more compressed forms than its caliphal prototypes. All the leaves of the capital and its decoration are subordinated to the volume of the capital as a whole; the parts of the capital itself are schematized. One of these schematized parts becomes a band at the base of the capital that holds the inscription "The Dominion is ʾAllah's"; another is the abacus, which alternates that invocation with others, including "The power is ʾAllah's."

The use of inscriptions on capitals was rare before the advent of Islam on the peninsula, and can be seen as one of the means by which Muslims introduced a didactic iconography into this architectural decoration. This tradition continued later in Toledo's *Tránsito* synagogue (see no. 58).

BIBLIOGRAPHY Clara Delgado Valero, *Materiales para el estudio morfológico y ornamental del arte Islámico en Toledo* (Toledo, 1987), 90–91; Basilio Pavón Maldonado, *Arte Toledano: Islámico y Mudéjar* (Madrid, 1973), 99–100; Klaus Brisch, "Sobre un grupo de capitales y bases islámicas del siglo XI," *Cuadernos de la Alhambra* no. 15-17, (1979-81): 156–58; Matilde Revuelta, *Taller del Moro, Toledo* (Toledo, 1979), 74.

—*JD*

55 **Capital**

Toledo, twelfth or thirteenth century

Limestone: carved

7⅞ x 6¼ x 16½ in (20 x 16 x 42 cm) (perimeter of the base)

Toledo, Museo Sefardí, no. 25

This limestone capital is decorated with both a Hebrew and an Arabic inscription, separated by a band of delicate vegetal decoration. The collar is decorated with a motif consisting of a band of diagonal lines surmounted by column-shaped verticals that appear to support a leaf-like canopy. Above this section, the Hebrew inscription is rendered in a single band around the lower part of the capital. It reads: "Blessed shall you be in your comings, and blessed shall you be in your goings" (Deut. 28:6).

Above the Hebrew inscription is a garland formed by pine branches alternating with pinecones around which a serpent is entwined. The Arabic inscription, in semi-kufic characters, appears above this garland, on the abacus. The inscription reads: البركة اليمن التوفية والامن "Blessing and happiness, success and peace"

In the uppermost zone, among the motifs surmounting the Arabic inscription, are flowers, shells, volutes, and (possibly) a lion cub.

The capital was discovered amidst debris in the cloister of San Juan de los Reyes in Toledo. F. Cantera believed it must have come from an old Toledan synagogue, no longer extant, which is mentioned in a poem by Yaakov Albeneh. The two languages of the inscription are a visual testament to the bilinguality of most Spanish Jews during the Middle Ages.

BIBLIOGRAPHY F. Cantera Burgos and J. M. Millás Vallicrosa, *Inscripciones Hebraicas de España* (Madrid, 1956), 333–35 (with additional bibliography); Ana María López Alvarez, *Catálogo del Museo Sefardí Toledo* (Madrid, 1986), 55–56; Madrid, Ministerio de Cultura, *La vida Judía en Sefarad,* exhibition catalogue, Sinagoga del Tránsito, Toledo, 1991-92, no. 8.

—*AMLA*

56 Decorative Stucco Fragments from the Córdoba Synagogue

Córdoba, 1314–15

(a) 42⅛ x 23⅝ in. (107 x 60 cm)

(b) 41⅜ x 15¾ in. (105 x 40 cm)

Stucco: carved

Córdoba, Delegación Provincial

These fragments are from Córdoba's only surviving synagogue, founded by Isaac Meḥab. Although of modest size, it displays finely crafted Mudejar stucco carvings of the Nasrid style.

Panels are covered with a low-relief geometric pattern including six-pointed stars, four-pointed stars, and the geometrical shapes formed by their intersection. Fragment (a) includes an inscription on a band near its top. The integration of calligraphic inscriptions with geometric patterning is typical of the Alhambra in Granada, and reminds us of the evolving relationship between Mudejar style under Christian hegemony and contemporary developments in Islamic art. The presence of this work in Córdoba's synagogue also evokes the particular way in which the Jewish community created a visual identity for itself that was closely linked to Islamic tradition.

BIBLIOGRAPHY F. Cantera Burgos, *Sinagogas Españolas* (Madrid, 1955), 3–32.

—*JD*

57 Dedicatory Inscription of the Córdoba Synagogue (Cast)

Córdoba, 1314–15 (original)

Plaster

21⅝ x 46⅞ in (55 x 119 cm) (original)

Córdoba, Delegación Provincial

This inscription comes from the only extant Cordoban synagogue.[1] It was placed in the east wall, next to the niche that served as a Torah ark. The text reads:

מקדש מעט ונוה תעודה שכללו
יצחק מחב בן הגביר אפרים
ודוה שנת שבעים וחמש כן שעה
(ה)אל וחיש לבנות ירושלם

> Isaac Meḥab, son of the honorable Ephraim, has completed this lesser sanctuary and he built it in the year 75 [1314-15] as a temporary abode. Hasten, O God, to rebuild Jerusalem.

As numerous writers have noted, the expression "this lesser sanctuary" does not refer to the small size of the Córdoba synagogue, which measures only 6.37 x 6.95 m or approximately 21 x 23 ft., but to the temporary nature of any synagogue in comparison with the eternity of the Temple in Jerusalem.

The donor's name "Meḥab" derives from the Arabic *muhibb* meaning friend or beloved. The name appears frequently in records from thirteenth-century Toledo and its environs.[2]

NOTES 1) That other synagogues existed in medieval Córdoba may be deduced from various documentary sources such as a bull from Pope Innocent IV to the archdeacon of Córdoba dated 1250 protesting the height of a new synagogue. For the text see R. Wischnitzer, *The Architecture of the European Synagogues* (Philadelphia, 1964), 30. 2) J. Pelaez del Rosal, *La Sinagoga* (Córdoba, 1984), 151.

SELECTED BIBLIOGRAPHY Otto Czekelius, "Antiguas sinagogas de España," *Arquitectura* 31 (1931), 326–41; Francisco Cantera Burgos, *Sinagogas Españolas* (Madrid, 1955), 1–32; Rachel Wischnitzer, *The Architecture of the European Synagogue* (Philadelphia, 1964), 27–30; Francisco Cantera Burgos, *Sinagogas de Toledo, Segovia y Córdoba* (Madrid, 1973), 151–86; J. Pelaez del Rosal, *La Sinagoga* (Córdoba, 1984), 123-64.

—*VBM*

58 Three Stucco Fragments from the *El Tránsito* Synagogue

Toledo, 1357

Stucco: carved

(a) 5½ x 8½ x 1⅛ in. (14 x 21.5 x 3 cm)[1]

(b) 4⅞ x 8⅞ x 1⅛ in. (12.5 x 22.5 x 3 cm)

(c) 6¼ x 5⅛ x 1⅛ in. (16 x 13 x 3 cm)

Toledo, Museo Sefardí/ Sinagoga del Tránsito, 243-23, 243-14/15, 243-7

These three fragments, with traces of polychrome decoration and Hebrew inscriptions, were originally part of the ornamental frieze that ran along the four walls of the women's gallery of the *Tránsito* synagogue in Toledo.

The first two fragments belonged to the upper part of the frieze section that decorated the southern wall. A band composed of diagonal lines and arcades with traces of red, green, and black paint, is partially preserved at the bottom of each fragment.[2] The Hebrew inscription on the first fragment reads: ["Thy throne given of God is for ever and ev]er; A sceptre of [equity is the sceptre of thy kingdom"] (Psalms 45:7). The inscription on the second fragment reads: "Thou hast loved right[eousness and hated wickedness; Therefore God, thy God, hath anointed thee]" (Psalms 45:8).

The third fragment belonged to the lower part of the frieze that decorated the southern wall of the women's gallery. Traces of red and black paint and *ataurique* or arabesque decoration are preserved on this piece.[3] The inscription reads: "[I]f [Thou, Lord, shouldest mark] iniquit[ies O Lord, who could stand?"] (Psalms 130:3).

58A

58B

NOTES 1) An additional centimeter should be added to the depth of this fragment, due to traces of mortar that served to affix the piece to the wall. 2) On the first fragment, only traces of red polychromy are preserved. 3) The *ataurique* decoration is also used on stucco decorations from the Convent of Las Dueñas (see no. 59).

BIBLIOGRAPHY F. Cantera Burgos, *Sinagogas Españolas* (Madrid, 1955, 143-44, 147-48, fig. 17); A.M. López Alvarez and T. Alvarez Delgado, "La galería de las mujeres de la sinagoga de El Tránsito: Nuevos hallazgos," *Sefarad* 47, no. 2 (1987): 301–14.

—*AMLA*

59 **Fragment of an Intrados from an Arch of the Convent of Las Dueñas, Córdoba**

Córdoba, fourteenth century

Stucco: carved

21⅝ x 18⅛ (55 x 46 cm)

Córdoba, Museo Arqueológico Provincial, no. 579

Like nos. 60 and 61 in this catalogue, this fragment is from the now destroyed convent of Las Dueñas in Córdoba. Here the Mudejar style appears at its closest to Islamic prototypes; and, as is typical of fourteenth-century Córdoba, the prototype seems to be a Nasrid work, like the Alhambra in Granada.

The intrados is divided into an interior panel and an epigraphic band. The panel is covered with *atauriques* or arabesques very similar to those that dominate the decoration of the Alhambra palace. The interstices of the interlacing forms are filled with another level of minute vegetal interlace.

The epigraphic band contains an elaborate decorative inscription in Arabic, with letters that end, at times, in leaves. The Arabic inscriptions in a Christian convent are not the secret graffiti of Muslim workmen as some have suggested; they were a conscious addition approved by the monastery's patrons, a testimony to the extent to which the Arabic language, like Islamic style, had become part of the fabric of life on the Iberian peninsula.

Unpublished

—*JD*

60 **Stucco Relief in Cartouche from the Convent of Las Dueñas, Córdoba**

Córdoba, fourteenth century

Stucco: carved

21⅝ x 17¾ in. (55 x 45 cm)

Córdoba, Museo Arqueológico Provincial, no. 577

60

This enframed cartouche from the destroyed Convent of Las Dueñas (see also nos. 59 and 61) relies on rich sensual curves to create a continuous decoration based on vegetal forms. Unlike the other examples of stucco work in this exhibition that come from Las Dueñas, these motifs are not geometric, but part of a stucco tradition that extends as far back as the ninth century in Islamic Iraq. The more recent prototype was Nasrid work, such as that of the Alhambra in Granada.

Similar designs and like manners of conceiving decoration are found in synagogues such as that of Samuel Halevi in Toledo. All of the stucco from Las Dueñas shows how the most traditional forms, derived from a long history of abstract ornamentation in Islamic art, later passed to Jewish and Christian art on the Iberian peninsula.

Unpublished

—*JD*

61

61 Panel with Expanding-Star Motif from the Convent of Las Dueñas

Córdoba, fourteenth century

Stucco: carved

28 x 28 in. (71 x 71 cm)

Córdoba, Museo Arqueológico Provincial, no. 584

This stucco panel typifies the use of Mudejar style by Christian foundations after the Christian conquest of Córdoba in the thirteenth century, and reminds us that Islamic art was considered the finest and most elegant on the peninsula, even as the power of Islamic states was waning. For the church, the intrinsic power of Islamic style overcame any negative implications of its association with Islam.

On this piece the use of fine, biplanar stucco carving and of continuous bands interlacing to create a never-ending sequence of stars shows that Mudejar craftsmen were aware of great Nasrid monuments like the Alhambra. Very similar expanding-star motifs in stucco can also be found in Córdoba's fourteenth-century synagogue.

Unpublished

—JD

This white marble fountain is carved in thirty-two curved sections (*gallones*) on both its interior and exterior, and has a hole at center to allow the inflow of water. Since the fountain has no perforation for a water outlet, the water may have overflown, sliding over the exterior when the fountain was in use. It was probably placed on the ground, as are the fountains preserved in the Court of the Lions at the Alhambra, and it may have been part of a decorative network of thin water channels.

62 White Marble Fountain

Alhambra, Nasrid period, fourteenth century

White marble: carved

H 4½ in., diam. 24¾ in. (11.5 x 63 cm)

Granada, Museo Nacional de Arte Hispanomusulmán, No. reg. 428

The use of water as both a functional and an ornamental element is constant in Hispanomoresque architecture in general and in the Nasrid period in particular. Water was used in ponds, channels, and fountains of different shapes and sizes, adding to the beauty of the architecture with its reflection and its sound.[1]

The use of curved sections or *gallones* as an ornamental theme in circular fountains is not foreign to the Nasrid period and important examples have been preserved of large fountains such as the one in the Alhambra Court of the Lindaraja bearing zigzag decorations and an epigraphic band on its exterior. The *agallonada* (carved with *gallones*) shape can be traced to the caliphal period, as can be seen in the fountain from Casa Chapiz (Granada) preserved in the Museo Arqueológico Provincial of Granada.[2] During the Nasrid period the *agallonada* shape received *gallones* of different forms and sizes, using white marble and serpentine as material. There are also some small ceramic fountains preserved from this period with golden and blue figurative decoration of fish, an appropriate theme for a water fountain and one that appears both in the western Islamic world as early as the caliphal period and in the Orient.[3]

NOTES 1) Jesús Bermúdez Pareja, "El agua en los jardines musulmanes de la Alhambra," in *Les jardins de l'Islam,* UNESCO (Granada, 1973), 184–91; Antonio Fernández Puertas, "Los jardines hispanomusulmanes del Generalife según la poesía," ibid., 196–200. 2) Darío Cabanelas, "La pila árabe del Museo Arqueológico de Granada y la casa del Chapiz," *Miscelánea de estudios árabes y hebraicos* 29–30 (1980–81): 21–34. 3) Purificación Marinetto Sánchez, "Dos pilas califales inéditas," *Arqueología medieval española,* vol. 2, (Madrid, 1987), 756–64.

Unpublished

—*PMS*

The geometric decoration is composed of a weave of octagonal shapes forming eight-pointed stars and squares. The stars alternate with the squares along the diagonal resulting in a pattern of stars and crosses.[1] These forms are outlined by gilding.

63 Longitudinal Stucco Panel

Arjona (?) (Jaén), Nasrid period, fourteenth century

Stucco: carved and polychromed

21⅝ x 38¾ in. (55 x 98.3 cm)

Granada, Museo Nacional de Arte Hispanomusulmán, No. reg. 2.225

The interior of some stars is decorated with palm motifs whose stems establish an axis of symmetry. The background is filled with alternating bands of green and red. Inside other stars is a vase decorated with alternating red and white bands; each corner of the star is painted red while the background of the octagonal shape in which the star is inscribed is filled with blue paint.

The carving of the different motifs of this panel is clear, and the traces of original polychromy emphasize the similarity of this kind of decoration to that found on textiles. This kind of stucco decoration covered the walls of summer residences while silk textiles were used to cover the walls of winter residences.[2] Color defined spaces, and differentiated one motif from another. The use of gilt adds to the richness of this panel.

The panel was once part of the collection of Francisca Pérez de Herrasti.

NOTES 1) Antonio Prieto Vives, "La simetría y la composición de los tracistas musulmanes," *Investigación y progreso* 6, no. 3 (1932): 40–41, figs. 22–23; Antonio Fernández Puertas, "El lazo de ocho occidental o andaluz: su trazado, canon proporcional, series y patrones," *Al-Andalus* (1975): 199–203; idem., "Notas sobre el lazo hispano-musulmán," *Epsilon* (Granada, 1987), 43–44. 2) Antonio Fernández Puertas, "Un paño decorativo de la Torres de las Damas," *Cuadernos de la Alhambra* 9, (1973): 51–52.

BIBLIOGRAPHY *Museo de Arte Hispano-Musulmán de la Alhambra,* 2d ser. 2, no. 1, (1981): 4.

—*PMS*

64 **Shaft with mosaic tile (*alicatado*) decoration**

Spain, Nasrid period, fourteenth century

Ceramic: glazed

H 10¼ in. diam. 7½ in. (26 x 19 cm)

Granada, Museo Nacional de Arte Hispanomusulmán, No. reg. 7.165

This engaged (*entrego*) shaft, with a base in the shape of half an octagon, is decorated with symmetrical lace-like patterns formed of eight-pointed stars in black, green, or white paint surrounded by black or green pentagons (*zafates*) and white almond-shaped motifs (*almendrillas*) following an octagonal symmetry.[1]

Socles of *alicatado* decorated with various geometric motifs are often found in the Alhambra since their decoration protected the supports from the humidity of the ground and from soiling. The preserved socles with their original polychromy show diverse chromatic designs in stucco work.[2]

Other examples of *alicatado* work are found on engaged columns; their decoration is similar to that of socles, forming a continuous unit adapted to the curved or polygonal shape of the shaft, as in this case. During the reign of Muḥammad V columns are used as decorative elements in stucco panels or as pseudosupports in freestanding or engaged arches. In the latter case, the decorative character of the shaft is enriched as it appears surrounded by an *alicatado* panel.[3] This architectonic solution occurs in several places at the Alhambra allowing us to contemplate *in situ* the effect of the geometrical and chromatic richness that covered the rooms of the palace from ground to ceiling.

The use of engaged shafts covered with *alicatado* is found in various places at the Alhambra: the central rooms of the Hall of the Comares and the Hall of the Kings. Sometimes the shafts have a semicircular base and sometimes an octagonal base.

NOTES 1) Antonio Prieto Vives, "La simetría y la composición de los tracistas musulmanes," *Investigación y progreso* 3 (1932): 43–44. 2) Purificación Marinetto Sánchez, "La policromía de los capiteles del palacio de los Leones," *Cuadernos de la Alhambra* 21 (1985): 79. 3) Purificación Marinetto Sánchez, *El capitel en el Palacio de los Leones: génesis, evolución, estudio y catálogo* (Granada, 1985), 229–41.

Unpublished

—*PMS*

65 **Ceramic fragment with mosaic tile (*alicatado*) decoration**

Cerro del Sol, Dar al-Arusa (?), Granada, Nasrid period, fourteenth to fifteenth century

Ceramic: glazed

45½ x 51½ in. (115.5 x 131 cm)

Granada, Museo Nacional de Arte Hispanomusulmán, No. reg. 1330

This panel decorated with *alicatado* is framed along the upper border by a black crenellation motif (*almenado*) set in a white ground and framed by a green band. The remainder of the panel is divided into rhomboids composed of black pentagons (*zafates*) and twelve-pointed stars in the angles. Each rhombus is divided in half by vertical lines composed of blue pentagons (*zafates*), forming two equilateral triangles filled with other motifs.

The geometric decoration and protection of the lower part of inner walls with panels of glazed and polychromed ceramics became popular during the Nasrid period. The variety of examples preserved facilitates the study of the evolution of geometric patterns and the use of color that makes the weave more complex and enriches the final result.

The *alicatado* as an architectural ceramic, created piece by piece, in a chosen color, serves both as a basis for and a study of geometric solutions to be used in other materials. It is perfectly proportioned to its designated space; a complex decorative solution well planned and enframed. This means of arranging a geometric theme in a precise space will disappear in the Mudejar period when the *alicatado* is supplanted by tile work that consists of the execution of repetitive themes on a small scale, imitating but losing the richness and perfection of the magnificent *alicatado* compositions.

Unpublished

—*PMS*

66 **Fragment of a double (*geminado*) arch**

Alhambra (Granada), Nasrid period, fourteenth century

Stucco: carved

20 x 29¾ in. (50.6 x 75.6 cm)

Granada, Museo Nacional de Arte Hispanomusulmán, No. reg. 958

This carved stucco fragment was the central part of a double (*geminado*) arch that formed a window. Each opening has a decentered extrados arch that left more space for decoration at the height of the keystone, here decorated with a palmette. Along the lower border are decorations in the shape of palms and peppers that spring out of serpentine stems. Carved in the middle of the spandrel (*albanega*) is the Nasrid shield bearing the dynastic motto, "Only God is triumphant." Framing the lower part of the shield is a kufic band with the apexes of the letters enveloping the bottom of the shield. Along its upper half, the shield is flanked by two inscriptions, one being the mirror image of the other, doubled for aesthetic effect.[1] The kufic inscription with its elongated letters is interlaced above the shield. The background of the spandrel (*albanega*) is filled with vegetal motifs.

NOTE 1) This kind of decoration also occurs in small symmetrical cartouches on capitals; (Purificación Marinetto Sánchez, *El capitel en el Palacio de los Leones: génesis, evolución, estudio y catálogo* [Granada, 1985], 370–72, figs. 160–63).

Unpublished

—*PMS*

67 **Stucco fragment**

Patio de los Leones, Alhambra, Granada, Nasrid period, fourteenth century

Stucco: carved

24 x 28⅛ in. (61 x 71.5 cm)

Granada, Museo Nacional de Arte Hispanomusulmán, No. reg. 2277

This fragment was originally part of the open-work stucco spandrel (*albanega*) of an arcade in the gallery of the Court of the Lions at the Alhambra Palace in Granada. The decorative design is composed of three sets of interwoven rhomboid motifs or *sebcas*: the main one is formed of protruding moldings that interlace with the horizontal molding above the arcade (*alfiz*); the second is composed of superimposed palms forming arches; the third consists of decorative bands interlaced with kufic letters for the word *baraka* (blessing). This last motif occurs on other capitals in the same courtyard.[1]

The decorative program of interwoven motifs (*sebcas*) is reminiscent of the crossed arches that were first built in the Córdoba Mosque under the rule of al-Ḥakam II and continued in the *taifa* period in a magnificent way in the Aljafería of Saragossa.[2] Variations of this decorative program were still in use during the Almohad period and evolve further in the Nasrid period.

While the supporting architecture in the Alhambra is composed of graceful columns surmounted by pillars that support lintels, the decorative program is composed of arched shapes that appear to support marble or stucco columns. The space between the arch and the lintel is filled with carved stucco panels with complex motifs and cut-out rhomboid shapes (*sebcas*) that alternate and form a decorative rhythm, for example, in the Court of the Arrayanes. In the Court of the Lions there are different decorative types in the capitals and in the columns, presenting a geometric solution that changes in each zone and element. These interlace with one another giving the impression of highly refined decorative purposes and symbolism.[3]

NOTES 1) Antonio Fernández Puertas, *La escritura cúfica de los palacios de Comares y Leones* (Granada, 1974), 112; Purificación Marinetto Sánchez, *El capitel en el Palacio de los Leones: génesis, evolución, estudio y catálogo* (Granada, 1985), 357–59, figs. 144–46. 2) Christian Ewert, *Spanish-Islamische Systeme sich Kreuzender Bögen: III, die Aljafería in Zaragoza* (Berlin, 1978). 3) Georges Marçais, *L'Architecture Musulmane d'Occident* (Paris, 1954), 348; Purificación Marinetto Sánchez, *El capitel en el palacio de los Leones,* 230, 300–307.

Unpublished

—*PMS*

68 **Fragments with Arabic inscriptions**

Alhambra, Granada, Nasrid period, fourteenth century

Stucco: carved

(a) 9¾ x 24⅝ in. (24.7 x 62.6 cm)

(b) 9¾ x 18¾ in. (24.7 x 47.5 cm)

(c) 9¾ x 16⅜ in. (24.7 x 41.6 cm)

Granada, Museo Nacional de Arte Hispanomusulmán, No. reg. 909, 910, 913

These are three of five extant fragments from a carved stucco frieze of the Alhambra Palace whose decoration is framed by two golden bands that interlace at intervals. The space between these two bands is filled by a small blue band and the resulting shape is an elliptical cartouche with lobed ends. The inner part of the panel is filled by a cursive inscription whose apexes are drawn in gold paint. The entire background, in red paint, is filled with palm motifs that spring from a serpentine stem.

The preserved fragments indicate that the longitudinal cartouches were separated by lobed circles filled with blue and decorated with the Nasrid shield, but without the dynastic motto (probably painted over). The shield is flanked by palms with six leaves and stems similar to the palms carved in areas of the Alhambra contemporary with the Palace of the Lions built by Emir Muḥammad V early in the last quarter of the fourteenth century. Other palm motifs appear on a red ground in the spaces between the cartouches and the circles, along with nodes of interlaced gold bands. During the period in which these fragments were executed there was an increased use of naturalistic forms like the palms and flowers used in different compositions in wall decorations.[1]

The richness of color, the beauty of the carving, and the composition of these fragments hint at the beauty and quality of the original frieze.

NOTE 1) Purificación Marinetto Sánchez, *El capitel en el Palacio de los Leones: génesis, evolución, estudio y catálogo* (Granada, 1985), 489–93; idem, "Apuntes sobre la decoración arquitectónica bajo el período emiral y califal," *Historia y cultura del Islam español* (Granada, 1988), 167.

Unpublished

—*PMS*

69 **Stucco fragment**

Convent of Zafra, Granada, Nasrid period, fourteenth century

Stucco: carved

15½ x 23½ in. (39.5 x 59.5 cm)

Granada, Museo Nacional de Arte Hispanomusulmán, No. reg. 3.758

This stucco panel consists of a double weave of rhomboid motifs or *sebcas*: one formed by crossed arches of palms and the other by the prolongation of the apexes of kufic letters. The inscription repeats the word "health": it starts at the base of the panel by forming intercrossed arches and ends in the upper part with the ascenders parallel to the upper border. All free spaces are filled with small cartouches with cursive writing and palms.

This panel shows clear signs of the ornamental decadence occurring at the end of the Nasrid period: the ornamentation is carved on only one plane; the different themes are hardly worked; and there is no real attempt to emphasize the independent decorative elements as had been done on the magnificent panels carved on varying planes in the mid-fourteenth century.

Unpublished

—*PMS*

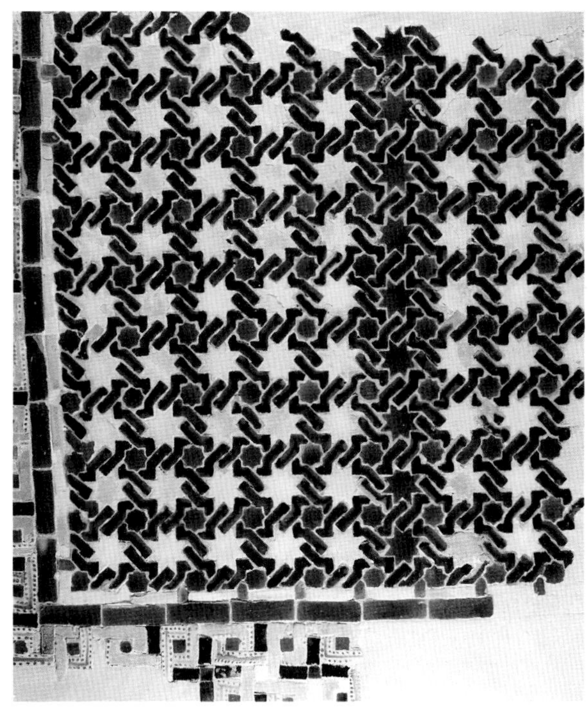

71

70 **Twelve-sided Wellhead with Inscription**

Spain, fourteenth or fifteenth century

Marble: carved

18¾ x 19¾ diam. in. (47.6 x 50.2 cm)

Yonkers, N.Y., Iona College

Carved wellheads were popular from the caliphal to the Nasrid periods. Used to mark the position of a well and to protect its opening from impurities, wellheads were also a sign of the presence and control of water, a prestigious power in Spain.

Although this piece is typical of Islamic tradition in its expanding star pattern, it might well be a Mudejar piece, since its use and style were shared by all the religious traditions on the Iberian peninsula.

Unpublished

—JD

71 **Mosaic Tile Panel**

Spain, end of fifteenth century

Tile

26⅛ x 26⅜ in. (66.5 x 67 cm)

Barcelona, Museu de Ceràmica, 62425

This mosaic tile panel or *alicatado* is fashioned of hundreds of tiny tile fragments cut to measure and assembled like a puzzle. Great precision was necessary to compose this tight, complex pattern of six-pointed stars and interwoven bands.

Such mosaic tile compositions were used on the dados of buildings, in particular in courtyards and gardens, and on floors. Their designs were often continued in stucco carving on the upper walls. In later times, after the fifteenth century, Christian monuments include imitations in painting, or in large square tiles with painted decoration, or in *cuerda seca* ceramic tiles, which uses an oily line to separate glazes so that they create the impression of mosaic tile. This example of genuine mosaic tile work probably comes from Seville, and could have been created under either Christian or Islamic rule. But its tradition was originally an Islamic one.

BIBLIOGRAPHY Alice Frothingham, *The Hispanic Society of America Handbook* (New York, 1938), 114.

—JD

72 **Panel of four tiles with geometric decoration**

Spain, end of fifteenth or beginning of sixteenth century

Ceramic: worked in the *arista* technique with reinforcement of *cuerda seca*

10⅞ x 10⅞ in.
(27.5 x 27.5 cm)

Granada, Museo Nacional de Arte Hispanomusulmán, No. reg. 3.974, 3.975, 3.976, 3.977

This panel is composed of four tiles of interlacing white bands that together form a wheel with twelve spokes. It was executed in the technique of *arista,* which uses a mold probably made of wood and soft mud, and later reinforced with *cuerda seca* (see cat. no. 71). The star of twelve points at the center of the wheel is filled with honey-colored paint, and is surrounded by blue pentagons (*zapates*) and almond-like shapes (*almendrillas*), which form the remainder of the wheel. In the angles of the panel are parts of eight-pointed stars that, when linked to other tiles, would have completed the composition.

The *arista* technique appears in the area of Toledo toward the end of the fifteenth century.[1] The diffusion of this technique, which made tile work faster and easier than the mosaic tile or *alicatado,* reached as far as Valencia and its surroundings.[2] From this period on, we will not find large mosaic tile panels with complex geometrical compositions, and the *alicatado* technique will be supplanted by the *arista* technique in all the areas under Mudejar influence.

This panel, executed toward the end of the fifteenth or the beginning of the sixteenth century, still reflects a Nasrid influence in its decoration. It differs from the Sevillan tilework introduced at this time in the Secano area of the Alhambra where traces of ceramic kilns were found, indicating that the ceramic work was produced in the palace itself.

NOTES 1) Juan Ainaud de Lasarte, "Cerámica y vidrio," *Ars Hispaniae,* 10: 240. 2) Manuel González Martí, "Alicatados y azulejos," *Cerámica del Levante español: siglos medievales* (Madrid, 1952), 244, plate XI.

—*PMS*

73 **Capital**

Northern Spain or southern France, ca. 1100

Limestone: carved

18 x 18½ x 18⅓ in.

(45.7 x 47 x 46.6 cm)

New York, The Metropolitan Museum of Art, Fletcher Fund Purchase, 22.219

73

A lion is carved in profile on each of the four faces of this capital. Two carry nude male riders; as these sides of the capital are more carefully carved, perhaps the capital was placed in such a way that these two faces were most easily seen.

The style of the carving and the forms reveal the influence of the workshop that carved the sculpture of Jaca (Huesca) Cathedral. For example, one hallmark of the cathedral's sculptures is snakes, such as the herringbone examples found here. Sculpture influenced by Jaca is found in both northern Spain and southern France, which makes more exact attribution of this work difficult.[1]

NOTE 1) This entry is based on the work of Professor David Simon, Colby College.

BIBLIOGRAPHY J. Breck, "The Capital of the Sour Lions, *Bulletin of The Metropolitan Museum of Art* 18 (1923), 29.

74 **Relief of a Kneeling King**

Castile (?), twelfth century

Sandstone: carved

20 x 10¼ in.

(50.8 x 26 cm)

New York, The Metropolitan Museum of Art, 29.158.758

74

This crowned king wears mail over a padded garment and a short sword. He kneels in an act of submission or reverence; the lack of context for the relief renders the exact meaning of the action uncertain. The contrast between the busy, repetitive pattern of the mail and the broad, smooth areas of the body contributes to the visual appeal of the work.

Prior to entering the collection of The Metropolitan Museum, the relief was in the Bashford Dean Memorial Collection.[1]

NOTE 1) We are indebted to Dr. Charles Little of the Medieval Department, The Metropolitan Museum of Art, for the information on which this entry is based.

BIBLIOGRAPHY J. Martinez Santa-Olalla, "La iglesia romanica de Moradillio de Sedano," *Archivo español de arte y arqueologia* 6 (1930), 267, fig. 17.

Ceramics

75 *Salero de Pellizcos* **(Salt or Spice Container)**

Paterna, first half of the fourteenth century

Tin glaze pottery: painted in copper and manganese

Max. ht. 2 in., Max. diam. 4⅞ in. (5 x 12.5 cm)

Collection of the Ayuntamiento de Valencia, 598 in deposit at the Museo Nacional de Cerámica "Gonzalez Martí" of Valencia

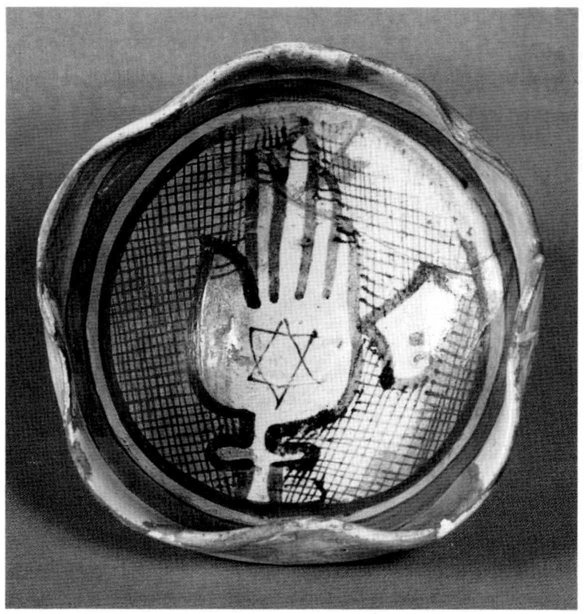

75

This piece was uncovered in the excavations of the Testar del Molí of Paterna. In the 1940s, it was restored with colored stucco.

Originally part of a table service, this vessel was used either as a salt or spice container. Made with the calcareous paste typical of Paterna, it was first turned on the wheel and then pressed with the five fingers of the hand, thus its name *salero de pellizcos* (salt container of pinches). At the bottom of the container is a ring with a small hole through which a thread could be passed in order to hang the container on the wall when not in use.

In the decoration, the manganese serves to mark the outlines while the green of the copper is used to fill figures. At the base of the container is the Seal of Solomon or Star of David inscribed in the Hand of Fatima or *ḥamsa.* Although these two symbols are frequently used in ceramics and other forms of Islamic art, their occurrence together on one vessel is quite rare. In Valencia, only one ceramic bowl is known to bear a small hand inscribed with the star.

Although the piece was made by Muslim craftsmen who worked under Christian rule, its symbolism is purely Muslim in origin. The *convivencia* of different cultures led to different interpretation of the same symbols.

BIBLIOGRAPHY M. González Martí, *Cerámica del Levante español,* 3 vols., vol.1 (Loza), (Barcelona, 1944), 168, fig. 196; J. Martínez Ortiz and J. de Scals Aracil, *Colección cerámica del Museo Histórico Municipal de Valencia: Paterna-Manises* (Valencia, 1968), fig. 45; J. Pascual and J. Martí, *La cerámica verde-manganeso bajomedieval de Valencia* (Valencia, 1986), 133, figs. 90–92; M. P. Soler Ferrer, *Cerámica valenciana, segles XIII a XIX* (Valencia, 1980), 15.

—*MSF*

The jar is in the shape of a truncated cone with four handles evenly spaced around its body, and bears green and purple decoration. Its exact function is uncertain; it may have been used as a small pitcher.

76 **Earthen Jar of Jewish Origin**

Teruel, fourteenth or fifteenth century

Glazed ceramic

H 5½ in., diam. 5⅜ in. (14 x 13.7 cm)

Teruel, Museo de Teruel, I. G. 8.575

The decoration is geometric with purple lines framing white and purple squares forming a checkered pattern. The handles are covered by a series of small horizontal lines. The checkered pattern belongs to a group of themes and decorative motifs that is very popular in the bicolor pottery from Teruel and is closely related to the aesthetics of brick architecture. The piece was uncovered in the excavations of the Plaza de la Judería of Teruel.

No information is available about the beginning of the Jewish settlement in Teruel, one of the most important communities of Aragón. The Jewish quarter, located on the northeastern part of the city, had one synagogue and a cemetery.[1] Several anti-Jewish riots errupted in Teruel (1321, 1348, 1391, 1417), and many Jews converted to Christianity induced by the preachings of the Dominican friar Vincent Ferrer (ca. 1350–1419) during his visit to the city (ca. 1414).[2] In 1484, the situation of the Jewish community suddenly worsened when two inquisitors settled in Teruel, later ordering the confinement of the Jews to a separate quarter until their expulsion in 1492.[3]

NOTES 1) F. Cantera Burgos, *Sinagogas españolas* (Madrid, 1955), 317–18. Several pieces of jewelry have been uncovered in the excavations of Teruel's Jewish cemetery. Some of these findings have been published in *La vida judía en Sefarad,* exhibition catalogue (Toledo, 1991-92), 278–80, cat. nos. 87-95. 2) *Encyclopaedia Judaica,* 6:1235–36. 3) Ibid., 15: 1022–23.

—*JVR*

77 **Earthen Jar**

Teruel, fourteenth or fifteenth century

Ceramic: glazed

H 5⅛ in., diam. 5⅛ in. (13 x 13 cm)

Teruel, Museo de Teruel, I. G. 7.321

This jar, in the shape of a truncated cone with four evenly spaced handles, was found in Teruel. The decoration, in green and purple applied to a white tin glaze, totally covers the piece. Its function is uncertain; it could have been used to store solid food or as a jar for liquids.

The decorative motifs are arranged in two registers. In the upper register the decoration consists of parallel vertical lines intersecting a horizontal line. The lower register around the handles has pinecone motifs inscribed in rectangular shapes. The handles are decorated with thick short horizontal lines.

The pinecone, a symbol of happiness, is frequently found on the decorated pottery from Teruel. The motif may have originated in the Orient and clear parallels to its use on ceramics can be found toward the end of the thirteenth century in the golden and blue pottery from Málaga and later, at the beginning of the fifteenth century, on the ceramics of Manises.

This jar is a clear example of the *horror vacui* that characterizes the overly decorated ceramics from Teruel, in which one motif occupies the central space and the rest of the body of the piece is filled with minor themes.

BIBLIOGRAPHY M. Almagro and L. M. Llubiá, *La cerámica de Teruel* (Teruel, 1962), plate XXXVI, fig. 1364.

—JVR

78 **Deep Dish (*Brasero*)**

Valencia (Manises), 1420–30

Earthenware: tin-enamelled

Diam. 18⅛ in. (46 cm)

New York, Lent by The Metropolitan Museum of Art, 56.171.27

Tin-enamelled ceramics or lusterware were introduced into Spain by the Muslims. Through their distinctive glazing processes, Muslim ceramicists were able to produce wares with the gloss of metals such as gold and silver. Techniques for producing the characteristic blue and gold glazes were first developed in Egypt by the mid-eleventh century, and were known in Spain by the thirteenth century.

The composition of the Metropolitan's *brasero* also appears on a number of pieces in other collections.[1] On all of these, an eight-pointed star formed of two interlocking squares is at center. Large bands of decoration consist of debased kufic writing. Smaller bands are filled with floral and geometric motifs.

NOTES 1) E. A. Barber, *Hispano-Moresque Pottery in the Collection of the Hispanic Society of America* (New York, 1915), frontispiece; M. P. Soler Ferrer, *Cerámica valenciana,* segles XIII-XIX (Valencia, 1980), 144, a piece in the Museo González Martí, Valencia.

Unpublished

—VBM

79 **Hanukkah Lamp (fragment)**

Teruel, fifteenth century

Glazed ceramic

2⅝ x 19⅝ in. (6.5 x 50 cm) (dimensions of reconstructed piece)

Teruel, Museo de Teruel, I. G. 7.167

The present lamp is one of two fragmentary Hanukkah lamps uncovered by the Teruel Museum in 1978, during the excavations of the Plaza de la Judería. A fragment of a third lamp was found in the same location in 1977, during the excavations of what is believed to be the site of the old synagogue.

These three Hanukkah lamps are the only known examples made in the glazed ceramic technique of Teruel. This lamp, which belongs to the green and purple series of Teruel ceramics, has been partially reconstructed: five ceramic oil receptacles that were originally missing have been added, one of these larger in size than the others. The spouts of the oil receptacles are flanked by painted eyes while the base is decorated with simple geometric motifs.

BIBLIOGRAPHY P. Atrian, "Lámparas de Hanukkah en cerámica popular turolense," *Teruel* 66 (1981): 175–80; Madrid, Ministerio de Cultura, *La vida judía en Sefarad,* exhibition catalogue (Sinagoga del Tránsito, Toledo, 1991–92), no. 37.

—JVR

80 Mortar of Jewish Origin

Teruel, fifteenth century

Glazed ceramic

H 5½ in., diam. 6⅝ in. (14 x 17 cm)

Teruel, Museo de Teruel, I. G. 5.252

The mortar, in the shape of an inverted truncated cone with three handles and a spout, is decorated in green and purple on a white ground. This kind of mortar, known in Teruel as the *mamelot,* was used to chop food and prepare sauces.

The mortar's decoration follows a compositional organization frequently used on the ceramics of Teruel: space is divided by using green stripes framed by thin purple lines. The upper register is decorated with alternating pyramidal motifs and a thin winding line. The lower register, divided by the handles, is decorated with fern leaves (a traditional motif on Teruel ceramics) and striped rectangles.

The mortar, uncovered during the 1979 excavations of the Plaza de la Judería of Teruel, was found on the ground floor of a large building, in an area probably used as a storeroom. The discovery of the mortar in the Jewish quarter along with other pieces of exclusive Jewish use (like the Hanukkah lamp, see no. 79) indicates that the mortar was used by the Jewish population of Teruel.

BIBLIOGRAPHY Madrid, Instituto Occidental de Cultura Islámica, *Exposición de arte, tecnología y literatura hispano-musulmanas: II Jornadas de Cultura Islámica celebradas en Teruel,* exhibition catalogue, 1988, 141, no. 107; Madrid, Ministerio de Cultura, *La vida judía en Sefarad,* exhibition catalogue, (Sinagoga del Tránsito, Toledo, Toledo, 1991-92), no. 72.

—JVR

81 Earthen Bowl

Teruel, fifteenth century

Glazed ceramic

H 1⅜ in., diam. 3⅞ in. (3.5 x 10 cm)

Teruel, Museo de Teruel, I.G. 7.696

This bowl, with small horizontal handles or *orejetas,* was executed in the characteristic technique of Teruel ceramics and is part of the green and purple series. The bowl was part of a table service and was used as a soup or broth dish.

The decoration on this bowl is similar to that of bowl 7.146 (see no. 82) in its decoration with a face in profile surrounded by fern leaves. The *orejetas* are decorated with the forms of two human eyes.

Similar examples can be found among early fifteenth-century ceramics from Teruel, Paterna, and Manises. Although this bowl was not found in an excavation, its discovery in the subsoil of the Jewish quarter indicates its association with pieces uncovered in the excavations of the Plaza de la Judería.

Unpublished

—JVR

82 Earthen Bowl

Teruel, fifteenth century

Glazed ceramic

H 2⅜ in., diam. 1⅛ in. (6 x 3 cm)

Teruel, Museo de Teruel, I. G. 7.146

This glazed ceramic bowl is decorated with green (copper oxide) and purple (manganese oxide), applied to a base of white tin varnish. The bowl has two triangular handles or *orejetas* and its function is purely domestic: It is meant to be used as a soup or broth dish.

The inner surface is decorated with fern leaves (a frequent motif on ceramics from Teruel) and a bust, possibly of a man, with a rather elaborate coiffure wearing a green mantle and a tunic decorated with a wheat-stalk motif.

These decorative motifs are used frequently in the ceramic production from Teruel and ceramics related to it, such as those from Paterna, Manises, and Muel. The fern-leaf motif, derived from pottery of Arabic-Egyptian origin, acquires a distinctive personality and treatment when used on Teruel ceramics.

BIBLIOGRAPHY M. Almagro and L. M. Llubiá, *La cerámica de Teruel* (Teruel, 1962), plate LI, fig. 2125; M. I. Alvaro, *Cerámica aragonesa,* vol. 1 (Saragossa, 1976), fig. 37; *II Tornadas de Cultura Isalmica Celebradas en Teruel, Exposición de arte, tecnología y literatura hispano-musulmanas:* Madrid, Instituto Occidental de Cultura Islámica, exhibition catalogue, 1988, 140, no. 105.

—JVR

83 **Oil Container**

Teruel, fifteenth century

Glazed ceramic

6⅝ x 5⅜ in. (17 x 13.5 cm)

Teruel, Museo de Teruel, I. G. 7.166

The bell-shaped vessel with a trilobed mouth and a handle opposite the spout was used to pour liquids, most probably oil. The container was covered with a layer of impermeable tin varnish on which the decoration in green and purple was applied.

The decoration consists of two eyes flanking the spout and a simple heraldic motif at the front of the vessel formed of a small shield with the stripes of Aragón surrounded by stylized vegetal motifs. This decorative theme is frequently found in the ceramic production from Teruel of the thirteenth and fourteenth centuries and is also found in several examples of the fifteenth century and later.

BIBLIOGRAPHY M. Almagro and L. M. Llubiá, *La cerámica de Teruel* (Teruel, 1962), plate XLVII, fig. 2059; Madrid, Instituto Occidental de Cultura Islámica, *Exposición arte, tecnología y literatura hispano-musulmanas: II Jornadas de Cultura Islámica celebradas en Teruel,* exhibition catalogue, 1988, 141, no. 108.

—JVR

84 **Mortar**

Teruel, fifteenth century

Glazed ceramic

H 5⅛ in., diam. 5⅞ in. (13 x 15 cm)

Teruel, Museo de Teruel, I.G. 7.150

This mortar is in the shape of a rounded truncated cone to which eight strips of clay were added. The piece has two small perforated handles or *mamelones*. It formed part of a table service and was used for grinding food.

The green and purple decoration, applied to the white tin varnish base, includes typical decorative motifs: wheat stalks, winding lines, semicircles, and dots, all of them executed rapidly. Thin lines in the shape of eyelashes surround the handles converting their perforations into eyes.

BIBLIOGRAPHY M. Almagro and L. M. Llubiá, *La cerámica de Teruel* (Teruel, 1962), plate LII, fig. 2158.

—JVR

85 **Ceramic Plate with Five Depressions**

Teruel, fifteenth century

Ceramic: tin, copper, and manganese glaze

Diam. 13⅜ in. (34 cm)

Barcelona, Museu de Ceràmica, Ajuntament de Barcelona

This plate, a typical example of Teruel ceramics, has green and purple decoration applied to a white tin varnish base. It has been assumed that this plate's receptacles served to hold hard-boiled eggs or vinegar. However, the presence of five receptacles may indicate a Jewish use, their function being to keep the different symbolic foods for the Passover seder: the roasted egg, the shankbone, the *maror* or bitter herbs, the *ḥaroset* (a paste made of fruit, spices, and wine), and the *karpas* (vegetable used for dipping). If this is so, then this plate would be among the earliest examples of a plate specifically used for the seder.

Another example of an early seder plate is the one probably produced in Valencia in the same technique as plates for Muslim and Christian use (see nos. 78 and 86 and fig. 66). In Teruel there are other examples of ceramics made for Jewish ritual purpose such as the Hanukkah lamps uncovered in the excavations of the Plaza de la Judería (see no. 79).

The decoration, which covers all the plate's surface, consists of two main motifs that repeat themselves: a stylized hand and a bird. The hand represents the hand of Fatima or *ḥamsa*, a motif found on other ceramic vessels such as the salt or spice container from Paterna where the Seal of Solomon or Star of David is inscribed in the *ḥamsa* (see no. 75).

85

BIBLIOGRAPHY D. Davidovitch, "Ceramic Seder Plates from Non-Jewish Workshops," *Journal of Jewish Art* 2 (1975): 51–54; M. González Martí, *Cerámica del levante español: siglos medievales* (Barcelona, 1952), 595, fig. 700.

—*CN*

86 Dish with Arms of the House of Castile-León

Manises (Valencia), late fifteenth century

Earthenware: tin-enamelled

Diam. 18⅞ in. (48 cm)

New York, Lent by The Metropolitan Museum of Art, The Cloisters Collection, 1956, ex. coll. William Randolph Hearst, 56.171.141

The coat of arms at center is that of an unidentified member of the House of Castile-León. It is surrounded by two larger bands of corrupted Latin and smaller bands of flowers and net patterns. The inner inscription band reads: SURGE . DOMINE . ADOUA . DM . SURGE DOMINE. ADOAI, while the outer band reads: SURGE . DOMINE . ADOUA . M . SURGE . DOMINA . ADOUA . M . SURGE . DOME . ADOU. These texts seem to be a corruption of *Exsurge Domine ad liberandum nos* ("Rise up Lord to free us").[1]

The appearance of Latin texts as decoration on pottery meant for Christian patrons signifies a reinterpretation of compositional schemes originally developed for Muslims. There is also extant a single example of a dish with Hebrew inscriptions from the fifteenth century whose text is similarly corrupt (see fig. 80).

NOTE 1) Description in Metropolitan Museum Records.

Unpublished

—*VBM*

Ivory and Wood

87 **Pyxis**

Madīnat al-Zahrā᾿,
ca. 950-75

Ivory, carved

4⅝ x 4³⁄₃₂ in.
(11.8 x 10.6 cm)

New York, Lent by The Metropolitan Museum of Art, The Cloisters Collection, ex. coll. Ernst Kofler, Lucerne, 1970.324.5

Pyxides or cylindrical boxes were among the ivory pieces produced in the ateliers of Madīnat al-Zahrā᾿ (see no. 88). Their shape resulted from slicing the tusk crosswise. This pyxis is missing its domed cover and the gold plugs for which little holes were drilled throughout the surface.

The carving of the surface of the ivory into pairs of animals (lions, gazelles, and parrots) arranged along a vertical axis is one of the decorative schemes found on the caskets and pyxides of the caliphal ateliers. Other examples are in the Museo Arqueológico, Madrid, and in the collection of the Hispanic Society, New York.[1] Similar compositional schemes appear on Islamic textiles and stone carving.

NOTE 1) John Beckwith, *Caskets from Córdoba* (London, 1960), plate 6.

BIBLIOGRAPHY E. Kühnel, "Eine spanisch-maurische Elfenbein-Pyxis," *Pantheon* 18, no. 1 (1960): 1–3; E. von Philippowich, *Elfenbein* (Brunswick, 1961), 125, fig. 94; H. Schnitzler, F. Volbach, P. Bloch, *Skulpturen: Elfenbein, Perlmutter, Stein, Holz, Europäisches Mittelalter: Sammlung E. und M. Kofler-Truniger Luzern,* vol. 1 (Lucerne and Stuttgart, 1964-65), no. S 28.

—VBM

88 **Ivory Casket with Musicians and Drinkers**

Probably Córdoba, early eleventh century

Ivory: carved

8½ x 10⅝ x 6½ in.
(21.5 x 27 x 16.5 cm)

London, Victoria and Albert Museum, 10-1866

Lent by the Trustees of the Victoria and Albert Museum

The palace Madīnat al Zahrā᾿ on the outskirts of Córdoba became the seat of ᶜAbd al-Raḥmān's court after its completion in 958. The complex included workshops for luxury goods, among them an atelier specializing in the carving of ivory that produced a series of caskets with kufic inscriptions referring to their owners, all members of the Ummayad house or their followers.

This casket, although lacking its inscription panels due to eighteenth-century repairs, is linked to the Córdoba casket group by its shape, its subject matter, and the style of its carving. Pairs of animals and of human figures drinking or playing musical instruments, single hunters mounted on horseback, animals preying on one another, an abbreviated image of a male ruler riding in a howdah on the back of an antelope, and numerous single birds, animals, and leaves form a rich network of forms in the carved ivory.[1] Ultimately, many of these motifs can be traced to Islamic textiles and architectural carvings.[2]

An inscription on another casket from Córdoba, now in the Hispanic Society of America collection, indicates the uses that these caskets served: "Beauty has invested me with splendid raiment, which makes a display of jewels. I am a receptacle for musk, camphor and ambergris."

NOTES 1) See John Beckwith, *Caskets from Córdoba* (London, 1960), plates. 14–24. 2) Ibid., figs.15–20, 21, 22.

BIBLIOGRAPHY John Beckwith, *Caskets from Córdoba* (London, 1960), 29–30, plates. 27–30.

—VBM

This chess rook was uncovered amidst the debris of a Muslim house in the Sanctuary of Tiscar in the district of Quesada, in Jaén. It has been dated prior to 1319, the year in which Don Pedro, Alfonso XI's uncle and regent, took possession of the Alcazaba (fortress) of the Sanctuary of Tiscar as well as several other fortresses located near the border between the Christian area and the Muslim kingdom of Granada.

89 **Chess Rook**

Sanctuary of Tiscar (Jaén), Nasrid period, before 1319

Bone: carved

H 3⅞, lower diam. 1⅛ in., upper diam. ⅞ in. (10 x 2.8 x 2.2 cm)

Granada, Museo Nacional de Arte Hispanomusulmán, No. reg. 2.840

The chess rook has a cut-out base forming crenellations that curve outward and are decorated with incised lines. This base is surmounted by an elongated spherical shape and ends in a truncated cone decorated with parallel incisions. The crenellated end might appear to be the upper part of the rook. Its lack of stability due to its being the widest and heaviest part of the piece, however, as well as the fact that the piece can be easily held by the other end, leads us to think that the crenellated portion is indeed the base of the rook and not its top.

This piece can be compared with other chess pieces made in bone that were uncovered in various locations, such as Córdoba, Ceuta, Mallorca, Vascos,[1] Mértola, Silves, Ebora, and Vale do Boto.[2] The variety of locations demonstrates the diffusion of chess in the Hispanomoresque regions earlier and in the Christian zone later on.[3] That chess was widespread in Christian Spain is documented in the miniatures of the *Libros de ajedrez, dados y tablas* (*Books of Chess, Dice and Backgammon*) of Alfonso X the Wise, where Arabs, Christian courtiers, Jews, children, physicians, and others are depicted playing the game.

All the extant bone chess pieces present a similar shape with slight differences in their forms and small incised decorative elements. They are carved from natural bone, making use of the shape and presenting the inner part hollow and irregular. None of the extant pieces has closed ends.

The piece was once owned by Mata Carriazo and later became part of the collection of M. Gómez Moreno who donated it to the Museo Nacional de Arte Hispanomusulmán of Granada.

NOTES 1) R. Izquierdo Benito, "Excavación en la ciudad Hispano-musulmana de Vascos (Navalmoralejo-Toledo): Campañas 1975–1978," *Noticiario Arqueológico Hispano* 7, (1979): 363. 2) Rafael Azuar Ruiz, *Castillo de la Torre Grossa (Jijona)* (Alicante, 1985), 116. 3) Félix M. Pareja Casañas, *Libro del Ajedrez, de sus problemas y sutilezas de autor árabe desconocido* (Madrid, 1935), lxxii-lxxxviii; idem, "Un torneo de ajedrez al estilo árabe," *Al-Andalus* (1957): 209–14; Rachel Arié, *L'Espagne musulmane au temps des Nasrides (1232–1492)* (Paris, 1990); Alfonso X el Sabio, *Libros de ajedrez, dados y tablas* (Madrid, 1987).

BIBLIOGRAPHY Juan de la Mata Carriazo, *Tartesos y el Carambolo* (Madrid, 1973); Claudio Torres, "Uma proposta de interpretaçao funcional para os conhecidos "Cabos de Faca" em osso já com longa histórica na arqueologia Ibérica," *Actas del I congreso de Arqueología medieval española*, vol. 1 (Huesca, 1985).

—PMS

This game board, uncovered in a Castilian convent, consists of a chessboard on one side, and on the other side, a backgammon board. The board, which has a protruding frame studded with round-headed nails, was decorated with *taracea*. This inlay technique utilizes a base of walnut wood that is cut out to receive pieces of wood of a lighter color for the squares and pieces of other woods and bone (of both natural color and green) for the geometric decoration.

90 **Inlaid Chess and Backgammon Board**

Granada (?), Spain, Nasrid period, fourteenth to fifteenth century

Wood and bone: inlaid

18$\frac{5}{16}$ x 14⅛ x 1¾ in. (46.5 x 36 x 4.5 cm)

Granada, Museo Nacional de Arte Hispanomusulmán, No. reg. 3.968

The chessboard is framed by a decorative rope-like stripe that defines two rectangular spaces at each end of the board for placing pieces that are out of play. These rectangular areas are decorated with three eight-pointed stars created by the intersection of two squares that, in turn enclose similar smaller stars. All are decorated with small pieces of bone painted green and with checkered patterns. Although the three stars are similar in composition, the central star is different in its *taracea* work encompassing different colors and geometric shapes. Between the three stars are two diamond shapes filled with small pieces of bone that form a checkered pattern. A game board with similar decoration composed of six-pointed stars and golden nails in the outer frame is depicted in the miniature that appears on folio 9 of the *Libros de ajedrez, dados y tablas* of Alfonso X.

On the opposite side of the board is the backgammon panel that is similar to the one described in the *Libros de ajedrez:* "Rectangular shape, made of wood, and with a division in the middle called *barra* which allows one to fold the board in two or to unfold it for play. The board is divided into four *quadras* (quadrants), in each *quadra,* six *casas* (houses) making a total of twenty-four." According to the text, the *casas* should be marked on the border of the board by being "carved in the shape of half a wheel." The half-wheels accommodate the round thick pieces (*tablas*) that gave the game its name.[1]

The decorative theme of the central space is similar to that used on the sides of the chessboard: eight-pointed stars enclosing other stars and diamonds, all decorated in the *taracea* technique. An ornament unique to this side of the board is a lace design encompassing five squares set at the center.

A metallic plaque with attached ring is affixed to one side of the board and allows it to be hung up when not in use.

Although it is known that chess was introduced into Europe through Muslim Spain, the origin of the term "chess" may have been introduced to Arabic from Persian, and before that from India into Persia.[2] It appears that chess (*ŝiṭranŷ*), which was known in the peninsula since the ninth century, may have been introduced by a musician named Ziryab or by another Iraqi immigrant.[3] It became widespread and several rulers professed fondness for it. For example, al-Muʿtamid (eleventh century) owned boards made of precious woods such as ebony and sandalwood with gold fittings.[4] During Alfonso X's reign both chess and backgammon were favorite forms of entertainment. Under Nasrid rule a curious episode took place: Yūsuf III, heir to the throne, who had been imprisoned in the fortress of Salobreña and was to be executed, asked to finish a game of chess with the mayor of the fortress. Yusuf managed to prolong the game until he was freed.[5]

Backgammon was introduced to Hispanomoresque Spain in two different forms: the classic game known in Rome since the first century (*alea* or *tabula*), and the oriental version called *nard.*[6] *Nard,* like chess, was introduced into Muslim domains by way of Persia. It was widely played, for example, in the Abbasid court by the caliphs Harun al-Rasid and his son al-Maʾmūn.[7]

NOTES 1) Ricardo Calvo, "El Libro de los juegos de Alfonso X el Sabio," *Alfonso X el Sabio, Libros de ajedrez, dados y tablas* (Madrid, 1987), 137. 2) Félix M. Pareja Casañas, *Libro del ajedrez de sus problemas y sutilezas de autor árabe desconocido,* vol. 2 (Madrid, 1935), lvi. 3) E. Lévi-Provençal, "Instituciones y vida social e intelectual," *España Musulmana hasta la caída del Califato de Córdoba (711–1031 de J.C.)* vol. 5 of *Historia de España* (Madrid, 1957), 288. 4) Henri Pérès, *Esplendor de al-Andalus: La poesía andaluza en árabe en el siglo XI: Sus aspectos generales, sus principales temas y su valor documental* (Madrid, 1983), 347. 5) R. Arié, *L'Espagne musulmane* (Paris, 1990), 409; Luis Seco de Lucena Paredes, *El libro de la Alhambra: Historia de los sultanes de Granada* (León, 1988), 54. 6) Ricardo Calvo, "El Libro de los juegos de Alfonso X el Sabio," *Alfonso X el Sabio: Libros de ajedrez, dados y tablas* (Madrid, 1987), 138. 7) Ibid.; Félix M. Pareja Casañas, *Libro del ajedrez* 2:lvi.

BIBLIOGRAPHY Purificación Marinetto Sánchez, "Tablero de ajedrez," *Andalucía y el Mediterráneo* (Seville, 1990), 181.

—PMS

91 **Inlaid Octagonal Box**

Spain, fifteenth century

Wood, ivory, gilt bronze

H 5⅞ in (14.9 cm)

New York, Lent by The Metropolitan Museum of Art, Rogers Fund, 50.86

The major decorative motif is an eight-pointed star that is repeated on all sides of the box. It is set off by narrow geometric borders. The eight-pointed star is commonly found on works of art from Spain, on textiles, ceramics, and even on the pages of Hebrew manuscripts, where it was used to represent the *matzah* in Passover hagaddot.

Similar boxes are in the collections of Miguel y Badia, Barcelona, and the Valencia de Don Juan, Madrid.

BIBLIOGRAPHY New York, Parke Bernet Gallery, *Edwin Berolzheimer Collection,* sales catalogue, March 9, 1950, no. 148.

—VBM

Metalwork

92 **Lamp from the Mosque of Medina Elvira**

Elvira, (Granada), tenth century

Bronze: cast

Diam. dish: 13¾ in. (33.5 cm)

Granada, Museo Arqueológico y Etnológico Provincial de Granada, no. 548

This mosque lamp is composed of a bronze discus, or dish, pierced with geometric motifs. Its small handles were once suspended by bronze chains whose links welded to the discus during a fire in Medina Elvira in the year 1010. Circular openings held glass containers of wax or oil, and small lamps.

The form of this mosque lamp follows Roman-Byzantine tradition while adapting it to Muslim aesthetics. These lamps have a unique value, as they were used to commemorate the founding of a mosque or were donated for other special events. Since the lamps had symbolic value, they were often objects of pillage when cities were plundered. Because of their rarity, the lamps are a treasured find for archaeologists.

Light has long been associated with ancient religions, especially with places of worship. Lamps not only served as a light source, but also as a symbol of divine presence making the place of worship holy. In the Qurʾān, the light of God is said to be similar to "a niche containing a lamp, the lamp is in a crystal and the crystal is like a shining star." A common liturgical practice of burning wax joined three great religions that developed in the Mediterranean and lived together in al-Andalus: Judaism, Christianity, and Islam.

BIBLIOGRAPHY *Ars Hispaniae,* 3:322, fig. 385 (bottom left).

—*EFP*

93 **Astrolabe with Arabic Inscription**

Spain

Signature: not legible.

Brass

Diam. 4⅝ in. (11.8 cm)

Washington, Smithsonian Institution, National Museum of American History, 3643

This is an Arabic astrolabe whose origin is not precisely known except that it is presumed to have been made in Islamic Spain: in common with other such instruments from the western Islamic world it is inscribed with kufic letters and, unlike the Hebrew and Latin astrolabes in this volume, has no astrological tables. Instead, it is inscribed with a zodiacal calendar with which the user could match the position of the sun with a date in the Christian calendar. On a *ṣafīḥa* or disk mounted on the front of the instrument, the times of the canonical morning and afternoon Islamic prayers are designated, as well as projections for important places in the Islamic world, including Córdoba, Seville, Toledo, Fez, and Marrakesh.

BIBLIOGRAPHY S. Gibbs and G. Saliba, *Planispheric Astrolabes from the National Museum of American History,* Smithsonian Institution (Washington, D.C., 1984), 177–79.

—*TG*

The decoration of this cylindrical mortar is reduced to forms that are also functional. The body bears pyramidal shapes that alternate in orientation, a type of decoration that was frequently used on bronze pieces from the caliphal period onward. The mortar has only one handle, rounded and perforated. Other extant examples, however, bear two to four handles.[1] From its provenance, it is known that this mortar once had a chain that is now lost. The decoration of this piece is reduced to the shapes, which are also functional.

This piece is a product of the magnificent caliphal workshops that continued to work during the Almoravid period in the area of Granada, producing pieces of exceptional beauty under Nasrid rule.

NOTE 1) Manuel Gómez Moreno, "El arte árabe español hasta los almohades: arte mozárabe," *Ars Hispaniae,* 3:324–36; Guillermo Rosselló Gordoy, "Bronces árabes de Mallorca," *Al-Andalus* 27 (1962): 229–32.

Unpublished

—*PMS*

94 **Mortar**

Abrucena (Almería), Almoravid period, twelfth century

Bronze: cast

H 3¾ in., diam. 3¾ in. (9.5 x 9.5 cm)

Granada, Museo Nacional de Arte Hispanomusulmán, No. reg. 380

Hebrew inscription on rim of upper circular part:

מלך המלכים יפתח * מלך כל הארץ יבוא

("The King of Kings shall open, the King of all earth shall enter").
Castilian inscription: "Dios abrirá rey entrará" ("God shall open, the King shall enter").

The silver original, today in the cathedral of Seville, was presented to Ferdinand III, king of Castile and León (ruled 1217–1252), by the Jewish community of Seville upon his capture of the city in 1248.[1] The use of the Castilian language instead of Latin in one of the inscriptions may have been a recognition of Ferdinand's efforts to encourage the use of Castilian as the official language of his kingdom.[2] The coat of arms of Castile with its three turrets is depicted on the key along with the figure of the lion, symbol of León, representing the two kingdoms over which Ferdinand ruled.

During Ferdinand's reign, the situation of the Jews improved, and their privileges were confirmed in several cities in recognition of their services during the Reconquest. In Seville, the king allowed the Jews to remain in their old quarter and granted lands to several Jewish public officials as part of his plan to redistribute property. The three mosques located within the boundaries of the Jewish quarter were ceded to the Jews and converted into synagogues. Most of these measures, however, were carried out by Ferdinand's son Alfonso X after his father's death in 1252, a few years after the conquest of Seville.[3]

NOTES 1) F. Cantera Burgos makes reference to a manuscript by Argote de Molina entitled *Elogio de los Conquistadores,* in which is mentioned that while the Jews presented Ferdinand with the key to the *judería* (the Jewish quarter), the Muslim community gave the king the key to the city bearing an Arabic inscription. *Las Sinagogas Españolas* (Madrid, 1955), 291. See also idem, "La epigrafía hebraica en Sevilla," *Sefarad* 11 (1951): 386–88. 2) J. F. O'Callaghan, *A History of Medieval Spain* (Ithaca, N.Y., and London, 1975), 354. 3) Y. Baer, *A History of the Jews in Christian Spain,* vol. 1 (Philadelphia, 1961), 111–12; F. Cantera Burgos, *Las Sinagogas Españolas* (Madrid, 1955), 292.

BIBLIOGRAPHY Y. Baer, *A History of the Jews in Christian Spain,* vol. 1 (Philadelphia, 1961), 111–12; F. Cantera Burgos, "La epigrafía hebraica en Sevilla," *Sefarad* 11 (1951): 386–88; idem, *Las Sinagogas Españolas* (Madrid, 1955), 291–304; *Encyclopaedia Judaica,* 14:1202 and fig. 2; *Jewish Encyclopaedia,* 5:363.

—*CN*

95 **Cast of the Key presented to Ferdinand III by the Jewish Community of Seville**

Seville, 1248 (original)

Bronze: cast

7⅓ x 6 ⅙ in. (18.6 x 15.7 cm)

Jerusalem, Lent by Shmuel Hadas

96 **Hanukkah Lamp**

Northern Spain–Southern France, thirteenth or fourteenth century

Bronze

5⅞ x 5¾ in.
(15 x 14.5 cm)

Paris, Musée national du Moyen Age, Thermes de Cluny, Inv. Cl. 12248

The earliest surviving lamps made expressly for Hanukkah date to the thirteenth century and stem from the regions of present-day Spain, France, and Germany. Nearly all are wall-hung examples of bronze and include a servitor; both features are innovations compared with the form of earlier lamps as it can be reconstructed from literary sources.

This lamp belongs to a subgroup decorated with horseshoe arches surmounted by a rose window, two features of contemporary architecture in southern France and northern Spain.[1] The lamp was found in the ancient Jewish quarter of Lyon during the nineteenth century, which indicates a date prior to the expulsion of the Jews from France in 1394.

NOTE 1) Bezalel Narkiss, "Un objet de culte: la lampe de Hanuka," *Art et archéologie des Juifs en France médiévale,* ed. Bernhard Blumenkranz (Toulouse, 1980), 190–91, n. 5.

BIBLIOGRAPHY [Georges Stenne], *Collection de M. Strauss: Description des objets d'art religieux hébraïques* (Poissy, 1878), no. 14, plate V; Mordecai Narkiss, *The Hanukkah Lamp* (Jerusalem, 1939),(Hebrew), 9, plate VI, 21; Bezalel Narkiss, "Un objet de culte: la lampe de Hanuka," *Art et archéologie des Juifs en France médiévale,* ed. Bernhard Blumenkranz (Toulouse, 1980), 191 and fig. 5; Paris, Musée de Cluny, *Catalogue raisonnée de la collection juive du Musée de Cluny,* exhibition catalogue by Victor Klagsbald (Paris, 1981), no. 17; Jerusalem, Israel Museum, *Jewish Treasures from Paris,* exhibition catalogue, by Victor A. Klagsbald, 1982, no. 82; Berlin, Berliner Festspiele, *Jüdische Lebenswelten: Katalog,* exhibition catalog, ed. A. Nachama and G. Sievernich, (Berlin, 1992), no. 20: 6/25.

—*VBM*

97 **Seal of Seneor Son of Rabbi Don Samuel**

Spain, thirteenth to fifteenth century

Bronze

1⅛ x 1⅛ x½ in.
(3 x 3 x 1.2 cm)

Seville, Museo Arqueológico de Sevilla, ROD 3063

Seal Impression, plaster, 1½ x 1½ in.
(3.8 x 3.8 cm), New York, The Jewish Museum, 1986-86, Gift of Daniel M. Friedenberg

Hebrew inscription:

שניאור בן הרב דון שמואל

(=Seneor son of Rabbi Don Samuel)

(Latin inscription unclear)[1]

The depiction at the center of the seal has been described as a stylized tree or a stylized menorah, the seven-branched candelabrum of the Temple.[2] While the image of branches coming from a central stem is certainly tree-like, the selection of seven branches and the inclusion of a tripodal base identify this symbol as a menorah. The button-shaped "leaves" could allude to the knops (ornamental knobs) and flowers mentioned in the biblical description (Exodus 25:31–40, 37:17–24). Two small shapes at the left side of the candelabrum's base may be stylized depictions of two other Temple implements that traditionally accompany the menorah, the *etrog* or citron, and the incense shovel.

The use of personal seals among Jews became widespread in Spain from the thirteenth century onward. Jewish seals were distinguished from Christian seals by their use of the Hebrew language and the absence, in most cases, of the human figure.[3] Since the seal makers generally did not sign their work, it is uncertain whether Jews were involved in seal production. However, the fact that the Hebrew inscription is correctly rendered while the Latin inscription is poorly executed with several reversed letters might indicate that a Jewish craftsman was employed in this case.

This seal has been attributed by Cantera and Millás to the family of Abraham Seneor (ca. 1412–ca. 1493), one of the most prominent Jewish courtiers. The use of the family name Seneor at the beginning of the inscription instead of the customary first name, and the poor execution of the seal, however, make this attribution unlikely.[4]

NOTES 1) F. Cantera and J.M. Millás, *Las inscripciones hebraicas de España* (Madrid, 1956), no. 251, read the Latin *Seneor Fil Bona* (Seneor Son of Bona or Seneor Son of the Good One). F. Menéndez Pidal and E. Gómez Pérez, however, read the inscription as follows: *Seneor d'Ebora [Matrices de sellos españoles (siglos XII al XVI)* (Madrid, 1987), no. 221]. 2) D. Friedenberg describes the central motif as a stylized tree with seven branches; *Medieval Jewish Seals from Europe* (Detroit, 1987), 130, no. 54. F. Menéndez Pidal and E. Gómez Pérez describe the central depiction as a stylized seven-branched candelabrum; *Matrices de Sellos Españoles,* no. 221. 3) A rare example bearing a human face has been described by Friedenberg, *Medieval Jewish Seals from Europe,* 142–43, no. 68. 4) Ibid., 128, no.52.

97

BIBLIOGRAPHY F. Cantera, "Dos sellos hebraicos inéditos," *Sefarad* 14 (1954): 369–71; F. Cantera and J. M. Millás, *Las inscripciones hebraicas de España* (Madrid, 1956), no. 251; D. Friedenberg, *Medieval Jewish Seals from Europe* (Detroit, 1987), 127-29, no. 52; J. L. Lacave, *Sefarad, Sefarad: La España Judía,* Comisión Quinto Centenario, Sefarad 92 (Barcelona and Madrid, 1982), plate 96 (center left); F. Menéndez Pidal and E. Gómez Pérez, *Matrices de Sellos Españoles (siglos XII al XVI)* (Madrid, 1987), no. 221 p. 113; Madrid, Ministerio de Cultura, *La vida judía en Sefarad,* exhibition catalogue, Sinagoga del Tránsito, Toledo, 1991-92, no. 79.

—*CN*

98 **Seal of Abraham bar Saadia**

Spain, thirteenth to fifteenth century

Bronze

1¼ x 1⅛ x½ in. (3.2 x 2.7 x 1.4 cm)

Seville, Museo Arqueológico de Sevilla, ROD 2981

Seal Impression, plaster, 1½ x 1½ in. (3.8 x 3.8 cm)

New York, The Jewish Museum, 1986-85, Gift of Daniel M. Friedenberg

Hebrew inscription:

אברהם בר סעדיה

(=Abraham bar Saadia)

The seal, with the fleur-de-lis at its center, is similar in its use of the quatrefoil to the seal of Todros Halevi, son of Don Samuel Halevi, chief treasurer of the King of Castile, Peter IV the Cruel (ruled 1350–69).[1]

The attribution of this seal is unclear. Baer mentions a certain Abraham Saadia, who held a public office in Saragossa under the rule of James I the Conqueror, king of Aragon 1213–76.[2] As discussed by Friedenberg, if this is the same Abraham Saadia as in the inscription, this seal would predate the Todros Halevi seal by a century and could have served as a model for the latter.[3]

NOTES 1) The seal is in the collection of the British Museum. See D. Friedenberg, *Medieval Jewish Seals from Europe* (Detroit, 1987), 124–27, no. 50. 2) Y. Baer, *A History of the Jews in Christian Spain,* vol. 1 (Philadelphia, 1961), 144. 3) D. Friedenberg, *Medieval Jewish Seals from Europe,* 127, no. 51.

BIBLIOGRAPHY F. Cantera, "La epigrafía hebraica en Sevilla," *Sefarad* 11 (1951): 388; idem., "Sellos hispano-hebreos," ibid., 13 (1953), 110–11; idem., "Dos sellos hebraicos inéditos y algunas consideraciones mas sobre estos," ibid., 14 (1954): 371; F. Cantera and J. M. Millás, *Las inscripciones hebraicas de España* (Madrid, 1956), no. 251; D. Friedenberg,

Medieval Jewish Seals from Europe (Detroit, 1987), 127, no. 51; J. L. Lacave, *Sefarad, Sefarad—La España Judía,* Comisión Quinto Centenario, Sefarad 92 (Barcelona and Madrid, 1987), plate 96 (center); F. Menéndez Pidal and E. Gómez Pérez, *Matrices de sellos españoles (siglos XII al XVI)* (Madrid, 1987), 115, no. 227; Madrid, Ministerio de Cultura, *La vida judía en Sefarad,* exhibition catalogue, (Sinagoga del Tránsito, Toledo, 1991-92), no. 96.

—CN

99 Silver Ring with Hebrew Inscription

Soria (Old Castile), twelfth to thirteenth century

Silver: engraved

Diam. ring: ¾ in. (2 cm)
Diam. bezel: ⅜ x ½ in. (1 x 1.2 cm)

Soria, Museo Numantino, 81/1/568

Hebrew inscription:

ינֿיהו

("they will lament" [?])

This ring and no. 100 were found in the Jewish necropolis of Deza, in the city of Soria, along with several other pieces of jewelry.[1]

A Hebrew inscription, probably of funerary meaning, is engraved on its bezel between palmettos. On the back of the bezel the number "36" is engraved, probably indicating the number of the tomb to which the ring belonged; however, the tomb has not yet been identified. Similar finds were uncovered in the Jewish cemeteries of Montjuich in Barcelona and in Teruel, both in Aragón.[2]

The beginning of Jewish settlement in Soria is unknown but there is evidence that the Jewish quarter was among the most populated *aljamas* in Castile. During the second half of the fifteenth century, however, restrictive measures against the Jews of Soria increased and in 1477 they were confined to a special quarter until their expulsion in 1492.[3]

NOTES 1) J. Casanovas Miró and O. Ripoll López, "Catálogo de los materiales aparecidos en la necrópolis judaica de Deza (Soria)." *Celtiberia* 65 (1983): 138. 2) For discoveries in the cemetery of Teruel see *La vida judía en Sefarad,* exhibition catalogue (Sinagoga del Transito, Toledo, 1991-92), 278–80, nos. 87–95. Some of the jewelry uncovered in Montjuich has been published in J. L. Lacave, *Sefarad, Sefarad: La España Judía,* Comisión Quinto Centenario, Sefarad 92, (Barcelona and Madrid, 1987), fig. 145. 3) For a document ordering the confinment of the Jews of Soria, see L. Suárez Fernández, *Documentos acerca de la expulsión de los judíos* (Valladolid, 1964), 133–34, no. 25.

BIBLIOGRAPHY J. Casanovas Miró and O. Ripoll López, "Catálogo de los materiales aparecidos en la necrópolis judaica de Deza (Soria)," *Celtiberia* 65 (1983): 138 and fig. 3, no. 568; *La vida judía en Sefarad,* exhibition catalogue, (Sinagoga del Tránsito, Toledo, 1991-92), no. 85.

—CN

98

100 **Ring with Hebrew Inscription**

Bronze

Soria (Old Castile), twelfth to thirteenth century

Diam. ring: ⅞ in. (2.2 cm)
Diam. bezel: ½ in. (1.4 cm)

Soria, Museo Numantino, 81/1/571

Hebrew inscription: ניהי

This ring, like no. 99, was found in the excavations of the Jewish necropolis of Deza, in Soria. The Hebrew inscription engraved on its bezel is either a variation or a misspelled version of the inscription on no. 99. The ring belonged to tomb 28 although it bears the number "51" on the back of its bezel.[1] (See no. 99).

NOTE 1) J. Casanovas Miró and O. Ripoll López, "Catálogo de los materiales aparecidos en la necrópolis judaica de Deza (Soria)," *Celtiberia* 65 (1983): 139.

BIBLIOGRAPHY J. Casanovas Miró and O. Ripoll López, "Catálogo de los materiales aparecidos en la necrópolis judaica de Deza (Soria)," *Celtiberia* 65 (1983): 139 and fig. 3, no. 571.

—CN

101 **Astrolabe with Latin Inscription**

Spain, 1498

Unsigned

Brass: Cast and Hammered

16⅛ x 12 11/16 in., diam. 1 1/16 in., (41 x 32.2 cm, diam. 4.3 cm)

Chicago, Adler Planetarium, History of Astronomy Collection, M 28

This astrolabe can be dated according to its astronomical parameters to 1498. The spider shows the positions of thirty-five stars, all with Latin names. The chief interest of this instrument is the dorso, which has a double calendar made up of four rings, three fixed and a movable civil calendar ring with the names of the months in Latin. This unusual arrangement made it possible continuously to revise the sun's position in the zodiac.

On the back plate, a circle of degrees is inscribed on which the altitude of the sun or a star could be read by rotating the sight or alidade. Curiously, this model has two such sights, with four counterchanged arms; thus the multiple alidade could have been used as a surveyor's cross. The "shadow square" is divided into twenty-four half parts with the letters *umbra versa* (designating the shadow thrown by the horizontal gnomon on the vertical plane) and *umbra extensa* (vertical gnomon on horizontal plane, usually called *umbra recta*).

BIBLIOGRAPHY R. S. and M. K. Webster, *The Adler Planetarium Catalogue* (in preparation).

—TG

102 **Astrolabe with Hebrew Inscription**

Europe, mid-sixteenth century

Unsigned

Brass: Cast and hammered

W. 5/16 in., diam. 4½ in. (W. 0.85 cm, diam. 11.5 cm)

Chicago, Adler Planetarium, History of Astronomy Collection, M 20

This astrolabe, one of the few surviving with Hebrew lettering, was made somewhere in Europe in the mid-sixteenth century. The "spider," whose pointers designate particular stars, displays the Hebrew names for the zodiacal signs as well as twenty star names, of which seventeen are in Hebrew and three in Judeo-Arabic (Arabic written in Hebrew characters), attesting to the relationship of this instrument to Arabic prototypes.

On a removable disk (*ṣafīḥa*) on which is portrayed a stereographic projection of the heavens for a particular latitude, the names Bologna and Paris are inscribed. On the back of the instrument are Hebrew alphabetic numerals for each zodiacal sign, a Julian calendar, and a shadow square, also with Hebrew alphabetic numerals from 2 to 12, at intervals of 2, written four times each.

BIBLIOGRAPHY B. R. Goldstein, "The Hebrew Astrolabe in the Adler Planetarium," *Journal of Near Eastern Studies* 35 (1976), 251–60.

—TG

Stone

103 Fragment of a Sundial

Córdoba, ca. 1000

Marble: engraved

13⅝ x 9½ in.
(34.5 x 24 cm.)

Museo Arqueológico Provincial, Córdoba, no. 12700

This fragment belongs to a group of eight sundials stemming from Muslim Spain. It was discovered in 1956 in the course of excavations on the site of an ancient road in Córdoba.

The engravings indicate six of the daily hours, the cardinal points, and the equinox. An interesting part of the inscriptions is the phrase "the work of Aḥmad ibn al-Saffar." It does not necessarily indicate that the sundial was made during al-Saffar's lifetime, but that the instrument was copied from one of his or that his name was invoked as a sign of the excellence of the instrument.

In medieval Muslim communities, sundials were particularly important because they were used to summon the faithful to prayer.

BIBLIOGRAPHY Samuel de los Santos Jener, "Un reloj de sol hispano-árabe hallado en Córdoba," *Boletín de la Real Academia de Córdoba* 26 (1955): 299–305; D. Cabanelas, "Relojes de sol hispano-musulmanes," *Al-Andalus* 23(1958): 394–96; Córdoba, *La Mezquita de Córdoba: siglos VIII al XV,* exhibition catalogue, 1986, no. 20; Carmen Barcelo and Ana Labarta, "Ocho Relojes de Sol Hispano-Musulmanes," *Al-Qantara* 9 (1988): 240–41.

—VBM

104 Container for Alms

Spain, 1319–20

Stone

H 5½ in., diam. 4⅞ in.
(13.2 x 12.5 cm.)

Paris, Musée national du Moyen Age, Thermes de Cluny, No. Inv. Cl. 12974

104

Everyday objects found in Spain suggest that Jews, Muslims, and Christians shared common forms. This container is very similar to a bronze mortar in the Museo Nacional de Arte Hispanomusulmán in Granada (see no. 94), which was probably used by Muslims.

The poor condition of most of the inscription does not permit a definitive reading of the entire text. One phrase gives the date *sh'nat et* (in the year 79=1319–20) and the Judeo-Spanish phrase: *Rey Ahashveros y la Reyna Esther* (King Ahasuerus and Queen Esther). Another phrase seems to indicate a reading, "[in] remembrance of the miracle."

BIBLIOGRAPHY I. Levi, "Une aumônière judéo-espagnole en pierre," *Revue des études juives* 25 (1892): 78–80; F. Cantera and J. M. Millás, *Las Inscripciones Hebraicas de España* (Madrid, 1956), 397; Cologne, Kölnischen Stadtmuseum, *Monumenta Judaica* (Cologne, 1963), no. E 691, fig. 166; Victor Klagsbald, *Catalogue raisonné de la collection juive du Musée de Cluny* (Paris, 1981), no. 87; Jerusalem, Israel Museum, *Jewish Treasures from Paris from the Collections of the Cluny Museum and the Consistoire,* by Victor Klagsbald, exhibition catalogue, 1982, no. 107; Madrid, Ministerio de Cultura, *La vida judía en Sefarad,* exhibition catalogue, (Sinagoga del Tránsito, Toledo, 1991-92), no. 29.

—*VBM*

Textiles

105 **Mounted Horsemen in Roundels (Fragments)**

Spain, ca. 1246

Silk: gold and silk threads

E: 5¼ x 4⅜ in. (13 x 11 cm)

F: 4⅜ x 4¾ in. (11 x 12 cm)

New York, The Cooper-Hewitt Museum, National Museum of Design, Smithsonian Institution, Given by John Pierpont Morgan from the Miguel y Badia Collection, 1902–1–218 E and F

These fragments are but two of eight large roundels (in addition to a set of smaller roundels) that originally belonged to the same textile. Their subjects include human figures confronted across a sacred tree, confronted harpies with a sacred tree, and mounted horsemen (as on these pieces from the Cooper-Hewitt). The remaining kufic border design on several of the roundels reads: "There is no god but ᵓAllah," the beginning of the Muslim affirmation of faith.

The quality of the weaving and the sumptuousness of the materials (the gold background in the large roundels, for example) mark these textiles as among the finest from the Islamic world. They stem from the tomb of Bishop Gurb of Barcelona who died in 1284, and must have been used as a tomb cloth. Related weavings were found on a pillow in the tomb of Queen Berenguela of Castile who died in 1246. Since those from Bishop Gurb's tomb show signs of reuse, they must date from before 1284 or ca. 1246, the date of the queen's demise.

Some writers understand the subjects in the large roundels as unrelated, largely decorative themes. Dorothy Shepherd, however, has interpreted them as part of an integrated iconographic scheme, the "Banquet and the Hunt," symbols of heroization and apotheosis in Sassanian art and, later, "symbols of the paradise that Islam promised to all true believers."[1] The harpies, birds with male heads, serve as guardians of the Paradise represented by the banquet and the hunt.

NOTE 1) D. G. Shepherd, "A Treasure from a Thirteenth-Century Spanish Tomb," *Bulletin of The Cleveland Museum of Art* (April 1978): 119.

BIBLIOGRAPHY D. G. Shepherd, "A Treasure from a Thirteenth-Century Spanish Tomb," *Bulletin of The Cleveland Museum of Art* (April 1978), 111–34.

—VBM

106 **Textile with Drinking Ladies**

Spain, thirteenth century

Silk

6⅞ x 13¾ in. (17.6 x 34.8 cm)

New York, The Cooper-Hewitt Museum, National Museum of Design, Smithsonian Institution, Given by John Pierpont Morgan from the Miguel y Badia Collection, 1902-1-82

The composition, paired figures within a roundel, first appears in Hispanomoresque art on the carved ivories of the tenth-eleventh centuries (see no. 88). Figures are either drinking or playing musical instruments, reflecting the activities of gatherings among the upper classes. They are set within a pearl border, a type of frame that may derive from Persian art.

The representation of animals and human figures is prohibited not in the Qurᵓān, but in the Tradition of the Prophet. Attitudes toward images varied over time and place in the Islamic world. In Spain, images appear as on this example, but they are rare. A related textile is in the Cleveland Museum; another fragment is in the Metropolitan Museum of Art.

BIBLIOGRAPHY Dorothy Shepherd, "The Hispano-Islamic Textiles in the Cooper Union Collection," *Chronicle of the Museum for the Arts of Decoration of the Cooper Union* 1, no. 10 (1943): 383–86, fig. 16.

—VBM

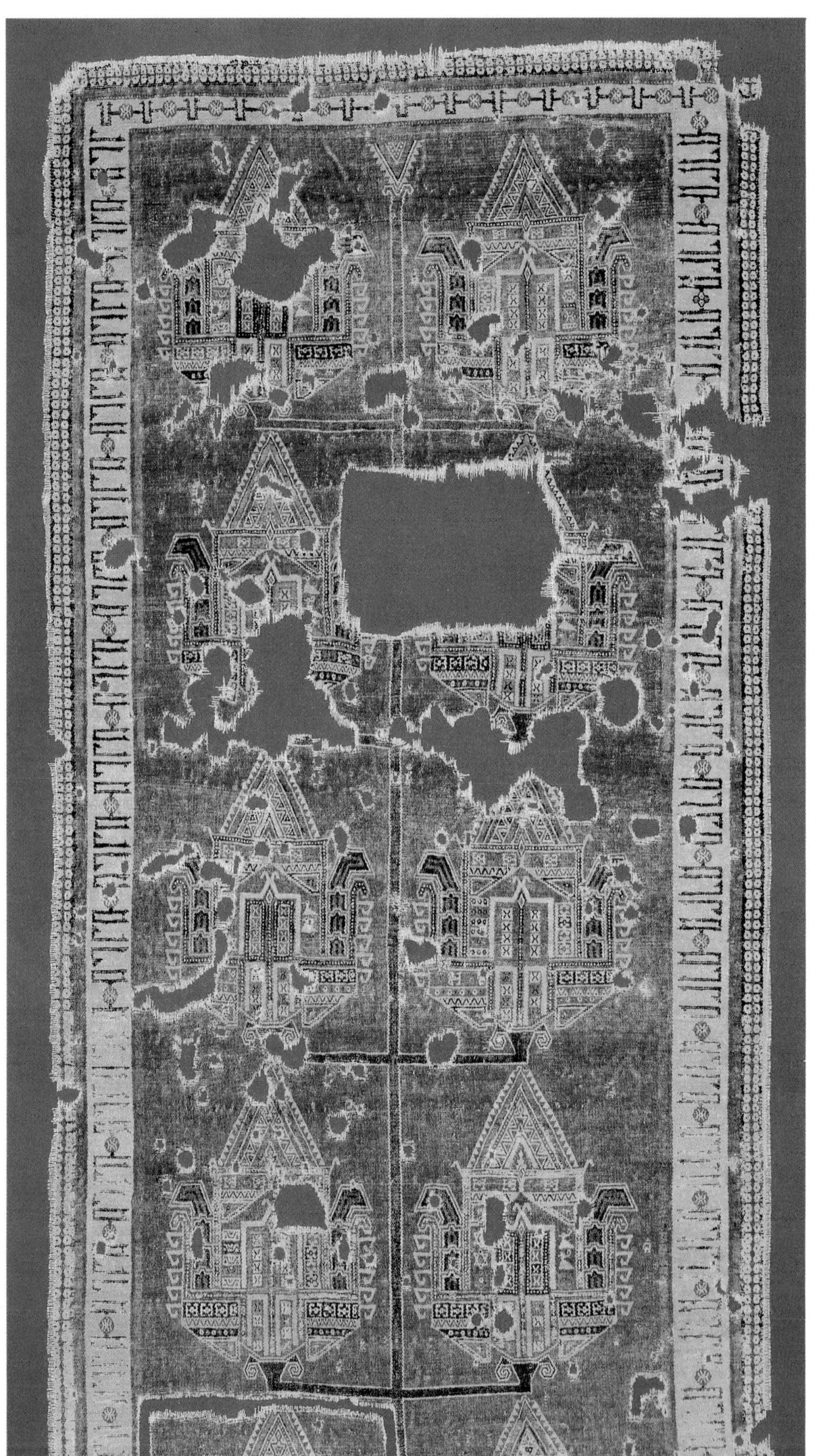

107

107 Synagogue Rug

Spain, fourteenth century

Wool

125 x 37 in.
(317.5 x 94 cm)

Berlin, Staatliche Museen zu Berlin, Islamisches Museum, I.27

By the first quarter of the fourteenth century, Jews were using rugs in synagogues for two purposes: seating, and hanging beside the Torah ark as decoration. These uses are attested to by a responsum of Rabbi Asher ben Yeḥiel who arrived in Spain in 1304 and who died in 1327.[1] Rabbi Asher discusses the issue of a rug used as a prayer rug that was decorated with an image of the *kaʾba*. Since Muslims prostrated themselves in prayer on such rugs, Rabbi Asher forbade their use as decoration on the walls flanking the Torah ark and even for seating. Prayer rugs were still an issue during the time of his son, Rabbi Judah (1270–1349), who received a similar inquiry from his nephew, Rabbi Asher ben Solomon.[2]

The problem posed by the rugs in question was due to their iconography, which raised the possibility of idolatry in the minds of the rabbis. Their answers suggest that a rug with Jewish iconography would have been acceptable, which may have been the impetus for the creation of rugs such as the one on exhibition. Its basic design is a flowering tree surrounded by geometric borders and a border with kufic writing. Unusual is the form of the flowers, a small shrine with a horned gable roof and a double paneled doorway. Parallels for such shrines appear in Jewish art in the mosaic floors of synagogues erected during the Byzantine period,[3] and elsewhere on the large Coptic textiles which may have been hung in doorways.[4] On a Coptic textile now in the Textile Museum, Washington, D. C., the compartments of the paneled doorway are filled with birds and geometric motifs as are the compartments on the Berlin rug.

The long narrow shape of the rug suggests that it was used for seating rather than as decoration on the walls. The simplicity of the kufic border design and the unique iconography suggests a date earlier than the more numerous armorial rugs of the fifteenth century. The kufic may read: *Lā ilāh illā ʾAllah* (There is no God but the God).

NOTES 1) Rabbi Asher ben Yeḥiel, *Responsa,* section 5, no. 2. 2) Rabbi Judah ben Asher, *Zikhron Yehuda* no. 21. 3) For example, the mosaic floors of the Beth Alpha Synagogue and that of Hammath Tiberias. For illustrations, see Lee I. Levine, *Ancient Synagogues Revealed* (Jerusalem and Detroit, 1982), 15, 66. 3) Rachel Wischnitzer suggested a connection to an illuminated page of the tenth-century Leningrad Hebrew Bible from Egypt, but the comparison is not as close as that between the mosaic floors and the rug; Rachel Wischnitzer, *Symbolen der jüdischen Kunst* (Berlin, 1938), 24. 4) Linda Woolley, "Pagan, Classical, Christian," *Hali* 48 (1989): 29 and fig. 9.

BIBLIOGRAPHY Wilhelm von Bode, *Vorderasiatische Knupfteppiche aus älterer Zeit,* Monographien des Kunstgewerbes (Leipzig, [1902]), 117, fig. 115; W. G. Thomson, "Hispano-Moresque Carpets," *Burlington Magazine* 18 (1910–11): 100–107, plate IIc; Friedrich Sarre, "A Fourteenth Century Spanish 'Synagogue' Carpet," *Burlington Magazine* 56 (1930): 89–95; Friedrich Spuhler, *Oriental Carpets in the Museum of Islamic Art Berlin* (Washington, D.C., 1988), 118; London, Hayward Gallery, *The Eastern Carpet in the Western World from the 15th to the 17th Century,* by Donald King and David Sylvester, exhibition catalogue, 1983, no. 3; Berlin, Berliner Festspiele, *Jüdische Lebenswelten: Katalog,* exhibition catalogue, ed. A. Nachama and G. Sievernich, (Berlin, 1992), no: 20, 12/4; Vivian B. Mann, "The Use of Muslim Rugs in Spanish Synagogues: the Evidence of the Responsa Literature," *Textile Museum Journal* (forthcoming).

—VBM

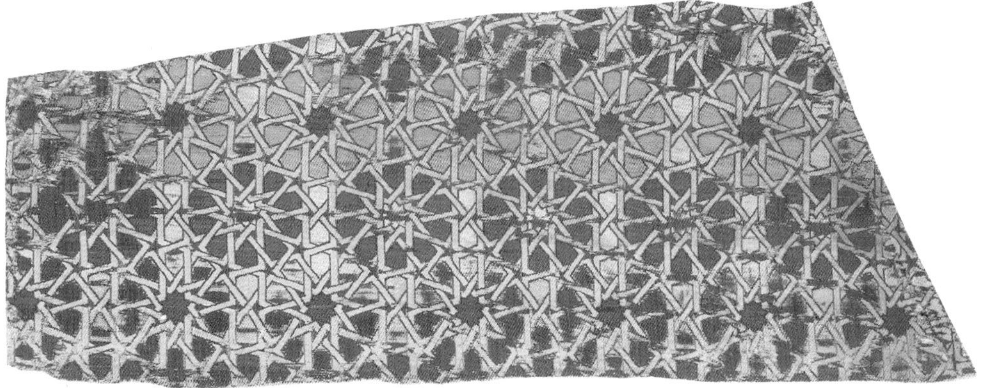

108

108 **Textile with Expanding-Star Motif**

Granada, fourteenth century

Silk

19 x 7 in. (48.3 x 17.8 cm)

Washington, The Textile Museum, 84.32

Later Hispanomoresque textiles, dating from the fourteenth and fifteenth centuries, are often based, as is this one, on patterns appearing earlier in other media. The expanding-star motif appears on a faience tile design from the Alhambra that dates to the thirteenth century.[1] Similar textiles are in the Hispanic Society collection, New York (H 918), and in the Museo de Indumentaria, Barcelona (39.918 and 896).

The shape of the textile suggests that it was cut as a sleeve for a now lost garment.[2]

NOTES 1) Florence May, *Silk Textiles of Spain* (New York, 1957), 190, fig. 122. 2) Textile Museum Records.

BIBLIOGRAPHY A. C. Weibel, *2000 Years of Silk Weaving,* (New York, 1944), 37, no. 132; Florence May, *Silk Textiles of Spain* (New York, 1957), 190, fig. 122; Washington, The Textile Museum, *Weaving through Spanish History, 13th Century-17th Century,* exhibition checklist, 1973, no. 9.

—*VBM*

109

109 **Nasrid Textile with Inscription "Glory to Our Lord the Sultan"**

Spain, fifteenth century

Silk: compound weave with one selvage preserved

10⅝ x 21¼ in.
(26.9 x 53.9 cm)

New York, Lent by The Metropolitan Museum of Art, Rogers Fund, 1918, 18.31

This textile was produced under the Nasrid dynasty, the last Muslim rulers on the Iberian peninsula, the center of whose power was Granada. Characteristic of the fifteenth century are the large size of the inscription, its formation of elegant letters terminating in floral forms, and the narrow borders of arabesques. The inscription reads *Izz limaulana al-sultan* (Glory to our lord, the Sultan).

The letters are yellow silk on a red satin. The bands of arabesques are in yellow, red, and cream on a blue background. There are also bands of cream silk and narrow bands of green with red and blue lines. Similar pieces are in the collections of the Cooper-Hewitt Museum, New York, the Cleveland Museum, the Victoria and Albert Museum, London, and the Musées Royaux du Cinquantenaire, Brussels.

111

BIBLIOGRAPHY New York, The Metropolitan Museum of Art, "The Celestial Pen: Islamic Calligraphy," by Annemarie Schimmel, exhibition checklist, 1982.

—VBM

This textile is composed of three wide bands of geometric interlace forming a carpet pattern of stars and two narrow bands of a kufic inscription alternating with palmettos. The kufic forms the Arabic for "Beatitude." Another Arabic inscription is contained within cartouches in the star pattern, "Eternal Glory."

The design was created during the fifteenth century; it remained popular among North African workshops after the fall of Granada in 1492.

BIBLIOGRAPHY Berlin, Museum fur Islamisches Kunst Berlin, *The Arts of Islam, Masterpieces from The Metropolitan Museum of Art* (Berlin, 1981), no. 63.

—VBM

110 **Nasrid Textile with Star Pattern**

Spain, fifteenth century

Silk: compound weave with two selvages preserved

39½ x 45¼ in. (100.3 x 114.9 cm)

New York, Lent by The Metropolitan Museum of Art, Fletcher Fund, 1946, 46.156.16

Copes are worn by the officiants during Mass. The textile used here was produced in a Nasrid workshop, that is, one under the control of the Muslim ruler of Granada, and reflects the esteem in which these luxurious silks were held by all the inhabitants of the Spanish peninsula during the Middle Ages.

Bands of inscription formed of large elegant script are typical of fifteenth-century textiles. On this piece, they read "Glory to our lord, the Sultan," a common slogan found on other examples of different composition (see no. 109). The white letters are set off against a black ground bordered on either side by predominantly red and green bands. A similar treatment of the main inscription band appears on a textile in the Museo Valencia de Don Juan, Madrid (no. 2101).

BIBLIOGRAPHY Dorothy Shepherd, "The Hispano-Islamic Textiles in the Cooper Union Collection," *Chronicle of the Museum for the Arts of Decoration of the Cooper Union* 1, no. 10 (1943): 392 and cover.

—VBM

111 **Fragment of a Cope Made of a Nasrid Textile**

Possibly Granada, fifteenth century

Silk

20⅛ x 16¾ in. (51.2 x 42.4 cm)

New York, The Cooper-Hewitt Museum, National Museum of Design, Smithsonian Institution, Given by John Pierpont Morgan from the Miguel y Badia Collection, 1902-1-302

Bibliography

HISTORY

Alfonso el Sabio. *Las "Siete partidas" del rey don Alfonso el Sabio.* 3 vols, Madrid, 1807.

Ashtor, E. *The Jews of Moslem Spain.* Translated by Aaron Klein and Jenny Machlowitz, 3 vols. Philadelphia, 1973–84.

Assis, Y., and R. Magdalena. *The Jews of Navarre in the Late Middle Ages* (Hebrew). Jerusalem, 1990.

Bachrach, B. *Early Medieval Jewish Policy in Western Europe.* Minneapolis, Minn., 1977.

Baer, Y. *A History of the Jews in Christian Spain.* 2 vols. Translated by L. Schiffman, Philadelphia, 1961-66.

Beinart, H. *Conversos on Trial.* Jerusalem, 1981.

Ben Sasson, H. H. "The Generation of the Spanish Exiles on its Fate" (Hebrew). *Zion* 26 (1961): 23–42.

Ben–Sasson, M., et al. eds. *Culture and Society in Medieval Jewry.* Jerusalem, 1989.

Benson, R. L., and G. Constable, eds. *Renaissance and Renewal in the Twelfth Century.* Cambridge, 1982.

Burgos, Las Diócesis de Castilla y León. *Las Edades del Hombre: Libros y Documentos en la Iglesia de Castilla y León.* Exhibition catalogue, 1990.

Burns, R. I., ed. *Emperor of Culture: Alfonso X The Learned of Castile and his Thirteenth–Century Renaissance.* Philadelphia, 1990.

Cantera Burgos, F. "Christian Spain." In *The World History of the Jewish People: The Dark Ages,* 357–81. Edited by Cecil Roth. New Brunswick, 1966.

Carpenter, D. *Alfonso X and the Jews: An Edition of and Commentary on Siete Partidas 7.24 "De los judíos."* Berkeley, Calif., 1986.

———. "Fickle Fortune: Gambling in Medieval Spain." *Studies in Philology* 85 (1988): 267–78.

Casanovas, J., and O., Ripoll. "Catálogo de los materiales aparecidos en la necrópolis judaica de Deza (Soria)." *Celtiberia* 65 (1983): 135–48.

Castro, A. *The Structure of Spanish History.* Princeton, N.J., 1954.

———. *The Spaniards.* Berkeley, Calif, 1971.

Chazan, R. "The Barcelona 'Disputation' of 1263. Christian Missionizing and Jewish Response." *Speculum* 52 (1977): 824–42.

Chejne, A. G., *Islam and the West: The Moriscos: A Cultural and Social History.* Albany, N.Y. 1983.

Collins, R. *Early Medieval Spain: Unity in Diversity: 400–1000.* London, 1983.

Daniel, N. *Islam and the West: The Making of an Image.* Edinburgh, 1960.

Encyclopedia Judaica. 16 vols. Jerusalem, 1971.

Fernández, J. R. *Las juderías de la provicia de León.* León, 1976.

Gampel, B. *The Last Jews on Iberian Soil.* Berkeley, Calif., 1989.

García Iglesias, L. *Los judíos en la España antigua.* Madrid, 1978.

Glick, T. F. *Cristianos y musulmanes en la España medieval.* Madrid, 1991. Revised version of *Islamic and Christian Spain in the Early Middle Ages.* Princeton, N.J., 1979

———. "Darwinismo y filología española." *Boletín de la Institución Libre de Enseñanza,* n.s. 12 (1991): 35–41.

Grayzel, S. *The Church and the Jews in the XIIIth Century.* Philadelphia, 1933.

Guichard, P. *Al-Andalus: Estructura antropológica de una sociedad islámica en Occidente.* Barcelona, 1976.

Hillgarth, J. N. *The Spanish Kingdoms 1250–1516.* Oxford, 1978.

Isaacs, A. L. *The Jews of Majorca.* London, 1936.

Kaplan, Y., ed. *Jews and Conversos.* Jerusalem, 1985.

Kriegel, M. "La prise d'une décision: l'expulsion des juifs d'Espagne en 1492." *Revue Historique* 260 (1978): 49–90.

Lacave, J. L. *Sefarad, Sefarad: La España Judía.* Barcelona and Madrid, 1987.

Leroy, B. *The Jews of Navarre.* Jerusalem, 1985.

Lourie, E. "A Jewish Mercenary in the Service of the King of Aragon." *Revue des Études Juives* 137 (1978): 367.

———. "Complicidad criminal: un aspecto insólito de convivencia judeo cristiana." *Actas del III Congreso Internacional 'Encuentro de las Tres Culturas,'* pp. 93–108, Toledo, 1988.

———. *Crusade and Colonisation: Muslims, Christians and Jews in Medieval Aragon.* Aldershot, Hampshire and Brookfield, Vt., 1990.

Maccoby, H. *Judaism on Trial: Jewish-Christian Disputations in the Middle Ages.* Rutherford and East Brunswick, N.J., 1982.

MacKay, A. "Popular Movements and Pogroms in Fifteenth-Century Castile." *Past and Present,* 55 (1972), 33–67.

Mendes Dos Remedios, J. *Os judeos em Portugal.* Coimbra, 1895.

Menéndez Pidal, R. *España, eslabón entre la cristiandad y el islam.* Madrid, 1956.

Meyerson, M. D. *The Muslims of Valencia in the Age of Fernando and Isabel: Between Coexistence and Crusade.* Berkeley, Calif., 1991.

Netanyahu, B. *Don Isaac Abravanel: Statesman and Philosopher.* Philadelphia, 1968.

Neuman, A. A. *The Jews in Spain.* Philadelphia, 1942.

O'Callaghan, J. F. *A History of Medieval Spain.* Ithaca, N.Y., 1975.

Palencia, A. G. *Los mozárabes de Toledo en los siglos XII y XIII.* Madrid, 1928.

Pimenta Ferro, M. J. *Os judeus em Portugal no século XIV.* Lisbon, 1979.

———. *Os judeus em Portugal no século XV.* Lisbon, 1982.

Proctor, E. S. *Alfonso X of Castile: Patron of Literature and Learning.* Oxford, 1951.

Rabello, A. M. *The Jews in Visigothic Spain in the Light of the Legislation* (Hebrew). Jerusalem, 1983.

Ruether, R. *Faith and Fratricide: The Theological Roots of Anti-Semitism.* New York, 1974.

Sánchez Albornoz, C. *España: Un enigma histórico.* 2 vols. Buenos Aires, 1956.

Schirman, J. "Samuel Hannagid, The Man, The Soldier, The Politician." *Jewish Social Studies* 13 (1951): 99–126.

Septimus, B. *Hispano-Jewish Culture in Transition: The Career and Controversies of Ramah.* Cambridge and London, 1982.

Singerman, R. *The Jews in Spain and Portugal: A Bibliography.* New York and London, 1975.

Southern, R. W. *Western Views of Islam in the Middle Ages.* Cambridge, Mass., 1962.

Stillman, N. *The Jews of Arab Lands.* Philadelphia, 1979.

Tello, P.L. *Judíos de Toledo.* vols. I–II. Madrid, 1979.

Twersky, I., ed. *Studies in Medieval Jewish History and Literature.* Cambridge, Mass., 1976.

Valdeon Baruque, J. *Los judíos de Castilla y la revolución Trastamara.* Valladolid, 1968.

Vernet, J. *De ʿAbd al-Rahman I a Isabel II.* Barcelona, 1989.

Wasserstein, D. *The Rise and Fall of the Party Kings: Politics and Society in Islamic Spain 1002–1086.* Princeton, N.J., 1985.

Watt, W. M. *A History of Islamic Spain.* Edinburgh, 1965.

Wolff, P. "The 1391 Pogrom in Spain: Social Crisis or Not?" *Past and Present,* 50 (1971): 4–18.

Yerushalmi, Y. H. *A Jewish Classic in the Portuguese Language.* Lisbon, 1989.

LITERATURE

Alfonso el Sabio. *Cantigas de Santa María.* Edited by Walter Mettmann. 4 vols. Coimbra, 1959–72.

Arbos Ayuso, C. "Los judíos en la literatura medieval española (siglos XIII–XIV): los judíos y la economía; protecciones y privilegios." *Actas de las Jornadas de Estudios Sefardíes, Universidad de Extremadura.* Caceres, 1980.

Bagby, A. I., Jr. "Some Characterizations of the Moor in Alfonso X's *Cantigas.*" *South Central Bulletin* 30 (1970): 164–67.

Berceo, G. De. *Los milagros de Nuestra Señora.* Edited by Brian Dutton. London, 1971.

Blau, J. *The Emergence and Linguistic Background of Judeo-Arabic: A Study of Middle Arabic.* Oxford, 1965.

Brann, R. *The Compunctious Poet: Cultural Ambiguity and Hebrew Poetry.* Baltimore and London, 1991.

Cancionero de Baena, facsimile edition edited by H.R. Lang. New York, 1926.

Cantera Burgos, F. "El *Cancionero de Baena:* judíos y conversos en el." *Sefarad* 27 (1967): 71–111.

Carmi, T., ed. and trans. *The Penguin Book of Hebrew Verse.* New York, 1981.

Carpenter, D. "Abner de Burgos, *Libro de las tres creencias: The Spanish Manuscripts.*" *Manuscripta* 31 (1987): 190–97.

Carrasco Urgoiti, M. S. *El moro de Granada en la literatura (del siglo XV al XX).* Madrid, 1956.

Chavel, C. *Ramban: Writings and Discourses.* New York, 1978.

Deferrari, H. A. *The Sentimental Moor in Spanish Literature Before 1600.* Philadelphia, 1927.

Derenbourg, H. *Les manuscrits arabes de l'Escorial.* 3 vols. Paris, 1884–1941.

Duggan, J. J. *The 'Cantar de mio Cid': Poetic Creation in its Economic and Social Contexts.* Cambridge, 1989.

Dutton, B., ed. *El duelo de la Virgen, Los himnos, Los loores de Nuestra Señora, Los signos del juicio final.* London, 1975.

Fraker, C. F. *Studies on the 'Cancionero de Baena.'* Chapel Hill, N.C., 1966.

García-Arenal, M. "Los moros en las *Cantigas* de Alfonso X el Sabio." *Al-Qaantara* 6 (1985): 133–51.

Gilman, S. *The Art of "La Celestina."* Madison, Wis., 1956.

———. *The Spain of Fernando de Rojas: The Intellectual and Social Landscape of "La Celestina."* Princeton, N.J., 1972.

Goldstein, D. *Hebrew Poets from Spain.* New York, 1966.

Harīzī, Judah al. *Taḥkemoni.* Translated by V.E. Reichert. 2 vols, Jerusalem, 1965–73.

Ibn Daud, A. *Sefer Ha-Qabbalah.* Edited and translated by G. Cohen, Philadelphia, 1967.

Ibn Sahula, I. "'The Sorcerer' by Isaac Ibn Sahula." Translated and introduction by R.P. Scheindlin in *Rabbinic Fantasy,* Stern and Mersky, 295–311.

Ibn Saqbel, S. "'Asher in the Harem' by Shelomo ibn Saqbel." Translated and introduced by R.P. Scheindlin, in Stern and Mirsky, *Rabbinic Fantasy,* 253–67.

Ibn Shabbetai. "'The Gift of the Judah: The Misogynist' by Ibn Shabbetai." Translated and introduced by R.P. Scheindlin, in Stern and Mirsky, *Rabbinic Fantasy,* 269–94.

Libro del Alborayque. In N. López Martinez, *Los judaizantes castellanos y la Inquisición en tiempo de Isabel la Católica,* Burgos, 1954, 391–404.

Katz, I., et al. *Studies on the 'Cantigas de Santa María': Art, Music and Poetry.* Madison, Wis., 1987.

Loewe, R. *Ibn Gabirol.* London, 1989.

Maimonides. *The Guide of the Perplexed,* edited and translated by S. Pires, Chicago, 1964.

Malkiel, M. R. L. de. "El moro en las letras castellanas." *Hispanic Review* 28 (1960): 350–58.

Menéndez, Pidal, R. *Textos medievales españoles: ediciones críticas y estudios.* In *Obras completas,* vol. 12. Madrid, 1976.

Pagis, D. "Dirges on the Persecutions of 1391 in Spain." (Hebrew) *Tarbiz* 37 (1968): 355–73.

———. *Hebrew Poetry of the Middle Ages and the Renaissance.* Berkeley, Calif., Los Angeles, and Oxford, 1991.

Resnick, S. "The Jew as Portrayed in Early Spanish Literature." *Hispania* 37 (1951): 54–58.

Sánchez de Vercial, C. *Libro de los exenplos por A.B.C.* Edited by John E. Keller. Madrid, 1961.

Scheindlin, R. P. "Rabbi Moshe Ibn Ezra on the Legitimacy of Poetry." *Medievalia et Humanistica,* n.s. 7 (1976): 101-15.

———. *Wine, Women, and Death: Medieval Hebrew Poems on the Good Life.* Philadelphia, 1986.

———. *The Gazelle: Medieval Hebrew Poems on God, Israel, and the Soul.* Philadelphia, 1991.

Schirmann, J. "The Function of the Hebrew Poet in Medieval Spain." *Jewish Social Studies* 16 (1954): 235-52.

———. *Hebrew Poetry in Sepharad and Provence* (Hebrew). Jerusalem and Tel Aviv, 1954-56.

Scholberg, K. "Minorities in Medieval Castilian Literature." *Hispania* 37 (1954): 203-9.

Shepard, S. *Shem Tov: His World and His Words.* Miami, Fla., 1978.

Smith, C. *Christians and Moors in Spain.* 2 vols. Warminster, 1988-89.

Smith, G. "Christian Attitudes Toward the Jews in Spanish Literature." *Judaism* 19 (1970): 444-51.

Spiegel, S. "On Medieval Hebrew Poetry." *The Jews: Their History, Culture and Religion,* 3rd ed. Edited by Louis Finkelstein. 3 vols. Philadelphia, 1960, vol. 2, 854-92.

Stern, D., and D. Mirsky. *Rabbinic Fantasy.* Philadelphia, 1900.

Twersky, I. *Rabbi Moses Nahmanides (Ramban): Explorations in His Religious and Literary Virtuosity.* Cambridge, Mass., 1983.

Weinberger, L. *Jewish Prince in Moslem Spain: Selected Poems of Samuel Ibn Nagrela.* University of Alabama, 1973.

SCIENCE

Abed, S. B. *Aristotelian Logic and the Arabic Language in Alfarabi.* Albany, N.Y., 1991.

Amasuno, M. V. *La materia médica de Dioscórides en el Lapidario de Alfonso X el Sabio.* Madrid, 1987.

Andalusi, S. al-. *Kitab Tabakat al-Umam (Livre des Catégories des Nations).* Edited by Régis Blachère. Paris, 1935.

Bossong, G., et al., eds. *De Astronomia Alphonsi Regis.* Barcelona, 1987.

Burnett, C. "A New Source for Domenicus Gundissalinus' Account of the Science of the Stars." *Annals of Science* 47 (1990): 361-74.

Cabanelas, D. "Relojes de sol hispanomusulmanes." *Al-Andalus* 23 (1958): 394-96.

G. Contamine, ed. *Traductions et traducteurs au moyen age.* Paris, 1989.

Daffa, A. A., al-, and J. J. Stroyls. "Transmission of Science and Technology Between East and West During the Period of the Crusades." *Studies in Exact Sciences in Medieval Islam,* 1-18. New York, 1984.

Dunlop, D. M. "Philosophical Predecessors and Contemporaries of ibn Bajjah." *Islamic Quarterly* 2 (1955): 100-116.

Dictionary of Scientific Biography. 16 vols., New York, 1970-80.

Gandz, S. *Studies in Hebrew Astronomy and Mathematics.* New York, 1970.

García Ballester, L. *Historia social de la medicina en España de los siglos XIII al XVI: I La minoría musulmana y morisca.* Madrid, 1976.

Gil, J. *La escuela de traductores de Toledo y sus colaboradores judíos.* Toledo, 1985.

Goldstein, B. *Ibn al-Muthannā's Commentary on the Astronomical Tables of al-Khwarizmi.* New Haven, Conn., 1967.

———. *Al-Bitrūjī: On the Principles of Astronomy.* 2 vols. New Haven, Conn., 1971.

———. "The Hebrew Astrolabe in the Adler Planetarium." *Journal of Near Eastern Studies* 35 (1976): 251-60.

———. "The Survival of Arabic Astronomy in Hebrew." *Journal for the History of Arabic Science* 3 (1979): 31-39.

———. "The Hebrew Astronomical Tradition: New Sources." *Isis* 72 (1981): 237-51.

———, and G. Saliba. "A Hispano-Arabic Astrolabe with Hebrew Star Names." *Anali dell' Istituto e Museo di Storia della Scienza di Firenze* 8 (1983): 19-28.

Haskins, C. H. *Studies in the History of Medieval Science.* Reprint ed., New York, 1960.

Instrumentos astronómicos en la España medieval: su influencia en Europa. Santa Cruz de la Palma, 1985.

Johnston, M. D. "A Catalan Astronomical Manuscript of the Fifteenth Century: Newberry Library Ayer Ms. 746." *Proceedings of the Illinois Medieval Association* (1984): 76-101.

Kunitzsch, P. "Al-Khwārizmī as a Source for the *Sententiae astrolabii.*" *Annals of the New York Academy of Sciences* 55 (1987): 227-36.

Leibowitz, J. O., and S. Marcus, eds. *Sefer Hanisyonot: The Book of Medical Experiences attributed to Abraham ibn Ezra.* Jerusalem, 1984.

Levey, M. "The Encyclopedia of Abraham Savasorda: A Departure in Mathematical Methodology." *Isis* 43 (1952): 257-64.

———. "Abraham Savasorda and his Algorism: A Study in Early European Logistics." *Osiris* 2 (1954): 50-64.

Lindberg, D. C., ed. *Science in the Middle Ages.* Chicago, 1978.

Mendelsohn, E. *Transformation and Tradition in the Sciences.* Cambridge, 1984.

Millás Vallicrosa, J. M. "Un nuevo tratado de astrolabio de R. Abraham ibn Ezra." *Al-Andalus* 5 (1940): 1-29.

———. *Estudios sobre historia de la ciencia española.* Barcelona, 1949.

———. "Una traducción catalana de las Tablas astronómicas (1361) de Jacob ben David Yomtob de Perpiñan." *Sefarad* 19 (1959): 365-71.

———. *Nuevos estudios...española.* Barcelona, 1960.

Molina, L. *Una descripción anónima de al-Andalus.* 2 vols. Madrid, 1983.

Puig Aguilar, R. *Los tratados de la construcción y uso de la azafea de Azarquiel.* Madrid, 1987.

Romano, D. "Le opere scientifiche di Alfonso X e l'intervenuto degli ebrei." *Accademia Nazionale dei Lincei: Atti dei Convegni* 13 (1971): 677-711.

Samso, J. "La astronomía de Alfonso X." *Investigación y Ciencia* 45 (1984): 91-103.

Sola Sole, J. M. *Sobre árabes, judíos y marranos y su impacto en la lengua y literatura españolas.* Barcelona, 1983.

Vernet, J. "Los médicos andaluces en el 'Libro de las Generaciones de Médicos,' de ibn Yulyul." *Anuario de Estudios Medievales* (Barcelona) 5 (1968): 445-62.

———. *La cultura hispanoárabe en Oriente y Occidente.* Barcelona, 1978.

———, and M. A. Catala. "La obras matemáticas de Maslama de Madrid." *Al-Andalus* 30 (1965): 15-45.

Winter, H. "Petrus Roselli." *Imago Mundi: A Review of Early Cartography* 9 (1952): 1-11.

Wolfson, H. A. "The Classification of Science in Medieval Jewish Philosophy." *Hebrew Union College Jubilee Volume.* Cincinnati, 1925.

———. *Crescas's Critique of Aristotle.* Cambridge, 1929.

ART AND ARCHITECTURE

Alamagro, M., and L. M. Llubiá. *La cerámica de Teruel.* Teruel, 1962.

Alvaro, I. *Cerámica aragonesa.* Zaragoza, 1976.

Baños árabes en el País Valenciano. Valencia, 1989.

Beckwith, J. *Caskets from Cordoba.* London, 1960.

Cabanelas, D. "La pila árabe del Museo Arqueológico de Granada y la casa del Chapiz." *Miscelánea de estudios árabes y hebraicos,* 21-34. Granada, 1980-81.

Cantera Burgos, F. *Sinagogas españolas.* 2d ed. Madrid, 1984.

———, and J. M. Millás Vallicrosa. *Las inscripciones hebraicas de España.* Madrid, 1956.

I Congrès Internationale de Céramique Médiévale dans le Méditerranée Occidentale. Paris, 1980. *II. Congrès*...Madrid, 1986. *III. Congrès*...Florence, 1986. *V. Congrès*...Mertola, 1991.

II Congreso de Arqueología Medieval Española, 3 vols. Madrid, 1986.

III Congreso de Arqueología Medieval Española. Oviedo, 1989.

Córdoba, Mosque. *La mezquita de Córdoba: siglos VIII al XV.* Exhibition catalogue, 1986.

Czekelius, O. "Antiguas sinagogas de España." *Arquitectura* 13 (1931): 326-41.

Delgado Valero, C. *Toledo islámico: ciudad, arte e historia.* Toledo, 1987.

———. *Materiales para el estudio morfológico y ornamental del arte islámico en Toledo.* Toledo, 1987.

Dodds, J. D. *Architecture and Ideology in Early Medieval Spain.* University Park, Pa., and London, 1990.

Epalza, M. de, ed. *Ars Hispaniae: Historia universal del arte hispánico.* Madrid, 1947-.

Ettinghausen, R. "Notes on the Lustreware of Spain." *Ars Orientalis* 1 (1954): 133-56.

Ferrandis, J. *Marfiles Hispano-Musulmanes.* Madrid, 1940.

Friedenberg, D. *Medieval Jewish Seals from Europe.* Detroit, 1987.

García Teizeria, F. A. *A antiga sinagoga de Tomar.* Lisbon, 1925.

Gómez Moreno, M. "El arte árabe español hasta los almohades. Arte mozárabe." *Ars Hispaniae* 3.

———. "El Cristo de Don Fernando y Doña Sancha." *Cuadernos del Instituto Central de Restauraciones* 1 (1966).

———. *Iglesias Mozárabes,* Madrid, 1919.

González Martí, M. *Cerámica del Levante Español: Siglos Medievales.* 3 vols. Madrid, 1944-52.

Halperin, D. A. *The Ancient Synagogues of the Iberian Peninsula.* Gainesville, Fla., 1969.

Izquierdo, R. "Los baños árabes de Vascos." *Noticiario Arqueológico Hispánico* 28 (1986): 193-242.

Jerusalem, Israel Museum. *Jewish Treasures from Paris.* Exhibition catalogue by V. A. Klagsbald, 1982.

Krinsky, C. H. *Synagogues of Europe: Architecture, History, Meaning.* New York and Cambridge, 1985.

Kühnel, E. *Die islamischen Elfenbeinskulpturen des VIII-XIII Jahrhunderts.* 2 vols. Berlin, 1971.

La casa hispano-musulmana: Aportaciones de la arqueología. Granada, 1990.

J. A. Gutiérrez González and R. Bohigas Roldán. *La cerámica medieval en el norte y nordeste de la Península Ibérica: Aproximación a su estudio.* León, 1989.

Llubiá, L. M. *Cerámica medieval española.* Barcelona, 1967.

López Álvarez, A. M. *Catálogo del Museo Sefardí Toledo.* Madrid, Ministerio de Cultura, 1986.

———, and T. Álvarez Delgado. "La galería de las mujeres de la sinagoga de El Tránsito: nuevos hallazgos." *Sefarad* 47 (1987): 301-14.

López Cuervo, S. *Madinat al-Zahra': Ingeniería y formas.* Madrid, 1985.

Marinetto Sánchez, P. *El capitel en el Palacio de los Leones: génesis, evolución y catálogo.* Granada, 1985.

———. "Dos pilas califales inéditas." *Arqueología medieval española* (1987): 756-64.

May, F. *Silk Textiles of Spain.* New York, 1957.

Menéndez Pidal, F. and E. Gómez Pérez. *Matrices de Sellos Españoles (siglos XII al XVI).* Madrid, 1987.

Menéndez Pidal, R. ed. *Historia de España,* vol. 5. Madrid, 1957.

Muñoz, M., and M. Domínguez. *Cerámica hispano-musulmana en Almería: loza dorada y azul.* Almería, 1989.

Palol, P., and M. Hirmer. *Early Medieval Art in Spain.* New York, 1967 (originally published in German by Hirmer Verlag München, 1967).

Pascual J., and J. Martí. *La cerámica verde-manganeso bajomedieval de Valencia.* Valencia, 1986.

Pavón Maldonado, B. *Arte Toledano: Islámico y Mudéjar.* Madrid, 1973.

Sabar, S. "The Beginnings and Flourishing of *Ketubbah* Illustration in Italy: A Study in Popular Imagery and Jewish Patronage During the Seventeenth and Eighteenth Centuries." Ph.D. dissertation, University of California, Los Angeles, 1987.

Santos Gener, S. "La sinagoga de Córdoba." *Anales de la Comisión Provincial de Monumentos Históricos y Artísticos de Córdoba, 1927-28.* Córdoba, 1929, 65-85.

Shepherd, D. "The Hispano-Islamic Textiles in the Cooper Union Collection." *Chronicle of the Museum for the Arts of Decoration of the Cooper Union* 1 (1943): 383-86.

———. "A Treasure from a Thirteenth-Century Spanish Tomb." *Bulletin of The Cleveland Museum of Art* (1978): 111-34.

Santos Simões, J. M. *Tomar e a sua juderia.* Tomar, 1943.

Stern, H. *Les mosaïques de la Grande Mosquée de Cordove.* Berlin, 1976.

Madrid, Instituto Occidental de Cultura Islámica. *Exposición de arte, tecnología y literatura hispano-musulmanas.* Exhibition catalogue, 1988.

Toledo, Museo de Santa Cruz. *Alfonso X.* Exhibition catalogue, 1984.

Toledo, Museo Sefardí. *La vida judía en Sefarad.* Exhibition catalogue, 1991-92.

Torres Balbás, L. "Arte almohade: Arte Nazarí." *Ars Hispaniae* 4. (1949)

———. *Ciudades Hispanomusulmanas.* Madrid, n.d.

Weibel, A. C. *2000 Years of Silk Weaving.* New York, 1944.

Wischnitzer, R. *The Architecture of the European Synagogue.* Philadelphia, 1964.

Zozaya, J. "Aproximación a la cronología de algunas formas cerámicas de época taifa." *Actas de las I Jornadas de Cultura Arabe e Islámica,* 277-285. Madrid, 1978.

———. "Joyería altomedieval española." *Un siglo de joyería y bisutería española: 1890-1990.* Palma de Mallorca, 1991.

———. "Fortification Building in al-Andalus." *Spanien und der Orient.* Berlin, forthcoming.

———. "Recientes estudios sobre la arqueología andalusí: la Frontera Media." *Recientes aportaciones a la historia de al-Andalus: Arqueología y sociedad.* Zaragoza, forthcoming.

MANUSCRIPTS AND PRINTED BOOKS

Amsterdam, Jewish Historical Museum. *The Image of the World: Jewish Tradition in Manuscripts and Printed Books.* Exhibition catalogue. Amsterdam-Leuven, 1990.

Avrin, L. *Hebrew Micrography: One Thousand Years of Art in Script.* Jerusalem, 1981.

Bucher, F. *The Pamplona Bibles.* New Haven, Conn., and London, 1970.

Calvo, R. "El Libro de los juegos de Alfonso X el Sabio." *Alfonso X el Sabio: Libros del ajedrez, dados y tablas.* Madrid, 1987.

De Ricci, S. *Census of Medieval and Renaissance Manuscripts in the United States and Canada.* New York, 1935.

Edelman, R. *Hebraica from Denmark: Manuscripts and Printed Books in the Collection of the Royal Library, Copenhagen.* New York, 1969.

Garel, M. "The Rediscovery of the Wolf Haggadah." *Journal of Jewish Art* 2 (1975): 22-27.

Goff, F. R., ed. *Incunabula in American Libraries.* New York, 1964.

Loewe, H. *Hand List of Hebrew Manuscripts in the University Library at Cambridge.* (n.p.) (n.d.)

Malibu, J. Paul Getty Museum. *The Vidal Mayor: Feudal Customs of Aragon.* Exhibition brochure, 1990.

Marx, A. *Bibliographical Studies and Notes on Rare Books and Manuscripts in The Library of The Jewish Theological Seminary of America.* New York, 1977.

Meiss, M. "Italian Style in Catalonia and a Fourteenth-Century Catalan Workshop." *Journal of the Walters Art Gallery* 4 (1941): 45-87.

Metzger, M. *La haggada enluminée.* Leiden, 1973.

Metzger, T. "Les objects du culte, le sanctuaire du désert et le Temple de Jérusalem dans les Bibles hebraïques médiévales enluminées en Orient et en Espagne." *Bulletin of the John Rylands Library* 52 (1966): 397-436; 53 (1970-71): 175-185.

———. *Les manuscrits hébreux copiés et decorés à Lisbonne dans les dernières décennies du XVe siècle.* Paris, 1977.

Moritz, B. *Arabic Paleography: A Collection of Arabic Texts from the First Century of the Hidja till the Year 1000.* Cairo, 1905.

Narkiss, B. *Hebrew Illuminated Manuscripts.* Jerusalem, 1969.

———. et al. *Hebrew Illuminated Manuscripts in the British Isles. I. Spanish and Portuguese Manuscripts.* London, 1982.

Narkiss, B., and G. Sed-Rajna. "La première Bible de Josué Ibn Gaon." *Revue des études juives* 130 (1972): 255-69.

Neubauer, A. *Catalogue of Hebrew Manuscripts in the Bodleian Library and the College Libraries of Oxford.* 2 vols. Oxford, 1886-1906.

New York, The Jewish Museum. *Illuminated Hebrew Manuscripts from the Library of the Jewish Theological Seminary of America.* Exhibition catalogue by T. Freudenheim, 1965.

———. *The Book and its Cover: Manuscripts and Bindings of the Twelfth through the Eighteenth Centuries.* Exhibition brochure by V. B. Mann, 1981.

———. "Manuscripts and Printed Books from the Collection of The Royal Library, Copenhagen." *Kings and Citizens: The History of the Jews in Denmark, 1622-1983,* vol. 2. Exhibition catalogue by U. Haxen, 1983.

Nordström, C. O. "Some Miniatures in Hebrew Bibles." *Synthronon* 2 (1968): 89-105.

Probasco, H. *Catalogue of the Collection of Books, Manuscripts and Works of Art Belonging to Mr. Henry Probasco.* Cincinnati, Ohio, 1873.

Roth, C. "Jewish Antecedents of Christian Art." *Journal of the Warburg and Courtauld Institutes* 16 (1953): 24-44.

———. "The De Bry Psalter and the Norsa Family." *Revue des études juives* 125 (1966): 401-5.

Rye, R. A. *Catalogue of the Printed Books and Manuscripts Forming the Library of Frederic David Mocatta.* London, 1904.

Saenger, P. *A Catalogue of the pre-1500 Western Manuscript Books at the Newberry Library.* Chicago, 1989.

Sassoon, D. S. *Ohel David: A Descriptive Catalogue of the Hebrew and Samaritan Manuscripts in the Sassoon Library.* London, 1932.

Ethics of the Fathers: A Facsimile from a Fifteenth century Spanish-Portuguese prayerbook from The Library of The Jewish Theological Seminary of America. Introduction by M. Schmelzer. New York, 1987.

Sed-Rajna, G. *Manuscrits hébreux de Lisbonne.* Paris, 1970.

Ubieto Arteta, A., J. Delgado Echeverría, J. A. Frago Gracia, and M. del C. Lacarra Ducay. *Vidal Mayor: Estudios.* Huesca, 1984.

Williams, J., and B. Shailor. *A Spanish Apocalypse: The Morgan Beatus Manuscript.* New York, 1991.

Wormald, F. "Afterthoughts on the Stockholm Exhibition." *Konsthistorisk Tidskrift* 22 (1953): 75-84.

Yerushalmi, Y. H. *Leaves from the Oldest Illustrated Printed Haggadah.* Philadelphia, 1974.

Contributors to the Catalogue

DWAYNE CARPENTER is Associate Professor of Spanish at Boston College. He is the author of *Alfonso X and the Jews: An Edition and Commentary on Siete Partidas 7.24 "De los judíos"* and numerous articles on medieval Spanish literature. He is also contributor to the *Bibliography of Old Spanish Texts.*

JERRILYNN D. DODDS is Associate Professor of Art History at the City University of New York. She is a specialist in medieval Islamic and Christian Art, as reflected in her book *Architecture and Ideology in Early Medieval Spain,* in the catalogue she edited for The Metropolitan Museum of Art, *al Andalus, The Arts of Islamic Spain,* and in her articles on Christian-Muslim cultural exchange.

EDUARDO FRESNEDA PADILLA is Director of the Museo Arqueológico y Etnológico de Granada and of the Museo Nacional de Arte Hispanomusulmán.

BENJAMIN GAMPEL is Associate Professor of Jewish History at The Jewish Theological Seminary of America. He is a specialist on the history of Sephardic Jewry and the author of *The Last Jews on Iberian Soil 1479–98.*

THOMAS F. GLICK is Professor of History at Boston University and author of *Islamic and Christian Spain in the Early Middle Ages* and numerous other publications. Dr. Glick is also co-editor of the *Historical Dictionary of Modern Science in Spain.*

ANA MARÍA LÓPEZ ÁLVAREZ is Director of the Museo Sefardí of Toledo (Nacional de Arte Hispano Judío), located in the Sinagoga del Tránsito. She received her degree in Semitic Philology from the Universidad Complutense of Madrid. She is the author of *Catálogo del Museo Sefardí* and *Guía del Toledo judío.*

VIVIAN B. MANN is Morris and Eva Feld Chair of Judaica at The Jewish Museum. In the past decade she has organized and directed many of the Museum's most ambitious and acclaimed exhibitions, most recently, "Gardens and Ghettoes: the Art of Jewish Life in Italy."

PURIFICACIÓN MARINETTO SÁNCHEZ is Assistant Director and Curator of the Museo Nacional de Arte Hispanomusulmán de la Alhambra in Granada. She has published extensively on the subject of Hispanomoresque art.

CLAUDIA NAHSON is Curatorial Assistant in the Department of Judaica at The Jewish Museum.

RAYMOND P. SCHEINDLIN is Professor of Hebrew Literature at The Jewish Theological Seminary of America. He is the author of *Form and Structure in the Poetry of al-Mu'tamid Ibn Abbad* and *Wine, Women and Death: Medieval Hebrew Poems on the Good Life,* among other works.

GABRIELLE SED-RAJNA is Senior Research Associate at the National Center for Scientific Research (CNRS)/Institute for Textual Research and History (Paris). She is a specialist in illuminated manuscripts and the author of *The Hebrew Bible in Art* and *Ancient Jewish Art.*

MARÍA PAZ SOLER FERRER is the Director of the Museo Nacional de Cerámica González Martí, Valencia. She is the author of numerous scholarly articles on the subject of ceramics, and is the author of *Cerámica valenciana, siglos XIII a XIX.*

JAIME D. VICENTE REDÓN is Director of the Museo de Teruel and a specialist in the material culture of medieval Iberia.

JUAN ZOZAYA is Deputy Director of the National Archaeological Museum in Madrid and President of the Spanish Association of Medieval Archaeology. Dr. Zozaya is a specialist in Islamic archaeology and material culture and has published numerous scholarly articles on medieval Iberia.

Lenders to the Exhibition

The Adler Planetarium, Chicago
Archivo Diocesano, Astorga
Archivo General de Navarra, Pamplona
Archivo Histórico Nacional, Madrid
Exmo. Ayuntamiento de Avila, Archivo Histórico Provincial de Avila, Avila
Biblioteca Apostolica Vaticana, Vatican City
Biblioteca de El Escorial, Madrid
Bodleian Library, Oxford
Syndics of Cambridge University Library, Cambridge
The Cooper-Hewitt Museum, National Museum of Design, Smithsonian Institution, New York
Delegación Provincial, Córdoba
Carl Alexander Floersheim Trust for Art and Judaica
Daniel Friedenberg, Byram
Collection of the J. Paul Getty Museum, Malibu, California
Shmuel Hadas, Jerusalem
Iona College, Yonkers
The Library of The Jewish Theological Seminary of America, New York
The Metropolitan Museum of Art, New York
Monastery of San Miguel de Escalada, Province of León
Musée national du Moyen Age, Thermes de Cluny, Paris
Museo Arqueológico Provincial, Córdoba
Museo Arqueológico y Etnológico Provincial, Granada
Museo Arqueológico de Sevilla, Seville
Museo Nacional de Arte Hispanomusulmán, Granada
Museo Numantino, Soria
Museo Sefardí/Sinagoga del Tránsito, Toledo
Museo Taller del Moro, Toledo
Museo de Teruel, Teruel
Museu de Ceràmica, Ajuntament de Barcelona, Barcelona
The New York Public Library, New York
The Newberry Library, Chicago
Parroquia de San Juan Bautista, Avila
The Pierpont Morgan Library, New York
The Royal Library, Copenhagen
Smithsonian Institution, National Museum of American History, Washington
Staatliche Museen zu Berlin, Islamisches Museum, Berlin
Staatsbibliothek zu Berlin-Preussischer Kulturbesitz, Orientabteilung, Berlin
The Textile Museum, Washington
The Master and Fellows, Trinity College, Cambridge
The Library, University College London, London
Collection of the Ayuntamiento of Valencia, in deposit at the Museo Nacional de Cerámica "González Martí" of Valencia, Valencia
The Trustees of the Victoria and Albert Museum, London

PHOTO CREDITS

The Adler Planetarium, Chicago (figs. 21A, 22)

Exmo. Ayuntamiento de Avila (fig. 8)

© The Bodleian Library, University of Oxford (figs. 45, 48)

By permission of the British Library, London (fig. 55)

After Cantera Burgos, *Sinagogas Españolas.* Permission granted by Consejo Superior de Investigaciones Científicas, Madrid (figs. 25, 32, 37)

A. C. Cooper, London (fig. 30)

Courtesy of Cooper-Hewitt Museum, National Museum of Design, Smithsonian Institution/Art Resource, NY. Photo: Scott Hyde (fig. 5; cat. no. 111)

Jerrilynn Dodds (figs. 31, 34, 35, 60; cat. no 52)

Collection of the J. Paul Getty Museum, Malibu, California (figs. 1, 16; cat. no. 24)

Israel Museum/Photo Nachum Slapak (fig. 66)

Jewish Historical Museum Amsterdam/Collection Floersheim (figs. 20, 49; cat. no. 10)

The Jewish Museum: Frank Darmstadter Photo Archive (figs. 26, 38); Photo Archive (figs. 7, 14, 27, 28, 39, 42, 57, 58 [By permission of the Bodleian Library, Oxford], 59 [By permission of the British Library, London])

Courtesy of The Library of The Jewish Theological Seminary of America/Photo Suzanne Kaufman (figs. 6, 19, 44, 52, 53)

Courtesy of Carol Herselle Krinsky, *Synagogues of Europe: Architecture, History, Meaning* (fig. 41)

Vivian B. Mann (figs. 40, 51)

The Metropolitan Museum of Art: © By The Metropolitan Museum of Art, 1991 (figs. 3, 67; cat. no. 109); All Rights Reserved, The Metropolitan Museum of Art (figs. 12, 63; cat. nos. 73, 74)

Museo Arqueológico de Sevilla (cat. nos. 97, 98)

Museo Nacional de Ceramica González Martí, Valencia (cat. no. 75)

By Courtesy of the Museo Sefardí, Ministerio de Cultura: (figs. 2, 29); Foto Arte San José, Toledo (figs. 11; cat. nos. 58a, 58b)

Museo Taller del Moro, Toledo (cat. no. 54)

Museo de Teruel (figs. 62, 64, 65; cat. no. 76)

Museu de Ceramica, Ajuntament de Barcelona (cat. nos. 71, 85)

Gobierno de Navarra, Departamento de Educación, Cultura y Deporte, Archivo Real y General, Pamplona (cat. no. 44)

Courtesy of The Newberry Library, Chicago (figs. 18, 23)

Spencer Collection, The New York Public Library, Astor, Lenox, and Tilden Foundations (fig. 54)

Photographs provided and authorized by the Patrimonio Nacional, Madrid (figs. 9, 15, 24A, 24B)

© The Pierpont Morgan Library, 1992 (figs, 17A, 17B)

© PHOTO Réunion des musées nationaux (fig. 13)

The Royal Library, Copenhagen (figs. 43, 46, 47, 50)

Reproduced by courtesy of the Director and University Librarian, the John Rylands Library of Manchester (fig. 56)

Nicolas Sapieha, © The Jewish Museum, 1991 (figs. 4, 33, 36, 61; cat. nos. 53, 61)

Smithsonian Institution (fig. 21B)

The Textile Museum, Washington D.C. (cat. no. 108)

By Courtesy of the Board of Trustees of the Victoria and Albert Museum, London (fig. 10)